Imagine Hope

In this volume for the Social Aspects of AIDS series Watney presents a chronological selection of his writings from the 1990s, with new contextualizing introductory and concluding essays. Offering a chronicle of the changing and often confusing course of the epidemic in its second decade and the shifting responses to it, *Imagine Hope* is able to cast light on the failings and achievements of the voluntary sector response to AIDS and the obstacles faced by policy-makers. The author succeeds not only in bringing together major debates about policy and its implementation on one hand and about representation and cultural responses on the other, but in arguing that the two must be regarded as inseparable. Questions explored include:

- How gay identity has been affected by AIDS
- How gay men have responded to AIDS
- How AIDS policies have been established and put into practice
- What happened to AIDS in the 1990s

Written in plain English, using hands-on experience, *Imagine Hope* is essential reading for anyone wanting to understand the implications of the epidemic as it enters its third decade.

Simon Watney is a well-known writer and broadcaster, art critic, art historian and Director of the Red Hot AIDS Charitable Trust.

Social Aspects of AIDS

Series Editor: Peter Aggleton
(Institute of Education, University of London)

AIDS is not simply a concern for scientists, doctors and medical researchers, it has important social dimensions as well. These include individual, cultural and media responses to the epidemic, stigmatization and discrimination, counselling, care and health promotion. This series of books brings together work from many disciplines including psychology, sociology, cultural and media studies, anthropology, education and history. The titles will be of interest to the general reader, those involved in education and social research, and scientific researchers who want to examine the social aspects of AIDS.

Recent titles include:

Power and Community: Organizational and Cultural Responses to AIDS
Dennis Altman

Moral Threats and Dangerous Desires: AIDS in the New Media
Deborah Lupton

Last Served? Gendering the HIV Pandemic
Cindy Patton

Crossing Borders: Migration, Ethnicity and AIDS
Edited by Mary Haour-Knipe

Bisexualities and AIDS: International Perspectives
Edited by Peter Aggleton

Sexual Interactions and HIV Risk: New Conceptual Perspectives in European Research
Edited by Luc Van Campenhoudt, Mitchell Cohen, Gustavo Guizzardi and Dominique Hausser

AIDS: Activism and Alliances
Edited by Peter Aggleton, Peter Davies and Graham Hart

AIDS as a Gender Issue
Edited by Lorraine Sherr, Catherine Hankins and Lydia Bennett

Drug Injecting and HIV Infection: Global Dimensions and Local Responses
Edited by Gerry Stimson, Don C. Des Jarlais and Andrew Ball

Sexual Behaviour and HIV/AIDS in Europe: Comparisons of National Surveys
Edited by Michel Hubert, Nathalie Bajos and Theo Sandfort

Men Who Sell Sex: International Perspectives on Male Prostitution and AIDS
Edited by Peter Aggleton

The Dutch Response to HIV: Pragmatism and Consensus
Edited by Theo Sandfort

Dying to Care: Work, Stress and Burnout in HIV/AIDS Professionals
David Miller

AIDS in Europe: New Challenges for the Social Sciences
*Edited by Jean-Paul Moatti, Yves Souteyrand, Annick Prieur,
Peter Aggleton and Theo Sandfort*

Social Aspects of AIDS

Series Editor: Peter Aggleton Institute of Education, University of London

Imagine Hope

AIDS and Gay Identity

Simon Watney

London and New York

First published 2000 by Routledge
11 New Fetter Lane, London EC4P 4EE

Simultaneously published in the USA and Canada
by Routledge 29 West 35th Street, New York,
NY 10001

*Routledge is an imprint of the Taylor &
Francis Group*

© 2000 Simon Watney

Typeset in Times by J&L Composition Ltd, Filey,
North Yorkshire
Printed and bound in Great Britain by Biddles Ltd,
Guildford and King's Lynn

British Library Cataloguing in Publication Data
A catalogue record for this book is available from
the British Library

Library of Congress Cataloging in Publication Data
Watney, Simon.
    Imagine hope: AIDS and gay identity / Simon Watney.
        p. cm. – (Social aspects of AIDS.)
    'Published simultaneously in Canada.'
    Includes bibliographical references and index.
    1. AIDS (Disease)   2. Gays–identity.   I. Title.
    II. Series.
    RA644.A25 W376 2000   99–086533
    362.1′969792′008664–dc21

ISBN 1–841–42058–1 (hbk)

ISBN 1–841–42057–3 (pbk)

For Edward King

Contents

Acknowledgements

I would like to thank the staff of the National AIDS Manual, Gay Men Fighting AIDS, the National AIDS Trust, The HIV Project, the library of the Terrence Higgins Trust, and the Public Health Laboratory Service, for their always reliable help in providing statistics and other related data and information. I would also like to thank friends and colleagues for their personal support and guidance, in particular Dennis Altman, Neil Bartlett, Mark Breedon, Camilla Broadbent, James Cary-Parkes, Kay Cheese, Emmanuel Cooper, Martin Dockrell, Simon Edge, Jill Frances, Larys Frogier, James Gardiner, Gill Gilman, Simon Goodwin, Peter Gordon, Mark Harrington, Bill Jacobson, Peter Jones, Robert Kemp, Edward King, Angela Mason, Neil McKenna, Alfredo Monferre, Daniel Monk, John-Paul Philippe, Gareth Pritchard, Tom Sargant, Peter Scott, Eve Kosofsky Sedgwick, Jamie Taylor, Jeffrey Weeks, and Dr Mike Youle. I am also grateful to Donald Moffett for permission to use his artwork for the cover of this publication. Finally I would like to thank Professor Peter Aggleton, who first suggested the idea for this book, and the editorial staff at University College London Press, and Routledge, who encouraged and helped me through its production.

Introduction

'Epidemic! *What* epidemic?'

'Looking back I see how easy it is to fall into folly, how hard to get out of it.'
– Wislawa Szymborska[1]

This book consists of a sequence of essays written about many different aspects of HIV/AIDS in the 1990s. It thus reflects something of my own involvement with the course of the epidemic, and makes no claims to represent anyone else's views or experience.

'Epidemic! *What* epidemic?' These are words one often heard in Britain in the late 1990s, from all sorts of people. They are not often intended to wound. They are not usually malicious. But the voices are usually heterosexual, and behind them you can just about make out the inner voice, thinking: 'AIDS. The epidemic that never happened. The plague that was going to kill us all. All those years we used those bloody condoms! Anyway, they've got a cure now haven't they?' Thinking in terms of the great contagious plagues of the past that scythed overnight through cities and entire countries, many in Britain casually assume there is indeed no AIDS epidemic, and never was. Unsurprisingly, lay perceptions of epidemic illness tenaciously lag behind the many complex developments of modern clinical medicine. After all, everyone knew about plagues for millennia, and before the discovery of antibiotics there was little need to differentiate between them.

I still frequently come across such attitudes, in many different versions, and it therefore seems to me to be important to try in ways like this to continue to discuss AIDS in public, not least for ethical reasons. It is insupportable that the lives of so many hundreds of thousands of people should be so casually erased, along with their frequently long, drawn-out deaths. It also matters because perceptions of personal risk are often inaccurate. Some are obsessed with largely imaginary fears, whilst others delude themselves that they are magically safe. Other health scares in the 1990s concerning such issues as Bovine Spongiform Encephalitis (BSE) and genetically modified foods clearly demonstrated that there remains a yawning gulf between the types of information provided by doctors and epidemiologists, and their wider cultural reception and interpretation.

In 1996 Edward King explored the resemblances and differences between BSE and HIV:

> Both AIDS and Creutzfeldt–Jakob Disease (CJD), the human equivalent of BSE, are caused by infectious agents with long incubation periods. Infected cattle have entered the food-chain from as early as the 1980's. Additionally, both diseases are transmitted by unremarkable activities of human existence – feeding in the case of CJD, sexual intercourse with HIV. That the diseases assault two fundamentals of life accounts for their devastating profiles. But their differences are equally telling … If significant numbers of the population develop CJD, it is certain that they will receive public sympathy and understanding, that research will be adequately funded and without reference to other 'more deserving' diseases like cancer. These victims, after all, had no reason to imagine that eating British beef would put them at risk of a life-threatening disease 10 to 15 years later. But positive gay men came to be routinely treated as if their illness was a deliberately self-inflicted condition, undeserving of public sympathy or concern. It took years before any significant sum of money was so much as earmarked for the search for AIDS treatments.[2]

It is certainly true that in the United Kingdom we have had a disproportionately small epidemic by European standards. By the end of December 1998 there had been 33,764 cases of HIV in Britain, and 16,028 cases of AIDS. Gay men cumulatively account for 67 per cent of UK AIDS cases. The second largest group consists of heterosexuals infected overseas, who account for 13 per cent of cases, a high proportion of whom are Africans resident in Britain. By December 1998 more than 13,000 people had died from AIDS in the UK.[3] This should not, however, blind one to its only too tragic ongoing effects within the social groups at greatest risk. As the statistics clearly demonstrate, in Britain HIV infection has been overwhelmingly concentrated amongst gay men, and to a much lesser extent amongst injecting drug users and African women. A report published by the Department of Health in 1997, based on anonymous testing of blood samples, concludes that HIV 'has become endemic in the homosexual male community, especially in London. At least one in 200 young homosexuals attending GUM clinics in London is becoming infected every year. By the age of 25 three in every hundred of this group have undiagnosed HIV infection'. The authors soberly conclude with a call for 'targeted prevention work with homosexual and bisexual men'.[4]

British statistics doubtless reflect many factors, the most important of which is the continued community-based mobilization amongst gay men since the early 1980s, and the government's introduction of a national network of needle-exchanges since 1986. Together, these have contributed significantly to the relatively small scale of the UK epidemic, by comparison with demographically similar countries such as France.[5]

In the UK it has, moreover, been essentially a *private* epidemic, experienced as in all countries in the developed world mainly within already marginalized social constituencies. It has thus been largely invisible in the public sphere. Mrs Thatcher did not even mention AIDS in her memoirs.[6] As I have explained elsewhere, it is also a *slow-motion* epidemic.[7] There is often a considerable delay between infection and diagnosis. Few develop symptoms in the first years after getting infected. Personal battles with failing health are fought over many long years. Yet each year in Britain another 2,500 cases of HIV infection are reported, more than two-thirds of which are amongst gay men. This situation remained more or less constant throughout the 1990s.

Long and arduous campaigns to set up and sustain adequate services and education have been largely invisible to most people, for the simple reason that happily they have not needed them. Indeed, there is no reason why most people should have any particular in-depth understanding of the real history of AIDS in Britain, not least because of the widespread public confusion caused by the relentless work of publicity-seeking cranks and conspiracy theorists, ever eager to deny the very existence of HIV, or of AIDS in Africa, and so on. All along such people have enjoyed a disproportionately powerful voice in the mass media, always happy to sensationalize and trivialize human misery.[8] Over the years, much of my writing has been in response to such voices.

This has been one symptom of the steady decline in the overall standards and quality of British journalism since the 1980s which over time has doubtless affected public perceptions of AIDS. Caught up in increasingly ferocious circulation wars throughout the early years of the epidemic, the British press alternately either vastly exaggerated or denied the very possibility of any risk of heterosexual HIV transmission. They subsequently more or less dropped the issue altogether. AIDS was recast as a soap opera about 'rival boffins', or else as a long-running science-fiction drama about supposedly 'plucky dissidents' defying and 'exposing' a ruthless 'medical establishment' which cynically plugs 'the HIV myth'. The former issue is simply a distraction, whereas the latter is a deluded and dangerously misleading fantasy, not unlike similar talk of 'the "myth" of the holocaust'.

In the meantime, the UK epidemic has been effectively pushed well back out of public sight. There was no reporting of the cut in the overall AIDS allocation from the Department of Health early in 1999. On the rare occasions when HIV statistics are reported, it is almost invariably in terms of the familiar, long-established journalistic convention of: 'Young defy Safer Sex warnings', or words to that effect, frequently followed by tut-tutting exclamation marks. Thus the infected are automatically blamed for their own infections, as if everyone had access to reliable information about AIDS, and as if those with HIV had set out to get infected, and deserved what happened to them anyway.[9]

Journalist Oscar Moore wrote a powerful and widely read personal column in the *Guardian* for several years before his death in 1996. Since then, coverage has been spasmodic, though the written and broadcast work of

Nigel Wrench stands out for its intelligence and humanity.[10] By contrast, Andrew Sullivan, the darling of the British and American right-wing media, who is also HIV-positive has routinely exaggerated the benefits of treat ments, writing most misleadingly of the supposed 'twighlight of an epi- demic'. Sullivan is a fashionably ardent controversialist, routinely promoting the goal of 'gay marriage' in his writings. This predictably serves only to encourage polarized debates, 'for' or 'against' the idea, thus distracting atten- tion from the deeper and far more important underlying and much neglected question of the quality of *all* our personal relationships. He also routinely reports his own comparatively good health as if this represents the course of the entire global epidemic.[11] No wonder public opinion has been so confused, as reflected in a 1999 MORI poll which suggested that one in five British adults think there is an available cure for AIDS.[12]

Declining standards of journalism are particularly noticeable in British television news and current affairs programmes, which in recent years have been increasingly colonized by professional print journalists. Before the 1980s, BBC radio and television news and current affairs broadcasting were almost entirely independent of Fleet Street, with their own distinct voices and high professional standards. Nowadays it is almost taken for granted that newspaper editors and columnists routinely anchor and appear on TV and radio commentary programmes about the press. As a result, newspapers come under very little serious independent public scrutiny. This has had the entirely predictable but no less regrettable effect of rapidly dragging most TV news and current affairs broadcasting down to the generally sorry level of much British contemporary newspaper journalism.

Throughout the 1990s British TV and press journalists had been conspic- uous by their absence from almost all the major international conferences concerned with treatments and other issues. Britain was the only country in the developed world where reports of the new combination therapies announced at the 1996 Vancouver AIDS Conference were not headline news at the time. In the UK the story was hardly mentioned outside the gay press for a further three months. British journalism generally prefers stories claim- ing that 'too much' is being spent on AIDS, invariably based on highly mis- leading comparisons between very different types of illness. For these and other reasons, people who want reliable information increasingly turn to community-based specialist publications such as *AIDS Treatment Update*, and the *Body Positive Newsletter*, as well as to the Internet.

There may be less of a daily barrage of overt homophobia swilling out of the newspapers than was the case ten years ago, but tabloid culture still much prefers stories of phoney 'AIDS scroungers' claiming social security and other state benefits, to reporting on the real situation facing most people with AIDS in the UK. British journalists are much more excited by exotic horror stories about AIDS in the developing world, understood as a kind of vast, abstract tragedy, about which (supposedly) nothing can be done, than by the coarse nitty-gritty of AIDS on their own doorsteps.

AIDS has, however, passed into contemporary consciousness in a host of often indirect cultural ways. It is commonplace nowadays to hear of athletes or others 'testing positive' for drugs, a phrase that was never used before the introduction of HIV testing in 1984. Talk of 'risk groups' has also become widespread in Britain, whilst we frequently hear social groups referred to as communities, such as 'the country community', or 'the sports community', and of course 'the heterosexual community'. There has been a striking change here. Before AIDS, what we might think of as community-based self-awareness emerged largely in response to shared discrimination, embodied most clearly in the idea of 'the black community' or 'the gay community', and so on.

These were originally *minority* identities, defined in relation to larger, more powerful groups. Nowadays the larger groups themselves are beginning to claim new community status, which has tended rather to weaken the concept of community itself. The experience of racism in 'the white community' is not commensurate with the experience of 'the black community'. Heterosexual men who talk of belonging to 'the heterosexual community' do not experience the discrimination experienced by men from 'the gay community'. Yet many heterosexual men do indeed face shared social challenges that are not generally experienced by most gay men, most obviously in relation to the challenge and responsibilities of parenting. It is important to recognise that throughout the population, growing numbers of people are increasingly defining themselves in 'minoritist' ways. There is a steady proliferation of emerging micro-identities, many of which trespass across the older boundaries of class, gender, race and sexuality. This is part of a deep, social change as we slowly move into a more openly pluralistic and communitarian age.

The epidemic is also reflected in a general change in British attitudes towards the subject of risk. Until the 1980s, risk was a relative concept. It was recognized that risks might change, for better or for worse. If you gave up smoking you understood that you were reducing your statistical risk of lung cancer. Radiation, whether from the sun or from nuclear technology, was understood to be dangerous by degrees. Yet whenever the subject of genetically modified food is mentioned in the late 1990s, there are many voices stating categorically that '99 per cent is not safe' and demanding '100 per cent safety'. It is generally as unproductive to point out to such people that nothing in this world can be scientifically described as '100 per cent safe', as it is to try to dissuade those who insist that there is 'no such thing' as safer sex and that HIV can only be prevented by either celibacy or lifelong mutual monogamy.

Britain has become an increasingly risk-aware society since the advent of HIV, and this has affected public perceptions of many health-related issues, including environment and diet. It should not be forgotten that at least two generations of British school children grew up in an often frightening atmosphere in which AIDS was constantly in the headlines. AIDS has contributed significantly to the process by which we have consciously and unconsciously become a much more risk-averse society than we were twenty years ago.

At the very end of the century there was a steady trickle of news stories about potential treatment drugs, usually misleadingly announced as if some miraculous 'AIDS cure' were just around the corner, rather than in the earliest stages of laboratory development, years in advance even of any possibility of trials in human beings which might conclusively demonstrate their efficacy. There are also occasional reports of vaccine research. The epidemic is thus constantly made to seem a largely theoretical affair, and generally very far away. In the meantime perceptions of the real epidemic on our doorsteps drift further and further into the background of most people's everyday social awareness. For such reasons I still think it is important that people actively involved in the epidemic should continue to bear witness to what has really happened. In this situation, archives also take on a very special importance.

I was a writer long before the identification of AIDS in 1981, and like many of my generation I became involved in voluntary work relating to HIV/AIDS issues quite early on, largely because I had close personal contacts with the United States in the 1970s, where the epidemic was running approximately five years ahead of the European situation. Like many other early AIDS workers of my generation, I also had a developed sense of gay identity, which typically involves a strongly motivating sense of solidarity with others.

Many of us involved in the early days of the epidemic had known one another as young men on the gay scene. Most of us came from a broadly shared liberal, centrist, anti-conservative 1970s political culture that had revolved around the London Lesbian and Gay Switchboard, and many other organizations and groups, such as the newly invented Gaysocs that had emerged in colleges and universities in the wake of the Gay Liberation movement all around the country. Our politics were generally communitarian rather than party-political. Some were Christians. When the epidemic exploded out of nowhere we were mainly in our late twenties and early thirties.

In the early days, people were trying to devise effective prevention campaigns with no obvious precedents. We knew from the initially strange epidemiological tables which we'd taught ourselves to decode into practical terms, that we still had time to act meaningfully. We couldn't just walk on by. There were vitally important priorities, if lives were to be saved, and avoidable suffering prevented. I was not a scientist, but I understood and respected scientific method. In retrospect I am very grateful to the University of Sussex where, in the 1960s, all arts undergraduates were obliged to undertake a science subject in our first year of study.

If the epidemic was to be brought under control, it was crucial that people in the worst affected communities should understand the nature of the available scientific evidence concerning everything from modes of transmission and degrees of infectiousness, to average life-expectancies and the ethical conduct of clinical trials aiming to study the efficacy (or otherwise) of potential treatment drugs. I have never nurtured any personal ambitions of 'leadership' in the gay community. For one thing, I am far too shy. But I was in a very limited way a well known figure, and it did seem important to me at least to try to set out clearly in public, a set of principles and priorities that might form the basis for informed discussion and action within the wider gay community. Hence the importance of the availability of reliable, accessible information, which is a recurring theme throughout this book.

I have been involved in policy-making in a variety of ways, in relation to many different aspects of the epidemic. Indeed at various times. I have been an active campaigner, particularly in the late 1980s, when I argued strongly for resources for targeted education and prevention work for gay men, and also for accessible up-to-date medical information for everyone with HIV. These may sound perfectly reasonable demands today, but at the time the few of us making this case were widely and often bitterly criticised, often by other gay men. Some argued that focusing on the needs of gay men might encourage prejudice, as if reducing prejudice were a more important goal than reducing the incidence of new cases of HIV, and developing proper services and care for the already infected. Others insisted in the face of all the evidence that AIDS affects everybody alike.

Nor was there any initial support for the principle of 're-gaying' from any of the leading AIDS charities, or from the National AIDS Trust. The government-funded Health Education Authority was so cowed by the political pressures of the times that it did not even begin its first advertising campaign in the gay press until 1989. Each institution had to be persuaded, one by one. A decade later, at a Parliamentary committee meeting late in 1998, I heard a perfectly respectable senior politician pointing out the need to target prevention work at those at statistically greatest risk of infection. Everyone applauded. It had taken eight years, but the single most important argument concerning health promotion had been won, at least in principle. This is not to say that such policies have been consistently implemented. On the contrary, a recent survey of English Health Authorities revealed that they spend on average only 20 per cent of their HIV prevention budget on gay men, despite the fact gay men account for 60 per cent of newly reported cases of HIV each year, with around 1,500 testing positive of a national total of around 2,500.[13]

The Department of Health now requires that a minimum of 50 per cent of the HIV prevention allocation be spent on the recognized risk groups most vulnerable to infection, but its recommendations are unevenly observed, and infringements are not punished. For example, Liverpool Health Authority, overseeing an area with a high prevalence of HIV, spent only 11 per cent of its annual HIV prevention budget in 1997/98 on work with gay men, who make up 63 per cent of local cases, and underspent its budget by 4.5 per cent. In the case of Blackpool, the North West Lancashire Health Authority spent 15 per cent of its annual HIV prevention budget on work with gay men, who make up 75 per cent of local cases. Dorset Health Authority allocated a mere 6 per cent of its prevention budget for Bournemouth on gay men, who make up 75 per cent of local cases, and in spite of the fact that Bournemouth has an extensive gay population and is a nationally popular holiday resort for gay men.[14]

This is the latest in a long line of reports, which have chronicled the history of state funding policy for targeted HIV prevention work in the statutory and the voluntary sectors in Britain in the 1990s.[15]

The introduction of 'contract culture' throughout the National Health Service and local government has imposed a competitive model of market economics into health care and health promotion work.[16] One gain has been greatly increased public accountability within the voluntary sector. In the early 1990s it was vital that the emerging voluntary sector response to AIDS should be stabilized and professionalized if it were to remain effective. Yet tremendous challenges remain in the field of targeted prevention work for gay men.[17]

Health Authorities around the country nowadays 'purchase' specific services from different 'providers', usually charities. Other work has been directly commissioned on the basis of local needs assessments. On the whole, this has led to a raising of standards and efficiency. It does not *guarantee* equality of access to treatments all around the country, but it makes it possible to set this as a primary goal. It also permits future planning, and the establishment of appropriate budgets. Yet there is still no coherent national strategy on AIDS, although the government undertook a useful and wide-ranging series of consultations in 1998. Nor is the annual allocation of funds from the Department of Health for either treatment and care or prevention predictable from any one year to the next. Hospital departments frequently find themselves in intense competition for funds, just as hospitals are forced into hostile competition with one another. None of this helps matters.

There is widespread recognition that changing needs will require new responses in relation to different groups as the epidemic grinds on. For example, what does AIDS mean to the new generations of young men born after the beginning of the epidemic and now entering the gay scene for the first time? Few of them will have had adequate HIV education at school. What do they think or do about AIDS? Much important work addressing such issues has been funded on the basis of reports based on research designed and undertaken and published within the AIDS sector, sometimes in dialogue with a few key academic departments. A long sequence of such reports now presents a deep and wide-ranging view of gay men's lives in contemporary Britain. This entire literature deserves to be far better known unknown outside the HIV/AIDS sector.[18]

Like many others, I find the current statistics on targeted funding and the steady rate of new HIV infections amongst gay men unutterably depressing. As far as I was concerned, throughout the 1990s this was the single most outstanding political issue affecting gay men in Britain. Yet it is still *hardly even on the agenda* of most contemporary British national lesbian and gay politics. Like so much else concerning the epidemic amongst gay men, it is taboo.

Part of my own work has involved participation in the setting-up and management of new institutions in response to changing needs, in the form of specialist charities and not-for-profit companies. But whatever else I have been involved in, I was also at the same time always a writer. AIDS was all around me from quite early on, so of course I wrote about it. As a writer I have tried to address many different audiences. I have written both for the constituency most directly affected, as well as trying to describe what goes on *inside* the epidemic, to those on the *outside*, who are not directly affected by it every day of their lives. With so much confusion and fear and anti-rationalism in the air, I tried to find a voice which might make some kind of practical contribution to public discussion and debate.

I was very fortunate to frequently find myself working alongside many remarkable, brave, gifted men and women who brought much-needed courage and intelligence and professional expertise to the management of the epidemic. I tried to describe the epidemic as I saw it, and to identify issues I thought important from the perspective of one very small cog within the wider developing matrix of organizations that were laboriously set up in response to the changing patterns of infection, illness and death all around us at that time.

First there was the gay press, for which I wrote widely on AIDS until quite recently. I had written for the first modern British gay weekly newspaper *Gay News* from its beginnings in the early 1970s, and also wrote widely in the international gay press. It seemed important to me at the time to try to set out as clearly as possible, to other gay men, the priority issues as they emerged. The 1970s gay political culture of which I was a part had involved growing international contacts and dialogue between both individuals and groups. I had close personal connections with the early East Coast American response to AIDS, and I tried to report back from one side of the Atlantic to the other on what was going on in our respective communities. I also wrote about the then highly vulnerable world of AIDS-related charities, where vitally important policy decisions were being made. I was also sometimes very critical of those early charities. I tried to encourage informed debate, and thus perhaps inevitably became involved in a certain number of disputes.

In retrospect I would only comment that as far as I was concerned, these public debates were never *ad hominem*, and about personalities, but simply about policies and outcomes. I detest controversy, especially when it becomes personalised. But sometimes one has to speak out, especially in response to opinions which seem potentially dangerous, such as the *Sunday Times*'s misreporting of basic AIDS science throughout most of the 1990s, or the campaign in the early 1990s by some young gay journalists *against* attempts to do targeted HIV education for young gay men, on the (to my mind) bizarre grounds that this involved a form of 'stereotyping'. Readers may imagine the feelings of workers within the voluntary sector, trying to obtain very scarce resources to develop vitally important targeted prevention campaigns for young gay men, and finding the very idea sneered at by many of the leading politically correct voices of Queer fashion.

It has also been most important to defend the basic principles of scientific method against the kinds of superstition and conspiracy theory which have abounded on almost every issue, not least from the far left. Indeed, throughout the history of the epidemic, conspiracy theories have flourished with the vigour of weeds. I was still perhaps naïvely shocked very recently, meeting a vastly well educated and utterly charming young gay intellectual, who casually asked me what I thought of the supposedly 'new idea' that HIV is not the cause of AIDS. Such ignorance of the medical history of the epidemic is far from unusual. I briefly said something about the indisputable, constant statistical association between the two, demonstrated in countless epidemiological surveys everywhere since the late 1980s. On reflection, I realized of course that like most of his generation, he has no easy access to reliable accounts of the ways his community has responded to AIDS, and the history of all the struggles that have occurred over so many years now, involving so many people. Such themes recur throughout this collection.

From 1976 until 1986 I had been an academic, teaching art history and photographic studies at what is now the University of Westminster. By 1979 I had already done quite a lot of national radio and TV work, and had lectured and published widely overseas. Much of my academic work was about the subject of photographic representation, so it was inevitable that I would write in this context about AIDS. Indeed, in the 1980s I wrote a great deal, in many books, catalogues and other publications, from *Screen* to *Artforum*: In my writings I increasingly tried to be as accessible as possible, and over the years I have become increasingly impatient with unnecessary and often intimidating academic jargon.[19]

In the course of the 1990s I had gradually written less about AIDS. Many of the issues that most concerned me at the beginning of the decade were finally more or less properly resolved, as the result of a great deal of work by a large number of people. Like many other early campaigners, I needed to step back and deal more with my own responses to what had happened to me personally. I looked round one day, and half of my closest friends were dead. For a while I was overwhelmed with grief. I had also reached an age when it was necessary for me to turn back to deal with several important unresolved issues in my own past, before I could begin to move forward again in my life. Thus the changing priorities of my private life, as well as within the objective public world of AIDS work, are doubtless reflected in the sequence of chapters in this book.

People sometimes asked me to contribute articles for books they were putting together, and in such writings I tried to draw attention to subjects of which I had direct first-hand experience, and to issues that mattered to me at the time. Most of the chapters in this book come from such publications.

Often such articles brought together topics and themes that I had been writing about as a journalist, or had presented in the ephemeral form of lectures. As Chinua Achebe puts it so clearly: 'If something needs to be said right away, you don't put it in a novel, you write an essay'.[20] It is therefore only to be expected that there are changes of mind, and of emphasis, and of tone. You learn more. The situation changes, and if you are open-minded you change your mind. What was correct or appropriate at an earlier stage of the epidemic may no longer be appropriate later on.

Over the years my experience as an art historian and critic has shaped much of my work, and I have written much about changing cultural responses to AIDS. In the late 1980s I was closely involved with the earliest phase of American AIDS activism, and parallel cultural activist aesthetics associated with the work of the Gran Fury collective, the art of David Wojnarowicz, Keith Haring, and many others, the writings of Douglas Crimp and so on.[21]

Much of this activist work used art to draw attention to government neglect and profiteering on the part of the pharmaceutical industry. It was posed in opposition to more traditional approaches to representation, as provided by many documentary photographers at the time. In the late 1980s there was a most remarkable cultural and political response to AIDS in the United States, especially in New York. This work belonged to a moment of tremendous collective defiance, that could not of its nature be indefinitely sustained. The work of the commercial pharmaceutical sector still needed to be closely monitored, yet by the early 1990s it seemed to me that there was a real danger of *over-politicizing* the epidemic. Focusing *only* on government neglect and related political and economic issues, activist culture ran the risk of neglecting the most intimate, personal experience of the epidemic on the part of those in its midst, above all the experience of *loss*.

Activism is a politics of emergencies, and becomes necessary when powerful institutions stubbornly refuse to listen to reasonable, well informed, democratic arguments. It is a politics of last resort, necessary when all other attempts at dialogue and negotiation have failed. Community activism is, however, unfortunately vulnerable to organized interventions by political extremists, seeking to harness popular single-issue campaigns to their longer-term political ambitions. There are also always strident 'full-time activists' around, more concerned with the rhetoric and personal exhilaration of direct confrontation, than with actually achieving pragmatic goals. This in turn is related, if in complex ways, to the emergence of '100 per cent homosexuals', whose entire political, personal and professional lives are bound up full-time with their sexuality. Cut off from the rest of the world, this can all too easily provide a fertile breeding ground for dogmatism and fanaticism of many kinds.

For my part, I had seen for myself how far left entryists had disrupted and distracted British lesbian and gay politics throughout the 1970s and early 1980s.[22] It should always be remembered that the mid-1980s were very difficult times for everyone involved in AIDS work in the UK. We did not yet have reliable epidemiological predictions concerning the future course of the epidemic. Treatments were woefully inadequate. The political climate of the day was moralistic in the extreme, and we did not know whether or not we might seriously need an effective, clearly focused AIDS activist movement if the 'moral majority', 'pro-family' agenda of the then-influential far right were to become the basis for government policy, as seemed a distinct possibility at the time. In these circumstances it seemed not unimportant to strongly reassert the autonomy of lesbian and gay politics, with its own specific goals and aims. Alliances could come later.

As far as I was concerned, this was what OutRage was initially all about – sustaining the community awareness and confidence generated all round the country in relation to Section 28, in case we were to suddenly need an effective AIDS activist movement. In its early years, OutRage forcefully expressed something of the frustration of at least two generations of younger lesbians and gay men, whose lives had been blighted by the resurgent and widely legitimated homophobia of the 1980s. Rejecting consensus politics in their entirety, Thatcherism made activism an inevitability throughout British society in the 1980s, in many fields, from housing to health care. The government and news media constantly encouraged confrontation, by ruthlessly dividing the population all the time into insiders and outsiders. This was the immediate social context in which most of the contents of this book were written.

The first chapter in this book, 'Ordinary boys', was written in 1989 for a collection of articles about domestic photography by various writers, co-edited by my great friend the late photographer Jo Spence, and published in the following year. It was for me a rather personal piece of writing, partly about my own childhood. In this new context it serves to represent something of the overlap between my pre-AIDS career as a teacher, very much involved in questions of representation, and my subsequent work on the social aspects of AIDS and identity politics.

In 'School's out' I summarized for an American readership some of the implications as I saw them of a range of contingent political debates affecting lesbians and gay men in Britain, in particular the notorious Section 28 of the 1988 Local Government (Amendment) Act. This was aimed to prevent the supposed 'promotion' of homosexuality by local government agencies, with possibly severe implications for effective AIDS education in the UK. The long-term significance of Section 28 in drawing huge numbers of people all round the country together as a self-conscious constituency could hardly be exaggerated. As a piece of legislation it was always a damp squib, but looking back, Section 28 had important *unintended* consequences, since the widespread legitimate anger and resentment it provoked helped not inconsiderably to re-establish communitarian values just when we needed them most, in response to AIDS. Moreover, it brought lesbians and gay men together in a united response as never before.

'Queer epistemology' was first published in Australia, and was an attempt to consider the emergence of the new lesbian and gay and Queer activist organizations springing up in many parts of the Anglophone world. I had been closely involved in the setting up of the British organization OutRage, largely in response to Section 28, but I was very doubtful about the strategy of 'outing'. It has always seemed to me that unless 'coming out' is *voluntary*, it is meaningless. It was also increasingly clear that 'outing' was highly selective and politically motivated. Those 'outed' invariably came from institutions such as the Church of England or the House of Lords, of which the outers disapproved. Nobody on the left was ever 'outed'. The exposure of gross political hypocrisy is one thing, but the persecution of unhappy individuals, many of whom were doubtless already locked in hells of private misery, did not strike me as attractive. In many cases 'outing' caused lasting personal suffering, no less than would have derived from exposure in the *Sun*. This was not a politics with which I wished to be associated. There was also the pressing question of how the new 'Queer' politics of the early 1990s might relate to AIDS.

It was clear that like every new generation, the youth of the 1990s would establish their own identities, and would of course develop their own social and political organizations and forms of cultural expression. How might these relate to the older structures of lesbian and gay culture? How might all this relate to patterns of HIV transmission? What were the lessons for young AIDS educators, working with their peers? These were some of the questions I explored in 'Emergent sexual identities'. Writing for a broad spectrum of professional AIDS workers, from academic sociologists to local health authority workers, I warned against any assumption that gay identity is ever monolithic or unchanging. Out in night-time Clubland, a whole rich new youth culture was emerging, much of it more closely tied to the environmentalist movement than to the older sexual politics. What was *their* experience of the epidemic?

Such work about questions of sexual *identity* was above all concerned with trying to better understand perceptions of risk from HIV, especially amongst those who had little direct experience of illness in their immediate social environment, yet who were at demonstrably high statistical risk of infection. This was the context in which Gay Men Fighting AIDS (GMFA) was conceived and set up in 1991, as a new grass-roots organization involved in designing and conducting fully evaluated HIV and AIDS education and prevention work for gay men, and related community-based research. The older AIDS charities which had been established at a much earlier stage in the history of the epidemic were proving inflexible in their policies, and seemed unwilling or unable to adequately support such work, or the provision of reliable and accessible information about available treatments and related research. Hence the urgent need in the early 1990s to set up new charities with a specific mission to undertake these tasks efficiently.

For many years I have greatly admired and benefited from the research and policy work of the independent Treatment Action Group (TAG) in New York, which had begun its work as the Treatment and Data Group of ACT UP New York, before ACT UP lost its practical political grip on reality in the early 1990s. I was greatly impressed by the achievements of American treatment activism, which was extraordinarily focused and well informed in its demands concerning the immediate, practical health needs of people living with HIV and AIDS. Yet by late 1990 ACT UP had in effect been taken over by a coalition of pre-existing political constituencies, mainly of the far left, with agendas reaching far beyond the epidemic. I will give one symbolic example that must stand for many.

In October 1990 a cartoon appeared in the widely read New York lesbian and gay weekly magazine *Outweek*, by one of the magazine's resident cartoonists, which summed up everything that had gone wrong.[23] A skinny little man with AIDS is seen scuttling along the ground on his knees, hooked up to a mobile drip on wheels. He is being pursued by a huge, lumbering figure, on all fours, identified as the 'AIDS Movement'. On one arm is a bandage labelled 'ACT UP'. On its back is a big rectangular horizontal wooden container, with a large slogan on its side saying: 'Thousand Year Plan'. Seated inside the container is a heavy load of activists in T-shirts waving banners that proclaim: 'Gay & Lesbian Visibility!', 'End Sexism', 'End Racism!', 'Only Men Can Be Sexist!', 'Only White People Can Be Racist!', 'US Troops Out Of Middle East', and 'Solve It All'.

Sue Hyde from Boston and Eve Faber from Washington responded in *Outweek*, accusing Sotomayor of 'gross distortion', claiming that his cartoon 'represents AIDS in the exclusive context of white gay men'. They concluded that: 'we think confronting the hatred that has informed every governmental and corporate decision about HIV is as important as getting drugs into your body'. Sotomayor rejected their accusations briskly: 'Since I am a Puerto Rican who has been living with AIDS for the last three years, I find your accusation almost too absurd to warrant a response. But it's nice to know that two white, middle-class, HIV-negative women are around to point this AIDS-infected Puerto Rican towards the truth … If you find the PWA's right to stay alive a selfish "me-me-me" endeavour, what the hell are you doing in this movement?'[24]

It soon became impossible to do effective AIDS work within an activist movement which was increasingly driven by completely impractical Utopian extremists who entirely lacked the central sense of practical, focused urgency that had motivated ACT UP into existence in 1986, and which informed its remarkable early successes. The entryists insisted, amongst other things, on gender-parity in *all* issues, including equal funding for HIV prevention for lesbians. In spite of the lack of *any* evidence in several surveys for the sexual woman-to-woman transmission of HIV, the spectre of 'Lesbian AIDS' came to dominate the agenda, at the height of the epidemic amongst gay men and other clearly defined risk groups.

From the perspective of a political culture concerned with the quite separate cultural question of 'lesbian invisibility', the very absence of cases was cited by many lesbian feminists as conclusive 'evidence' of the extent of this supposedly 'hidden epidemic'. In both Britain and the USA a number of lesbians falsely claimed to have HIV, and went so far as to get actively involved in AIDS work. This was later justified by other lesbians on the extraordinary grounds that 'lesbians were being ignored'.[25]

Women and men who tried to draw attention to reliable, *reassuring* medical evidence concerning the minimal risk of woman-to-woman HIV transmission, were routinely publicly vilified. Gay men were ritually denounced as misogynistic agents of some sinister 'AIDS Mafia', deliberately putting women ('wimmin') in danger. Such were the political pressures of the times in America that by the early 1990s Gay Men's Health Crisis in New York was employing four full-time workers, devising HIV prevention campaigns for lesbians, against a non-existent mode of transmission. Reason had long since ceased to prevail. Writing in the leading national lesbian and gay magazine *The Advocate* in December 1991, Merle Woo of the San Francisco University Women's Studies program stirringly outlined the politically correct line for America's young Queer revolutionary cadres: 'We are the scapegoats for capitalism's literal bankruptcy ... Any liberation movement worth its salt has got to fight for everybody or none of us will be free ... Capitalism is going down in flames. We'll be right there fanning the flames and throwing on the butane.'[26]

Elsewhere lesbian activists dramatically announced: 'AIDS-Like Symptoms and Stigma Strike the Lesbian Community'. This was Chronic Fatigue Immune Dysfunction Syndrome, or: 'CFIDS: The Invisible Health Crisis'.[27] Reporter Victoria Brownsworth insisted: 'CFIDS *is* a medical crisis, though it may not present as terminal illness like AIDS or breast cancer', and she rounded angrily on the failure of the entire 'queer community' to form direct-action groups along the lines of ACT UP in order to engage with 'the politics of the CFIDS crisis', and so on and so forth.

Predictably enough, the sectarian elements which frequently dominated lesbian-feminist politics at that time had neither understanding of nor respect for the lives of most lesbians, least of all for many women's only too real and complex and often very painful experience of the epidemic, mainly in relation to the illness and death of close gay male friends. Meanwhile ACT UP had been turned into a kind of extremist political party, with a narrow 'party-line' required on a whole host of issues from domestic to foreign policy matters. By the early 1990s the *long-term* goal of creating a system of socialized medicine in America had became fixed as a higher priority than the *immediate* goal of finding better treatments and care for people with HIV and AIDS. This, in effect, is what happened to almost all the initially effective AIDS activist groups in the United States and elsewhere. Leading US treatment activist Mark Harrington later summed up the mood of the time that if *anything* important was to be achieved for people with HIV, there had to be a decisive move 'from therapeutic utopianism to pragmatic praxis'.[28]

Given the much smaller scale of the epidemic in Britain, and the real obstacles to obtaining adequate funding or government support for gay men's prevention work in Britain, it seemed that we might benefit from an activism directed towards the badly neglected field of targeted AIDS education. Our aim was to encourage well organized new forms of community-based 'prevention activism', as some of us thought of it at the time. This was part of the background to the formation of the organization Gay Men Fighting AIDS (GMFA). I wrote many articles on this subject in the gay press, of which two are included here, both of which also appeared in gay publications in the USA and Australia. At this time I was still writing a regular monthly column in *Gay Times* in Britain, and also writing regularly in the New York gay press. Included here is an article from *Gay Times* in 1993, 'Hard won credibility', which looked at the role and responsibilities of the gay press in relation to the reporting of AIDS issues.

'Read my lips' was written as a catalogue essay for the first exhibition in Britain of AIDS activist graphics, videos, and related artworks, curated by Nicola White, with whom I worked very closely. In 1989 I had worked closely with Director Saskia Baron on a *Late Show* special for BBC2 about the same subject. I interviewed a number of significant artists and activists, most of whom I already knew, and the programme was well received.[29] In the catalogue I wrote from a clear sense that the first 'classic' phase of AIDS activism associated above all with ACT UP New York was effectively over. There was a different mood. So many people were dying, and any residual hopes that AZT might prove a bridge-head leading to more effective treatments were dashed. As for so many others, the International AIDS Conference in Berlin at which the deeply disappointing Concorde trial results of AZT were reported in the summer of 1992 was one of the most depressing events of my life. For many it was a moment of terrible pessimism, often verging on despair.

In the meantime I was becoming increasingly disillusioned with the world of lesbian and gay studies, of which I had once felt very much a part. I had begun writing about AIDS from the perspective of the person I was before the epidemic. Now, many years later, I had become a very different person. I was also disappointed by and impatient with the fanaticism and lofty posturing of much of Queer and leftist politics as they had evolved in different ways in Britain and the USA. Inciting violent hatred and contempt for all heterosexuals never struck me as a particularly attractive feature of Queer politics, which had from the outset carefully established itself at a safe distance from the epidemic, as if anxious not to be defined in relation to the virtual decimation of an older generation of gay men. This in turn frequently reflected a growing but rarely acknowledged sense of division between the long-term interests of infected and uninfected gay men.

Many younger, self-styled Queer academics and journalists sneered at what they regarded as 'vulgar' notions of community and solidarity. They poured scorn on what they regarded as 'naïve' and 'essentialist' notions of stable sexual identities. They rejected the validity of all notions of gay community. They seemed to have nothing but contempt for the majority of gay men, from whom some of them in Britain strenuously distanced themselves in the self-designated name of 'anti-gay' politics. The anti-gays condescendingly dismissed gay identity as if it were completely monolithic and invariant – hedonistic and shallow and mindlessly consumerist, and somehow uniformly imposed on everyone. It also seemed that it was mainly working-class gay culture that they most looked down on.

Throughout the 1990s one would find their articles in the national press every June, or their joyless faces on national television, pompously informing us all why they couldn't possibly take part in anything as trivial and vulgar and naïve as the annual Lesbian and Gay Pride Festival. No wonder the national mass media loved them. By contrast, in spite of all its many glaring faults and failings, it seems to me that the modern lesbian and gay scene is on the whole a most remarkable *achievement*, of the greatest complexity and range, which was stubbornly brought into being over a long period of time, against a background of intense, entrenched homophobia. Not the least of the gains of recent years has been the greatly improved relations between so many younger men and women. This constantly mutating sense of gay community is not something that we have been forced into. On the contrary, it is a largely informal social space that we have ourselves successfully claimed in this society, as a result of decades of thankless organization and campaigning, in a host of different ways, on the part of vast numbers of folk.

The lesbian and gay scene is frequently inhospitable to older people. It is expensive. It is doubtless in many ways shallow. It is vulnerable to bloodsucking corporate interests. It does not look after its own very well. But then this is true of the entire contemporary world, and why should we expect the gay scene to be magically different? It may not be good enough, but it is *infinitely better* than what we had before the 1970s. The gay community is what we make of it. Of course it will be caught up in a constant process of reinventing itself in order to meet the needs of the always unimaginable future as that emerges. But for the time being at least, the gay scene (including its extensive Internet dimension), remains the main place where gay men meet and socialize. It is thus automatically the main terrain on which the fight against HIV will continue to be lost or won. This is why these debates *matter*.

It seemed to me at the time that the rampant individualism of much 1990s British Queer culture and politics, with its sometimes violent hostility to communitarian values and identities, was little more than an extreme, perverse reflection of the very forces it ostensibly opposed. Sectarian government breeds sectarian opposition, with its predictable tendency to intense internal rivalries and splintering.[30] It was a period in which bullies were given full licence in many walks of life, and aggression was the journalistic order of the day.[31] There were few positive political beliefs on display in the mass media, only a kind of aimlessly angry, fashionably embittered, intensely competitive, cynical individualism. Hired by the national press, the anti-gays could hardly wait to dissociate themselves from the communities from which they had come, which had made their early careers possible, and where their genius had perhaps been under-appreciated. Julie Burchill, Andrew Sullivan and, later, Camille Paglia pointed the way.

The latter's sophisticated grasp of the complexities of modern gay and lesbian history is conveniently summed up in her recent, sweeping pronouncement that all gay men today are entirely 'self-referential', and that the gay community is 'competitive and aggressive, whereas in pre-Stonewall days it was introspective and more honest'.[32] On the basis of such profound insights she feels confident to launch into equally sweeping assertions about all gay men's sexual behaviour.[33] For many years this intellectual giant has preached the same foolish and bigoted message that AIDS is somehow Nature's Revenge on gay men, for rejecting our proper place in the order of things as secretive, shame-driven (but 'artistic') second-class citizens, and for basing our lives (according to Paglia) solely on the basis of our 'carnal sexual identity'.[34]

Yet if you are actually *involved* in the AIDS sector you work all the time in relation to an extensive and vastly disparate social constituency which for lack of any better phrase we may best describe as the gay community, whose 'authenticity' is beyond any doubt. Try telling all those who gathered in Soho over the May Bank Holiday weekend in 1999, to express solidarity with the victims of the recent nail-bomb attack on the Admiral Duncan pub on Old Compton Street, that there is no such thing as a lesbian and gay community. Try explaining it to the hundreds of thousands of concerned telephone callers all over the country on the evening after the explosion. This always-changing community is where the epidemic is, and where it has to be fought. Those of us who question the 'anti-gay' dismissal of *all* notions of gay community and gay identity do so not because we seek controversy, but simply because we are not nihilists. We have seen in our lifetimes what well targeted collective action can achieve, and we are only too aware of how much more such work will be needed for the foreseeable future.

I persist in believing that most gay men face similar personal problems and challenges in our lives, and that however much things may generally be changing for the better in terms of social attitudes towards us, still, across the generations, we are likely to have in common a wide range of social and emotional experience, rooted in myriad ways in our shared homosexuality, however badly and inadequately we may deal with one another as mere mortals. To question this seems to me to question the most palpable reality in front of one's eyes. It suggests resistance to the very idea of *belonging*.

I had played a small role myself since the mid 1980s in attempts to draw attention to some of the inadequacies of the ways in which AIDS has been represented in the various branches of the mass media. I wrote a book and many articles on this subject in the 1980s, and frequently addressed the subject on British radio and television.[35] By the 1990s I had other, more pragmatic goals in my life and work, but I continued to be involved in various ways with questions of the cultural responses to AIDS, ranging from my direct involvement in the production of Safer Sex materials, including videos, for the Terrence Higgins Trust, and in much of my writing and other work.

Included here is 'Art from the pit', written for the catalogue of a major Australian exhibition in 1994 of international art responding to AIDS, and 'In purgatory', about the work of the young Cuban-American artist Felix Gonzalez-Torres, whom I knew very slightly, and greatly admired. I had initially met Felix at the Whitney Program in New York, where I gave a regular annual talk and seminar in the late 1980s and early 1990s. I also knew his partner Ross Laycock from pre-AIDS visits to Toronto. I particularly admired the way Felix's work addressed questions of medical research, and tragic loss, in an entirely non-didactic and non-dogmatic fashion. Ross died of AIDS in 1991, and Felix died in 1996.[36] It was a very great shame and scandal that none of the leading London galleries chose to bring his magnificent 1995 Guggenheim Museum retrospective to London, after its display in New York and Paris. It should also be noted that over the years the leading London galleries have all consistently refused to show major travelling exhibitions which have been displayed in major museums around the world, including AIDS-related work by artists as distinguished as Keith Haring, Ross Bleckner and David Wojnarowicz. It was thus all the more to the credit of the Victoria and Albert Museum that in the summer of 1996 it originated and displayed a small but important exhibition of international AIDS-related materials curated by Shaun Cole, titled *Graphic Responses to AIDS*.

'Acts of memory', 'AIDS awareness?', and 'Lifelike' were all reflective responses to what was going on around me in the mid-1990s. At the same time I was by this time myself running a small charity, aiming to raise much-needed funds to distribute to front-line and often controversial AIDS education projects, mainly in the developing world. 'Signifying AIDS' is included here as an example of my involvement in international aspects of the epidemic. Amongst other things it criticises the institutional homophobia of the World Health Organisation throughout its policies and practices on HIV and AIDS education.[37]

I also include an article from 1994 looking back over the history of the Concorde trial of AZT, which in this new context stands for an entire dimension of medical research issues with which I was for many years involved. For example, I was the first person to report the early stages of Protease Inhibitor research in the UK gay press, in 1989. It was a great relief to know by the early 1990s that there were many people far more scientifically competent than me to report on such vital issues.

The later essays in this volume were all written in response to requests from book editors, wanting articles from me. In all of them I tried to summarize particular aspects of recent history, and to explore some of the deeper long-term implications of the epidemic within the worst affected communities. Thus 'The politics of AIDS treatment information activism' offers a brief history of treatment activism in Britain and the USA.

'These waves of dying friends' examines many different aspects of mourning, and the widely differing degrees of experience of illness and death amongst gay men, and our many different responses. The article on statistics and epidemiology offers a similar retrospective overview of the 're-gaying' movement, which I had first named and subsequently worked hard for. It comes from the published papers from a 1996 conference at the Institute of Contemporary Arts (ICA) in London, where in 1988 I had helped to organize an earlier international conference bringing together cultural and political analysis, the papers from which were published.[38]

In 'Lesbian and gay studies in the age of AIDS' I looked at some questions concerning the ways in which AIDS has been approached within the emergent field of lesbian and gay studies, noting the many differences between the situations in different countries. The great challenge is the ability to understand the epidemic in relation to the other Big Issues within the field of lesbian and gay studies in such a way that AIDS is not marginalised. At the same time, it seemed to me that some within the Academy much preferred to think about AIDS as a purely theoretical issue, rather than as an ongoing social crisis, urgently requiring *practical* responses based on good research. Nothing could more graphically demonstrate the decadence of much contemporary academic 'theory' than its posturing on the subject of AIDS, from the early asides by Baudrillard[39] to later, more fully expanded postmodern versions of AIDS, for example, as a diagnosis which apparently 'exposes, in the course of all appropriations and manifestations of unity, the Being-not-one of time and the self, and sets off the impossible experience of this Being-not-one, experience of the uncertainty of all bounds and limits'.[40] And so on and so forth, *ad nauseam*. There are whole books of this kind of stuff, which use the epidemic as an excuse for any amount of obscure, narcissistic post-graduate pyrotechnics, which serve only to distract attention from the key issues.

'Imagine hope' was written for this collection, and considers something of the neglected history of the identities developed by people with HIV and AIDS in relation to their own lived experience. It also explores the relations between these diagnostically grounded social identities, and the contingent history of gay identity. Finally, readers may note that I have included a number of obituaries, some read at funerals, others published. At an earlier stage of the preparation of this book I took them all out, afraid that they might be found mawkish. Yet if we cannot sometimes stop to remember those who have died, why should we bother to try to understand the whole story of AIDS at all?

After all these years, we 'get used' to AIDS. We have to. It's the horror story that didn't go away. We find new coping mechanisms, new accommodations, new goals, new identities. Certainly the dead are no longer 'marching into our lives like an occupying army',[41] as they were throughout the early 1990s.

At the same time AIDS-related prejudice has certainly become less aggressive and vociferous than it was. Yet a decade later there is still, I believe, a widely prevalent and unacceptable social level of 'AIDS denial', which shares some features with Holocaust denial, as analysed so eloquently by historian Deborah Lipstadt.[42]

Certainly both the far right and the far left have long enthusiastically battened onto AIDS, using it in their deluded and generally paranoid propaganda wars against 'the scientific establishment'; 'the ruling class'; 'the myth of HIV'; 'the homosexual conspiracy to bring down the family'; 'the genocidal capitalist pharmaceutical industry', and so on. Like Holocaust denial, this is mainly 'a tactic designed to gain access to the mainstream'.[43] Their success is apparent in the widespread media (and academic) tendency to give equal weight to any and every opinion about AIDS, regardless of provable factual status. Loudly espousing the principle of free speech, careerists and fanatics of many persuasions have long attempted to hijack the epidemic, in order to use it to their own advantage, getting themselves onto television or into the press in order to 'reveal' AIDS as a medical hoax, a moral lesson, a government plot, a scientific cover-up, or whatever. This gives them further pseudo-respectability.

To take just one example, in *The Times Higher Education Supplement* in 1999, journalist Ayala Ochert interviewed 'maverick' scientist Kary Mullis, once hired as an expert witness by O. J. Simpson's lawyers, who claims there is no 'evidence' linking HIV to AIDS. Mullis's preferred metaphors are zoological: 'Think of the immune system as a camel. If the camel is overloaded it collapses. In the 1970's we had a significant number of highly mobile, promiscuous men sharing bodily fluids and fast life-styles and drugs ... our society was experimenting with a lifestyle and it didn't work. They got sick.'[44] This may be preposterous nonsense, and potentially dangerous, but it still gets an entire page of a prestigious academic publication.

Ms Ochert cheerfully described the way Mullis 'has gone out against the AIDS establishment all guns blazing'. Did Ms Ochert ask him about the scientifically incontrovertible epidemiological evidence for the clinical association between HIV and AIDS? She did not. And what ultimately is this sinister 'AIDS establishment'? In reality it consists of tens of thousands of over-worked, generally modest doctors (with exceptions to the rule, like any other social group), treating hundreds of thousands of HIV-infected people all around the world, on top of having already witnessed the deaths of hundreds of thousands of others in their daily care over the years. It also consists of all those struggling to get access to costly treatment drugs in backward countries such as the USA which lack socialized medicine. If HIV doesn't cause AIDS, why should anyone worry about safer sex? It was all those dirty Seventies queers, wasn't it, who brought this whole thing on themselves? And what of the grim HIV and AIDS statistics in Harare, or Calcutta? Or of haemophiliacs around the world, infected via contaminated blood plasma? The mere fact that *The Times Higher Education Supplement* can provide an uncritical platform for this kind of misleading and self-promoting nonsense tells us more than we would like to know about current levels of supposedly serious British journalism.

Deborah Lipstadt helpfully summarizes anthropologist Marshall Sahlin's description of this process as it tends to operate within the academic arena:

> Professor X publishes a theory despite the fact that reams of documented information contradict his conclusions. In the 'highest moral tones' he expresses his disregard for all evidence that sheds doubt on his findings. He engages in *ad hominem* attacks on those who have authored the critical works in the field and on the people silly enough to believe them. The scholars who have come under attack by this professor are provoked to respond. Before long he becomes 'the controversial Prof. X' and his theory is discussed seriously by non-professionals, that is, journalists. He soon becomes a familiar figure on television and radio, where he 'explains' his ideas to interviewers who cannot challenge him or demonstrate the fallaciousness of his argument.[45]

It is in this context that we should also regard the type of fashionable postmodernism which denies the existence of *any* historical reality or truth outside language. Such work plays straight into the hands of those who seek, for whatever reasons, to deny the medical or the wider historical reality of AIDS. 'Epidemic! *What* epidemic?'

This is one more reason why truthful personal testimony remains so important.[46] As James Baldwin once observed: 'I'm a witness. That's my responsibility. I write it all down'.[47] The terrible mortality rates of the early 1990s may be behind us, but there is no cure, and people are still dying of AIDS every day. My friend the late Allen Barnett told the story of the Board of an American academic sociology journal which turned down an article on grief in the gay community on the grounds that gay men cannot suffer bereavement, since our relationships are 'too shallow'.[48] In such a world, as gay critic Timothy F. Murphy has wisely observed: 'Testimony for the dead is not driven by a desire to overcome death, but to prevent it from eroding the meaningfulness of life. Testimony, not death, is the last word'.[49]

Notes

1 *The Times*, Wednesday 12 May 1999, p. 17.
2 Edward King, 'Why we aren't such lucky cows', *Pink Paper*, Issue 424, 5 April 1996, p. 13.
3 *AIDS/HIV Quarterly Surveillance Tables, UK Data to End December 1998*, No. 42: 98/4, January 1999, Table 1, The Public Health Laboratory Service (PHLS), London, 1999. In future, regular HIV/AIDS statistics will be published by the PHLS at six-monthly intervals, rather than quarterly. These tables are also available on the Internet.
4 *Unlinked Anonymous HIV Prevalence Monitoring Programme in England and Wales: Report from the Unlinked Anonymous Surveys Steering Group* (Department of Health, 1997), p. 22.
5 See Simon Watney, 'Muddling through', in Simon Watney, *Practices of Freedom: Selected Writings on HIV/AIDS*, London: 1994; Durham, NC: Duke University Press, River Oram Press, 1994).
6 I would like to thank Colin Richardson for drawing my attention to this deafening silence.
7 Simon Watney, 'These waves of dying friends', 1996, Chapter 26 in this collection.
8 See the excellent analysis of the *Sunday Times*'s repeated assertion that there is no AIDS epidemic in Africa, in 'The myth that is killing a continent', by Julie Flint, *Independent on Sunday*, 2 January 1994, pp. 12–13. On the same subject see also Steve O'Connor, 'Newspaper is criticised over AIDS articles', the *Independent*, 9 October 1993.
9 For example, see Helen Rumbelow, 'HIV cases rise as the young spurn condoms', *The Times*, Wednesday 25 November 1998; Andrew Gumbel, 'The last seduction. Gay men are tired of living in fear of AIDS. So now they're turning risk into a thrill', *Independent on Sunday. Weekend Review*, 13 February 1999, p. 8.
10 For example, Nigel Wrench, 'The stigma that never goes away', *The Times*, Tuesday 24 November 1998, p. 16; *AIDS and Me*, BBC Radio Four, Tuesday 13 July 1999.
11 Andrew Sullivan, 'When plagues end: Note on the twighlight of an epidemic', *New York Times Magazine*, Sunday 10 November 1996, pp. 52–84; and *Independent on Sunday Review*, 16 February 1996, pp. 7–11. See also Andrew Sullivan, 'Hello life, I hardly recognise you', *Sunday Times News Review*, 1 November 1998, p. 10; and Gus Cairns, 'Too cute. Andrew Sullivan has an answer for everything', *Positive Nation*. Issue 39, London, February 1999, pp. 6–10.
12 'One fifth believes AIDS cure exists', *Pink Paper*, 16 April 1999, p. 4.
13 *Are Health Authorities failing gay men? HIV Prevention Spending in England 1997/98* (London: The National AIDS Trust, February 1999). The classic text in this debate is Edward King, *Safety in Numbers: Safer Sex and Gay Men* (London: Cassell, 1993)
14 *ibid.*
15 Major reports include: Michael Rooney, *Gay Men: Sustaining Safer Sex?* (London: The HIV Project, 1991); Edward King, Michael Rooney and Peter Scott, *HIV Prevention for Gay Men – A Survey of Initiatives in the UK* (London: North West Thames Regional Health Authority, 1992); Peter Scott and Les Woods, *HIV Infection and AIDS. Developing Services for Gay Men and Bisexual Men* (Luton: Local Government Management Board, 1993); Will Anderson and Ford Hickson, *Local Government, AIDS, and Gay Men, Results of a survey into the HIV and AIDS services of local government in England and Wales, with a*

particular emphasis on work with gay men and bisexual men (London: NAM
Publications, 1994); James Fitzpatrick, *HIV Funding In England. AIDS Funding
Research Bulletin*, no. 1 (London: National AIDS Trust, June 1994); Jeffrey
Weeks *et al.*, *Voluntary Sector Responses to HIV and AIDS – Policies Principles
and Practices, Summary Report* (London: HERU, Institute of Education, 1994); P.
Kelley, Peter Scott and Martin Dockrell, *A Survey of London Needs Assessments*
(London: Gay Men Fighting AIDS, 1995); Peter Scott and Ian Warwick, with H.
Durbin, *A Pilot Needs Assessment and Evaluation Training Project* (London: The
HIV Project, 1995); P. Kelley, Roger Pebody and Peter Scott, *How Far Will You
Go: A Survey of London Gay Men's Migration and Mobility*, (London: Gay Men
Fighting AIDS, 1996); Greg Lucas and Peter Scott, *Basic Building Blocks for
Population Needs Assessment in HIV/AIDS: Worksheets Developed From the
Findings of a Project to investigate Current Practice in Population Needs
Assessment* (Luton: Local Government Management Board, 1996); Peter Scott,
*Moving Targets: An assessment of the needs of gay men and of bisexual men in
relation to HIV prevention in Enfield and Haringey*, a report published by the
Enfield and Haringey Health Authority (London, 1996); Katie Deverell, *Building
Bridges, Linking Research and Primary HIV Prevention.* London: NAM
Publications, 1996; Peter Scott and Les Woods, *Critical Tolerance: A Gay
Community Led Model of Needs Assessment investigating the needs of HIV posi-
tive men, their partners and surviving partners.* (Brighton: Critical Tolerance,
1997) (available on the Internet at http://www.racoon.dircon.co.uk); Peter Scott
with Tony Coxon *et al.*, *Cottaging and Cruising in Barnet Brent & Harrow: Final
Report* (London: Barnet AIDS Education Unit, 1997); National AIDS Trust,
*Families and AIDS: A review of support services for HIV affected families and
carers in the UK* (London, 1998); Peter Scott, *The Zorro Report: An assessment of the HIV prevention needs of gay men in Brighton and the adequacy
of local HIV prevention services in meeting those needs.* Report 98–6 of
Project SIGMA (University of Essex, 1998) (available on the Internet at
http://www.racoon.dircon.co.uk); Greg Lucas and Peter Scott, *Charitable funding
in the era of combination therapies: next steps towards quality and effectiveness*
(London; Crusaid, 1998); Will Anderson and Peter Wetherburn, *Taking heart?
The impact of combination therapy on the lives of people with HIV*, SIGMA
Research Report (1999); *It's A Job Being Positive: The Back To Work Report*
(London: The UK Coalition of People Living with HIV and AIDS, 1999). It
should be noted that, taken together, these reports represent the theory and practice of one of the most important strands of the British community-based
response to the epidemic.

16 For a helpful practical guide to 'contract culture' in relation to AIDS, see Peter
Scott, *Purchasing HIV Prevention: A No-nonsense Guide for Use with Gay and
Bisexual Men* (London: Health Education Authority, 1995).

17 See Barry Evans, Simon Sandberg and Stuart Watson (Eds). *Working Where The
Risks Are* (London: Health Education Authority, 1992). See also Peter Scott, 'My
three big ideas. A strategy for 1999', *Pink Paper.* 27 November 1988, pp. 14–15.

18 See note 10.

19 See Chapter 13 and Chapter 28 in this book.

20 Chinua Achebe, *Another Africa* (London: Lund Humphries, 1998).

21 See Simon Watney, 'Representing AIDS', in Tessa Boffin and Sunil Gupta (Eds).
Ecstatic Antibodies: Resisting the AIDS Mythology (London: Rivers Oram Press,
1990), pp. 165–92; and Simon Watney, 'ART AIDS NYC', *Art & Text*, no. 38,
Sydney, Australia, 1991, pp. 51–98. See also Jan Zita Grover, *AIDS: The Artists'
Response* (Hoyt L. Sherman Gallery, The Ohio State University, 1989); and
Douglas Crimp and Adam Rolston (eds) *AIDS Demo Graphics* (Seattle: Bay
Press, 1990).

22 See Simon Edge, *With Friends Like These: Marxism and gay politics* (London: Cassell, 1995).

23 *Outweek*, New York, 17 October 1990.

24 Daniel Sotomayor, 'Letters', *Outweek*. no. 75, 5 December 1990, New York, pp. 5–6.

25 See Jo-Ann Goodwin, 'A marriage made in hell', *Guardian Weekend*. London, 17 December 1994, pp. 30–6. This contains an accidentally illuminating survey of UK attitudes at the time. Read the letters pages of the gay and lesbian press in New York or London through these years for a chilling resume of such madness, e.g. *Outweek* and *NYQ* in New York, *Capital Gay* and the *Pink Paper* in London. See also Amber Hollibaugh *et al.*, *The Lesbian AIDS Project Information Pack* (New York: GMHC, 1994); and GMHC's *Safer Sex Handbook for Lesbians*, published in 1993, a typical example of a widespread genre.

26 Merle Woo, *The Advocate*, no. 592, 17 December 1991.

27 Victoria Brownsworth, 'CFIDS: The invisible health crisis', *QW*, New York, 13 September 1992, p. 45.

28 Mark Harrington, 'Some transitions in the history of AIDS treatment activism; from therapeutic utopianism to pragmatic praxis', in Joshua Oppenheimer and Helena Reckitt (Eds) *Acting on AIDS: sex drugs & politics* (London: Serpent's Tail Press, 1997), pp. 273–87. See also Robin Hardy, 'Die harder. AIDS activism is abandoning gay men', *Village Voice*, New York, 2 July 1991, pp. 33–4.

29 Transcriptions of most of the interviews were later published in *Art & Text*, no. 38, Sydney, 1992.

30 See the brilliant analysis of sectarianism by Mary Douglas and Aaron Wildavsky in *Risk and Culture: An Essay on the Selection of Technological and Environmental Dangers* Berkeley, CA: University of California press, 1982).

31 See Madeleine Bunting, 'A phoney cry of freedom: the media's contempt for privacy and propriety', *Guardian* Wednesday 4 January 1994, p. 18; and Adam Gopnik, 'Read all about it', *New Yorker*. 12 December 1994, pp. 84–102.

32 Nick Stellmacher, 'Parlez-vous Paglia?', *Pink Paper*, Issue 585, London, 4 June 1999, pp. 20–1.

33 Camille Paglia, 'Ask Camille: Three-way sex with death', *Salon Magazine*, 17 February 1999, n.p.

34 Camille Paglia, *ibid*.

35 See Simon Watney, *Policing Desire: Pornography AIDS & The Media* (London, 1987 and 1997; University of Minnesota Press, 1988, 1989, and 1997); and Simon Watney, *Practices of Freedom: Selected Writings on HIV/AIDS* (London: Rivers Oram Press, 1994; Durham, N.C.: Duke University Press, 1994).

36 See William S. Bartman (Ed.) *Felix Gonzalez-Torres* (New York Art Resources Transfer Inc., 1993) New and Nancy Spector, *Felix Gonzalez-Torres* (New York: Guggenheim Museum, 1995).

37 See Neil McKenna, *On the Margins: men who have sex with men, and HIV in the developing world* (London: The Panos Institute, 1996); and Peter Aggleton (Ed.) *Bisexualities and AIDS International Perspectives* (London: Taylor & Francis, 1996).

38 See Erica Carter and Simon Watney (Eds.) *Taking Liberties: AIDS and Cultural Politics* (London: Serpent's Tail, 1989).

39 See Larys Frogier, 'Representation, identity, and minorities', *Texte Zur Kunst*, Cologne, Issue 17, February 1995, pp. 93–4.

40 Alexander Garcia Duttmann, *At Odds with AIDS: Thinking and Talking about a Virus* (Standford, CA: University Press, 1996), p. 16.

41 Allen Barnett, *The Body and Its Dangers and Other Stories* (New York: St Martin's Press, 1990), p. 115.

42 Deborah Lipstadt, *Denying the Holocaust: The growing assault on truth and*

memory (London: Penguin, 1994). (I am very grateful to Edward King for drawing my attention to this remarkable book.)

43 Lipstadt, *ibid.*, p. 218.

44 Ayala Ochert, 'Cresting controversy', *The Times Higher Education Supplement*, 23 April 1999, p. 17. See also Simon Watney, 'HIV-AIDS link irrefutable', Letters & Opinions, *The Times Higher Education Supplement*, 21 May 1999, p. 19.

45 Lipstadt, *Denying the Holocaust*, p. 27.

46 See Simon Watney, 'Powers of observation: AIDS and the writing of history', *Practices of Freedom: Selected Writings on HIV/AIDS* (London: Rivers Oram Press, 1994; Durham, N.C.: Duke University Press, 1994), pp. 256–65.

47 James Baldwin, 'Conversation with Ida Lewis', in F. L. Stanley and Louis H. Pratt (Eds) *Conversations with James Baldwin* (Jackson: University Press of Mississippi, 1989), p. 92.

48 Allen Barnett, 'Philostorgy, now obscure', *The Body and its Dangers and Other Stories*, (New York: St Martin's Press, 1990), p. 44.

49 Timothy F. Murphy, 'Testimony', in T. F. Murphy and Suzanne Poirier (eds), *Writing AIDS: Gay Literature, Language, and Analysis* (New York: Columbia University Press, 1993), p. 316.

1 Ordinary boys*

Only that historian will have the gift of fanning the spark of hope in the past who is firmly convinced that *even the dead* will not be safe from the enemy if he wins and this enemy has not ceased to be victorious.

Walter Benjamin[1]

But don't forget the songs that made you cry, And the ones that saved your life, Yes you're older now and you're a clever swine, But they're the only ones who always stood by you.

Morrissey[2]

The fiction of our invisibility remains influential.

Neil Bartlett[3]

In 1947, two years before I was born, The Camera Inc. of Baltimore, USA, published a very up-to-date handbook on *Portraiture* in their Camarette Photo Library series. The anonymous editors explained in their Foreword that: 'Amongst all the branches of photography, perhaps portraiture is the most fascinating, for it is the story of people and the interpretation of personality.'[4] This admirable and most illuminating text has much to say on such topics as Portraiture at Home (including sections on 'photographing thin subjects, photographing heavy subjects, groups of two, subjects with glasses', etc.); Glamour Portraiture ('star photographs, corrective make-up … glamour photographs for society and royalty', etc.); Hair-Dos in Portraiture; Principles of Portrait Lighting; Draping the Model; Child Portraiture (including 'timeless qualities in pictures, holding the child's attention', etc.); Portraits for the Home Record; and Portraiture of Men (including 'use of lighting to bring out features and hair, getting sitter at ease', etc.).

Needless to say, such manuals continue to proliferate in both Britain and the USA, setting the stage for lives which will in most cases be recalled only through photographic records. I have no idea whether my parents ever actually picked up a book on photography as such. They hardly had to. For the

* First published in Jo Spence and Patricia Holland (Eds) Family Snaps: The Meanings of Domestic Photography, *London: Virago Press, 1990.*

conventions of domestic 'family' photography are experienced as second nature, which precisely marks them as densely ideological – as formal as Noh plays, or a well-practised round of bell-pulls on Sunday morning. What fascinates me initially about the Camarette Photo Library book is its system of categories. More than two-thirds of the text is given over to portraits of women, usually alone but occasionally in pairs, all acknowledging the role of technique and lighting in constructing the impression of 'strength of character', 'motherliness', 'femininity' … Yet as soon as we turn to children, the desired values are very different. Here 'spontaneity' and 'humour' are the order of the day, with the strict injunction that 'eyes must see something', and so on.

This could hardly contrast more strongly with the portraits of grown men, who are presented as uniformly grim and unsmiling, or relentlessly avuncular. Yet I am loath to interpret these distinctions as if they simply express some natural order of patriarchal representation. For a start, it is difficult not to conclude that however much idealization is going on in the pictures of women, there is also an admission of the erotic, of a certain quality of play, the sense of pleasure in 'dressing up', 'looking good' … By the same token it is difficult not to feel the immense cultural pressures that have compressed the men into such monotonously joyless appearances, that force them to aspire to stereotypes of 'the rugged' or 'the intellectual' or 'the businessman' which are every bit as constrictive as the roles that their wives, mothers and older daughters are obliged to enact. Only the children seem to have fun, if in a calculatedly 'cute' way which means that they are especially droll when 'serious'. As everyone knows, a 'serious' child is an unhappy child, a child who will reflect badly on his or her parents' duty to keep them happy as nature (or photography) intended. Besides, there's something 'funny' about a serious child, something not quite right…

As a gay man approaching 40 who has kept a fairly thorough photographic record of my life since I left home more than twenty years ago, I compare the two sets of images of my life before and after I went away to college with a sense of curiosity and some anxiety. Photography was not much practised in my family, and only a couple of years ago my mother chucked out all the old negatives to 'make room'. Like many other gay men, I am acutely aware of the moment when I realized that I was not the 'nice' little boy in the holiday snaps, that a deception was being perpetrated. Yet it was *me* who felt like the deceiver, rather than my parents' image *of* me. I have almost no photographs of myself between the age of ten or so and my late teens. I was therefore very surprised, on a recent visit to my mother, to find several pictures of myself as a small boy. These are images which I had completely forgotten – as completely as I had forgotten the person I was and the world of childhood to which they offer a few moments of fragile, ambiguous access.

I grew up in the shadow of the various gay scandals of the 1950s, including the notorious Montagu case, though I cannot claim that at the age of five

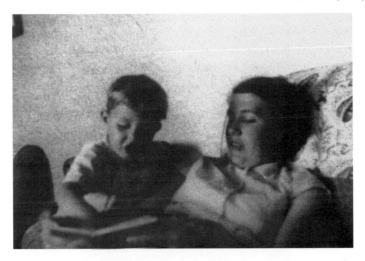

I was aware of the arrest and subsequent imprisonment of Lord Montagu and two other men for 'homosexual offences' in 1954. I do, however, remember very clearly only a few years later reading about other such unnatural monsters in my grandmother's Sunday newspaper, *The People*. Knowing instantly that I was 'one of them'. Knowing that *I* was this new word in my vocabulary, never to be said out loud: 'queer'. I have a photograph of myself learning to read. My mother tells me that it was taken on holiday, which explains its otherwise anomalous existence. She couldn't remember who the woman in the picture was. What amazes me is this simple fact: *the child is me*. And I look fine, a little boy just like millions of other little English boys in the mid 1950s. Yet I am shocked to discover that the picture reveals nothing of the terrible secret that drove me so deeply into myself for so many long irrecoverable years – years that, without photographs, do not exist.

Or perhaps there were signs? Another picture taken a couple of years later shows me hand in hand with a friend, up to our ankles in the sea. Who was he? What did I feel for him? These are questions we all ask ourselves of such images. There I was, steadily growing towards my eventual identity and life as a gay man, yet now I recall next to nothing of those early years. Again, a few years on, another beach with another friend, Midge, whom I adored, but who has now decayed to a single memory – that his parents lived in Kuwait. By this time I had read about myself in *The People*. I had also begun to have sex with other boys in a fumbling pre-public sort of way. By now I had any number of secrets, and was well aware of the degree to which my knowledge of myself conflicted with the ways other people saw me. What startles me now is a simple and painfully obvious displacement: I have always believed that I was a grotesquely fat and unattractive child, but the

little boy who stares back rather cautiously from under his sunhat is neither of these things. I thought I was fat and ugly because I thought I was *bad*.

Many people will have memories of this order, memories that signal some kind of dysfunction between one's sense of oneself and one's parents' expectations. These are folded in with the larger function of domestic photography, which is to impart the semblance of retrospective coherence to family life, usually more or less chaotic and unpredictable. This *narrative* function should not be lightly dismissed, for it provides a crucial psychic stabilizer to life – the sense of *purpose*. Yet gay children are particularly vulnerable to their parents' fantasies about who they are, fantasies that invariably fail us. The gay child can hardly be expected to understand this, though he feels the sense of failure. How is a child to learn that he is perfectly OK as he is, and that his sexuality and feelings are not his problem but that of his family, and then through no real fault of their own? Who prepares parents for the entirely predictable and intrinsically unremarkable fact that their children may well grow up gay? Not many parents cope as well as Mrs Dumbo. *Dumbo* is *our* film.

All too few parents ever have the opportunity or encouragement to imagine parenting in terms that differ significantly from the ways in which they themselves were parented. In a world of great uncertainty, where most pleasures and humiliations alike are lived in silent isolation, it is not surprising that parents should tend to veer towards what they feel to be the safety of the familiar. Not many parents would nod their heads in agreement with John

Ashbery's assertion that we are saved only by what we could never have imagined.[5] Gay children are always to some extent the victims of such familiarity, and we learn many ways to hide our cloven hooves, often at terrible personal cost. The gay child who loves and wishes to be loved spares his parents' feelings at the expense of his own. This pattern may take a lifetime to unlearn. It is often clearly visible to those who know what they are looking for in the smiling photograph of an unmarried son or daughter, framed discreetly on a dressing-table in any household in the land.

We are what our parents most dread, what they have read about in *The People* and the *News of the World* and, for that matter, in the *Observer*. Yet we are also the Family Face. We therefore tend to learn from an early age that appearances are not much to be trusted, that nothing is necessarily what it seems, least of all ourselves. Thus gay children tend not infrequently to lead lives of intense privacy, knowing far more than they can ever reveal, ill at ease with other children, who always find us out ... We are there, and we are not there. Yet I am not convinced that we should simply blame photography for the narrowness of its conventional pictures of family life. Indeed, the very determination to put a brave face on things, to show us all smiling as our teeth chattered on the frozen windswept beach or at the washed-out picnic, only demonstrates our more or less desperate desire to be happy: a dumb, clumsy, inchoate awareness that somehow life could be better than it is. This is the poignancy and potency of so much domestic photography. It is where we see our past follies and illusions grow clearer (or more damaging) year by year, as much in repetitions as in changes. There I am, standing on the beach, facing the camera. If only I could talk to the child I was, tell him not to worry, tell him that he's all right as he is, and lovable! Perhaps we spend our entire lives coming back to stare at pictures of the people we once were, mouthing the same reassuring messages that we could never hear when we most needed them? Perhaps this is secretly what family photographs are all about, always giving back the same forlorn and incompatible messages: 'How happy I was' and 'If only I'd known'...

And then we leave home, though home is always there in our head as we struggle to break with the immensely powerful role models offered by our parents, to be ourselves. I look at the generic 'family' snaps of my parents with myself and my sister. It's as if we were all invisible away from the seaside, as if we came to life only as a family on holiday. My father died when I was sixteen. Now, when I shave, I see his face starting back at me from the bathroom mirror: at least his look, if not his actual looks. This was *it*, their marriage, with all its crushing load of symbols and duties (and relations) that marriage entails. Oh, and love too, if you're lucky. My Extended Family albums are so very different. This difference might be summarized in the observation that whereas heterosexuals have separations and divorces, gay men usually make friends from the wreckage of failed love affairs. A high proportion of names in my address book, and faces amongst my photographs,

are ex-lovers, and in this respect I think I am entirely typical rather than an exception. My photographs and my life coincide with the emergence of modern gay culture. As Neil Bartlett points out, this is 'something to be struggled for, not dreamt or bought. At this point, our rewriting of history becomes a truly dangerous activity.'[6]

Our photographs help us learn to be generous and forgiving to ourselves. This is especially important for people who often have to overcome a heavy sense of personal failure: the failure to be what our parents expected. Sadly, some of us never learn that this was our parents' failure, not ours. So I look back to myself at the age of twenty and cannot help but think how little I had to model my life on that might have given me a stronger sense of self-esteem. In the two decades between that image and pictures of myself with my lover John-Paul today, I am very much aware of the presence of tens of thousands of people like me, who have worked to construct our culture, however uneven and contradictory it may be. Such images carry us through life, like the songs you learn as a teenager – in my case the songs of Dionne Warwick, Aretha Franklin, Billie Holiday – images, like the songs, that do some justice to the complexity of life, its risks and passions, its memories and forgettings. My Extended Family albums contain pictures of my first hitchhiked trips to Europe, the first ever British Gay Pride march, many demonstrations, many parties, many days out and many days at home. Different places, different careers, different lovers, different homes. Yet everywhere I go, the little boy on the beach who I was goes with me.

I am still trying to make up to him for what he went through, trying to make amends.

I could not finish this piece without saying something about AIDS. Looking through my own photographs this afternoon – a clear, bright January afternoon – I saw friends who are now sick, some now dead. Beautiful, gifted young gay men who, like me, spent their childhoods in prisons of guilt, finding their feelings reflected and validated in the voice of Judy Garland, or watching Bette Davis in *Dark Victory*, or reading Cavafy or Auden. We all took great risks, my generation, because great damage and injustice had been done to us, because we had so much catching up to do, through no fault of our own. In a very brief period of time we have defined our own forms of domesticity, perhaps a little more honest and flexible than those we fled – or that threw us out. We were ordinary girls and ordinary boys, growing up and 'coming out' at an extraordinary time. There is nothing that the human immunodeficiency virus or its many human allies can do to undermine the historic achievements of the Gay Liberation movement in the lives of literally millions of lesbians and gay men around the world. It is important, however, for us to try to understand the full extent to which we are hated and feared, the extent to which powerful institutions regard gay men as entirely disposable.[7] AIDS demonstrates with grim clarity the full extent to which even the dead are not safe from such pathological malice. I fear for my friends, as I fear for myself, yet in circumstances in which I am more than ever thankful to be gay. As Robert Gluck has written: 'AIDS creates such magnitude of *loss* that now death is where gay men experience life most keenly as a group. It's where we learn to love, and where we discover new values and qualities in ourselves.'[8] Like most of my friends, I am still in many respects in a state of shock, and there is so much to be done. Yet I still find time to take photographs, especially of my friends, whom I had always previously taken for granted. My Extended Family album is now something more than a partial record of my life: it has become an archive, one fragment of the much greater enterprise that is modern gay history. All around the world lesbian and gay archives are currently under threat. I hope my photographs survive, not just for personal reasons but because they show something of who we were, and what we made happen against all the odds.

Notes

1 Walter Benjamin, 'Theses on the Philosophy of History', in *Illuminations* (Cape, 1970), p. 257.
2 Morrissey, 'Rubber Ring'.
3 Neil Bartlett, *Who Was That Man? A Present For Mr Oscar Wilde* (Serpent's Tail, 1988), p. 128.
4 Anon., *Portraiture* (Baltimore: The Camera Inc., 1947), p. 6.
5 John Ashbery, *Three Poems* (New York: Viking Press 1970), p. 104.
6 Neil Bartlett, p. 229.
7 Robert Gluck, 'HIV 1986–1988', *City Lights Review* (San Francisco, 1988), p. 45.
8 *Ibid.*

2   Vito Russo: 1946–90*

Whatever time of day it was that Vito Russo was born, it must have been under the sign of the Ruby Slippers. Like so many other gay men, Vito loved the movies because they had helped him make sense of his feelings as a gay kid, and he never lost that sense of films as *friends*. When you visited his New York apartment he would always be bursting to show you some rare recent find – the fluttering image of a camp butler in some unknown Thirties comedy, a dizzy blonde smoking langorously as she waves goodbye to the last of the lifeboats, Judy Garland doing something absolutely extraordinary, whatever.

Vito also had the most wonderful and passionate sense of the importance of our knowing about the real history of our communities. He was a tremendous advocate for lesbian and gay culture and did as much as anyone else to encourage the emergence of modern gay cinema all round the world.

For the past five years Vito had been living with AIDS, and he played a central role in the emergence of ACT UP in New York. This is how he describes telling his parents he had AIDS: 'There was silence and no hysteria. Finally, my mother said "Do you know why I'm not hysterical? I suspected this all along and I was just wondering when you were going to decide to tell us." My father cried a little, held both of my hands and told me that everything would be alright and that we would get through this together. They are not strong or highly intelligent people, but they were being strong for me' (*Surviving and Thriving With Aids Vol 2*). I know that this helped Vito to be strong for so many other people.

It is typical of Vito that he should have been the person who managed to get Bette Midler to come along and calm down a near-riot after New York's first ever Gay Pride march, and that when I last spoke to him on the phone a few weeks ago he was just off to see her for tea.

When I visited him this summer on Fire Island, where he was convalescing after massive chemotherapy, he was appalled that I'd never seen Cher in *Moonstruck*, and promptly proceeded to rent the video that same evening. A group of us sat around as Vito introduced the film in his inimitably lively way, drawing deeply on his own roots in New York's Italian community, alert

* *First published in* Gay Times, *December 1990.*

and sensitive as ever to the cultural values and the achievements of the marginalized – always intolerant of injustice.

Vito was the most palpable link between the historic lesbian and gay struggles of the Stonewall period in the USA, and the AIDS activist movement. Moreover, he never abandoned his commitment to the process of learning about the history of our communities, and until very recently he was still tearing about the world delivering ever-changing versions of his famous lecture on the history of lesbians and gay men in cinema. The way in which he managed to combine his work as a teacher, historian and articulate advocate of gay culture with his AIDS activism was a constant source of inspiration to all around him.

On May 8th, 1988 he gave a particularly powerful and moving speech at an ACT UP rally in Albany, the capital of New York State. What he said then is just as true today:

'Aids is not what it appears to be at this moment in history. It is more than just a disease which ignorant people have turned into an excuse to exercise bigotry they already feel. It is more than a horror story to be exploited by the tabloids. Aids is a test of who we are as people. When future generations ask us what we did in the war, we have to be able to tell them we were out here fighting. And we have to – for the generations of people who will come after us – remember that someday the Aids crisis will be over. And when that day has come and gone there will be people alive on this earth – gay people and straight people, black people and white people, men and women – who will hear that once there was a terrible disease and that a brave group of people stood up and fought and in some cases and so that others might live and be free.

He was a marvellous public speaker. It is entirely fitting that we should remember and pay tribute to one of the very rare gay men whose achievements were truly international in both scope and significance. He died peacefully in his sleep on the morning of November 6th, having been lovingly cared for by a close circle of friends, just as he had cared for so many others.

3   School's out*

How Childhood tries to reach us, and declares that we were once what took it seriously.

Rainer Maria Rilke[1]

The most crucial aspect of psychoanalysis ... is its insistence that childhood is something in which we continue to be implicated and which is never simply left behind ... It persists as something which we endlessly rework in our attempt to build an image of our own history.

Jacqueline Rose[2]

Introduction

The American artist Tim Rollins has recently argued that

> one of the most cherished ideas in America, the rationale for compulsory education and public schooling in this country, is the belief that a genuine democracy cannot exist without the full education of all its citizens.[3]

Much the same could be said of most people's attitudes towards education in the United Kingdom. Yet when I was at school in the 1960s the subject of homosexuality only existed as a pretext for sniggers and insults. Little has significantly changed in either country. Two subsequent decades of debate and action in the direction of multi-culturalism in the classroom have had, at best, only uneven results. But the question of homosexuality remains in total abeyance. Which is to say that the question of *sexuality* remains in abeyance, since our respective education systems manifestly fail to acknowledge the actual diversity of human sexuality within the curriculum or outside it. In effect, children are taught that homosexuality is beyond consideration. This is bad for everyone in education, but most especially for lesbian and gay

* First published in Diana Fuss (Ed.) Inside/Out: Lesbian Theories, Gay Theories, *New York: Routledge, 1991.*

teachers, and lesbian and gay students. In this article I want to consider briefly the immediate legal and ideological circumstances that frame the subject of homosexuality in schools, for unless we understand the historical and institutional dimensions of anti-gay prejudice, we will not be able to develop effective counter-strategies.

Section 28 and the 'Wolfenden Strategy'

On May 24, 1988, Section 28 of the Local Government (Amendment) Act came into force in the United Kingdom. The Act states that

(1) A local authority shall not
    (a) intentionally promote homosexuality or publish material with the intent of promoting homosexuality;
    (b) promote the teaching in any maintained school of the acceptability of homosexuality as a pretended family relationship.
(2) Nothing in subsection (1) above shall be taken to prohibit the doing of anything for the purpose of treating or preventing the spread of disease.

This was the culmination, to date, of more than a decade of increasingly polarized debate and controversy focused around so-called 'family values', which has involved a special emphasis on education in the broadest sense, from the formal curriculum in schools, to plays, films, and art exhibitions housed or in any way financed or supported by local government. In other words, we are witnessing an increasing acknowledgment of the role that culture plays in the construction of sexual identities, and it is the field of cultural production that is ever more subject to frankly political interventions, in Britain as in the United States.[4]

Yet it would be a mistake to regard Section 28 as something entirely new. On the contrary, in many respects it may be seen to stand in the mainstream of modern British legislation concerning homosexuality, which has never aimed to establish or protect the rights of lesbians and gay men. Rather, it has always aspired to protect our imaginery victims – those whom the law regards as especially 'vulnerable', including the feeble-minded, women, and above all children. However, the concept of childhood remains highly elastic in relation to all aspects of homosexuality, as in the most obvious example of the legal age of consent for sex between men, which is still firmly fixed at 21, five years more than the age set for heterosexuals.[5] Far from ushering in a new age of sexual enlightenment, the famous Sexual Offences Act of 1967 paved the way for the implementation of what Beverley Brown has named the Wolfenden Strategy, which has established ever more effective control of sex and sexuality by the state, but also by many other non-state institutions, from the mass media to clinical medicine. Indeed, the Sexual Offences Act of 1967 clearly enacted the legal moralism of the Report of the Wolfenden

Committee on which it was belatedly modelled, which explicitly regretted the 'general loosening of former moral standards'.

Sadly, there has never been any question of English law turning its archaic attention to the rising tide of anti-gay prejudice and discrimination and actual violence in contemporary Britain. This is largely a result of the absence of any effective discourse of civil rights within Parliamentary politics in the UK.[6] On the contrary, the workings of the Wolfenden Strategy have consistently, if unconvincingly, attempted to define 'acceptable' human sexuality in strict relation to reproductive sex between married couples, and to contain all forms of non-reproductive sex, from homosexuality to prostitution, in a legally defined private sphere where they are permitted to exist, but not to be culturally validated in any way. Hence it is no surprise that British lesbians and gay men are at the very bottom of the line in terms of available police protection, way behind women or racial minorities. In 1989 the Metropolitan Police launched a major poster campaign in London to combat racism. Yet a parallel campaign against anti-gay discrimination remains entirely unthinkable. In the meantime, police prosecutions of gay men in Britain in 1990 have reached the worst levels of the notorious witch-hunts of the mid-1950s.[7] This wider question of anti-gay prejudice in Britain, and the United States, must also be related to the worsening tragedy of HIV/AIDS in both countries, which are distinguished in international terms by governmental refusal to establish proper national policies which would take the epidemic seriously, and by the constant harassing of health education and non-government AIDS service organizations whose work is deemed to 'promote homosexuality' or 'drug abuse'.[8] And in both countries the political opposition party has equally failed to challenge official government policies, or their absence, for fear of association with the dreaded 'electoral liability' of lesbian and gay issues. The assault against lesbians and gay men in the field of education, whether as students or teachers, must be viewed in this wider perspective if its full significance is to be understood, and if effective strategies are to be developed to remedy the situation. Section 28 simply put into law the previous recommendations of the Department of Education, which published an official Circular in November 1987 that baldy stated

> There is no place in any school in any circumstances for teaching which advocates homosexual behaviour, which presents it as 'the norm,' or which encourages homosexual experimentation by pupils.[9]

These brief yet densely written clauses already speak volumes about the attitudes and beliefs that constitute anti-gay prejudice, and the laws it brings about and sanctions. Indeed, they provide a startlingly clear insight into the world that the prejudiced inhabit, a world that is mainly defined by *fear* – fear of gay couples being accepted just like other couples, a world in which homosexuality is a perpetual and terrifying menace, a world in which the young are always thought to be in danger of corruption, and in which they

can never be sufficiently protected. If we want to understand the force of
anti-gay prejudice, and the role that it plays across the entire field of modern
education, we must begin by considering the ways in which heterosexual
adults are encouraged to identify with children. This requires a close understanding of the discourse of 'promotion' that unites both Section 28 in
Britain, and the Helms Amendment which banned safer sex education for
gay men in the USA for several years in the late 1980s.[10] Yet at the same
time, such laws also serve paradoxically to draw attention to the fact that
fundamental definitions of sexual identity and sexual morality are historically contingent, and by no means 'natural'. They also further demonstrate
the confidence of the institutions which insist that the existing power relations of sexuality and of gender must be vigorously defended, pre-emptively
if necessary.

Certainly no area of social life has been subjected to more violent ideological contestation in the modern period than sex education, and the whole
vexed question of homosexuality in schools. As we have already seen, this
has now culminated in the state's claim to distinguish between supposedly
'real' and 'pretended' families. At a time when a third of babies in Britain are
born into single-parent families, it would appear that underlying, long-term
changes in the nature of adult sexual relations and patterns of child-raising
are encouraging ever stronger patterns of resistance, retrenched around a
powerful fantasy of how 'family life' used to be, and should be in future. Sex
is the central and heavily overdetermined focus of such fantasies, which
involve a sharp distinction between the world of marriage and the home, and
the lives of lesbians and gay men. Since homosexuality cannot be acknowledged within the ordinary workaday world, it must of necessity be thought of
as the completely different inversion of the heterosexually known and familiar. Indeed, it is vitally important that lesbians and gay men should be able to
understand the mechanisms of displacement and denial that inform heterosexual projections about us as people, for these projections determine the
world in which we must live our lives. Furthermore, as public attitudes gradually change over time, it would appear that there has been a consolidation
of prejudice at the level of institutional politics, where the subject of homosexuality can easily be exploited, or else ignored as a supposed electoral
'liability'. Hence the need for broad cultural strategies in relation to 'public
opinion', as well as specific strategies targeting the state, and the very
concept of 'politics'.

Promoting homosexuality

Throughout the long debate which accompanied the publication and the
eventual passing into law of Section 28, journalists and other commentators
frequently referred to the Bill's aim to prevent the promotion of homosexuality in schools. The concept of 'promotion' behind the Bill was rarely questioned, except in legal opinions sought by the teaching trade unions and

others in order to oppose it. Thus by analogy with British company law, Lord Gifford concluded his written Opinion with the observation that

'promote homosexuality' involves active advocacy directed by local authorities towards individuals in order to persuade them to become homosexual, or to experiment with homosexual relationships.[11]

While Section 28 does not supersede the legal authority of previous legislation concerning sex education in Britain, it has nonetheless had a wide cultural impact – not least in establishing the notion of homosexual 'promotion' as never before. In this respect it is helpful to note the way in which the wording of Section 28 binds together a theory of the formation of sexual identity with a theory of representation. On the one hand it is assumed, within the wider terms of the Wolfenden Strategy, that 'the vulnerable' may be easily seduced into sexual experimentation, and into a rejection of supposedly 'natural' heterosexuality. On the other hand it explicitly targets representations in any medium that depict lesbian or gay relationships as equivalent to heterosexual families. The unconscious logic thus runs that homosexuality can only exist as a result of the seduction of minors by predatory older perverts. This seduction may, however, be indirect, and effected via *cultural* means. In other words, there is a clear recognition that sexual identities are culturally grounded, and an acknowledgment that gay identity does not follow automatically from homosexual desire or practice. Something else is needed – the active presence of a confident, articulate lesbian and gay culture that clothes homosexual desire in a stable, collective *social* identity.

In this respect, the strategic significance of Section 28 lies in the way it harnesses a theory of (homo)sexual identity to a theory of representation which is remarkably like crude 'copy-cat' theories concerning the supposed influence of pornography on its users, and especially on those who supposedly come across pornography 'by accident'. What in effect is acknowledged is the *pedagogic value* of gay culture in developing and sustaining gay identities. In all of this, it is the imagined vulnerability of heterosexuality that is most significant, together with the assumed power of homosexual pleasure to corrode the 'natural' order of social and sexual relations. This is evidently a response to the long-term impact of gay culture in modern Britain, where the Government's Inspectorate of Schools concluded in 1986 that 'given the openness with which homosexuality is treated in society now it is almost bound to arise as an issue in one area or another of a school's curriculum'.[12] They therefore conclude that

Information about and discussion of homosexuality, whether it involves a whole class or an individual, needs to acknowledge that experiencing strong feelings of attraction to members of the same sex is a phase passed through by many young people, but that for a significant number of people these feelings persist into adult life. Therefore it needs to be dealt with objectively and seriously, bearing in mind that, while there has been a marked shift away from the general condemnation of homosexuality, many individuals and groups hold sincerely to the view that it is morally objectionable. This is difficult territory for teachers to traverse, and for some schools to accept that homosexuality may be a normal feature of relationships would be a breach of the religious faith upon which they are founded. Consequently LEAs (Local Education Authorities), voluntary bodies, governors, heads and senior staff in schools have important responsibilities in devising guidance and supporting teachers dealing with this sensitive issue.[13]

In all of this it should be noted that there is no consideration of the consequences for lesbian and gay teachers or students. Indeed, it is the very open-endedness of the Inspectors' Report, published by the Department of Education, which seems to have been an immediate trigger behind the lobby that orchestrated Section 28. For the Report unambiguously recognizes a reality, 'a marked shift away from the general condemnation of homosexuality', that the authors of Section 28 equally unambiguously wish to deny.

Section 28 thus exemplifies an extreme registration of the changing sexual politics of the past twenty years. In one sense it evidently belongs to the long tradition of anti-Freudian thought that denies infantile sexuality, whilst at the same time it is almost *too* eager to concede that sexuality may be 'artificially' conjured into being via sexual 'experimentation'. This sense of homosexual desire as a kind of omnipresent potential contagion is wholly in keeping with Michel Foucault's prophetic observation in 1980 that, in the future,

> Sexuality will no longer be a form of behaviour with certain precise prohibitions but rather a kind of danger that lingers … Sexuality will become the threat looming over all social bonds, relations among generations as among individuals. On this shadow, on this phantom, on this fear the power structure will assume control by means of a seemingly generous and blanket legislation thanks largely to a series of timely interventions that will probably involve judicial institutions supported by the medical profession. And there will arise a new order of sexual control … Sex will be decriminalized only to reappear as a danger, and a universal one at that. There lies the real danger.[14]

Certainly we are presently witnessing an unparalleled struggle between values and identities forged within the sexual categories of the late nineteenth century, and rival values and identities that have emerged in the twentieth century. This struggle is waged with special ferocity in those areas of social life where sexual identity is most contested, of which education is perhaps the most significant. Education has clearly long been targeted by anti-gay traditionalists because it is identified as the site at which the supposed 'threat' of homosexuality is most acute, and where pre-emptive manoeuvres are most needed. Yet public opinion polls in both Britain and the United States suggest that broad levels of prejudice are actually in decline. For example, 71 per cent of Americans recently polled thought that lesbians and gay men should have equal job opportunities to heterosexuals, compared to only 59 per cent in 1982.[15] Meanwhile in Britain a still more recent survey suggests that 60 per cent of heterosexual men and 62 per cent of women think that gay men should be allowed to adopt children, while over 60 per cent of men and over 80 per cent of women think that no gay person should be barred from any job on the grounds of their sexuality.[16] It is thus far from clear that popular consent could actually be won in relation to any attempt to recriminalize homosexuality as such, and it is highly significant that there has been no serious attempt in either Britain or the US to introduce legislation to proscribe specific 'sexual acts', in the manner of pre-modern laws. The contestation that is currently being fought out in relation to education involves a fight to the death between the diverse forces of radical sexual pluralism, including single-parent families, pro-abortion campaigners, and all whose lives are invalidated by 'family values', and those who devotedly subscribe and submit themselves to 'family values'. Insofar as school represents a double threshold, between the privacy of the home and public space, as well as between the categories of child and adult, it was inevitable that education would find itself caught in the cross-fire between fundamentally incompatible definitions of what it means to be a man or a woman in the late twentieth century, an adult or a child. In this context it is imperative that we appreciate the new significance of the discourse of 'promotion', whether it is employed to justify attacks on gay culture as in Britain, or on safer sex education, as in the United States.[17]

For gay identity can undoubtedly be promoted, in circumstances where homosexual desire might otherwise have little opportunity of providing the ground for an integrated sense of self. Section 28 aims to restore a world of exclusively heterosexual values, identities, and institutions, in which homosexual desire could only be lived within the compliant, subservient terms of 'homosexual' identity. 'Homosexuals' are thus envisaged as a discrete number of invisible individuals, who preferably do not act on the basis of their desires. This is the picture of homosexuality and 'homosexuals' that traditionalists wish to impose on young people and as far as possible, throughout the rest of society. 'Homosexuals' are thus depicted as a uniform type, an abstract, generalized, and thus dehumanized menace – especially dangerous because they cannot necessarily be readily identified. Unlike people of colour, lesbians and gay men cannot immediately be recruited to constitute a visible, immediate definition of otherness in relation to which heterosexuality can be positively contrasted. It is therefore imperative that the cultural iconography of 'the homosexual' has precedence over any representations that might reveal the actual diversity and complexity of sexual choice. Hence the traditionalists' obsession with the *representation* of family life, and their violent iconoclasm in relation to images that contravene their codes of 'acceptable' gender imagery. It is precisely at this point that anti-pornography campaigners often unwittingly find themselves in alliance with another, parallel social-purity movement, rooted in anti-gay prejudice and strict patriarchal values. Ultimately, the conflict of contemporary sexual politics concerns the unreconcilable conflict between power relations that seek increasingly to define and divide people along the lines of sexual object-choice, and a politics which aspires to transcend the power relations of the categories of sexuality altogether, along with the identities they produce. This conflict is currently being waged with special ferocity around rival definitions of the meaning of childhood. On the one hand, there is evidently a growing demand that sexual diversity should be acknowledged in schools, while on the other it is insisted that homosexuality should only be represented as a hideous perversion of heterosexuality, understood as a 'natural' domain of unassailable, rigidly gendered characteristics organized around the prime purpose of sexual reproduction and the 'protection' of asexual children.

Theorizing childhood

In his celebrated *Introductory Lectures on Psychoanalysis*, Freud succinctly argued that

> to suppose that children have no sexual life – sexual excitations and needs and a kind of satisfaction – but suddenly acquire it between the ages of twelve and fourteen, would (quite apart from any observations) be as improbable, and indeed senseless, biologically as to suppose that they brought no genitals with them into the world and only grew them at the time of puberty. What *does* awaken in them at this time is the reproductive function, which makes use for its purposes of physical and mental material already present.[18]

Those who refuse to accept this 'are committing the error of confusing sexuality and reproduction and by doing so you are blocking your path to an understanding of sexuality, the perversions and the neuroses'.[19]

It is important at once to note that, for Freud, 'perversion' was simply a descriptive term used to theorize all aspects of sexuality that do not have a reproductive aim, and one of the most productive tensions within his work concerns the way he often contradicts himself in relation to the supposed reproductive ends of adult sexuality. For elsewhere he insists that 'in man the sexual instinct does not originally serve the purpose of reproduction at all, but has as its aim the gaining of particular kinds of pleasures'.[20]

From Freud's perspective, it is above all *education* which serves to restrict the aim of sexual pleasure, and to channel it into socially and culturally acceptable directions – in other words, into the familiar patterns of marriage and, we must note, of homophobia. Nor is this aim simply that of sexual reproduction. On the contrary, for Freud education aims

> to tame and restrict the sexual instinct when it breaks out as an urge to reproduction, and to subject it to an individual will which is identical with the bidding of society. It is also concerned to postpone the full development of the instinct till the child shall have reached a certain degree of intellectual maturity, for, with the complete irruption of the sexual instinct, educatability is for practical purposes at an end.[21]

In other words, according to Freud, perhaps the central aspect of education is the inculcation of certain specific rules and attitudes towards sex, which will guarantee the subsequent sexual workings of (patriarchal) society, including the familiar double-standards of sexual morality in relation to women and men of which he was a particularly bitter critic. With the benefit of hindsight we can also recognize that attitudes towards homosexuality are also thus an indispensable target of education, since it is always at least potentially available as a site of alternative sexual satisfaction to heterosexual sex, a site moreover which must therefore be rigorously controlled. In all of this, however, we should also note that neither Freud nor his followers have ever demonstrated much concern for the fate of young lesbian and gay people within a pedagogic environment which has as its central business the production of compliant heterosexual identities, largely by means of demonizing homosexuality. This is precisely where we pick up psychoanalysis in the late twentieth century. For the vital point is that young people do not lack sexuality: what they are frequently *denied* is an identity in relation to their sexuality.

This is largely effected by means of the establishment of the widely pervasive belief that there indeed exists a distinct 'world of childhood', quite separate from and independent of adult life. While this is generally felt to be in the child's own best interests, it actually dooms children – and especially gay children – to very considerable misery, since the ordinary relations between adults and children are arbitrarily severed. As Hannah Arendt has pointed out, this can easily have disastrous consequences for the child for, by being 'emancipated' from the authority of adults, he or she

> has not been freed but has been subjected to a much more terrifying and truly tyrannical authority, the tyranny of the majority … either thrown back upon themselves or handed over to the tyranny of their own group, against which, because of its numerical superiority, they cannot rebel, with which, because they are children, they cannot reason, and out of which they cannot flee to any other world because the world of adults is barred to them.[22]

This strikes me as a peculiarly accurate depiction of the dilemmas facing most young gay people at school.

Nor can most gay children expect any understanding of this dilemma at home, where their marginalization and vulnerability is only likely to be reinforced. Hence the familiar strategies such children so frequently develop as self-defence mechanisms – the semblance of ultra-conformism to conventional gender roles, excessive zealousness in competitive sports or academic pursuits, and so on. Somehow we have to develop ways to defend young lesbians and gay children from the consequences of their own defensive strategies, with which they will often closely identify for obvious reasons. Much later unhappiness is undoubtedly rooted in such common childhood experience. This is one clear reason why we should not lie to children about the (homo)sexuality of historical or contemporary cultural figures, including scientists, writers, artists, and athletes. For good education involves helping children to learn how to make and exercise choices. This is not to say that one's sexuality is in any simple sense 'chosen', at least in the same way that one might choose a career. However, the choices one makes on the basis of one's sexuality should be respected and encouraged, and this must include sexual experimentation, which in turn involves (for most of us) both success and failure. What we have to end is a world in which young lesbian and gay students often feel no real sense of belonging, and where they have precious little opportunity to develop a sustaining sense of their own self-esteem. Given the grotesque denial of safer sex education to young gay men in schools, and our increasing understanding of the role of self-esteem in relation to preventing the transmission of HIV, this is now more urgently important than ever. We must never forget that great violence is routinely perpetrated against all young lesbians and gay men in the name of 'education', violence which is generally continuous with the emotional violence of heterosexual domesticity and 'family values' which would deny our very existence, let alone the dignity and significance of our particular emotional and sexual needs, whether as young people or as adults.

From this perspective we may invert the usual question of what children supposedly want or need from education, and ask what it is that adults want or need of children in the name of 'education'. For it is in relation to theories of childhood that the practices of adult power relations may be very productively analysed, and nowhere more so than in the wholesale denial of children's sexuality. As Michel Foucault has pointed out:

> When it comes to children, the first assumption is that their sexuality can never be directed towards an adult. Secondly they are deemed incapable of self-expression. Thus no one ever believes them. They are believed to be immune to sexuality, and unable to discuss it.[23]

It is especially ironic that this position is generally presented within the context of a heavily vulgarized version of psychoanalysis itself, harnessed to the most reactionary (and anti-Freudian) purpose of denying children's sexuality altogether. In this respect we should recognize the high priority of targeting the domain of 'educational psychology' that underpins so many aspects of the training of teachers. This in turn involves acknowledging the erotic component that plays so central a part in *all* educational environments. As long as education is imagined to be entirely non-sexual, the actual erotics of the pedagogic situation can be displaced away in the imaginary likeness of the evil pervert, 'promoting' his or her sexuality with 'innocent' children. The question is *not* whether or not children are sexual beings, but how adults respond to children's sexuality, in ways that range from total denial to an untroubled acceptance.

Conclusion

Behind the rhetoric that identifies the supposedly widespread and perilous 'promotion' of homosexuality lies a particularly dense core of fantasy and denial that needs to be carefully unpacked if the rhetoric is to be successfully countered. On a descriptive level we may easily detect deep-seated fears that cross over the familiar social barriers of class, gender, and culture. These fears constitute a narrative, according to the logic of which 'vulnerable' (i.e. non-sexual) children are in constant danger of being seduced into homosexuality via sexual 'experimentation' stimulated by the depiction of gay and lesbian relationships as fully equivalent to 'family' (i.e. heterosexual) relations. The discourse of 'promoting homosexuality' thus articulates real anxieties on the part of many people, as well as providing an imagined solution to the problem in the form of new laws and other extraordinary measures. These are rationalized as forms of defence against what is perilous, yet they are in fact transparently aggressive and preemptive, since powerful legislation already exists to deal with the complex realities of actual child abuse. We may therefore be justified in suspecting that the 'reality' that this discourse addresses is not that of concrete social relations but of the unconscious.

In a sense this should already be apparent from the sheer tenacity of the ways in which the narrative returns to the imagined spectacle of the child's seduction, and his or her *acceptance* of the seducer, which is most dreaded. In other words, the narrative of 'homosexual promotion' should be regarded as a powerful fantasy which permits some heterosexuals to legitimately dwell on the image of children's bodies as objects of (homo)sexual desire, and, moreover, as its active *subjects*. In this respect the narrative reveals significant parallels to other fantasy-narratives that also possess widespread contemporary currency, from those of Satanic child abuse, to demonic possession, and so on. All of these share a heavily overdetermined investment in the 'innocence' of childhood, and the depravity of the surrounding adult world, from which it is considered to be the primary responsibility of parents to protect the young. In all these respects the discourse of the 'promotion' of homosexuality should be recognized as an essentially pre-modern construction, that is only able to conceptualize homosexual desire in the likeness of sinister, predatory perverts, luring innocent victims to their doom, having corrupted them from within. It articulates 'the homosexual' in the image of nineteenth-century Christian popular culture as an essentially *immoral* figure against which 'the heterosexual' is left to define 'morality'. In these terms, homosexuality is to all intents and purposes a metaphysical force rather than a human characteristic, and the resurgence of the discourse of 'promotion' may best be explained as a last-ditch attempt to resist the larger implications of the emergence of gay politics, which insist on giving lesbians and gay men ordinary human features. This perhaps is what is most terrifying of all to those who conceptualize themselves and other people in brutally archaic terms. For as long as 'the homosexual' is not regarded as human, individual lesbians and gay men can continue to be marginalized and persecuted. The greatest threat that gay politics offers to this ideological formation is the risk of acknowledging that, on the contrary, we are as human as everyone else. It is precisely this threat that the discourse of 'promotion' aims to forestall. What is new is the tacit recognition that there is no going back to the strategy of criminalizing sexual acts, and with this we witness a displaced concern with the role of *representation*, as in so many other areas of contemporary moralism. The discourse of 'promotion' therefore aims to saturate the image of 'the homosexual' with the traditional connotations of depraved sexual acts, and to prevent the cultural acceptability of gay identity, and sexual diversity rooted in the principle of sexual choice. It is choice that the discourse of 'promotion' wishes to deny, and it is on this level and around these terms that gay politics will undoubtedly have to fight its major battles in the 1990s.

Notes

1 Rainer Maria Rilke, 'How childhood tries to reach us', *Selected Works Volume 2, Poetry*, ed. J. B. Leishman (London: The Hogarth Press, 1967), p. 322.
2 Jacqueline Rose, *The Case of Peter Pan, or the Impossibility of Children's Fiction* (London: Macmillan, 1984), p. 12.
3 Tim Rollins, 'Education and democracy', in *Democracy: A Project by Group Material*, ed. B. Wallis (Seattle: Bay Press, 1990), p. 47.
4 For example, see Lisa Duggan, 'On sex panics', *Artforum* 28, no. 2 (October 1989), pp. 26–7.
5 See Simon Watney, *Policing Desire: Pornography, AIDS, and the Media* (Minneapolis: University of Minnesota Press, 1989).
6 See Simon Watney, 'Practices of freedom: "citizenship" and the politics of identity in the age of AIDS', in *Identity: Community, Culture, Difference*, ed. J. Rutherford (London: Lawrence & Wishart, 1990).
7 Indecency prosecutions against gay men in the UK have risen from 857 in 1985 to an astonishing 2,022 in 1989.
8 See Simon Watney, 'Introduction', in *Taking Liberties: AIDS and Cultural Politics*, ed. Erica Carter and Simon Watney (London: Serpent's Tail Press, 1989).
9 Department of Education and Science, *Circular 11* (1987).

10 See Douglas Crimp, 'How to have promiscuity in an epidemic', in *AIDS: Cultural Analysis, Cultural Activism*, ed. Douglas Crimp (Cambridge, MA: MIT Press, 1988).
11 Quoted in Madeleine Colvin with Jane Hawksley, *Section 28: A Practical Guide to the Law and Its Implications* (London: National Council for Civil Liberties, 1989), p. 12.
12 *Health Education from 5 to 16* (London: Her Majesty's Stationery Office, 1986).
13 *Health Education from 5 to 16.*
14 Michel Foucault, *Semiotext(e) Special, Intervention Series 2: Loving Children* (Summer 1980), pp. 41–2.
15 Michael R. Kagay, 'Homosexuals gain more acceptance', *New York Times*, 25 October 1989, A24.
16 'Is it still OK to be gay?', *New Woman* (October 1990): 16–20.
17 See Crimp, 'How to have promiscuity', p. 10.
18 Sigmund Freud, 'The sexual life of human beings', in *Introductory Lectures on Psychoanalysis* (Harmondsworth: Penguin, 1972), p. 353.
19 *Ibid.*
20 Sigmund Freud, '"Civilised" sexual morality and modern nervous illness', *Penguin Freud Library Vol. 12* (Harmondsworth: Penguin, 1977).
21 Freud, 'The Sexual Life', p. 353.
22 Hannah Arendt, 'The crisis in education', *Between Past and Future: Eight Exercises in Political Thought* (Harmondsworth: Penguin, 1977), pp. 181–2.
23 Foucault, *Semiotext(e)*, p. 42.

4   Queer epistemology: activism, 'outing', and the politics of sexual identities*

> Cultural identities come from somewhere, have histories. But, like everything which is historical, they undergo constant transformation. Far from being fixed in some essentialised past, they are subject to the continuous 'play' of history, culture and power.
>
> Stuart Hall[1]

Introduction, November 1993

This article was written in 1991 for a publication in which it did not eventually appear. A slightly edited version was printed in the Australian gay magazine *Outrage*, and in *Artforum*.[2] It was originally intended as an initial response to the sudden emergence of Queer identity in the field of lesbian and gay politics and culture in many different countries around the world. I have subsequently explored the significance of newly emerging sexual identities in other published work.[3]

The nineties have already seen a remarkable upsurge in lesbian and gay political activism all around the world, from New York to London, from Sydney to Vancouver. Powerful activist organizations such as Queer Nation in the US and OutRage in Britain have emerged in response to a shared sense of cumulative anger concerning escalating levels of anti-gay prejudice, discrimination, and actual violence. Furthermore, the entire diaspora of lesbians and gay men is in turmoil over the vexed question of 'outing', and the validity or otherwise of the emergent category 'queer', which is increasingly being used by women and men alike as a term of primary identity. Much of this international energy derives its inspiration from the rhetoric and tactics of Queer Nation, founded early in 1990 in New York City.

Queer Nation came into existence as a vigilante group, commemorating the victims of gay-bashings, and organizing street patrols against would-be bashers. Its methods are frankly confrontational. For example, groups go into straight bars to conduct impromptu anti-homophobia education sessions, and

* First published in Critical Quarterly 36, 1, 1991.

the very streets of Greenwich Village were eloquently stencilled in the spring of 1991 with messages that starkly proclaimed, 'My beloved was queer-bashed here', or asked 'Would you feel safe walking hand in hand with a lover on this street?' Yet some lesbians and gay men have questioned the use of the word 'queer', which has long been a term of personal abuse in both Britain and the US. It has been argued that 'queer' cannot simply be reappropriated, and that its revived usage only serves to fuel existing prejudices, and may even lead to an increase in discrimination and actual violence.

Such criticism frequently comes from older lesbians and gay men, and it forcibly reminds me of the strong resistance put up by many self-styled 'homosexuals' to the adoption of the term 'gay' in the late sixties and early seventies. For many who grew up in the fifties, 'queer' is evidently still closely associated with painful memories of insults and low self-esteem. Yet it is also often forgotten that 'queer' has also long been used by many people, of themselves, in a way that is quite open and positive. Thus, throughout the post-war period 'queer' has always been available for conflicting meanings, very much depending on the user.[4] Far from being trivial issues, such questions of change and contestation at the level of intimate personal identities are fundamental to our understanding of the workings of power within the wider framework of modernity, and are the site of a complex biopolitics. There are two sets of issues that need to be briefly established. The first concerns the generational divide between those who 'came out' in the sixties and seventies, and those who have 'come out' in the eighties and nineties. The second concerns the dominant system of sexual classifications, established since the late nineteenth century, which are fleshed out and lived in different sexual identities.

Most criticism of the emergent 'queer' identity has come from older lesbians and gay men who clearly find it difficult to identify with younger people who have 'come out' since the beginning of the AIDS epidemic. Whilst the subject of homosexuality has never previously attracted so much public attention, most of this has amounted to little more than a barrage of terrifyingly hostile prejudice and misinformation. It would be difficult to exaggerate the extent to which public AIDS commentary has associated the term 'gay' with AIDS in the minds of the young, who have received almost no health education which accepts and respects their homosexuality. The results, tragically, are plain to see. One report at the seventh annual International AIDS Conference suggested that, for example, whilst the overall rate of new seroconversions in the San Francisco Bay Area has fallen in recent years, this was far less marked amongst the young. In San Francisco County 34.8 per cent of gay men under 25 attending STD clinics for HIV antibody tests are HIV-positive. The same survey revealed that no less than 54 per cent of young black gay men under 25 are seropositive in San Francisco County, compared to 27 per cent of whites and 11 per cent of Latinos.[5] Moreover, suicide and attempted suicide rates amongst gay teenagers depict an intolerable experience on the part of countless young people who are effectively denied any access to effective support and counselling services as a result of discriminatory age of consent legislation in countries such as the UK, and a wider refusal to recognize young gay people's needs and entitlements, above all to sexual love.

At the same time, a substantial proportion of young lesbians and gay men have grown up in a period when overt racism and sexism are decreasingly culturally legitimate, whilst profound homophobia remains endemic and goes largely unremarked by non-gays. It is hardly surprising that many young people accuse older lesbians and gay men of complacency in regard to levels of anti-gay discrimination and violence. Furthermore, many of today's young 'queers' feel much more in common with one another as women and men than they do with older lesbians or gay men, who have long tended to be divided along the lines of gender, and by numerous political boundary disputes, such as those concerned with explicit sexual materials. The great convenience of the term 'queer' today lies most immediately in its gender and race neutrality. This is only to remark that for many young Americans the term 'gay' is widely understood to mean 'white', 'male', 'materialistic', and 'thirty-something'. On the contrary, 'queer' asserts an identity that celebrates differences within a wider picture of sexual and social diversity.

Meanwhile, in Britain 'queer' has emerged within a very different political culture, where lesbian and gay politics have long been strongly influenced by far left entryists, who frequently regard gays as little more than potential recruits to so-called 'revolutionary' politics. Such an approach denies any real specificity to the politics of sexuality, and has contributed greatly to the marginalizing of lesbian and gay issues within national politics. This is the context in which the influential activist organization OutRage was formed early in 1990, only a few weeks after the birth of Queer Nation in New York. OutRage has carefully targeted its demonstrations and other activities in relation to local British questions of discriminatory policing, censorship, and homophobia, with conspicuous success. For the first time in Britain, a 'queer' activism flourishes which rejects traditional hierarchical Marxist–Leninist structures, and insists on the autonomy of sexual politics from other sites of struggle. Yet certain aspects of the new 'queer' politics remain international.

The up-side of 'queer' lies in its ability to articulate the complex, shifting contemporary alignments of class, race, gender, age and sexuality in the lives of individuals who frequently face multiple oppressions. The downside of 'queer' lies in its tendency to romanticize such differences. Within the broad terrain of queer nationalism there remains a crucial unresolved conflict between an overall critique of the categories of sexuality and the unequal power relations they impose on *everyone*, and a kind of unthought-through separatism. Yet 'queer' is obviously an identity that has emerged in an emergency, and we should not rush in to criticize it for failing to resolve *all* the many questions surrounding the politics of sexual identities. On the contrary, the very passion with which 'queer' identity is currently being asserted should oblige us to think rather more seriously than is perhaps customary about the larger contemporary crisis of sexual epistemology – the theory of knowledge which informs the classificatory system which defines and regulates modern sexual identities. Certainly the conventional homo/heterosexual dualism seems increasingly unable to give adequate expression to late-twentieth-century sexual beliefs and behaviour. This is most apparent in the painful tensions surrounding 'bisexuality', a category which simultaneously threatens and reinforces the dominant homo/hetero dualism.

All discussion of the changing modern categories of sexuality must proceed from a consideration of *desire*, understood as an irreducible element in human nature. However, as Foucault, Weeks, and many others have argued, desire is lived and sensuously experienced in a multitude of ever-changing social and historical circumstances.[6] Far from being scientific, descriptive categories, the classifications of desire within Western epistemology have profound political, ethical, and psychic implications. In this manner, the question of which gender (or genders) one is sexually attracted by becomes the ground for fundamental power relations of privilege and underprivilege. The epistemology of sexuality should thus be recognized as a strategy which positions and aligns *all* human beings, in a basically dualistic theory of sexuality, which has little relation to the diversity and complexity of sexual desire as it is lived in the actual lives of individuals, or communities organized around shared sexual desires, or indeed of entire societies. It is one indication of the underdeveloped nature of contemporary sexual politics that we are still obliged to talk of 'homosexual object-choice' as that which unites people who call themselves 'homosexual', or 'gay', or 'lesbian', or 'dykes', or 'queers'. Yet such terms are not doing the same kind of ideological or psychic work.

For example, to describe oneself as 'a homosexual' is immediately to inhabit a pseudo-scientific theory of sexuality which more properly belongs to the age of the steam engine than to the late twentieth century. The most that 'homosexuals' can (politely) ask for is 'tolerance', since the 'homosexual' has already accepted marginalization in his or her core identity. Homosexual identity should thus be understood as *a strategic position which privileges heterosexuality*. It is thus extremely convenient to the power relations of sexuality that people should *voluntarily* accept its categories as if they derived from some timeless essence of personal being. In this manner the strategic power relations of sexuality remain invisible and unchallenged. Theorized as a 'wrong' object-choice, 'the homosexual' is permitted to occupy a strictly policed private zone, which encourages the fantasy that public space is intrinsically and exclusively heterosexual. The entire history of sexual legislation in the past century has been principally concerned with constructing and preserving these differential zones of sexualized space. The culture of 'homosexuality' is thus always in collusion with the wider epistemology which gives it (limited) meaning. The only movement of resistance from within this framework is the familiar and curious claim that 'homosexuals' constitute a distinct 'minority' by analogy with race or gender, and that its members possess admirable gifts of sensibility, sensitivity, and so on. Yet it is precisely on these highly unstable (because unconvincing) grounds that most 'homosexuals' plead for 'toleration'.

It was against this modern epistemology of sexuality that one major strand within Gay Liberation originally posed 'gay' identity, understood as a fundamentally *political* response to the individualism of 'homosexual' identity, and its tendency to pose sexual politics as an issue of achieving 'equal rights' with heterosexuals. In this manner the categories of sexuality themselves remained unquestioned within 'homosexual' culture and politics. Gay Liberation insisted, on the contrary, that what lesbians and gay men share is not some identical, *personal* essence of homosexual desire, but the *social* experience of discrimination and prejudice, which are mobilized by the workings of power – the law, the press, education, the Church, social science, and so on – upon the terrain of sexuality *as a whole*. Yet in the mass media as well as amongst many 'gay' men, the word 'gay' is still frequently used as if it were simply synonymous with the word 'homosexual'.

This reflects on the one hand the strong institutional and discursive resistance to the word 'gay' that has characterized most subsequent mass-media commentary since the late sixties, and on the other hand the continued inability of gay politics (especially when dominated by the far left) to grasp the full political significance of the epistemological struggles which take place on the terrain of sexual categories and classifications. Moreover, there has long been a marked tension between gay *political* strategies such as 'coming out', which regard 'gay' very much as a collective as well as a personal identity, and gay *culture*, which on the contrary has tended to promote a rather narrow and puritanical picture of 'gay' life, especially in relation to sex. Thus, mainstream lesbian and gay political culture has often promoted the concept of 'positive images' which would supposedly counter and replace 'negative images', and so on. The implication behind such strategies is that there is indeed some available, uniform 'truth' about all gay people, a 'truth' which in practice has an unfortunate tendency to censor out the whole question of our actual diversity as a social constituency, in favour of a 'politically correct' line which does not look very favourably on drag queens, for example, or S&M dykes. Thus, whilst gay political theory was trying to take on board the wider question of the overall organization of sexual identities and power relations, gay culture tended to lapse back into a 'minoritist' approach, which had (and has) strong continuities with the older 'homosexual' culture, and its problematic notion of 'gay sensibility'. Furthermore, this 'minoritist' position depicts lesbians and gay men as if we were self-evidently a coherent 'minority', by analogy with race or ethnicity, with the dangerous assumption that anything labelled 'gay' can supposedly represent *all* lesbians and gay men. Lesbian and gay cultural theory and practice has also tended to be extremely limited by its anxiety about the so-called 'objectification' of the body in visual representations, having imported wholesale the very questionable values and beliefs of Radical Feminism. Yet sexual desire and fantasy could not even exist without some degree of psychic objectification. Put simply, we do not love or desire people in their totality, whatever that might be. In Britain, as in the US, it has been the sanctimonious moralism of so much lesbian and gay culture which has played a central role in stimulating the new 'queer' politics.

Thus, by the early 1980s the term 'gay' had become widely associated with just the type of plea for 'toleration' or 'equality' that had characterized 'homosexual' political culture, and which provoked Gay Liberation into being in the first place. This is nowhere more obvious than in the continued use of notions such as 'the homosexual community' by gay men *and* by an intensely homophobic mass media. In this respect it should be recognized that the fundamental strategic problem facing contemporary gay politics is not the word 'queer' but the word 'homosexual', together with its acceptance as a term of personal identity. Having lost sight of its initial contestation of the classificatory systems of sexuality, Gay Liberation has increasingly seemed to regard lesbian and gay issues as if they were only relevant to lesbians and gay men, again imagined as a discrete minority. In reality today the main conflict is not simply between older 'gay' assimilationists, who merely want admission to the American Dream, or to 'equal rights' with heterosexuals, and 'queers' asserting their 'queerness'. Rather, it is between those who think of the politics of sexuality as a matter of securing minority rights, and those who are contesting the overall validity and authenticity of the epistemology of sexuality itself. This is nowhere more obvious than in relation to the notorious question of 'outing', which has now emerged as a serious issue in the UK.

As in America, the issue of 'outing' has been a pretext for any amount of outraged protest in the national daily press, which never seriously imagines 'out' lesbians or gay men amongst its readers. The national press expresses sympathy with the plight of unfortunate 'homosexuals', whose privacy, it is argued, must be protected at all costs. What is so ideologically brilliant about the British 'outing' strategy has been the way it has revealed the depths of anti-gay prejudice amongst journalists who themselves work for publications which have long profited from the public exposure of closeted 'homosexuals'. Yet these same papers evidently also require the category of 'the homosexual', since it plays such a key role in stabilizing heterosexuality, and heterosexual identities.[7] Nonetheless, non-British readers may be somewhat startled by the tone of vitriolic hatred that has informed mainstream British press coverage around 'outing'. Thus, under the headline 'This Fascist Gay Army Doomed To Failure', we were recently treated to a report from *Daily Mail* hack George Gordon in New York about Queer Nation, and its supposed 'witch-hunt of desperation – a vicious hypocritical and smearing propaganda stunt', and so on.[8]

Yet from the outset it has been clear just who is being hypocritical in such reporting, given that the *Daily Mail* is given to predictable bouts of extreme homophobia. Hence Mr Gordon's conclusion that:

> the whole outing exercise was in fact the last desperate throw of angry gay activists who had failed to convince the world that AIDS was as much a threat to the community at large as it was to homosexuals. Figures were manufactured, scare propaganda was widespread, but the reality was that, by and large, AIDS remains a lethal illness of choice and the majority of victims are homosexuals, and junkies who exchange needles.[9]

Meanwhile another very well known female journalist wrote of 'outers' as:

> the dreariest, most vindictive people in the world with which they can't cope. They have no self-respect, esteem or confidence to proudly live out their sexuality without crudely flaunting it. They're not in the same class as the good old boring heterosexual Joneses who just get on with it, and shut up about it, between their private sheets which the rest of us have no desire to hang out and examine.[10]

There was also much else besides about 'a shrill band of homegrown fanatics'.[11] Such commentary exemplifies the press *requirement* of a wholly private sphere for homosexuality, in which 'homosexuals' may be tolerated as long as they are both invisible and inaudible. As soon as we are visible we begin to threaten the heterosexual claim for public space, and are therefore seen to be 'flaunting'. As soon as we make ourselves audible we similarly interrupt the heterosexual claim for public discourse, and are therefore dismissed as 'shrill', regardless of what we actually say. What was so strategically incisive in Britain was the loud announcement of a major 'outing' campaign along American lines, which was designed in fact to draw attention not to closet 'homosexuals', but rather to the gross sexual hypocrisy of the British mass media. A small campaigning group, FROCS (Faggots Rooting Out Closet Homosexuality) announced at a subsequent press conference that the entire 'outing' story, complete with leaks about gay Members of Parliament and members of the royal family to key journalists, had been designed to expose the 'hysterical, homophobic media'.[12] One tabloid journalist was overheard to remark bitterly: 'We've been shafted by the buggers'.[13]

Yet 'outing' does continue to raise genuine problems, not least because it so often loses sight of the vital aspect of *choice* which has always lain at the heart of progressive sexual politics. Moreover, it runs the risk of falling back into an extremely conservative notion of what it means to be 'gay' in the first place. Indeed, 'outing' usually tends to depict questions of sexual identity very much from *within* the normative values of the dominant sexual epistemology. Gay political theory has emphasized that there is no simple or automatic connection between homosexual desire and individual senses of identity. On the contrary, gay theory has stressed that homosexual desire is the ground on which different sets of fantasies, behaviours, and senses of sexual identity are constructed at different times and in different societies. 'Outing', however, pictures an immediate and exact fit between hidden, secret sexual *behaviour*, and 'gay' *identity*. In this manner the entire political significance of the word 'gay' is eradicated, and its use as a term of identity is equated with 'homosexual'. 'Outing' presumes that there is a simple, uniform 'truth' of homosexuality, and that everyone is equally aware of this private 'truth' of their nature. Yet what of a man who has never had sex with another man, but has always wanted to? Is he 'gay'? Or what of a married woman in her forties who has just begun her first-ever sexual relationship with another woman? Is she 'gay', or a 'dyke', and if so, in what sense? And what of 'bisexuals'?

This tendency to essentialize gay identity in 'outing' strategies has a significant parallel in the widely held defence that 'outing' can be justified as a means of providing 'positive role models' to young lesbians and gay men. This strikes me as an especially bizarre claim, since it is difficult to understand how isolated gay teenagers are going to benefit much from the sad spectacle of the reluctant 'outing' of deeply damaged and often unhappy people, regardless of their social prestige and standing. If Jason Donovan were in fact a closet 'homosexual', would his young gay fans be much empowered by discovering that he is too frightened and/or ashamed to 'come out'? Celebrities can only really help gay teenagers by openly coming out as 'gay', or 'queer', as an act of *choice*. That indeed is an excellent role model, as singers such as Jimmy Somerville attest. The claims that 'outing' can provide 'positive role models' simply take us back to the older, conservative picture of lesbian and gay culture, rooted in the dubious practice of rejecting the validity of all images and representations of homosexuality that could not be easily identified as 'positive'. Behind both the 'outing' picture of 'role models' and the older gay cultural theory of 'positive image' lurks a dangerously simplistic picture of how individuals respond to images and representations, and of how sexual identities are forged. Of course it is important that societies should be persuaded not to censor or stereotype all images of homosexuality. But we should not delude ourselves into thinking that *any* single image of homosexuality can truthfully represent the entire latitude of homosexual desire, and all the many sets of pleasures and identities that homosexual desire may provide the grounding for. What we urgently *need* to target are the objective forces of homophobia which so often cause whole lifetimes of guilt and suffering. As George Eliot observed long ago:

> there is much pain that is quite noiseless; and vibrations that make human agonies are often a mere whisper in the roar of hurrying existence. There are glances of hatred that stab and raise no cry of murder;

robberies that leave man or woman forever beggared of peace and joy, yet kept secret by the sufferer – committed to no sound except that of low moans in the night, seen in no handwriting except that made on the face by the slow months of suppressed anguish and early morning tears.[14]

This strikes me as a not inaccurate depiction of life in the closet, as lived by many people. The major problem with 'outing' remains that its vision of supposedly 'rescuing' people from the closet ignores both the personal and the political significance of *choice* in 'coming out', as well as leaving the closet itself intact at the end of the day.

Conclusion: 'queer' culture

It is clear that not all lesbians and gay men will come to accept the term 'queer' in relation to themselves, even if they fully understand why other people find it of practical use. This is entirely for the good, since it serves to acknowledge that there is no *natural* or *inevitable* connection or essence uniting *everyone* whose sexual identity is formed on the basis of *involuntary* homosexual object-choice. On the contrary, there are complex, shifting unities and divisions within and between different sexual constituencies, just as there are conflicts and divisions within the individual. For example, not a few ardent S&M dykes were once equally ardent campaigners against what they deemed 'pornography', just as not a few of the original supporters of Gay Liberation are now equally stalwart conservatives.

Yet it is important that the new 'queer' politics should not be regarded as if it were totally distinct from the older lesbian and gay political culture, for there are many continuities between the two. In this respect Queer Nationalism raises different issues in different countries, according to the local history of lesbian and gay politics, and the current situation. Thus, as the US lurches increasingly to the right, 'queer' issues are likely to appeal to large numbers of people who feel the need to aggressively counter fundamentalism in all its various guises, and are increasingly likely to attract the wrath of the 'pro-family' lobby. In Britain 'queer' emerges in an almost exactly opposite political scenario, with the far right on the retreat, in the context of a widespread desire to re-establish social democratic political consensus after a decade of divisive Thatcherism. With the possibility of achievable legal reforms in the near future, 'queer' politics in Britain are more likely to be attacked by the mainstream of lesbian and gay politics, on the grounds that it is too 'extremist'. All the more reason, I should say, in both countries, for getting queerer and queerer!

It is, however, evident that whatever the opponents of the term 'queer' may think, it has effectively ushered in a new phase in the history of sexual politics. For 'queer' identity forces us to think again about the aims and objectives of 'the gay movement', and its history. Everything we know about the history of sexual identities teaches us that identities change over time, in the lives of individuals and of societies. 'Queer' does not magically resolve all the problems of sexual epistemology, but it serves to alert us to some of the most pressing problems which lesbian and gay politics have not been able to resolve, especially the relations *between* lesbians and gay men, and the general tendency of gay politics to suppress the actual diversity of 'queer' sex in the name of 'gay community' values. Thus an account of 'queer' culture would have to be woven around such glamorous if disparate figures as Oscar Wilde (and the rent-boys he employed), Rimbaud, Ronald Firbank, Divine, Morrissey, Tom of Finland, Charles Ludlam, Derek Jarman, Madonna, and so on. What these all have in common is the way their work and their lives have challenged the authority of the dominant epistemology of sexuality. In this sense 'queer' stands for a sexual politics which proceeds from a recognition of the fundamental inconsistency within a lesbian and gay politics which challenges the authority of 'homosexual' identity, but which leaves 'heterosexuality' more or less unquestioned. 'Queer' culture appears as that which aims to trouble and destabilize the overall discursive legitimacy of modern sexual classifications, and the power relations they sustain and protect.

'Queer' thus articulates contradictions and tensions within the older lesbian and gay politics, and permits us to think of 'gay' politics in a wider historical perspective. Hence we may begin to distinguish, broadly, between 'homosexual' culture, 'gay' culture, and 'queer' culture. 'Homosexual' culture proceeds from the assumption that gay men share some kind of metaphysical essence of 'good taste' and 'artistic sensibility'. Thus we appear 'exotic', different, but deferential. 'Homosexual' culture can only ultimately demonstrate our supposed 'tastefulness', with accompanying pleas for 'toleration', or at most 'equality'. Gay culture on the contrary has historically been closely involved in asserting lesbian and gay identity, in challenging what it regards as the twin perils of 'stereotyping' or 'invisibility'. In practice this has led to the widespread dissemination of a set of highly normative pictures of 'gay life'. Objections to 'stereotypes' often proceed from an unstated uneasiness with the particular *type* of lesbian or gay man represented, with whom the critic very much wishes not to be associated. But this is exactly the problem. No single image of a lesbian or gay man can ever represent the entire latitude of lesbian and gay identities. Our real enemy is not so much the images of which we tend to complain, but the theory of representation which leads people to imagine that single representations of individual members of large, complex social groups can *ever* be 'representative'. Similarly, the problems facing us do *not* proceed from our supposed 'invisibility', but, on the contrary, from the ways in which other people project their fears and fantasies on to us whatever we say or do. The notion of 'invisibility' simply fails to illuminate the processes by which we are made to embody and encode social meanings which largely derive from the dominant system of sexual identities, and its rationality.[15]

This is precisely the terrain on which 'queer' culture operates, revealing the multitude of ways in which 'public' speech and images marginalize us. It also points to continuities of pleasure and identity *across* the barriers of both gender and sexual object-choice. This is, for example, the 'queerness' of dykes who fist-fuck gay men and vice versa, or of the heterosexual woman who shares with some gay men a primary sexual identity as a 'Bottom', or a gay man and a straight man who share a primary interest in foot fetishism. Terrified of 'objectifying' the body, gay culture has tended to shy away from such issues, which have, however, remained current within the older cultures of drag and S&M, which we might in any case want to think of as 'queer'. 'Queer' culture is thus above all opposed to all forms of sexual censorship, whether called for from the left or the right, from homophobes or from lesbians or gay men. 'Queer' culture and politics thus seem to me to be in some vital sense *above* party politics. They identify the fundamental legitimacy of 'queers' to work in their own interest against the numerous oppressions and exclusions we experience. 'Queer' culture can thus never settle for 'equality', since it is so apparent that this involves total subjection to the rationality of 'normal' sexuality, and its identities. Hence the great danger, for example, of simplistic calls for 'gay marriage', which wholly overlook the wider political/ideological/economic significance of marriage as an institution. 'Queer' culture is about sexual choice, for everyone, not only lesbians and gay men.[16]

Thus 'queer' culture refuses to regard lesbians or gay men simply as distinct 'minorities', since this is so obviously to accept the validity of the larger structure of sexual classifications organized around the homo/hetero dualism. 'Queer' emerges as the site of a hugely ambitious politics of alibis and conundrums, of naming-games with private rules, and of interventions against the authority and legitimacy of the most fundamental sexual categories on which modern state power and 'governmentality' depend.[17] Right now there is an urgent need to launch major initiatives around most of the key terms put into mass circulation during the epidemic: 'the gay lifestyle', 'sexual addiction', 'self-oppression', etc., and the insultingly banal picture of sexual behaviour and sexual identities that lurks not far behind them. Yet if there is one problem with all of this it concerns our responses to AIDS, at a time when community mobilization around gay identity has proved to be the only demonstrably effective grounds for ongoing Safer Sex. Indeed, the 1991 Florence Conference provided very alarming figures from the Bay Area which strongly suggested that recognition of the unconditional need for Safer Sex may be undermined for some people by the belief that they belong to a new 'queer' vanguard, which is magically immune to HIV.[18] It would certainly be a terrible and tragic irony if hostility to lesbian and gay culture on the part of today's young 'queers' were to make them *more* vulnerable to HIV.

Belatedly in the history of the epidemic, epidemiologists 'discovered' the existence of gay men. Modelling their questions and assumptions on 'heterosexuals', they proceeded to ascertain our 'lifestyle', and to isolate objective 'risk factors'. In this way they never had to confront us as people who live differently from heterosexuals in *most* cases, not least because of the effects of prejudice and discrimination. The HIV epidemiologists have still not recognized that there are gay teenagers who have the same emotional and sexual needs as everyone else, yet magnified by the neglect and isolation so many feel when at school, and subsequently. The only reliable indicator for unsafe sex is loneliness and isolation, and these are the direct consequences of our homophobic societies – societies so deeply afraid of young 'queers' that they cannot imagine their existence, let alone see that they might have the greatest entitlement *of all* to supportive health education in this terrible emergency. In this respect, it cannot be sufficiently emphasized that the most immediately important task for 'queer' culture is to make unsafe sex uncool, to make safer sex 'queer'.

Out of the old, fragmentary order of sixties and seventies identity politics there is evidently emerging, fitfully and unpredictably, a new sense of human sexuality as a political terrain which is quite distinct from other arenas of social change and contestation. Sexuality is a terrain where individuals and social groups are not necessarily coherent and unified, where the basic ethical and political principles are *choice* and *consent*. It seems likely that increasing numbers of people will come to associate such a politics with the term 'queer', with which they will themselves identify. 'Queer' is certainly not going to go away, but nor I think is it going to take the place of earlier classifications and identities in any absolute sense. On the contrary, 'queer' identity recognizes that no single term, including 'queer', can ever resolve all the epistemological and political problems that are inscribed within the current dominant rationality of sexuality and sexual identities. Counter-identities will continue to come and go, to flare up and to become dormant. Who knows, 'gay' men may have ceased to exist as a commonly lived identity in fifty years' time, only to be revived, with a new significance, another fifty years later. In all of this, however, our enemy is not the closet 'homosexual', but the system of sexual classifications that imprisons her, and us all.

Notes

1 Stuart Hall, 'Cultural identity and diaspora', in J. Rutherford (Ed.) *Identity, Culture, Difference* (London: Lawrence & Wishart, 1990), p. 225.
2 *Artforum*, New York, November 1991.
3 See Simon Watney, 'Emergent sexual identities and HIV/AIDS', in P. Aggleton *et al.* (Eds) *AIDS: Facing the Second Decade* (London: Falmer Press, 1993), pp. 13–29.
4 See, for example, Douglas Plummer, *Queer People: The truth about homosexuals in Britain* (London: W. H. Allen, 1963).
5 T. A. Kellogg *et al.*, 'Prevalence of HIV–1 among homosexual and bisexual men in the San Francisco Bay area: Evidence of infection among young gay men', *Seventh International AIDS Conference Abstract Book*, vol. 2, 1991 (W.C.3010), p. 298.

6 See Jeffrey Weeks, *Against Nature: Essays on history, sexuality and identity* (London: Rivers Oram Press, 1991).
7 See Simon Watney, *Policing Desire: Pornography, AIDS & The Media* (Minneapolis: University of Minnesota Press, 1989).
8 George Gordon, 'This fascist gay army doomed to failure', *Daily Mail*, London, Tuesday 30 July 1991.
9 *Ibid.*
10 Jean Rook, 'Shameful revelations by a bunch of nasty bullies', *Daily Express*, London, Wednesday, 31 July 1991, p. 9.
11 'Witchhunt is a disgrace', *Daily Star*, London, Monday 29 July 1991, p. 8.
12 Quoted in Alex Renton, 'Press misses out as homosexuals remain in the closet', *Independent*, London, Thursday 1 August 1991, p. 1.
13 *Ibid.*
14 George Eliot, *Felix Holt* (1866) (Harmondsworth: Penguin Classics, 1987), p. 84.
15 I have discussed these points in greater detail in '*Wet Holes/Wet Dreams': The Queer Art of Donald Moffett* (New York: Simon Watson Gallery, 1991).
16 These points are explored in Anna Marie Smith, 'The end of the rainbow', *Marxism Today*, February 1991, pp. 24–5.
17 On the useful concept of governmentality, see Graham Burchell *et al.* (Eds) *The Foucault Effect: Studies in Governmentality, with Two Lectures by and an Interview with Michel Foucault* (London: Harvester Wheatsheaf, 1991).
18 Robert B. Hays, 'Understanding the high rates of HIV risk-taking among young gay and bisexual men. The Young Men's Survey', Presentation M.C. 101 *Seventh International AIDS Conference*, Florence, 1991.

5 Emergent sexual identities and HIV/AIDS*

In reality the lesbian and gay community has always been a network of communities, primarily split between a political community which pursues an ideal of political power and representation, and the communities of the night, which encompass the genuine diversity which political activists seek to represent.

(Alcorn, 1992: 14)

Cultural identity ... is a matter of 'becoming' as well as of 'being'. It belongs to the future as much as to the past. It is not something which already exists, transcending place, time, history and culture.

(Hall, 1990: 225)

An extensive modern literature demonstrates that *all* sexual identities are intensely contingent (Weeks, 1986). Thus, while the underlying forms and forces of human sexual desire seem relatively stable, the lived identities of groups and individuals vary greatly in relation to different changing historical circumstances. Moreover, sexual identities are sites of varying degrees of conflict and contestation for groups and individuals, as the relations between women and men, and adults and children change over time, together with attendant bodies of belief and theory. Nowhere is this more obvious than in relation to the wide range of identities which have flourished in different societies and in different periods on the shared basis of homosexual desire.

It seems highly probable that within most urban societies groups of men have developed specific sexual identities on the basis of their shared, local relations to homosexual desire, and also in relation to sexual roles. The factors determining the form of such sexual identities vary greatly over time from varieties of nationalist hostility to homosexuality, rationalized as a foreign perversion, to the cultural control and policing of gender relations.

* First published in *Peter Aggleton* et al. *(Eds)* AIDS: Facing the Second Decade, *London: Falmer Press, 1993.*

Certainly what we know of pre-modern sexual identities rooted in homosexual desire and experience suggests that marginality and persecution played a central role in framing identity, for individuals and for collectivities. For at least 300 years, however, we may trace the rise and fall of (homo)sexual identities which are also confident, articulate and socially organized, with their own cultures and institutions.

For example, as Greenberg (1990) points out, the self-consciously 'effeminate' mollies and margeries of the late seventeenth and eighteenth centuries:

> were at the center of a newly emerging male homosexual subculture in London and perhaps some of the larger English towns. The mollies were men drawn largely from lower and lower-middle class backgrounds, who dressed as women, took female names, adopted exaggerated feminine mannerisms and speech habits, and engaged in sexual relations with other men ... By 1709, when Edward Ward published his *The Secret History of Clubs*, which devotes a chapter to the mollies, they had evolved their own rituals, including mock marriages, child-births and baptisms. The mollies' visibility made them a particular target of the reforming societies' anti-sodomitical crusades. (Greenberg, 1990: 96)

The tenacity and richness of these various homosexual subcultures can hardly be sufficiently emphasized, especially in relation to the homophobic amnesia which afflicts so much of British academic social historiography. Nor should it be forgotten that (homo)sexual subcultures have always courageously challenged the law. Thus for centuries the members of such collectivities have lived complicated lives, subject to imprisonment and even death as a direct result of their sexual object choice (Senelick, 1990). Equally remarkable is the tenacity of British national homophobia, at all levels of society, and its constitutive institutions of education, law, politics, medicine and popular culture. In other words, homosexuality has long played a very special role in the make-up of British national identity, and has been a subject of heated controversy throughout the modern period. In considering the history of emergent (homo)sexual identities, therefore, we are not simply considering the discrete history of a 'minority' but the complex, frequently contradictory process whereby *all* sexual attitudes are generated, sustained, contested and eventually replaced. Nor should it be imagined that we are dealing with a neat, chronological sequence of sexual identities. On the contrary, such identities frequently overlap in time, as individuals and societies age and change in unpredictable and uneven ways.

In this context it should be recognized that 'homosexual' identity was a particular response to particular historical conditions. One hundred years ago 'the homosexual' was an emergent sexual identity in Britain, just as today it is almost entirely redundant, save within heterosexual culture and discourse, which have never fully accepted the category 'gay'. Homosexual identity emerged reactively to the new claims of late-nineteenth-century science, and the state, in relation to the classification and management of human sexuality as a whole. Indeed, as Silverstolpe (1987) has argued: '"Science" in the modern age has been an agent of social control to an extent that might be compared to the religious inquisition of the medieval age' (Silverstolpe, 1987: p. 206). Moreover, the emergence of the 'homosexual' category was not simply a product of scientific and state authority but can also 'be attributed to the emancipatory needs, interests and innovative politics of homosexually interested people themselves' (Silverstolpe, 1987; p. 206).

Thus homosexual identity, and the many negative uses to which it is still frequently put, should be properly understood in the wider context of previous and subsequent (homo)sexual identities. The category of 'the homosexual', together with the wider system of sexual classifications which make up the modern ideology of sexuality, is no more scientifically rigorous, natural or descriptively accurate than the category of the molly or of the gay man. All are equally historically specific, equally contingent, equally provisional and equally transitory. They are all also equally strategic responses to periods of special crisis in the overall political and cultural management of homosexuality in Britain, and their painful consequences in the lived experience of a substantial proportion of the population who were vulnerable to discrimination and prejudice as a direct result of their sexual object choice. It is thus possible to chart the complex, overlapping chronology of British sexual identities founded in homosexual desire as a series of changing and advancing claims for social legitimacy and acceptance, in the face of fluctuating levels of legal and cultural persecution.

Yet in the lives of *individuals*, sexual identity is often thought of as if it were a direct, unmediated product of homosexual desire itself. As Vance has pointed out, our new understanding of the ways in which sexual categories are produced at the level of culture and history 'does not mean that individuals have an open-ended ability to construct themselves, or to reconstruct themselves multiple times in adulthood. (This is not to deny individuals' experiences of sexual malleability and change, which are probably considerably more extensive than our cultural frames and our own biographical narratives admit)' (Vance, 1989; p. 17).

This is especially apparent in the gradual replacement of homosexual identity in the early 1970s by the then emergent category 'gay'. Homosexual identity was the private, lived aspect of a general strategy which sought law reform by parliamentary means, and which found its cultural equivalent in calls for 'tolerance' and so on. Homosexual politics thus tended to consist of lobbying groups, often drawn from middle-class men and women who wished to end their own personal stigmatization, in association with support from leading liberals, churchmen and others. Homosexual identity embraced a late-nineteenth-century picture of sexuality, and accepted and inhabited its classification system uncritically.

Gay identity, on the contrary, regarded the oppression of lesbians and gay men as one immediate aspect of a wider political crisis in the categories and management of sexuality *as a whole*. Gay liberation aimed at nothing less than a transformation of the ways in which *all* sexual object choice is valued, policed and actually lived. It was taken as axiomatic that prejudice, discrimination and violence against lesbians and gay men were closely related to the larger questions surrounding gender roles and gender relations. Unlike homosexual identity, gay identity was not founded on the assumption that all gay men are somehow the same, on the basis of shared homosexual object choice. Rather, gay identity has always emphasized the role of key institutions – medicine, the churches, governments, the law, the mass media, the police and so on – as forces of oppression. What gay men share in the name of gay identity is this recognition that we are marginalized and hurt by homophobia regardless of our individual identities (Weeks, 1985). Gay culture thus emerged with a very strong sense of the diversity of ways of being gay, unlike homosexual identity, which implies uniformity underneath its umbrella. Gay identity was also unconcerned by questions of sexual *roles*. In other words, what one likes to do sexually with a member of the same sex is quite distinct from one's overarching sense of being 'gay'.

This is very clear from the range of institutions generated directly by gay identified men, often working with lesbians, who are understood to be victimized by similar forces of oppression. Thus a widespread variety of publications has existed for gay men and for lesbians throughout the UK since the early 1970s, as well as counselling and information services such as the Lesbian and Gay Switchboard network. Gay identity remains very strong in Britain, not least because of continued institutionalized prejudice which dictates how we are represented throughout the newspaper industry, and measures such as Section 28 of the 1988 Local Government Act (Watney, 1991a).

Yet after twenty years gay identity is showing signs of wear and tear. This is hardly surprising, since the wider social circumstances in which gay men live have changed considerably. For example, many gay men have also developed identities and institutions in relation to particular areas of sexual pleasure, such as consensual sado-masochism, especially when these continue to be the target of venomous and increasing policing. There have now been several distinct generations of gay men, 'coming out' at different moments in British socio-economic history. A gay man of 25 is likely to have a very different experience of gay identity from a man of 35, who in turn is likely to share very little with a selfidentifying 'homosexual' in his 60s. The advent of HIV has also had profound consequences on gay identity, not least because of the broadly homophobic response of the UK media, which have tended to identify HIV as if it were a direct symptom of homosexuality as such.

Such questions concerning the development and mutation of sexual identities over time are of the greatest significance in relation of HIV prevention work and the development of appropriate, targeted education. Far too often HIV and AIDS education materials assume a homogeneity to gay identity as if it were unchanging, and at the same time obliterative of all other aspects of social, economic and cultural difference. In the same way as material circumstances in which gay identity is acquired, developed and lived over the course of a lifetime change, so gay identity may alter and vary in relation to perceptions of risk from HIV. This is an especially important question in countries such as Britain, where the epidemic is most prevalent among gay men, while being disproportionately small by international standards. For example, one man's confident gay identity may lead him to excessive anxieties about possible infection, while it may full others into complacency. It should moreover be noted that the response of so-called 'gay community' organizations to HIV has not been uniformly excellent. Indeed, through northern Europe it seems that the long-term goals of established lesbian and gay rights organizations have sometimes led them to regard HIV as an inconvenient distraction from the supposed priorities of law reform and the wider relations between lesbians and gay men (Watney, 1993).

Furthermore, political assults against the so-called 'promotion of homosexuality' have frequently led to self-censorship within independent AIDS service organizations, fearful of losing state funds, and to unwanted controversy. Such problems have been exacerbated by the concentration of research for HIV education strategies for gay men within academic departments of psychology, which have no theoretical model for thinking about distinctions between homosexual behaviour and sexual identities, or any sense whatever of homosexual desire as a factor independent of either behaviour or identity. Lacking any sensitivity to the cultural issues determining gay identities, behavioural psychologists spend much of their (expensive) time chasing chimerical invariant indicators of risk, regarding individual personalities as a whole as either 'risk taking' or 'risk avoiding'. There is thus little or no sense in the dominant social scientific literature on HIV and risk perception of the ways in which perceptions *change* in context within the lives of individuals and collectivities. Nor is there any sense of the ways in which perceptions of risk may be contradictory, ambivalent or related to unconscious mechanisms of projection or defence.

These are vital issues if we wish to try to predict HIV and AIDS education needs in the long term, for it would be most unwise to assume that gay identity will be the same as it is today by the end of the century. There are, moreover, very particular implications for younger men in all of the above. In recent years much research has been done concerning 'younger gay men', a term which is very elastic and usually unhelpfully inclusive. The emotional and sexual world of a 17-year-old teenager living at home with his family in the suburbs will differ considerably from his needs in five years' time, when he is perhaps 'out' about his sexuality, has other gay friends, and is very much on the gay scene. Yet in both situations he is regarded as a 'younger gay man'. Modern social science has long privileged class and gender as key elements in the formation of identities, alongside race, age and so on. In all of this homosexuality has been largely neglected, save as a supposedly uniform 'deviance' from what are uncritically presented as 'norms'.

All sexual identities are historically specific, even and especially when they are regarded as if they were immutable and inevitable. All sexual identities have histories, and they are all heading in directions which are never entirely predictable. They are intensely intimate, especially on the part of the marginalized, whose personal identities respond in different ways to the shared experience of being, or having been hated, feared, despised and so on. They express our sense of similarity to some people, as well as our sense of difference from others. Such identities thus provide a level of social belongingness which is unavailable elsewhere. A gay man will feel 'safe' in a gay bar with other gay men, in ways that have no real parallel for heterosexual men. This is why perceived challenges to the authenticity or authority of given, existing sexual identities are likely to be met with strong resistance on the part of individuals who may feel personally threatened. We cannot expect current or future emergent sexual identities grounded in homosexual desire or behaviour to be welcomed with open arms by lesbians or gay men whose political and personal loyalties lie with the strategic aims and values of the older cultural formation which came into being with gay liberation in the early 1970s. Indeed, we should learn from the strong resistance on the part of many 'homosexuals' to the emergent gay identity in the 1970s. It is salutary to consider that had HIV emerged only a decade or two earlier this century, there would have been only the most fragile institutional framework from which to have launched health promotion and education, since the notion of community was never part of homosexual identity, which was highly individualistic and could not conceive of notions of 'community' or similar social and political claims which are so characteristic of lesbian and gay culture and identity today.

Sexual identity and risk perception

The anthropologist Mary Douglas has produced the most distinguished body of theoretical work in Britain in recent years concerning risk perception (see for example, Douglas and Wildavsky, 1983; Douglas, 1987). In a recent summary of her position, she observed how the meaning of the word 'risk' is changing from a neutral concept taking account of the probability of losses and gains, to a much more direct sense of *danger:* 'the word has been pre-empted to mean bad risks' (Douglas, 1990). Douglas's work is strongly critical of social scientific attempts to isolate risk perception from its cultural context. She traces the ways in which individuals and groups tend to delegate decision-making processes about possible risks to trusted institutions. From this briskly commonsense perspective she notes, 'Refusing to take all dangers into account is not behaving irrationally' (Douglas and Wildavsky, 1983: 73).

In Britain, as elsewhere, lesbians and gay men are well aware of the failure and refusal of state agencies to accept the equal validity of homosexuality and heterosexuality. We are also likely to be somewhat sceptical about the mass media's concern for our health, since their wishes towards us are so transparently malicious This means that gay men are likely to delegate responsibility for reliable information and policy on HIV/AIDS issues to community-based institutions which are understood, rightly or wrongly, to be part of the wider gay community. Hence the significance of the role of the gay press, for example, or gay television shows. Far beyond any direct informational role, such services represent the idea of a community responding to a crisis on its own terms and in its own best interests.

It should, however, be remembered that gay identity is frequently acquired only after a long period of social and sexual isolation as a teenager, when homosexual desire has often been lived as an anxious or guilty secret. Thus, paradoxically, gay identity may lead to a form of collective amnesia on the part of gay adults about their lives as children or teenagers, whom I shall term queer teenagers in relation to their primary sense of difference from heterosexuals, prior to their sense of subsequent identification with other gay men within the social relations of the gay scene. Community-based organizations and institutions may also be timid about targeting younger people with HIV education for fear of attracting homophobic controversy or police attention. It should certainly not be assumed that something called 'the gay community' is always able to identify and meet the changing needs of different groups of sexually active gay men. As lesbian and gay youth culture broadens and develops, it is far from clear that it will remain visible and recognizable from the political and cultural centre of lesbian and gay culture. At the opposite extreme, it seems likely that the very concept of 'middle age' and 'old age' will be radically transformed as the first post-Gay Liberation generations of politically and personally self-confident lesbians and gay men reach retirement age.

While armies of social scientists quarry away to identify abstract 'risk factors' in the lives of gay men, especially in relation to drugs and alcohol, the changing conditions in which we live our lives and experience the epidemic are almost entirely neglected. Indeed, we can learn a very great deal about contemporary social science, and wider politics, from the fact that it is all but impossible to articulate the basic sexual and emotional rights of queer children in either ordinary or official public discourse. This is precisely why queer teenagers may be described as vulnerable to HIV – not because of any intrinsic pathological vulnerability, but because their very existence is all but completely denied as a constituency at serious statistical risk from HIV. A recent survey of *Gay Times* readers, for example, showed that no less than 42 per cent of men aged between 16 and 25 had unsafe sex before learning about safer sex (*Gay Times*, 1992).

Nor is this all that surprising. As Wetherburn (1992) and Project SIGMA pointed out recently, discriminatory age of consent legislation in the UK prevents young gay men getting the sexual education they need at school. Recent figures show a rise in unintended teenage pregnancies in Britain from 58.7 per 1,000 in 1980, to 69 per 1,000 girls in 1990 (Hall, 1992). If a 13-year-old girl can become pregnant in 1992 because she thinks she's too young to have a baby, how much can we reasonably expect a 13-year-old

Isolated queer teenage boy to understand about HIV transmission? As Kosofsky Sedgewick (1991) points out bluntly, the denial of targeted HIV/AIDS education amounts to nothing less than 'punishing young gay people with death'.

Yet one powerful strand of political gay male identity has consistently opposed the special targeting of HIV education for gay men, together with the very concept of 'risk groups'. From this perspective it is considered discriminatory to define gay men of any age as a 'risk group', even though 3,034 of the 3,708 men who died from AIDS in Britain between January 1982 and July 1992 were gay or bisexual. Thus a gay politics of the far left, seeking as a priority to achieve tactical coalitions with other marginalized social groups, is able to neglect the most serious medical and political crisis in its own social constituency. A political vision which privileges class struggle as the all-determining site of power and resistance is unlikely to make very much practical sense of an epidemic which is still overwhelmingly concentrated among gay and bisexual men, across class boundaries.

This is a very serious issue, since historically gay identity has always been the object of far leftist 'entryist' ambitions. Furthermore, the familiar British absence of politically neutral or independent civil rights organizations and principles has tended to make party politics the model for sexual politics, with generally unfortunate results. Thus gay and lesbian politics have long tended to align themselves with other groups in relation to national and international political issues, while lacking any very developed sense of what might be specific to lesbians and gay men themselves. The emergence of a determined challenge to the forces of sectarian leftism, in the form of the direct action organization OutRage, is indicative of changes within British gay culture in the 1990s. Yet it is surely significant that OutRage has flourished successfully since 1990 because it recognized and responded to the fact that most younger lesbians and gay men were much more alarmed about everyday levels of anti-gay violence and prejudice in their lives than they were about the epidemic. OutRage belongs neither to the inherited tradition of political lobbying nor to the sectarian left. It may thus be regarded as indicative of the political goals of lesbian and gay men who have 'come out' since the AIDS crisis began, yet who up to now have had little space within mainstream lesbian and gay politics to articulate their specific experience as younger people.

OutRage has also embodied a certain principle of 'fun politics'. Its demonstrations and graphics are direct, theatrical and at the same time very carefully targeted. It is as much a street party as a political movement, and it is also very stylish. This perhaps marks the beginning of a breakdown of previously rigid distinctions between the domains of lesbian and gay politics and our everyday lives and culture. For, as Alcorn, one of OutRage's founders, has forcefully argued: 'In this disintegrating social order, it's inevitable that we invent new notions of community, just as we choose to recycle notions of family in order to defend ourselves' (Alcorn, 1992: p. 14).

Looking over the contemporary commercial London gay scene, Alcorn observes:

> Dance clubs like Troll, Trade and Chemistry provide a sense of community which is quite different from the political community. These are communities of the body rather than the imagination, and they probably provide more powerful collective experiences (for young gay men) than anything else in our society. Meanwhile, the SM scene is becoming a place of pilgrimage for many people who want their sexuality to remain political at a time when gay identity is being evacuated of its capacity to shock or threaten the society that half-tolerates it. (Alcorn, 1992: p. 14)

In reality, though,

> the lesbian and gay community has always been a network of communities, primarily split between a political community which pursues an ideal of political power and representation, and the communities of the night, which encompass the genuine diversity which political activists seek to represent. These range from the nightclubs to all the other privatised activities through which lesbians and gay men meet together. They provide not only a means of meeting new partners, but also of belonging to a group in which sexuality is the common factor. (Alcorn, 1992: p. 14)

If, as is suggested, the members of these new 'communities of the night' feel little sense of identification with the category gay, beyond the annual tribal gathering of Lesbian and Gay Pride Day, HIV education needs to find out whether previous strategies targeting gay men are still appropriate for the post-gay dance generation. This is especially important, since there is still comparatively little direct experience of HIV among the young in London, compared to Paris or New York for example, and most of those already infected in their teens are unlikely to become symptomatically ill until their mid- or late 20s.

Safer sex versus safe sex

Turning back to Mary Douglas, we need to mark her observation that 'the neutral vocabulary of risk is all we have for making a bridge between the known facts of existence and the construction of a moral community' (Douglas, 1990: p. 15). In gay safer sex education we are not seeking to identify 'guilty' or 'dangerous' individuals. Rather, it is a collective consensus that is sought, in order to establish risk reduction practices while supporting gay men in their everyday lives, which are often hard enough even without HIV as an issue. Unfortunately, most public discourse on HIV and risk tends, on the contrary, to establish the notion of defective, dangerous

'AIDS carriers', dangerous sexual acts and dangerous identities. Seeking not *risk reduction* but *risk elimination*, much contemporary HIV education targeted at heterosexuals and women, including lesbians, may actually serve to undermine strategies developed by and for gay men, who, it must always be recognized, are at far greater risk from HIV than anybody else. This is not because our sexual pleasures are intrinsically dangerous, but for the simple reason that HIV affected us before it affected other people. It is surely extremely significant that recent best-selling popular books such as Magic Johnson's *What You Can Do to Avoid AIDS* expect far more of intended heterosexual readers than is usually expected of gay men.

In this context we may distinguish between the demonstrably effective risk reduction strategies developed by and for gay men in the name of safer sex, and strategies apparently aiming at total risk elimination, which we may term 'safe sex'. Exceeding any demonstrably necessary precautions against HIV transmission, safe sex becomes little more than an instrument for exercising social control of people's sexual behaviour through the use of fear. Such an approach typically tends to whip up anxieties about oral sex, for example, and is always ready to tell people not to have sex. While monogamy and celibacy are always options, they do not realistically address the sexual needs of most teenagers, and least of all the most basic needs of those at greatest risk, who need and deserve all the help they can get in achieving a strong sense of collective solidarity with others like themselves, whether they identify as gay, or bisexual or queer.

There is also an international dimension to this dilemma, since gay identity and culture are always diasporic to a greater or lesser extent, and there is strong evidence of a growing disparity between the goals of US HIV/AIDS education aimed at gay men and strategies developed in Britain, Canada and Australia, for example. It cannot be sufficiently emphasized that the entire concept of risk in American society is largely different from the concept in other Anglophone societies. The US gay and lesbian community response to HIV/AIDS has been overwhelmingly focused on questions of treatment research and drugs, service provision and care, for the obvious reason that such a vast number of people are already ill or dead. Prevention work has been badly neglected, and what does exist is, to say the least, uneven. For example, the celebrated STOP AIDS campaign in San Francisco now uses a badge which simply reads '100 per cent', meaning 100 per cent *safe* from HIV. But is this realistic? Or is it a potentially dangerous approach, not least in its most fundamental assumption that risks are complex and may vary by minute percentage points, rather than a question of sexual identity and *cultural* solidarity?

Even worse is a recent poster campaign from the San Francisco AIDS Foundation which smugly states that: 'Research shows that some gay men still have unsafe sex. Unsafe sex must be completely eliminated if we are to triumph over AIDS. There are no excuses.' The poster proceeds to list seven 'Excuses', concluding, 'If you have *any* unsafe sex – STOP NOW.' Unsafe sex is defined as 'fucking without a condom, having oral sex, licking someone's ass (rimming), fisting without a latex glove, and sharing sex toys'. Such victim blaming is sadly not unusual in US HIV education for gay men, together with its misleading and excessive embargo on all forms of oral sex and rimming. Much of this kind of campaigning, aiming at 100 per cent risk elimination, is based upon the misguided concept of 'relapse' which dominates most university-based US HIV prevention research. Given the diasporic nature of international gay culture, there is a real risk that US models of safe sex education will increasingly come into conflict with European and other safer sex initiatives, aiming for the more modest, yet pragmatically achievable goal of risk reduction, rather than the chimerical goal of risk elimination, which is in reality only likely to put people at *increased* risk of HIV by exaggerating danger and expecting too much. There is a yawning chasm between the world as it is imagined by the designers of such excessively demanding safe sex strategies and the real world in which gay men live and have sexual relationships of many different kinds.

Nor are such approaches unknown in Britain. It will doubtless one day be widely recognised that one of the most tragic aspects of the UK AIDS epidemic concerned the way in which state-funded HIV prevention policy and work since the late 1980s was based directly on supposedly reliable 'scientific' research conducted by academic statisticians and epidemiologists who understand nothing about the significance of sexual identities, or the complex cultural processes that form and underpin them. At the same time, official HIV/AIDS advertising continues to be generated from a hellish fusion of the commercial advertising industry, which refuses to consult or listen to informed, community-based expertise, and a Health Education Authority which has long seemed even more keen to distance itself from the vulgar nitty-gritty of gay men's lives than its political masters in Whitehall and Westminster.

Yet as Douglas and Wildavsky (1983) remind us, questions about acceptable levels of risk:

> can never be answered just by explaining how nature and technology interact. What needs to be explained is how people agree to ignore most of the potential dangers that surround them and interact so as to concentrate only on selected aspects. (Douglas and Wildavsky, 1983: p. 9)

Thus, she maintains:

> In risk perception, humans act less as individuals and more as social beings who have internalised social pressures and delegated their decision-making processes to institutions. They manage as well as they do ... by following social rules on what to ignore: institutions are their problem-solving devices. (Douglas and Wildavsky, 1983: p. 80)

From her perspective:

> Current theories of risk perception steer badly between overintellectual-
> ising the decision process and overemphasising irrational impediments
> … Shared values do more than weight the calculation of risks. They
> work on the estimates of probabilities as well as on the perceived
> magnitude of loss. (Douglas and Wildavsky, 1983: 84)

Such conclusions have profound implications for HIV educators working
with gay men, since we may or may not accept the authority of state institutions which speak on the subject of AIDS. Since many lesbians and gay men
will have perfectly good, rational reasons for not trusting demonstrably
homophobic institutions such as the government, political parties or the
National Health Services, a tremendous responsibility falls on known lesbian
and gay institutions, to whom the most vital problem-solving aspects of the
epidemic are delegated. The question here is of *plausibility*, which depends on
sufficient numbers of people accepting and consciously sharing particular
moral or ethical principles. For example, what happens when such community-
based lesbian and gay institutions close ranks against the perceived threat of
emergent, post-gay homosexual identities? The shocking rate of new infection
among young American men strongly suggests that nobody is successfully
getting through to those at greatest risk, who do not necessarily identify with
gay culture at all.

The 'men who have sex with men' myth

The continued widespread use of such misleadingly monolithic notions as
'the gay community', or worse, 'the gay lifestyle', throughout the field of
HIV prevention research demonstrates how little is actually understood
about the diversity of sexual behaviour and identity in Britain. Taking their
own identities for granted, as if they were natural and timeless, heterosexual
researchers and policy-makers have effectively colluded to ignore the actual
complex world of homosexual behaviour and identities. Indeed, the bizarre
fantasy that all gay men share a single 'lifestyle' speaks volumes about the
homophobic agenda implicit within most academic HIV prevention research
and policy. This is even plainer in the increasing adoption work targeted at
so-called 'men who have sex with men' (MSMs).

The category of the 'man who has sex with men' emerged from the convergence of two very different sets of pressures. On the one hand, it was very
convenient within institutions in Britain such as the Health Education
Authority, which have not wanted to be seen 'promoting' homosexuality. At
the same time it also expresses a basic misunderstanding of an important
insight about the nature of sexual identity. Correctly recognizing that homosexual behaviour is not the same as gay identity, and that the latter is culturally acquired and sustained, the notion of 'MSM' was developed to describe

men who do not have a gay identity, but who may be at risk from HIV as a result of unprotected sex with other men. This supposed group has special significance in academic research since it is thought of as the main route of possible HIV transmission from 'the gay community' to 'innocent' heterosexuals. It is thus an intensely liminal category, containing those assumed to be 'hard to reach', since they do not necessarily identify as gay. Yet this is also to assume that such men have no sexual identity whatsoever. In other words, the category of MSMs is little more than a reconceptualization of the earlier concept of the 'bridging group', imagined as a Trojan horse full of 'AIDS carriers' inside 'the heterosexual community'. Besides, as Scott has pointed out, it is most unlikely that such men will only have sex with one another (Scott, 1992). In reality, they either identify as heterosexual or bisexual.

The main problem is that the category of heterosexuality is proving stubbornly resistant to any acknowledgment of the sexual diversity which it so evidently contains. The MSM is thus primarily a product of projective homophobic fantasy, concerning what is perceived as the most immediate source of possible contamination to heterosexual men. It is, furthermore, far from clear whether the contamination which is most dreaded is HIV or homosexuality. Ironically, the notion of MSM has been widely seized upon in a period of massive ongoing neglect of out gay men's HIV education, as a means of getting funding, especially in the independent sector. There is thus a formidable coalition of interests at work in sustaining the largely imaginary spectre of a hidden sexual underworld of secretly bisexual married men, busily having unsafe sex with one another!

However, if one accepts that there are many powerful obstacles to the acquisition of gay identity, then the correct response to the question of men whose behaviour may be asymmetrical with their sexual identity would be to combat and minimize such obstacles. Yet this would require a detailed analysis of, and challenge to, the forms and forces of homophobia within contemporary British culture and society. In this context the most important aspect of HIV education based on the aim of targeting MSMs has concerned queer teenagers, prior to their coming out on the gay scene at a time when powerful voices still publicly oppose *any* form of HIV education in schools which does not strictly conform with Department of Health guidelines stressing 'the importance of self-restraint' and 'the benefits of stable married and family life and the responsibilities of parenthood' (Watney, 1992). Yet the very category of MSM can only serve to obscure the concrete social processes of personal and institutional prejudice which may put queer teenagers at *increased* risk of HIV by effectively delaying or even preventing their adoption of confident gay or post-gay identities. It is thus also a potentially very dangerous distraction from the most important underlying issues, which continue to involve the denial of adequate resourcing for community-based work with gay and bisexual men of *all* ages, within the terms of their own cultural identities, whatever they may be or become (Watney, 1992). The idea of MSMs is little more than the latest way of 'de-gaying' AIDS.

Post-gay Identities

In all of the above it is important to recognize that sexual identities are not immanent or necessarily tied to sexual behaviour; they are, above all, cultural constructs which help people make sense of their own desires and emotions. At the same time they are intensely symbolic, providing boundaries which run across the entire social formation, independently of other aspects of identity grounded in race, class, gender, age and so on. Such boundaries constitute a fundamental level of social relations, the full significance of which is only rarely acknowledged within mainstream British social or political analysis. Furthermore, they have become increasingly important in a period of intense social transition, when the older basic social organizing categories of family and class have been widely eroded. Sexual identities emerge and decline in strict relation to their capacity to provide coherent and persuasive accounts of sexual desire and related emotions as they are lived by the individuals and collectivities who inhabit them. Certainly, there is already abundant evidence that the models of lesbian and gay identities established in the early 1970s are proving inadequate to increasing numbers of people who, as it were, inherit them in the 1990s, and for many different reasons, which are all to a greater or lesser extent related to the epidemic.

This is precisely why the growing reliance upon the fiction of MSM is so disturbing, since it demonstrates so clearly that academic and other professional researchers and policy-makers are unable or unwilling to engage with existing identities such as gay, lesbian or queer. Instead, it is simply assumed that gay identity exists as a monolithic, universal type of person. In other words, the meaning of the term 'gay' as it is used and understood by gay men is often automatically translated by heterosexuals to mean something synonymous with the older 'homosexual' identity. As an American queer activist stated in 1990: 'Straights think they've done everything we've demanded simply by changing the language they use to patronise us' (cited in Alcorn, 1992: p. 14). Such opinions are also increasingly common in the UK. The stridently confident climate of homophobia in Britain in the 1980s angered hundreds of thousands of lesbians and gay men, who constitute our usually largely invisible communities. Furthermore, younger people became increasingly impatient with what they often regard as the complacency of older lesbians and gay men, especially in relation to questions of street violence and police harassment. Moreover, many younger lesbians and gay men associate the word 'gay' with the celebratory promiscuity of the late 1970s, and this has led to rifts both within and between different generations of gay men. Indeed, nothing could be more indicative of the tensions and stresses within gay identity than the many recent debates between older gay men about the nature and significance of their sexual behaviour before the epidemic. In the meantime, younger men are either on the whole much more selective about prospective sexual partners, or much more intensely committed to sexual pleasure and the proud assertion of sexual difference.

At the same time, the major institutions of gay culture are also in a state of flux. The established gay press in Britain has never dealt with AIDS as well as it could and should have. *Gay Times* did not begin a regular monthly column on HIV/AIDS until early 1988, and the weeklies *Capital Gay* and the *Pink Paper* are uneven in their coverage, with the latter, for example, allowing only 600 words per article in its weekly column on HIV/AIDS. In this context the emergence of a highly successful new weekly, *BOYZ*, is extremely significant, *BOYZ* contains very little from the older, surrounding gay culture. Targeted at young gay men on the commercial scene, it affirms a defiantly cheerful, sexually confident youth culture, focused closely on the pleasures of being young – fashion, sport, holidays, dancing and music, but, above all, relationships and sex. *BOYZ* is much the most impressive gay publication in relation to safer sex. Indeed, it is perhaps the only gay paper in Britain which evidently has a clear and consistent policy on HIV prevention issues, presenting HIV as a very important question which is constantly addressed, but as a reminder rather than with a sledge-hammer, always around, but never obtrusively.

Parallel to changes in the gay press are changes on the gay scene itself, most obviously with the belated emergence in both Manchester and London of inner city districts where gay bars, cafés, clothes shops and so on are to be found in close proximity, as in Old Compton Street in London's Soho district. Such changes are at least as important in the history and development of sexual identities as gay political movements, for they speak of popular demand for services and facilities which heterosexuals invariably take for granted wherever they go. Thus debates about 'outing' or 'the new queer cinema' should be properly regarded as indicative of a culture in the process of rapid change, not least in response to the prejudices of the surrounding society, whether of the left or the right (Watney, 1991b; McKenna, 1991).

In any case, it is always salutary to consider what gay youth culture *might* have become, had it not been for the epidemic and measures such as Section 28 of the 1988 Local Government Act, which have tended on the whole to stabilize an 'overhead' validity to gay identity as the older lesbian and gay subcultures appear retrospectively fuddy-duddy and mutually separatist, rather than collectively anti-straight. For example, the ongoing emergence in Britain and the US of a confident and frankly sexual lesbian youth culture is directly reactive to what is widely perceived as the moralistic, dour, anti-sex culture of much earlier lesbian feminism. Indeed, the new lesbian youth culture, with its stylishly 'boyish' look and aggressive assertion of explicit sexual roles, which were widely previously dismissed as 'stereotypes', seems to be making similar claims for lesbian sexuality and identity to those that Gay Liberation made for men in the 1970s.

There is also a great deal of cultural overlap between young women and men within the emergent queer culture associated with OutRage and the thriving late-night commercial dance/drugs/rave scene. Here lesbians and gay men meet in what Gregg Bordowitz has aptly described as the 'newly constituted disease identified community', which is the meaning of queer in the 1990s (Bordowitz, 1992). Queer identity thus reacts both to the earlier lesbian and gay subcultures as well as to the shrill homophobia against the background of which this generation has come of age. As Keith Alcorn has written, queer is:

> an incendiary device planted in the heart of 'gay pride'. Nothing makes liberals – gay and straight – squirm more than calling yourself queer. It reminds them of the degree to which they ignore homophobia every day by talking about 'gay' people … It was the AIDS epidemic that caused the rehabilitation of the label 'queer'. The AIDS epidemic hit gay men, and brought home the message that we are still queers in the eyes of society. (Alcorn, 1992: p. 14)

While every centre has its margins, so every margin has a centre or focus point. Queer identity is organized around an angry assertion of sexual difference on the part of a generation which has 'come out' at a uniquely horrible moment in history, facing both the extremes of Thatcherite legal moralism and its popular cultural expressions and the complex reality of HIV. It may involve many different kinds of personal and cultural responses to the epidemic, from the steady growth of a gymnasium-based physical cultural movement, which often appears as a thinly veiled reaction to the presence of so much illness and death in our midst, and doubts about our own HIV status, to the fast growing club-based sexual fetish scene, which transfers much of the intensity of pre-AIDS gay sex into equally specialized sexual expression, which has little or no risk of HIV transmission. It is for this volatile, complex constituency that effective safer sex education strategies must be developed as a matter of high priority, since there is always the risk that HIV will be culturally associated only with the older gay culture, while confidence about safer sex may not yet have been empirically acquired. As the epidemic worsens, and we move from a predominantly HIV epidemic into a full-scale AIDS epidemic, we can only expect queer identity, or other as yet unestablished sexual identities, to flourish, whether or not they also accept an overarching gay identity as a political strategy, as seems currently to be the case.

While we cannot predict the forms or values of future, emergent post-gay identities grounded in homosexual desire, we should recognize that such developments are responses of a profound, spontaneous nature, to ongoing prejudice, discrimination and the stress and trauma of the epidemic, as well as to changing demands and cultural expectations (Alcorn, 1992). If we are seriously concerned with questions of risk perception on the part of those at greatest potential risk of HIV infection, we cannot afford to ignore the most basic social arena in which such perceptions are constantly being defined, revised and replaced – namely, the 'communities of the night'. Statistics can provide us with a valuable, continually updated profile of new cases of HIV and shifting patterns of infection, but they cannot even begin to explain why these are taking place. Avoiding HIV is not a matter of luck, or of mathematical probability, but of socially learned skills, rooted in collective experience and shared morality. Sadly and scandalously, these are topics about which most contemporary HIV-related social science research and mathematical modelling can tell us precisely nothing.

References

Alcorn, K. (1992) 'Communities of the night', *Capital Gay*, London, 18 September, p. 14.

Bordowitz, G. (1992) 'Identity crisis: Queer politics in the age of possibilities', *Village Voice*, New York, 30 June, p. 28.

Burrows, L. (1992) 'No to gay sex at 16', *Daily Telegraph*, 7 June.

Douglas, M. (1987) *Risk Acceptability According to the Social Sciences*, London: Routledge and Kegan Paul.

Douglas, M. (1990) 'Risk as a forensic resource', *Daedalus*, 119, 4, p. 3.

Douglas, M. and Wildavsky, A. (1983) *Risk and Culture: An Essay on the Selection of Technological and Environmental Dangers*, Berkeley, Calif.: University of California Press.

Gay Times (1992) Reader's Survey, *Gay Times*, November, p. 12.

Greenberg, D. F. (1990) 'The socio-sexual milieu of the love-letters', *Journal of Homosexuality*, 19, 2.

Hall, C. (1992) 'Family planning services fail to reach the young, *Independent*, 6 November, p. 8.

Hall, S. (1990) 'Cultural identity and diaspora', in J. Rutherford (Ed.) *Identity: Community, Culture, Difference*, London: Lawrence and Wishart.

Kosofsky Sedgwick, E. (1991) 'Queer and now', personal communication.

McKenna, N. (1991) 'Outing's bitter truths', *Independent*, 29 July.

Scott, P. (1992) 'Beginning HIV prevention work with gay and bisexual men', *Healthy Alliances in HIV Prevention*, eds. B. Evans *et al.*, Health Education Authority, London, 1993, pp. 148–64.

Senelick, L. (1990) 'Mollies or men of mode? Sodomy and the eighteenth-century London stage'. *Journal of the History of Sexuality*, 1, 1, pp. 33–68.

Silverstolpe, F. (1987) 'Benkert was not a doctor. On the non-medical origin of the homosexual category in the nineteenth century', in D. Altman *et al.* (Eds) *Homosexuality, Which Homosexuality?*, London: Gay Men's Press.

Strickland, S. (1992) 'Too many condoms, not enough morals', *Independent*, 9 July.

Vance, C. S. (1989) 'Social construction theory: Problems in the history of sexuality', in Altman, D. *et al.* (Eds) *Homosexuality, Which Homosexuality?*, London: Gay Men's Press.

Watney, S. (1991a) 'School's out', in D. Fuss (Ed.) *Inside/Out: Lesbian Theories, Gay Theories*, New York, Routledge.

Watney, S. (1991b) 'Troubleshooters: On outing', *Artforum*, New York, 16–18 November.

Watney, S. (1992) 'Gay politics, gay teenagers', *Gay Times*, December, p. 14.

Watney, S. (1993) 'The killing fields of Europe', in *Practices of Freedom: Selected Writings on HIV/AIDS*, London: Rivers Oram Press.

Wetherburn, P. (1992) 'Family planning services fail to reach the young', *Independent*, 6 November, p. 8.

Weeks, J. (1985) *Sexuality and Its Discontents: Meanings, Myths and Modern Sexualities*, London: Routledge and Kegan Paul.

Weeks, J. (1986) *Sexuality*, London: Tavistock.

6   The killing fields of Europe*

Things are going very badly indeed at almost all levels of HIV/AIDS education and prevention work for gay men throughout Europe. Some examples:

- In Germany the leading AIDS service organization, Deutsche AIDS-Hilfe, is currently threatened with severe financial cuts, while safe sex campaigns for gay men have to be produced with non-government money as a direct result of previous censorship of sexually explicit materials.
- Two planned campaigns from the Stop AIDS organization in Switzerland have been scrapped as a result of right-wing pressure on the government, and older education material has been censored.
- The new conservative government in Sweden continues the previous Social Democrat policy of regarding HIV antibody testing as if it were a form of primary HIV prevention rather than a means of access to treatment and care. Swedish saunas have long since been shut down.
- In Holland the saunas are open, but with little evidence of education materials or condoms, largely as a consequence of the Dutch government's HIV education policies, which until last year simply told gay men 'don't fuck': hardly a helpful message.
- In socialist France the situation is already quite literally catastrophic, with more than 300,000 people officially thought to be HIV-infected, and some 25,000 cases of AIDS to date. There are still no needle-exchanges in France. There is no counselling available before or after HIV antibody testing, and specialist hospital wards are already full to the point of overflowing.

Gay men's entitlements in the ongoing HIV/AIDS crisis are not being adequately or sufficiently met anywhere in Europe. This is not an issue of the Left or the Right. Rather, it reflects a crisis of European culture, which remains deeply homophobic across all social and national boundaries. As a leading French doctor told me last week, with tears of frustration and exhaustion in his eyes: 'We've lost the first round against HIV.' We must

* First published in Outrage, *Melbourne, July 1992.*

conclude that government policies throughout Europe have guaranteed the virtual inevitability of an almost entirely preventable disaster.

Homophobia, prejudice and stupidity

On top of this dismal picture of the consequences of prejudice and stupidity, we have to address the overwhelming evidence of massive homophobia, leading to the wholesale denial of our rights as gay men to resources appropriate to our needs and entitlements as the group most vulnerable to HIV infection in Europe. But homophobia does not just have one clearly identifiable face. Thus here in Britain we all know the type of loud, confident anti-gay prejudice which has resulted, for example, in such crude manifestations as Section 28, or the Isle of Man situation before law reform was enacted in May. Yet in countries such as France things are rather different.

The French Constitution theoretically offers equal rights to all French citizens, but in practice homosexuality is hardly acknowledged in France, save as a private issue, for individuals. While British homophobia tends to operate more by explicit commission, French homophobia tends to work implicitly, and by omission. So pervasive is this political obliteration of homosexuality that there is very little in France resembling Anglophone gay identity, let alone gay politics.

French homosexuals tended to present AIDS as a general problem, for everyone, perhaps in order to avoid an imagined anti-gay backlash. Instead, they have a catastrophe in their midst. The results are only too tragically apparent in French HIV/AIDS statistics. Putting this bluntly, one need only compare Britain with France. Both countries have similar economies and populations. Yet there have already been more than 12,000 deaths from AIDS in France, compared to some 3,000 in the UK.

Britain was at least fortunate to possess an energetic lesbian and gay press, and an unbroken tradition of lesbian and gay community organizations going back to the period of Gay Liberation, and earlier. Yet things are far from rosy in Britain. The original AIDS service organizations, which were largely set up in an *ad hoc* manner in the early 1980s by gay men with a background in community politics, have been professionalized out of recognition. An understandable concern with questions of direct service provision to people with HIV or AIDS has, until very recently, tended to eclipse any active involvement with treatment issues.

HIV education for gay men has also been badly neglected, partly because it was naïvely assumed that it had 'already been done', but also because such work has tended to attract the critical attention of the press and politicians. In order to 'protect' the funding of the new, large AIDS service outfits, prevention work for gay men was left to volunteers, and largely sacrificed. For example, the Terrence Higgins Trust, Britain's oldest and largest AIDS service organization, has a total staff of 60. Of these, only one is a gay man doing HIV prevention work for other gay men! We have excellent new leaflets, but few resources, especially for younger people who have come out during the epidemic.

The failure of the gay movement

Questions of sexual identity are absolutely central to our ability to design and implement effective education strategies. Yet the shocking paradox of the Second European Conference on Homosexuality and HIV, attended by some 300 delegates in Amsterdam in February, was the evidence that a powerful and perhaps central strand of northern European post-Gay Liberation lesbian and gay politics is hopelessly unable to acknowledge, let alone confront, the catastrophe that already surrounds us.

Indeed, the tragedy of the Amsterdam conference lay in the fact that there appears to be a widening gulf between the aims and objectives of the international lesbian and gay political movement founded long before the emergence of HIV, and needs of the epidemic. In the name of a conference on 'Homosexuality and HIV' it seemed that relations between lesbians and gay men frequently had a higher priority than the AIDS crisis!

The most fundamental questions were not asked. Surely the starting point for any European conference on homosexuality and HIV should be a concern with the unavailability of adequate resources, access to clinical trials, and so on. What is the latest reliable information about levels of HIV infectivity among gay men? What are differing patterns of disease progression among gay men in Europe, or of life expectancy? Yet such questions were nowhere in evidence.

As Peter Scott, Editor of the *British National AIDS Manual*, concluded, 'it was absolutely criminal to leave out the single most important issue of the second decade of the epidemic: the utter mismatch between the levels of risk facing gay men, and the ludicrously small resources available to us. This appalled, outraged, and amazed me.' Of the 100 or so panels and workshops, only one was dedicated to the subject of clinical trials for potential new treatment drugs, and even this was sorely inadequate.

Nonetheless, it would be highly misleading not to mention the large number of inspiring individual sessions at the conference, which offered a wealth of information about specialist issues. To provide just a few examples from amongst the sessions I attended, both Theo Sandfort from Utrecht and Gary Dowsett from Sydney addressed the vital subject of how to conduct behaviour surveys amongst gay men, while Carsten Hinz from the Deutsche AIDS Hilfe gave an excellent paper on outreach work with gay teenagers in Germany. Marc Anguenot-Franchequin also spoke movingly of the appalling situation in France.

Gay men, lesbians and HIV

Yet the fundamental inability of the conference to identify the central issues facing us became most starkly apparent in the talk given by Dianne Richardson from Sheffield University immediately following this grim account of France's genocide by negligence. As if nothing of any real consequence had been said, she launched into a regrettably misleading talk which claimed that gay men have been all but washed away in a tidal wave of HIV education campaigns and leaflets, contrasting this to the supposedly 'unexamined' issue of woman-to-woman transmission.

This warmly received paper suggested much about the unchanged agenda of European lesbian and gay politics. It should by now be plainly obvious that the only ways in which lesbians are potentially at risk from HIV are via unprotected intercourse with HIV-infected men, or from sharing infected needles. There has not been one demonstrable case of sexually transmitted HIV infection from woman to woman in the entire history of the European epidemic. It is therefore quite unethical to try to compare HIV transmission between lesbians, and between gay men, as if there were indeed some scientific, epidemiological principle of parity, needing to be established. There is not.

There is, however, a genuine irony underlying much of the confusion and uncertainty surrounding the whole question of how lesbians and gay men relate to AIDS. Many lesbians and gay men have long worked closely together in European countries. HIV emerged at a time when gay culture as a whole was beginning to consolidate, ten years after Gay Liberation. It would certainly be unreasonable to expect a uniform lesbian response to the increasingly confident gay male culture of the late 1970s and early 1980s. Moreover, the relations between lesbians and gay men have inevitably been fractured to a great extent by divisions within feminism, and divisions between feminist and non-feminist lesbians.

The result has been a formidable amount of confusion. This has been largely focused on oral sex, about which many gay men are still badly informed and unnecessarily anxious. Thus, by a bitter irony, the general paucity of HIV education available to gay men, who are at most risk of being infected, has a knock-on effect among lesbians, who are at least risk. It cannot be sufficiently emphasized that risk is determined by scientifically verifiable, virological factors: not by homosexuality as such. Rather than complaining about the supposed 'neglect' of what is in fact an imaginary health hazard to lesbians, influential lesbian commentators should surely be seeking to allay unnecessary and doubtless sometimes debilitating fears among other lesbians, and to reassure them about their sexual behaviour.

Ludicrously distracting debates

At a time when less than 5 per cent of British state funds for HIV education have gone to gay men, who last year yet again made up over 70 per cent of new cases of HIV infection, it is dishonest and totally unacceptable to argue, like Dianne Richardson, that women's resources are inadequate. On the contrary, European women have received vastly more resources than gay men. If lesbians have been badly served, it is not the fault of gay men.

It is unhelpful for gay men simply to dismiss lesbian anxieties as 'AIDS envy'. Yet at the same time we cannot collude with misinformation. All gay men face the epidemic head-on every time we have sex. We have mostly learned to live with this, though God knows the personal costs are high for very many of us. This is not how lesbians live. To fail to recognize this is to insult the only too real experience of gay men in relation to the epidemic, wherever we live, and trivializes our experience. Worse still, it encourages the kind of ludicrously distracting debates that we all had repeatedly to endure in Amsterdam.

This difficult issue draws me back to the wider historical problems confronting us. For example, throughout the conference, reports of mass arrests and a subsequent suicide on the Isle of Man were widely circulated, together with a petition of complaint to the British government. Yet what did this really have to do with a conference about HIV? It seemed to me indicative of another crisis alongside the epidemic. For ultimately the Isle of Man situation, however cruel, is of a legal and political nature, and is subject to legal and political resolution and redress. In other words, it seems easier for many in the lesbian and gay politics movement to think about such civil rights issues, than it is for them to think seriously about the specific problems raised by HIV.

We may also detect a similar situation in the way that many involved in traditional pre-AIDS lesbian and gay politics can only seem to acknowledge HIV/AIDS in relation to questions of social and legal discrimination. However vitally important it of course is to challenge such discrimination, we should note that there has been little or no equivalent attention to questions of medical or sociological research, let alone to the wholesale neglect and censorship of HIV education. Why no petition from Amsterdam to François Mitterand concerning the genocide taking place in France? Why no petition to John Major about the censorship of Safer Sex materials in Britain by Customs and Excise officials?

Wherever we look in Europe, existing traditions of lesbian and gay politics seem unable to grasp the desperate needs of gay men in this epidemic. Moreover, the lesbian and gay movement may even be subtly or not so subtly hostile to what is sometimes seen as 'giving ground' to HIV/AIDS, as if the epidemic were merely an inconvenient distraction from our previous civil rights agenda.

'De-gaying' and 'De-AIDS-ing' in collusion

The great strength of the lesbian and gay movement lay in its capacity to articulate together our common interests, as well as our differences, without ever imagining that there is any simple, or natural, or inevitable unity between us, either as lesbians or as gay men. That flexibility of outlook seems sadly unable to stretch to HIV/AIDS, and the principal victims will continue to be younger gay men, and other newcomers, entering a gay identity and a gay social scene which is woefully unprepared to meet their specific emotional and sexual needs. and their extreme potential vulnerability to HIV.

On top of the 'de gaying' of AIDS service organizations throughout Europe, we must now confront the effective 'de-AIDS-ing' of mainstream European lesbian and gay politics. This at any rate is the risk. Nobody in the field of HIV/AIDS work is claiming that lesbian and gay rights campaigns should cease. It does, however, seem necessary to recognize that the type and scale of anti-gay prejudice and discrimination which determine HIV/AIDS funding and policies throughout Europe constitute the most important political crisis in our lives. At this time we know that the only demonstrably effective means at our disposal to combat HIV is condom education for men having sex with men, targeted closely in relation to class, race, age, sexual tastes, and so on. In effect this means reconstructing gay identity in such a way that the very word 'gay' comes to signify safe sex, individually and socially. This is our major task in HIV/AIDS education, and it is political, whatever else it may also be.

As Edward King from London's Terrence Higgins Trust argued, the next conference should be renamed the First European Conference on Gay Men and HIV. That way the real issues cannot again be so easily neglected, and a genuine sense of European solidarity in the face of this ever growing disaster might emerge. Without such international solidarity it is difficult to know how we are going to be able to support the needs of gay men in Eastern Europe, the former Soviet Union, or even Portugal and Greece.

There is now increasing European co-operation between AIDS service organizations concerning treatment issues, and biomedical research, but there is no forum at which the crisis of HIV education can be addressed. As things are currently going, we run the risk of doing little more than campaigning for the equivalent to comfy chairs in the cattle-trucks conveying hundreds of thousands of European gay men to the latest killing fields on this unhappy continent.

7 Charles Barber: 1956–92

Memorial Service, 1992.

Charlie Barber came into my life one sunny afternoon in 1977. We had mutual friends here in London where he was then living. There are always Americans living in London, thank God! Vito Russo was also living over here at the time. I was working on a book about early twentieth-century British art, and Charlie and I found we had a lot of things in common – the way you do in your twenties, with that wonderful pleasure in finding that other people actually understand and even share one's most passionate enthusiasms. In our case these included the poetry of Frank O'Hara and Elizabeth Bishop, the films of Bette Davis and Katharine Hepburn; Joni Mitchell, Aretha, Shakespeare, Virginia Woolf. A thousand and one things. We were both young, and single, and over the years we saw one another through a lot of happy/sad love-affairs, and much else besides. We did the bars in London and New York. We wrote. We phoned. We stayed the closest of friends.

Charles got sick at my house in 1986. I was elected by Charlie to provide unconditional support, and I tried my best to supply it. These days I have a young friend here in London, a theatre director, madly stage-struck, very like Charlie at the same age. He's working on an unpublished Tennessee Williams play, the text of which Charlie had magically come up with. My English friend had read that Williams thought Roberta Flack the best singer of the seventies, but he'd never previously heard of her, let alone heard her voice. So I played him a few songs, including one that Charlie and I loved, in common with our entire pre-AIDS generation – the 'Ballad Of The Sad Young Men'. Many of you will doubtless remember how this was invariably played as a late-night smooch-song in bars and clubs in London, Paris, Amsterdam, New York, everywhere in the early and mid-seventies. Rickie Lee Jones does a heartbreaking version on her latest record, which Charlie played me last November. And we just clung together, and wept and wept for the sheer horror of all this. *And* trying not to hurt the catheter in his chest. How can we explain this? How do we carry on, with this endlessly accumulating immensity of loss, pressing us down and down and down?

Oddly, I never really perceived Charlie's great gifts as a poet until the very end of his life. Like many of us, Charlie had to do a lot of living in his twenties, to get beyond the pain of growing up in such a cruelly homophobic world. He had so many things still to do, amongst them a long-term project that he dearly cherished. This would eventually have been a full-length account of four generations of American gay writers, from the time of Henry James to the present – four generations variously scythed and sacrificed, by two wars, by Senator McCarthy, and now by this fucking virus. So now Charlie is himself a part of the very history that he didn't live to write, and which one increasingly fears will now never be written. I've been trying for days to write something for Charlie, sitting here at my typewriter, crying, getting up and striding around, sitting down, crying again. He was the bravest man I've ever known. Was it thirty times he was hospitalized, or was it forty? I know that many others have been bravely through this hell, but he was *my* friend. I suppose that if anything makes all this bearable it is the thought that we are all in this together, wherever we may be, and in whatever we do. For Charlie was, after all, an activist – in his poetry as much as outside City Hall with ACT UP. AIDS activism is above all a politics of friendship, of active caring solidarity. If you want to know what made Charlie Barber tick, read Vito's wonderful speech from the Albany demonstration. He would certainly have appreciated that I and many of his other friends couldn't be in New York today because we're busy doing our best at the Eighth annual International AIDS Conference, taking place in Amsterdam. But also watch a film of Merce Cunningham dancing, in his prime. And Pina Bausch. Listen to Callas singing Norma, to Billie Holiday singing 'I Wished On the Moon'. And also read Wallace Stevens' 'Evening Without Angels'. If we cannot acknowledge and creatively reimagine our losses, our anger will destroy us. Charlie knew this instinctively. It was one of the many things he taught me, which will stay with me, as we all live in one another's lives, always.

8   Read my lips: AIDS, art & activism*

for Mark Harrington

> AIDS is not what it appears to be at this moment in history. It is more than just a disease which ignorant people have turned into an excuse to exercise bigotry they already feel. It is more than a horror story to be exploited by the tabloids. AIDS is a test of who we are as a people. – Vito Russo, 1988[1]

Introduction: facts and figures

As I write, in the late wet London summer of 1992, it is reported that 6,279 people have so far been diagnosed with AIDS in the United Kingdom since the epidemic was first identified in 1981. Of these, 3,913 are already dead.[2] In the United States, however, which has between four and five times the population of Britain, there have been 230,179 cases of AIDS diagnosed, 41,598 of which were in New York.[3] Whilst in the UK it is estimated that there are between forty and one hundred thousand people infected by HIV, it is thought that at least one million people are infected in the US. Indeed, the American epidemic is fast approaching what epidemiologists refer to as a 'steady state'. That is, the annual rate of AIDS-related deaths is quickly catching up with the annual rate of new cases of HIV infection, currently running at around 50,000 per annum. Meanwhile the World Health Organisation (WHO) calculates that there are as many as ten million people infected worldwide, a projection that many experts think conservative.[4]

Such bald statistics suggest something of the sheer scale of the epidemic, and its changing international profile, but tell us little or nothing about the direct, lived experience of HIV and AIDS around the world. In order to understand how affected communities have identified and responded to local needs, it is necessary to look at more detailed figures. For example, in Scotland there have been 313 cases of AIDS, and a further 1,903 reported cases of HIV infection. Up to the end of 1985, 81 per cent of HIV cases in Scotland were amongst injecting drug users, 18 per cent amongst gay men, and less than 1 per cent resulting from heterosexual transmission. By the end of 1991 this picture had changed dramatically. Largely as the result of the

* First published in Nicola White (Ed.) Read My Lips: New York AIDS Polemic, *Glasgow: Tramway, 1992*

widespread introduction of state-funded needle-exchanges since 1986, the annual proportion of new cases of HIV amongst injecting drug users fell to 36 per cent of the total, whilst the proportion of new cases amongst gay men rose to 36 per cent. In the same period, heterosexual transmission also rose to account for 28 per cent of reported cases, with a significantly disproportionate impact amongst the female sexual partners of bisexual men and male injecting drug users.[5]

Such figures contrast greatly with the wider UK picture as a whole. Thus, looking at the annual HIV statistics for England, Wales and Northern Ireland, we find that by the end of 1991 there had been a cumulative total of 14,885 cases of HIV since the beginning of the epidemic. Up to the end of 1985, 93 per cent of non-Scottish UK cases of HIV were amongst gay men, and 5 per cent amongst injecting drug users, with 2 per cent resulting from heterosexual transmission, and less than 1 per cent resulting from mothers to infants (often referred to as 'horizontal' transmission). By the end of 1991, however, the annual rate of new cases of HIV amongst gay men had fallen to 65 per cent, with a further 25 per cent of new cases resulting from heterosexual transmission, 9 per cent from injecting drug use, and 1 per cent from mothers to infants. While the rate of new cases amongst gay men has gradually fallen, the rate amongst injecting drug users rose to 15 per cent in 1988, and has only subsequently fallen. Looking at the overall picture of AIDS in the UK, we see that 83 per cent of all cases have been amongst gay men, 9 per cent from heterosexual transmission, 6 per cent from injecting drug use, 1 per cent from mothers to infants, and 1 per cent undetermined.

In the second half of 1992 there are less than 3,000 people living with AIDS in the UK, out of a population approaching 60 million. Since more than two-thirds of British HIV and AIDS cases are in London, this means that few people in Britain have even knowingly met anyone living with HIV or AIDS. Whilst increasing numbers of gay men have friends who are infected, only a minority has had direct experience of AIDS. Two or three people on average die every day from AIDS in the UK. The contrast with the US situation, where on average 123 people die of AIDS every day, is a dramatic one. This is especially the case in New York, where it is thought that at least 50 per cent of all gay men are already infected.

The United States does not publish HIV statistics, but it seems likely that there are already several hundred thousand people infected in New York alone. Fifty-two per cent of New York male AIDS cases have been amongst gay men, and a further 4 per cent amongst men who have sex with men who are also injecting drug users, whilst 37 per cent of cases have been amongst heterosexual injecting drug users. Less than 1 per cent of male AIDS cases have resulted from heterosexual transmission with women at risk – a total of only 12.

Amongst women, 60 per cent of cases have resulted from injecting drug use, a total of 3,892. The much greater efficiency of male-to-female transmission than female to-male transmission is graphically demonstrated by the 1,625 cases of AIDS amongst women who were infected by men at risk – 25 per cent of the female total of cases. It is also vitally important to understand the dimensions of race and ethnicity in the US epidemic. For example, 44 per cent of AIDS cases amongst African-American men have been amongst men having sex with men, compared with 36 per cent from injecting drug use, and a further 7 per cent amongst injecting drug users who also have sex with men. No less than 47 per cent of AIDS cases amongst Hispanic men have been amongst men having sex with men, compared with 38 per cent from injecting drug use, and a further 8 per cent amongst injecting drug users who also have sex with men. By contrast, 80 per cent of AIDS cases amongst white men have been amongst men having sex with men, and only 7 per cent from injecting drug use, with a further 7 per cent amongst injecting drug users who also have sex with men.

Although women are evidently much more vulnerable to HIV from heterosexual or bisexual men than men are from women, we should also note that AIDS in America has had a vastly disproportionate impact amongst men overall. By the end of April 1992 there had been 22,607 cases of AIDS amongst American women, compared to 192,002 amongst men. However, the impact of AIDS amongst women has been disproportionately felt within the black and Hispanic communities. For example, whilst 2,409 white women have contracted AIDS from injecting drug use, there have been 6,569 cases amongst African-American women who inject drugs, and 2,304 amongst Hispanic women who have shared needles.

It cannot be sufficiently emphasized that these harrowing statistics reflect a shocking national failure to respond to the realities of the epidemic. There is only a handful of needle-exchanges in the United States, and many of these are illegal. Little has been done for gay men by way of effective, community-based health education. Those most at risk of HIV have been consistently denied proper HIV education, or means of protection. In the absence of socialized medicine, and given the general failings of the US health care system in a period of widespread economic recession, the results have been nothing less than catastrophic. In a word, New York is fast becoming a human charnel-house. The scale of suffering, trauma, and loss beggars belief. Furthermore, it is perfectly obvious that much if not most of this suffering could have been avoided if the needs of injecting drug users and men who have sex with men had been acknowledged, and properly responded to, as one might reasonably expect of a modern democracy, faced with the worst health crisis in its history. Tragically, the reverse has been the case. In order to understand the complex cultural responses to HIV and AIDS in New York, or elsewhere in the United States, it is necessary to consider what one might feel in such circumstances if one belonged to one or more of the social constituencies which have been scythed by the epidemic.

AIDS activism in New York

By the end of 1986, more than 10,000 people in New York had been diagnosed with AIDS, over half of whom were already dead. Many thousands more were beginning to experience pre-AIDS symptoms of HIV disease. Entire networks of friends were dying. Amongst injecting drug users' families, increasing numbers of children were being orphaned. But the great majority of deaths were amongst gay men. There were simply too many names to strike from one's address book, and it became a widespread custom simply to write the letters RIP across the names of the dead, until the pages began to resemble a mortician's diary. The gay community was in shock.

It was also painfully apparent that treatment and service provision were woefully inadequate, and unevenly available. Politicians prevented the establishment of needle-exchanges, whilst bigots of all political and religious persuasions managed to prevent effective health education for gay men. Those most at risk of HIV were being most systematically neglected. Above all, questions of access were increasingly occupying people's minds, from overflowing hospital emergency rooms (casualty departments), to beds in hospital wards, treatment drugs available in other countries yet unlicensed in the US, social security, housing benefits, life insurance, terminal care, and so on. Increasing numbers of people found themselves gradually pauperized by the costs of treatment and care, whilst many others had no means of accessing treatments at all because they lacked adequate health insurance, or indeed health insurance of any kind.

It was this immediate context of suffering, loss, trauma and rising anger on a massive, growing scale, that fuelled the emergent AIDS activist movement. The catalyst was a talk given by Larry Kramer, on 10 March 1987 at the New York Lesbian and Gay Center in which he 'articulated and helped focus the frustration and rage he shared with his audience over community inaction, governmental ineptitude and overt malice, unavailable treatments, underfunded research, and media distortions'.[6]

Two days later a group of some 300 people met to form an ad hoc community-based protest group, paying particular attention to the unavailability of treatment drugs, and the need for far more clinical trials which would be open to far more people living with HIV or AIDS. Thus the AIDS Coalition To Unleash Power (ACT UP) was founded, describing itself at every subsequent meeting as 'a diverse, non-partisan group of individuals united in anger and committed to direct action to end the AIDS crisis'.[7]

ACT UP had no formal membership, and its policies are decided by votes from the floor at weekly meetings. Various committees were eventually formed to handle different areas of research and policy, as well as to plan pro-active large-scale political actions, and reactive, on-the-spot 'zaps' of offending institutions, ranging from individual magazines to companies. Thus *Cosmopolitan* was 'zapped' for running an article (by a psychiatrist) claiming that women were not at any sexual risk from HIV, and many firms which had fired gay or HIV-positive workers found small armies of ACT UP demonstrators on and within their doorsteps. Hundreds of people attended the weekly meetings, and many tens of thousands more participated in 'zaps', actions, and so on.

Conceived as a coalition, ACT UP aimed to unite the various social constituencies affected worst by HIV and AIDS. It also set out to mobilize wider public opinion, and to influence those institutions most centrally involved in the production, testing, licensing and distribution of potential treatment drugs. Responding to criticism, ACT UP commentator James Brudner pointed out in 1990 that: 'The inflammatory charge that activists wish to redirect dollars to AIDS from other diseases is simply untrue. The bulk of activism is devoted to insuring the intelligent and humane use of funds already provided ... Because our obsolete drug research and approval system is incapable of selecting, testing or approving promising therapies with adequate speed, we will not move drugs from the test tube into people's bodies quickly enough to prevent millions of deaths. Under such conditions activists will not be silent, and our critics within the industry cannot expect the relief from scrutiny they disingenuously demand. As Dr Anthony Fauci of the National Institutes of Health has acknowledged, AIDS activism is a positive force that, despite opposition, has already helped prolong thousands of lives.'[8]

It is also significant that Brudner is himself a senior management analyst with the City of New York. ACT UP thrived because it was able to draw upon the professional expertise of an extremely broad cross-section of New York society, a cross-section as broad as gay identity, which is far more widely and openly accepted in urban America than in the UK. ACT UP's success has depended upon its ability to target specific institutions in relation to their role in the AIDS crisis. This precise targeting has involved specific, detailed demands, based upon formidable quantities of scientific research, and a thorough, pragmatic critique of the aims and methods of medical research. This has led to frequent confrontations with leading national state-funded agencies such as the Centers for Disease Control (CDC), the National Institutes of Health (NIH), individual hospitals, New York's City Hall and Health Department, as well as the commercial pharmaceutical industry.[9]

Since 1990, ACT UP has also organized a street-based outreach project, including needle-exchange facilities for injecting drug users, and currently serves around 1,000 users each week in the West Bronx, East Harlem, Manhattan's Lower East Side, and Bushwick and Williamsburg in Brooklyn. There are some 200,000 injecting drug users in New York City alone, 60 per cent of whom are thought to be HIV-positive. Yet New York remains one of eleven US states which criminalize the possession, use or sale of syringes without a medical prescription – thus literally driving drug users into sharing needles,[10] as was the care in Scotland until the late 1980s.

ACT UP emerged at a very particular moment in the history of the AIDS epidemic, and in a very particular place. Building on the complex legacy of the US lesbian and gay and Civil Rights movements, it constituted a refusal to accept the neglect and failings of the Reagan administration, and the wholesale prejudice surrounding most aspects of treatment, care and prevention work. Whilst organizations such as Gay Men's Health Crisis (GMHC) and the Association for Drug Abuse Prevention and Treatment (ADAPT) were doing excellent work, they were neither designed nor suited to the task of creating a grassroots movement, or of direct political confrontation. ACT UP has justifiably been described as the most significant American activist organization since the 1960s. Yet unlike the many protest movements ofthe sixties, ACT UP regarded the mass media not simply as a necessary evil, but rather as a primary target and site for political and cultural interventions. From ACT UP's perspective, the media were a vital part of the social and economic world, not merely a wicked conspiracy, to be shunned and despised.

Media politics and the AIDS activist style

In 1986 a small group of gay men who called themselves the SILENCE=DEATH Project designed and began to fly-post a poster that appeared all over downtown New York. As Douglas Crimp and Adam Rolston have explained: 'That simple graphic emblem – SILENCE=DEATH printed in white Gill Sanserif type underneath a pink triangle on a black ground – has come to signify AIDS activism to an entire community of people confronting the epidemic.'[11]

It was an uncanny image, amidst the burgeoning street furniture of New York. With no address or phone number, no summons to attend a rally or a meeting, it simply signified – in the most dramatic and striking way – that a catastrophe was taking place in the city, and furthermore, that nothing was being said in public, and not enough was being done. It is difficult to convey the nightmarish feeling of the time, which the SILENCE=DEATH logos symbolized so sparely and eloquently. It was hardly surprising that it was taken up by ACT UP as its founding emblem. For as Crimp and Rolston point out, its significance 'depends on foreknowledge of the use of the pink triangle as the marker of gay men in Nazi concentration camps, its appropriation by the gay movement to remember a suppressed history of our oppression … SILENCE=DEATH declares that silence about the oppression and annihilation of gay people, then and now, must be broken as a matter of our survival.'[12]

If prior to 1987, silence had indeed equalled death, then it was ACT UP which would articulate the demands upon which so many lives continue to depend. People flocked to ACT UP not *as if*, but *because* it was their only hope.

Unlike previous oppositional or counter-cultural movements, ACT UP from its origin contained significant numbers of accomplished, experienced media workers, from film, television, advertising, graphic design, and the print media. ACT UP was also informed by the Cultural Studies movement of the 1970s and 1980s, and its keen awareness of the role of context in defining the meaning of images. The powerful graphic simplicity of its very name established a 'house style' with which ACT UP remains closely associated. This style also provided a strong sense of personal and collective identity amongst American AIDS activists. From the very beginning, ACT UP was thus able to communicate its aims and objectives, and to announce its meetings and actions, with exemplary clarity and visual impact. Indeed, there is a close parallel between the precision of ACT UP's ability to target key institutions on the basis of reliable information and research, and its ability to produce clear, concise graphics, whether to summon people to demonstrations, or to translate activist messages directly into immediate television images.

Thus each major ACT UP action has had its own style, its own 'look', ranging from the sickly yellow-green, red-eyed AIDSGATE image of Ronald Reagan, to the celebratory READ MY LIPS images of World War Two sailors kissing, and of earlier twentieth-century lesbians kissing. Like many other designs, these were used on posters and T-shirts. Some designs also circulated as placards and stickers. Thus ACT UP fast became an instantly recognizable and always arresting part of the visual style of New York. It became fashionable, and this was one aspect of its political and cultural intelligence and perspicacity. It was in touch with its members, and its wider urban audience. Thus it was also (inevitably) criticized, especially from the Right, as well as the more conventional Left.[13]

The typical recycling of images and image-text relations from popular culture was closely related to wider cultural theory and practice. Thus critic and activist Douglas Crimp argues that the new AIDS activists graphics should be seen in the wider perspective of socially engaged art work in the United States, as well as in the context of a generation recently out of the art school: 'very familiar with the work of Hans Haacke, Barbara Kruger and Jenny Holzer. What interests me is that this whole discussion about appropriation, originality and so forth that took place in the art world in the late 1970's and early 1980's is something that these people are really putting to use. They take the style of Barbara Kruger's work for example, and use it for their own advantage. It doesn't matter that it was Barbara Kruger who invented this style. If it's useful, we will use it.'[14]

Much of the work most closely associated with ACT UP was produced by Gran Fury, a group of artists and designers who took their name from the blue Plymouth automobile driven by undercover New York police. For Gran Fury and many others, 'cultural activism' and 'direct action' are seen as 'expression of different communities' differing needs, and this process can range from poster projects to street demonstrations to free needle exchange to peer education.'[15]

They consistently attempt 'to situate our work in the "public realm" in an effort to include a diverse, non-homogeneous audience. Through appropriating dominant media's techniques, we hope to make the social and political subtexts of the AIDS epidemic visible and to incite the viewer to take the next step.'[16]

Gran Fury's work thus takes many forms. For example, in 1989 they participated in the American Foundation for AIDS Research (*Art On The Road AmFAR*'s project, which consisted of billboards, illuminated bus shelter signs, exterior and interior bus panels, store window displays, and so on, by more than thirty different artists and groups, including Barbara Kruger, Nayland Blake, Keith Haring, Cindy Sherman, Lorna Simpson, Brian Weil, Group Material, Robert Mapplethorpe, and so on. Much of this work was of uneven quality, and the use of commissioned work by famous artists served to highlight the paradox that artistic reputation does not guarantee anything in the way of AIDS awareness, or understanding of the complex role played by public imagery throughout the history of the epidemic.[17]

Gran Fury produced a pastiche Benetton advertisement for the side of buses, with three mixed race couples kissing – one heterosexual, one lesbian, and one gay – under the banner heading: KISSING DOESN'T KILL; GREED AND INDIFFERENCE DO. In March of the same year they also produced an edition of 6,000 copies of *The New York Crimes*, a near facsimile of *The New York Times*. As Avram Finkelstein explains, the project 'actually makes a historical reference to Dadaism the Fluxus movement in the 1960's. It's another type of political activism where we reproduced the authorative voice and mimicked the look of *The New York Times*, creating a double-page wrap-around that we put around 6000 copies of the *Times* in New York City. People took them to work with them assuming they were reading the *Times* and consequently read all of the news with our political spin from issues varying from AIDS behind bars, to AIDS and women, to the subtext between the pharmaceutical companies and how they are interrelated.'[18] The back page contains a quote from a spokesperson for the drugs company Hoffman-La Roche, saying 'One million (people with AIDS) isn't a market that's exciting. Sure it's growing, but it's not asthma.' As Finkelstein points out, this implies that 'it's not as profitable to research AIDS drugs as it is asthma drugs, because people with asthma don't usually die – they develop the product on its continuing basis. So its subtext is profit, the profitability of illness which is a reality but a horrifying one and which we think needs to be looked at.'[19] Amongst many projects, Gran Fury has also strategically invoked popular memory of the meaning of the American Civil War, with the rhetorical question: WHEN A GOVERNMENT TURNS ITS BACK ON ITS PEOPLE, IS IT CIVIL WAR? Such work exemplifies a particular AIDS activist aesthetic of the late 1980s, which sought to minimize redundancies in the relations of images to texts, and to force questions about social and government policies on AIDS.

Another Gran Fury member, Tom Kalin, has also worked in video and, more recently, in film. *They Are Lost To Vision Altogether* is a short montage of fair images of the epidemic, taken from US network television, alongside other images which problematize and 'trouble' the TV pictures, in a manner similar to the way in which the KISSING DOESN'T KILL project works on our preconceptions about the world of the supposedly 'united colours' of

Benetton. Indeed, video has played an important role for New York AIDS activism, not least because activist videos can be screened on cable television, which has a legal obligation to transmit a quota of 'community' programmes. Thus video collectives such as Testing The Limits function to generate a 'counter-practice' to the ways in which network television represents the epidemic.

Video makers such as Adam Hassuk and Bob Huff, John Greyson, and Catherine Saalfield have generated a substantial body of work, which is highly contingent, in so far as it deals with the immediate media issues of the moment. Thus Hassuk and Huff filmed the 1989 Republican Convention in Atlanta, Georgia, and *We Are Not Republicans* demonstrates the worst excesses of American prejudice about AIDS, as delegates congratulate HIV, and take its side, understood to be that of American 'family values'. The film ends as the videomakers are literally knocked to the ground inside the Convention Hall. Other video makers such as Gregg Bordowitz and Jean Carlmusto, based at GMHC, have been producing a cable TV series, *Living With AIDS*, since 1987. Like Saalfield, Hassuk and Huff, all were also closely involved in ACT UP.

The *Living With AIDS* series embodies the principle that minority communities can be empowered in relation to the field of representation, in which they are usually marginalized, on the assumption that the audience for network television is always white and heterosexual. *Living With AIDS* has been especially involved with issues concerning medicine, civil liberties, and health education, including sexually explicit Safer Sex music videos for use on the commercial gay scene. Many of these programmes, and other activist videos, are also broadcast nationwide on the Deep Dish satellite system. Yet video activism has also had its critics. As the late Ray Navarro explained: 'After the FDA demonstration (October 11, 1988), media makers were still being accused of being "MTV activists" – a pejorative term levelled against a form of activism that included a sense of style, a means of editing tapes that were going to be flashy and watchable by the general public. We tried to seize upon that term "MTV activism" and turn it around, calling it "More Than a Virus" activism. Yes, it's MTV activism. It's more than a virus that's killing us.'[20]

AIDS and the New York art world

New York is the hub of the American art market, and like London it is also a city to which large numbers of gay artists come to work, and to get away from small-town prejudice. The city's cultural life has thus been profoundly affected by AIDS, from the world of the performing arts, to film, fashion, and painting. The New York art world has responded to AIDS in many different ways, as has London's theatre community. One response has been that of straightforward fundraising. A recent donor of work commented: '"It's our way of feeling we're doing something for the health of the world,"

Mr Isaacson said, referring to the Donald Desky white Art Deco chest of drawers (estimate $5,000 to $7,000) that he and Mr McDonald have donated to the auction. A third partner in the gallery, Ralph Cutler, died of AIDS in 1989.'[21] Sotheby's alone had raised more than $4.5 million in auctions for GMHC by the Spring of 1991.[22]

However, Douglas Crimp dissents:

> There are several problems with art used as fundraising. First of all, it plays very much into what was initially the Reagan agenda, which is that volunteerism should deal with this crisis, that it wasn't somehow the government's responsibility. And to a certain extent every fundraising effort was saying this is our responsibility and not the government's. In addition, I think it accepts a certain notion of art as essentially alienated from society and from social problems, as something that can't in itself do anything directly. So there's a way in which the artist is simply asked to buy a relation to AIDS, or simply to take the position of the wealthy individual, to sort of buy someone else's work in relation to the crisis. One of the results of this is that there's a tendency to simply overlook, ignore, or not support works which attempt to take an activist position, to provide necessary information, or to incite social action.[23]

The position is not easy. As Tim Sweeney, Executive Director of GMHC pointed out in the catalogue to a Sotheby's benefit auction in 1991:

> GMHC has served 10,000 clients, more than one third of all cases diagnosed in New York City … Millions of people are reached through our extensive education programs … Through our Public Policy Department we aggressively fight on all levels of government for the release of new drug therapies, expanded access to healthcare, increased funding for cities hardest hit by the epidemic and civil liberties protection for people living with AIDS. As government funds for AIDS continue to decline, GMHC must rely on private individuals for more than 80% of our annual operating budget.[24]

By 1989 even ACT UP was organizing an annual art auction, though with a mere $5 admission charge, and chaired by Annie Leibovitz with David Hockney. The range of artists whose work was auctioned was much the same as at Sotheby's – Keith Haring, Francesco Clemente, Eric Fischl, as well as Gran Fury. The catalogue, however, was far less lavish than the Sotheby's equivalent, and contained a centrepage spread with a massive quote: 'I'd give all my money to AIDS activists and turn the Plaza Hotel into free Housing for People with AIDS. New York Lotto. All you need is a dollar and a dream.'[25]

More significant in some ways was another 1991 Benefit for AIDS, The Crown Auction, organized by Barney's, the famous New York department store.

Thirty-two artists, from Ross Bleckner to Paloma Picasso, Cindy Sherman and The Starn Twins, were invited to create crowns for display in Barney's windows, and subsequent auction at the second New York Love Ball. Thus artist David Carrino created a 'Crown And Cape For The Young Prince', together with a text: 'The function of a crowning is to honour, but more importantly to pay attention to an individual and his or her moment in history. I will participate in any ceremony or event that brings public attention and support to people with AIDS.'[26]

Andres Serrano constructed a 'Silver Crown', made from barbed wire with silver paint, commenting: 'It is important for every American to contribute whatever is in their power to help end the AIDS crisis. As an artist, I contribute my work.'[27]

The Crown Auction thus managed to raise money *and* issues, whilst also making the epidemic visible at an everyday, street level, publicly honouring people with AIDS, and the values of gay community celebrated at the spectacular annual Love Ball, and throughout gay dance and 'vogueing' culture.

Yet the most frequent critical response to the relationship between AIDS and art has concerned the supposed struggle for 'Art's Eternal Expression in the Age of AIDS', as the *New York Times* has described it.[28] Even the *Times*, however, has noted that in film and theatre 'a broader, more complicated gay experience is being depicted these days.'[29]

Professor of European Art History at New York University, Robert Rosenblum represents a more conservative strand of American criticism, arguing that there is little art can do about the AIDS crisis:

> There's been all kinds of political protest art throughout history, and not much of it is enduring … it would not seem that many very important artists have taken on the issue of AIDS directly … But as far as I'm concerned – and this is obviously a very personal judgement – the only art that I thought could match the harrowing quality of the epidemic and the sense of apocalypse that we have now is not the work here in New York, but in London: that of Gilbert and George … For me that was the only art directly in response to AIDS that was sufficiently shattering to meet the challenge.[30]

Writing in *Art in America*, Professor Rosenblum pursued this same theme in more detail, depicting Gilbert and George as:

> a modern Dante and Virgil travelling through the heavens and hells of contemporary London … Surrounded, like the rest of us in the art world, by the individual human facts of AIDS and the grim generalizations the

disease has prompted, Gilbert and George seem to have been destined to confront the tragedy in their art, and they have finally done so ... What they have done is to push their art to the brink of apocalypse. Everywhere in these new works is the red of blood and fire colliding with the green of nature ... It is a grim update to the kind of melancholic Symbolist allegory explored by artists like Hodler in the 1890's ... Such lucid, emblematic structures have long been used by Gilbert and George in their pictures of allegorical intention ... Like those artists who painted in Tuscany after the Black Death of 1348, Gilbert and George have tried to bridge the gulf between art and a devastating plague by making altarpieces, at once sacred and secular, that would exorcise the demons around us.[31]

The Gilbert and George exhibition FOR AIDS raised more than one million dollars for the UK charity CRUSAID, but the work itself hardly addresses any concrete issues to do with HIV or AIDS. There are several images of blood, and the familiar Gilbert and George scenarios in which they themselves appear, variously surrounded by leaves, flowers, teenage boys, and so on. This is typical of a pair of artists who have never been embarrassed to express their great admiration for Mrs Thatcher as Prime Minister, and their general lack of enthusiasm for other social issues: 'Unemployment is not an artist's problem. We're unemployed – we get our dole from the galleries. I mean, unemployed people can visit our exhibition.'[32]

For Rosenblum, and many others, Gilbert and George articulate a supposedly *universal* dimension of the epidemic. Yet it cannot be sufficiently emphasized that HIV, unlike the Black Death, or other 'plagues', is not a contagious condition. Rather than confront the specific, and often political and ideological dimensions of the epidemic, Rosenblum praises images that are 'shattering', apocalyptic, and so on. This is consistent with the message of a 1987 painting by Gilbert and George's close friend, the artist David Robilliard, whose death from AIDS in 1988 was one of the motives behind the FOR AIDS exhibition. '*Safe Sex*' contains six roughly painted heads, across which is superimposed a text which reads:

'I had Safe Sex Last Night'
'Really'
'Yes I Went Home Alone'

From such a perspective there is no such thing as Safer Sex, and no point in campaigning for gay men's (or anybody else's) AIDS education, or treatment drugs, and so on. Taken as an allegory, AIDS is almost required to be tragic, 'harrowing', or 'melancholic', but never a matter for anger, research, or political and cultural activism.

A similar dilemma afflicts a 1991 fundraising book, *Hockney's Alphabet*, edited by Stephen Spender, with drawings by David Hockney, and written contributions from numerous literary luminaries, including Martin Amis, Margaret Drabble, Doris Lessing, Susan Sontag, and so on. Spender explains in his Preface that the book was produced in order to raise money for the AIDS Crisis Trust, a London-based charity. He also notes complacently that only two of the twenty-six writers took AIDS as a subject, and one of those, John Updike, does so only to talk vaguely and insultingly about 'Nature's curse.'[33] Instead, we are treated to Doris Lessing's ruminations of the subject of pumpkins, Joyce Carol Oates on D for Death, and so on. Only Arthur Miller deals directly with the issue of AIDS. *Hockney's Alphabet* is fairly typical, I suspect, of the mainstream cultural response to AIDS in countries such as Britain, which have comparatively small epidemics, at least by European let alone North American standards of comparison. The idea that fundraising might be combined with some kind of practical relation to the language and imagery of the epidemic simply seems not to occur to people. Hence the timeliness of much of the work in this exhibition.

Photography, painting and AIDS

Much has already been written about the role of photography in the AIDS epidemic.'[34] It has been widely objected that photographers have tended to concentrate on the visible signs of extreme illness and mortality, at the expense of all other social aspects, including the everyday lives of people with HIV and AIDS who are 'vibrant, angry, loving, sexy, beautiful, acting up and fighting back' as one ACT UP flyer put it, in protest against the exhibition of Nicholas Nixon's photographs at the Museum of Modern Art (MOMA) in 1988. Moreover, there is a large section of lesbian and gay culture which campaigns for so-called 'positive images' of lesbians and gay men, in order to counter 'negative stereotypes'.

   This approach to imagery tends to be rooted in a rather crude theory of representation, which regards pictures out of context as inherently either true or false, helpful or harmful. This has resulted in a large number of doubtless heartwarming documentary photographic projects, but it is doubtful whether these ultimately tell us anything more about the complexities of the epidemic than the gloomier work of mainstream art photographers such as Nicholas Nixon. As Douglas Crimp has judiciously observed, single photographic images 'can't deal very well with the complexity of AIDS … One can feel pity or one can feel revulsion. But there's no way that these kinds of photographs (Nixon *et al.*) can tell us any of the things that we need to know about why these people are in the predicament they are.'[35] This is precisely why so many artists have turned to video, or else to more complex image-text work using photography as one important element. Others have simply preferred painting all along. Indeed, it may be fairly objected that we should not expect photography to be able to do what Crimp and many others seem to expect of it.

Hence the significance of the work of a number of New York based artists who address the AIDS crisis with a keen awareness of the role that representation has played in the epidemic, in establishing many misconceptions, from questions of individual risk perception, to treatment issues and health promotion. From a British perspective it is also important to understand how many American artists have responded in their work, and elsewhere, to a newly censorious cultural climate, and repeated attacks by Christian fundamentalists, and others, on the National Endowment for the Arts (NEA), which provides grants of state funds to experimental artists.[36] The question of freedom of speech, and of representation in general, have much concerned artists at the same time as the AIDS crisis has worsened. The two issues are of course further connected, since the censorship of Safer Sex materials for gay men preceded the assault on the work of Robert Mapplethorpe, Andres Serrano, Karen Finlay, Holly Hughes, Time Miller, and many others.

Conclusion: AIDS activism, cultural activism

Much of the work in this exhibition derives from a sense of public space that is very different to British perceptions. Posters and stickers coat almost every available surface, from telephone boxes to lamp-posts, in some parts of Manhattan. At the same time, the immediate urgency of HIV and AIDS is far more apparent in New York than anywhere in Europe, save perhaps in parts of Paris. American AIDS activism, and the cultural activism which is associated with it, were born of great pain and anger. They were also born of hope. In 1992 it is no longer the case that many people in New York feel even remotely optimistic about the future of the epidemic.

AIDS activism in Europe has lacked both the political traditions and the motivating crises surrounding questions of access which so forcefully shaped the US origins of ACT UP. European AIDS activism has thus tended largely to respond to the epidemic through preexisting models of political struggles, developed around other issues. Thus ACT UPs in Europe have rarely been involved in the kind of routine research around treatment issues that have been so central to ACT UP in New York and elsewhere in the United States. Certainly there has been very little AIDS activism of any significance in Europe, save in France, where grotesque levels of government neglect have led directly to a catastrophe of New York proportions amongst French 'homosexuals' and injecting drug users. Nor has the European response to AIDS involved anything like the attention to questions of medical research, and clinical trials, largely because most people with HIV are not encouraged to identify their long-term interest closely to those of people with AIDS. A great deal of attention has been paid to issues of service provision, and discrimination, but comparatively little to the leading institutions which direct and manage social and other policies around HIV and AIDS.

In New York the heroic moment of ACT UP is over. Doubtless many brave and necessary zaps and actions will continue to take place, but ACT UP no longer possesses its original sense of purpose. Almost inevitably, AIDS activism attracted many oppositional elements in American society who to a greater or lesser extent have hi-jacked the AIDS activist movement to other ends and purposes. The original aim of being 'non-partisan' has long since been abandoned. Indeed, as early as the spring of 1988, some activists were asking whether ACT UP had been created to oppose the Reagan administration's foreign policies in Central America.'[41] In any case coalitions are, by definition, volatile and unstable. In New York, ACT UP has been increasingly dominated by those who argue that the priority of the activist movement should be the establishment of socialized medicine for all. This is doubtless an honourable goal, which is earnestly to be desired. But it hardly addresses the real, immediate, short-term interests of people living with HIV and AIDS, who will almost certainly die unless better treatment drugs are found, fast.[42]

In New York, many are simply exhausted. Many of ACT UP's founders are themselves dead. Many, many more are sick, or dying. Large numbers of people are becoming increasingly involved with their own emotional reactions, and the cost of the daily trauma involved throughout the gay, and Hispanic and black communities. Yet the cultural activism of the late 1980s and early 1990s in New York stands as a unique moment in the history of politically informed cultural reactions to catastrophe. Nothing remotely of such quality has been seen since the Paris of 1968, and the comparison does not flatter the French. The most sophisticated treatment activists in the world continue to work in New York, though now mostly outside ACT UP, in a new organization called the Treatment Action Group (TAG). TAG also makes videos! This is what makes AIDS cultural activism so unique. It employs the most sophisticated aspects of media culture to communicate popular messages based upon the most sophisticated scientific thought and research. It has rallied an entire, vast modern city to a common cause. It has helped people make sense of the epidemic. It has inspired people. It has brought tens of thousands out onto the streets of New York. It has brought people together. It has been sexy *and* smart. The large question, however, remains, concerning how AIDS activism and cultural activism will be able to deal with the personal dimensions of the epidemic, as the situation worsens in the coming years. New York's recent experience proves that even the commercial gallery world, and that of the museums, can respond to social crisis. This is no threat to the significance of more purely aesthetic art practices than are represented here. The question of how we respond adequately or sufficiently to the AIDS crisis, wherever we live, depends upon our ability to analyse local circumstances, and plan forwards in time. Right now in the United Kingdom a new form of AIDS activism, is indeed emerging, at grass-roots level, in response to the scandalous neglect of gay men's health education. It is surely significant that the new organization Gay Men Fighting AIDS (GMFA) should already be taking their lead from Gran Fury in the style of their publications.[44] GMFA represents a form of *prevention activism* that we are likely to

set in many parts of the world, where the needs of those at *greatest* risk of
HIV infection are least met. Walking round this exhibition you may legitimately feel that you are looking at the record of a most remarkable moment
in modern history, when gay men, together with many from other marginalized communities, organized a political and cultural response to a terrible
health crisis which was being almost wholly mismanaged at every level,
from the White House to the local pharmacy. ACT UP has achieved the
extraordinary goal of democratizing the process surrounding treatment drug
research in the US. It has helped many thousands gain access to clinical
trials for which they would not previously have been eligible. It has changed
large sections of American public opinion about the epidemic. The role
played by the kinds of imagery you see in this exhibition cannot of course be
quantified. But nor can it be neglected. This is art which has made things
happen. It is art that has helped save lives.

Notes

1 Vito Russo, Speech at Albany AIDS Rally, 8 May 1988, reprinted in this
   catalogue.
2 Public Health Laboratory Service, Monthly AIDS Figures. 92/9, 24 August 1992.
3 HIV/AIDS Surveillance, First Quarter Edition. US Department of Health and
   Human Services, April 1992.
4 Erik Eckholm. 'AIDS, fataily steady in the US, accelerates worldwide'. *New York
   Times*, Sunday 28 June 1992.
5 AIDS/HIV Quarterly Surveillance Tables, Public Health Laboratory Service
   AIDS Centre, and the Communicable Diseases (Scotland) Unit, Data to end of
   December 1991, No. 14: March 1992.
6 Mark Bronnenberg, 'ACT UP', in *A His and Her Story of Queer Activism* by The
   Lesbian and Gay Activist History Project, with ACT UP, June 1989, p. 70.
7 *ibid.*
8 James Brudner, 'AIDS activism is good for research'. *New York Times*, Section 3,
   Sunday 30 September 1990.
9 Many of these actions are chronicled in *AIDS Demo Graphics*, by Douglas Crimp
   with Adam Rolston (Seattle: Bay Press 1990).
10 Needle Exchange: The Creation of a Community-Based Program in New York
   City, presentation at 8th International AIDS Conference. Amsterdam, July 1992.
11 Douglas Crimp with Adam Rolston, Needle Exchange page 14.
12 *Ibid.*
13 For a narrow, Leftist critique of ACT UP see Daniel Harris, 'AIDS and theory'.
   Lingua Franca: The Review of Academic Life. June 1991, and subsequent corre-
   spondence. For a more subtle Rightist critique, see Andrew Sullivan, 'Gay
   life, gay death', *New Republic*, 17 December 1990. For the wider context see
   Simon Watney. 'The possibilities of permutation: pleasure, proliferation, and the
   politics of gay identity in the age of AIDS', in James Miller (ed.), *Fluid
   Exchanges: Artists and Critics in the AIDS Crisis*, (Toronto: University of Toronto
   Press. 1992).
14 Douglas Crimp, Interview, in Simon Watney. 'ART/AIDS/NYC'. *Art and Text*
   No. 38, Sydney, January 1991, pp. 95–6.
15 Gran Fury Press Kit Statement, 1990.
16 *Ibid.*

17 For a thorough critique of the Art On The Road project, see Kristen Engberg, 'Art, AIDS, and the New Altruism', *New Art Examiner*, Chicago, May 1991.

18 Gran Fury, interview, in Simon Watney, 'ART/AIDS/NYC'.

19 *Ibid.* p. 64.

20 Ellen Spiro and Ray Navarro, interview, in Simon Watney, 'ART/AIDS/NYC', p. 68.

21 Ron Alexander, 'In honoring a friend an auction of art items also benefits AIDS', *New York Times*, Sunday 3 March 1991, p. 54.

22 *Ibid.*

23 Douglas Crimp, Gran Fury Press Kit p. 94.

24 Tim Sweeney, 'A letter from the Executive Director of GMHC', Sotheby's Arts Auction Catalogue. New York, 5 March 1991.

25 AUCTION FOR ACT UP, Programme, Sunday 3 December 1989.

26 The Crown Auction: A Benefit for AIDS, Wednesday June 5, 1991, Barney's New York, Catalogue, no. 5.

27 *Ibid.* no. 26.

28 Michael Cunningham, 'After AIDS, gay art aims for a new reality', *New York Times*, Sunday 26 April 1992. Section 2, p. 16.

29 *Ibid.* p. 17.

30 Robert Rosenblum, interview, in Simon Watney, 'ART/AIDS/NYC', p. 72.

31 Robert Rosenblum, 'Gilbert and George: The AIDS Pictures', *Art in America*, November 1989, pp. 153–4.

32 Dalya Alberge, 'Unhappy with double vision', *Independent*, Monday 17 April 1989, p. 16.

33 Stephen Spender (Ed.) *Hockney's Alphabet* (London: Faber and Faber, 1991).

34 For example, Simon Watney, 'Photography and AIDS', in Carot Squiers (Ed.) *The Critical Image: Essays On Contemporary Photography* (Seattle: Bay Press, 1990) and Jan Zita Grover, 'Visible lesions: Images of the PWA in America', in James Miller (Ed.) *Fluid Exchanges: Artists and Critics in the AIDS Crisis* (Toronto: University of Toronto Press, 1992); Robert Atkins, 'Photographing AIDS: difficult subject', *Village Voice*, 28 June 1988; and Ann Cvetcovich, 'Video AIDS and activism', *Afterimage*, Vol. 19, No. 2, September 1991.

35 Douglas Crimp, Gran Fury Press Kit, p. 95.

36 See Carole S. Vance, 'The pleasure of looking; The Attorney General's Commission on Pornography versus visual images', in Carole Squiers (ed.), *The Critical Image*; and Carole S. Vance. 'The war on culture', *Art in America*, September 1989.

37 See Jon Nalley, 'Aphasia by any other name', *OutWeek*, 25 February 1990; and Simon Watney, 'Wet holes: The queer art of Donald Moffett', Simon Watson Gallery, New York, January 1991.

41 For example, Hal Bramson, 'A plea for common sense', broadside distributed at ACT UP meeting, New York, Spring 1988.

42 See Peter Staley, 'ACT UP: Past, present and future', 4th National AIDS Update Conference, San Francisco, Monday 20 May 1991; and Robin Hardy, 'Die harder' AIDS activism is abandoning gay men', *Village Voice*, 2 July 1991.

43 See Simon Watney, 'Gay Brits take back the fight', *QW*. No. 43, New York, 30 August 1992.

9　How to have sax in an epidemic*

For more than a decade gay men have responded to the presence of HIV and AIDS in our personal lives in a wide variety of ways. At one end of the scale, some, sadly, have been terrified into celibacy or loveless monogamy; at the other, some evidently find safer sex difficult to sustain. Yet the great majority of gay men have found ways to feel confident about sex.

Community-based HIV education has insisted that safer sex is an issue for all gay men, regardless of our HIV-antibody status, and a remarkable collective response has emerged that is intimately informed by our awareness of the epidemic In our midst. HIV hardly interrupts our common need for love and sexual expression, and most of us have found ways to move through sexual relationships without being overwhelmed by anxieties on behalf of ourselves or our partners.

Disco music has been at the heart of gay youth culture for two decades, so it is hardly surprising that pop music has responded to the epidemic far more pragmatically and directly than any other cultural medium. Indeed, nothing is more indicative of our determination to live through this appalling tragedy than the intensity of contemporary gay dance and 'rave' culture, which articulates the complexity of our lives and feelings with passionate precision. No band has responded to this challenge with more integrity and musical imagination than the Pet Shop Boys, who more than anybody else have helped 'get us through' these bad times. They have done so, moreover, with grace, wit, and intelligence; and their latest album, *Very*, is their finest achievement to date.

Like the Smiths, Marc Almond, and Jimmy Somerville, the Pet Shop Boys emerged out of nowhere, in 1985, with an all-time-classic pop standard, 'West End Girls'. They are unlike other bands, however, In that their identity is extremely fluid: while they have released many singles and albums as the Pet Shop Boys, they have also produced records with other performers who have become part of their musical project by simple contingency. Liza Minnelli's 1989 album *Results*, for example, is in an important sense a Pet Shop Boys record, as is Electronic's magnificent 1992 *Disappointed*, or the music 'by' Cicero and Boy George for Neil Jordan's film *The Crying Game*.

* First published in Artforum, New York, 1993.

To understand this music it is necessary to understand (and respect, and probably love) the sensation of being one among hundreds of others on a packed dance-floor, dancing because dancing is what we enjoy most, and because dance music (like sex) binds us intimately.

Very exhibits in the highest degree the Pet Shop Boys' ability to produce classic pop songs that are also great dance music, while combining humour, pathos, and lyrical intensity. It opens with a song about a man who can't accept his homosexuality, though his attempts to pass as straight are transparent to his girlfriend because he dances to disco rather than rock. There follow two wonderful gay love-songs, about the excitement of falling in love for the first time, and the sense of liberation this can bring after years of adolescent guilt and loneliness. In this sense the album traces the whole narrative of coming out during the epidemic – falling in love, relationships going wrong, infidelity, insecurity, and so on. Yet the Pet Shop Boys' approach is not in the least didactic. On the contrary, by leaving the genders of the people who populate their songs open, they enlarge the number of people who can meaningfully identify with them.

Very also contains at least three great pop standards. 'Dreaming Of The Queen' Is an extraordinary and moving musical response to the epidemic: dreaming a tea party attended by the Queen and Lady Diana, as well as by Pet Shop Boys singer Neil Tennant and an unnamed other (taken as his boyfriend), the song offers us the astonishing scenario of the Queen asking why love doesn't often seem to last these days. To which Diana replies, in a chorus as harrowing and as instantly memorable as that of the Righteous Brothers' 'You've Lost That Lovin' Feelin'', "There are no more lovers left alive, no one has survived ... So that's why love has died.' The voice is simultaneously Tennant and Lady Di, in such a way that the concluding refrain of this repeated chorus – 'Yes it's true, it's happened to me and you' – speaks far more about the effects of the epidemic in gay men's lives than about a famously unhappy royal marriage. The song records the toll of loss in our lives with unnerving surreal accuracy.

'To Speak is a Sin' is about personal insecurity on the commercial gay scene, with all its pressures to look good, be cool, find love. One gay critic in the UK has written, 'The real sadness is that there's anyone who still thinks gay bars are like this', he seems to me to miss the point in a fairly spectacular way. To complain that the Pets don't make records full of 'positive images' of gay life is rather like complaining that Morrissey is depressing, or that you can't dance to Chet Baker. Some nights one feels good in the bars; some nights one doesn't. Indeed, one of the most immediate (and unpredictable) aspects of life in the epidemic is precisely such fluctuations of self-confidence, such intense varieties of projection onto other people.

Finally the hit single 'Go West' strikes me as one of the truly great pop records of my lifetime, a remake, with additional material, of an old Village People song from the now-all-but-unimaginable disco era before AIDS. Like previous Pets remakes, it was a choice of genius. For what the widespread interest in the 1970s on the contemporary international gay scene is surely all about is a fantasy about the present as it might have been. As such, the song embodies the sense of gay culture, and above all of the club scene, as an almost utopian domain of consensual choice and pleasure – things that are of course anathema to the grim moralists of the 1990s.

More than any other song I know, 'Go West' speaks profoundly of both our losses and our absolute determination to survive them, to come through all this, to go forward rather than backward, and to do so by insisting on the unbroken vitality of our culture. That is what 'Go West' 'means'. Far from being 'a melancholy lament for a paradise lost', as one critic has written, it is a defiant assertion of the values and tenacity of gay life in the 1990s.[1] If it makes one want to cry, this is at least as much because of its wildly romantic, anathemic assertion of gay pride and gay love as of its simultaneous reminder of our losses. On one song on *Very*, Tennant sings of himself as having 'been a teenager since before you were born', and this is his greatest gift. The Pet Shop Boys have long since demonstrated that they possess the most sophisticated, sensual, and thoughtful pop sensibility of our times. 'Go West' is the 'I Will Survive' of our times, of which *Very* is the finest musical expression to date.

Note

1 Sheryl Garratt, 'Martians in Moscow', *The Face* no. 60, London, September 1993, p. 103.

10 Hard won credibility*

The UK HIV/AIDS epidemic is somewhat unusual by international standards. First, our overall epidemic is disproportionately small, compared to similar countries such as France or Germany. Second, it is overwhelmingly concentrated amongst gay and bisexual men. Third, with the exception of the widespread implementation of needle-exchange facilities since the late 1980s, prevention work has consistently prioritized the needs of those at least risk of HIV infection to the virtual exclusion of those at greatest risk.

Fourth, we now have to deal with the whims of a stupid, arrogant, and viscerally homophobic Secretary of State for Health, who has cheerfully cut funds to the most needy and deserving community-based organizations at the front-lines of the epidemic. Fifth, we have a uniquely dreadful national mass media, which has consistently trivialized and sensationalized the epidemic.

In such circumstances, the gay press continues to play an absolutely vital, central role in communicating basic information and ideas to a large and extremely diverse social constituency. When our only supposedly 'liberal' national newspaper. The *Guardian*, can continue to run stories with headlines such as 'HIV "vampires" wreak revenge' as recently as July 15th this year, it is fairly obvious that we cannot trust our national mass media on any aspect of its HIV/AIDS coverage.

Hence the indispensable role of the gay press, since the gay press is the only institution which is able to reach significant numbers of gay men and lesbians with reliable, up to date information and debate. Furthermore, the gay press is the only area of the national media which respects the integrity and the dignity of our lives and feelings.

But what does 'information and debate' really mean? How is the UK gay press currently responding to the epidemic? Writing in *Capital Gay* on August 20th, the distinguished editor and gay journalist Graham McKerrow complained of censorship throughout the gay press, especially in relation to the ideas of those who question any meaningful association between HIV and AIDS.

It is undoubtedly true that over the years there has been a much greater emphasis on safer sex and HIV education, than on medical issues. This

* First published in Gay Times, *October 1993.*

is closely related to the fact that all along, we have had a much larger epidemic of HIV than of AIDS, with the result that treatment issues are only now becoming more widely discussed as increasing numbers of people are unfortunately becoming symptomatically unwell.

At the best of times most people tend to leave medical issues to doctors and other professional health care providers, and those of us who have been closely involved in medical issues for many years have until very recently had little or no active support in the gay press, or elsewhere.

Hence it has been necessary to set up organizations such as the National AIDS Manual, and regular publications such as AIDS Treatment Update, as independent, community-based companies and charitable trusts. I have argued in this column since early 1988 that health education and medical issues should always be given equal priority, both within AIDS service organizations, such as the Terrence Higgins Trust, and in the gay press, but until recently this has been to little avail.

We should feel proud of things like the National AIDS Manual, and Gay Men Fighting AIDS, for they are amongst the most remarkable achievements in the whole history of the modern gay movement.

How should the gay press be tackling the epidemic? Is it in fact letting its readers down?

To answer such questions it is necessary to recognize the major, arterial role the gay press plays in providing the kinds of information which spin out into gossip, hearsay, anecdotes and so on. The gay press is thus our nearest equivalent as it were to the old village 'parish pump', where local information and gossip was traditionally exchanged.

In an epidemic, however, it is clear that one major function for the gay press is precisely to challenge misinformation, and to put reliable ideas into the widest possible circulation. This is not as easy as it might at first sight appear. For example, AIDS is the very last thing some people want to read about in the weekly newspapers, distributed mainly through the commercial bar and club scene. This is not so much evidence of irresponsibility, but simply an acknowledgement of the great difficulty faced by writers and editors trying to raise levels of HIV/AIDS awareness at a time when direct lived experience of the epidemic is highly uneven, and patchy.

There is moreover a strange paradox in the fact that whilst direct experience of HIV or AIDS may stimulate an intense involvement in medical questions about potential treatment drugs, the experience of death and mourning may sometimes work to undermine such involvement.

Another important factor governing attitudes to medical research has been the widespread tendency to exaggerate the therapeutic potential of new drugs undergoing clinical trials, a tendency which may be as harmful as exaggerating their potential dangers. Hence my criticisms at the time of the way in which *Capital Gay* for example prematurely trumpeted AZT as a so-called 'early intervention' drug in 1989. Such claims can have two sets of harmful consequences. First, they may raise hopes in an unscientific and unethical manner, leading to otherwise avoidable subsequent disappointments. Second, they may undermine safer sex by giving the impression that effective anti-retroviral drugs are indeed just around the corner.

In the absence of other, reliable sources of information for lesbians and gay men, the gay press has particular duties. First, it is absolutely vital that we can read accounts of how we are variously facing and responding to the tragic human costs of the epidemic, where personal heroism is mostly private and unrecorded. We need the highest levels of testimonial writing for the plain ethical reason that nobody else is likely to record our lives and our achievements.

Second, we need regular information concerning the latest developments and research in the areas of both treatment and prevention, in order that these can be discussed widely, and pass into general gay social consciousness. Third, we need regular columns like this one, which are always there across the many different types of publications that constitute the gay press as a whole.

Few people probably read this, or any other column, on an absolutely regular monthly or weekly basis. That's not on the whole how any papers or magazines are consumed. Whilst I don't for one moment expect all my readers to agree with everything I say, I do think it vitally important that certain voices are understood to be basically trustworthy, and based over the years on absolutely reliable research. This question of trustworthiness strikes me as being completely central.

Furthermore, whilst the mainstream mass media moves continually through long cyclical periods of HIV/AIDS hysteria, followed by long periods of neglect, it is important that the gay press makes up for the 'peak and trough' effect of the national dailies which we all also read, by never letting the epidemic get out of focus.

This does not necessarily mean bashing people over the head with it all the time. This is why I very much admire the approach taken by *BOYZ* since its inception, where there are occasional features, but most of all a constant, 'low-level' awareness of the epidemic at every level. *BOYZ* may be criticized for sustaining a supposedly Bimbo-like identity for young gay men focusing on boyfriends, sex, holidays, fashion and so on. But such subjects shouldn't be dismissed as mere escapism. On the contrary, it is imperative that we retain our capacity for fun and pleasure. which are so central to gay identity and confidence. Indeed, this process of constantly reinforcing gay pride is one of the leading functions of the gay press in relation to the epidemic. For if we can't exercise choices about what we do want, we are less likely to be able to exercise choices about what we don't want, including HIV.

With new editors in charge at *Gay Times*, the *Pink Paper* and *Capital Gay*, it is an opportune moment to be thinking very seriously about such issues. Inevitably there will be commercial and other rivalries between different publications, but these should in no way be permitted to affect a deeper commitment to dealing properly with the epidemic, all the time. This will involve a certain amount of repetition, as new readers emerge, and old readers catchup on issues they'd not previously been particularly involved with.

We are at least fortunate in the UK to have a flourishing gay press, even if distribution is still a big headache. For example, cities as large as Paris and New York have nothing to compare with the resources provided by the British gay press.

In this respect it is not unreasonable to hope that the overall approach of the gay press to HIV/AIDS issues is consistent, and that there are not major policy conflicts either within or between different publications. Whilst conspiracy theories may flourish, the gay press should surely be able to distinguish between trustworthy experts, and mere cranks, of whom not a few have rushed into this field over the years.

If individual publications wish to support people like Professor Peter Duesberg and his various cronies, at an editorial level, then it is important that everyone understands the implications of such decisions. For example. Duesberg has consistently questioned the need for safer sex, since he thinks AIDS is 'caused' by excessive recreational drug use, and/or vast amounts of sex. He also denies that there is any kind of AIDS epidemic in Africa, and has even offered to inject himself with HIV which he denies has any relation to AIDS.

Those of us who have opposed Duesberg and his ilk over the years have done so on the basis of easily available statistics which demonstrate the exact statistical correlations between HIV and AIDS, both for individuals and communities.

This is not to take an entirely fatalistic line. On the contrary, as Keith Alcorn recently pointed out in *Capital Gay*, (September 3rd) 12 per cent of a group of 562 men in San Francisco infected by HIV at least ten years ago still have T-cell counts above 500, whilst 31 per cent of the group had not developed AIDS ten years after infection.

The point here is simple. Over the painful course of a decade we have worked incredibly hard to set up organizations providing reliable, trustworthy information. This level of gay community-based expertise should not be compared to the rantings of any small gang that happens to come along screaming that there is really no such thing as an AIDS epidemic, or that our doctors are all homophobic psychopaths trying to deliberately kill us.

It is simply absurd to expect some kind of 'balance' between reliable, scientifically verifiable information, and wild assertions that HIV has nothing to do with AIDS.

Nobody pretends that we understand everything about the pathogenesis of HIV (the precise mechanisms whereby it leads to AIDS), which is precisely why the accusations of supposed censorship are so insufferable. In point of fact. Duesberg's position has been featured many times over the years in the gay press, and if this attention has mainly been critical it is precisely because Duesberg's work is so deeply dangerous, not least in the way he manages to pass himself off to the gullible as if he were some kind of beleaguered genius, tyrannized by a sinister conspiracy of medical orthodoxy.

On the contrary, he is just a crank, but a crank with credentials, which makes him potentially very dangerous, not least in relation to HIV education, in which needless to say he doesn't believe!

Besides, one shudders to think what might have happened in the UK had the gay press all along taken the line that it had to 'balance' every article or advert about safer sex, with other articles insisting that HIV can be casually transmitted, or that condoms are entirely useless. The results would have been catastrophic, and the gay press would rightly have lost all its hardwon credibility.

I believe that the gay press has certain clear responsibilities in the AIDS crisis. First, it has to continue to do its best to undo and correct the mischief and malice that dominates the rest of the mass media coverage of the epidemic to which far more gay and bisexual men are routinely exposed than ever read the gay press. We also have a responsibility to counter cranks and bigots of all persuasions, who sow unnecessary doubt and confusion everywhere, and cause untold avoidable anxiety, especially to people living with HIV. But these are essentially reactive responsibilities.

We must also be able to help people make sense of the epidemic as it affects us as individuals, and as groups of friends. We have to do our best to explain what has been going on, and what needs to be done in the future. This is why it is so important that the gay press continues to mobilize opinion, and to inform and steer the many types of discussion about almost any aspect of the epidemic that crop up all the time.

Such responsibilities, however, are not discharged by those who seem either unable or unwilling to understand why Duesberg and his chums must always be calmly and confidently opposed by the voice of reason. We cannot afford to retreat into fantasies of neutrality on such fundamental issues.

11 Michael Callen: 1955–93*

When I first met Michael Callen in New York in 1985 he was already one of my heroes! Diagnosed with AIDS in 1982, he played an indispensible role in the establishment of the People With AIDS Coalition, and in 1983 was instrumental in the drafting of the celebrated 'Denver Principles' – the Founding Statement of the US PWA movement. In 1983 he also co-authored *How To Have Sex in an Epidemic*, together with his boyfriend Richard Berkowitz and his physician, Dr Joseph Sonnabend. Long before the identification of HIV, this 40-page booklet embodied an approach to AIDS education embodied in the principle of risk reduction, and respect for gay men's sexual needs. This was the most influential and inspiring model for those of us trying to develop similar initiatives at that very difficult time in the UK.

Michael subsequently worked at the foreground of the AIDS treatment movement. Always healthily sceptical about the claims made on behalf of AZT before the publication of proper clinical trial results, he also played an absolutely central role in the long campaign for effective PCP prophylaxis, as a direct result of which the average life-expectancy of people with AIDS has been radically improved. He also helped the newly diagnosed, not least with his exemplary 1987 publication *Surviving and Thriving with AIDS*, which he edited. His collected writings, *Surviving AIDS* (HarperCollins, 1990) tells his own story, and that of many other long-term survivors.

Michael was also an accomplished singer, with a fine, light tenor voice, which he used to great effect on his own records, and together with the gay singing group The Flirtations, with whom he regularly appeared. He last visited England in 1990, when he spoke at the London Lighthouse. Hearing of Michael's death in Los Angeles on December 27, I immediately thought how glad his old friend film-maker Stuart Marshall (who died here in London earlier this summer) would be to see him again. And Michael could continue his ceaseless, fascinated quest to find out whether everyone around him was 'really' a top or a bottom. Michael Callen was a brave, far-sighted, funny, sexy, clever, richly gifted gay man, who found his voice (like many others) in a crisis. I'm glad I was recently able to assure him that the influence of his

* *First published in* Gay Times, *1993*.

work lives on here in the work of Gay Men Fighting AIDS, and other groups. Gay life continues, the richer for his great contribution to our collective struggle against AIDS, which Michael Callen also always recognized as a struggle *for* our pleasures.

12 Dr Simon Mansfield: 1960–93

Read at his funeral.

The cruel, senseless tragedy of Simon Mansfield's recent death from AIDS is only too apparent in the dates of his all too short life. Simon burst into my life, an astonishingly vivacious and beautiful medical student, at a Pro-Choice demonstration in 1979. This seems somehow appropriate, since he was soon to become a pioneering doctor, always passionately committed to the principle of respecting and enlarging his patients' choices. In the early years of the AIDS epidemic he helped set up the exemplary Community Care unit for people with AIDS, attached to St Mary's, Paddington. The efficient, sensitive procedures he later instituted at the London Lighthouse were reliably in place for his own untimely funeral on April 30th. In recent years he played a central role at the Kobler Centre. And he was always deeply involved in the work of the voluntary sector, working tirelessly as a member of the Gay Men's Health Education Group at the Terrence Higgins Trust; as an active Trustee of (and contributor to) the National AIDS Manual; and with Streetwise, which was especially close to his heart.

To me Simon embodied everything that was most admirable about the early generations of gay men who 'came out' between Gay Liberation and the advent of HIV. Gay pride was a fundamental part of Simon's life, and it profoundly informed his considerable skills as a doctor. He was one of a generation which translated an inherited tradition of community politics into the many organizations which provide caring services for people living with HIV and AIDS, and effective education for all. My sister once remarked to me that the only possible consolation for being knocked down by a bus would be the wildly remote possibility that when one came round in Casually, he might be there leaning over you. The hundreds of people at his funeral attested to how widely he inspired love in others. But it is for his own great capacity for love, and joy, and goodness, that his friends will recall and miss him. He is survived by his partner, Gareth.

13 AIDS and the politics of queer diaspora*

Nineteen-ninety-three has been an exceptionally grim year in relation to HIV/AIDS.[1] The prospect of effective, available anti-HIV drugs seems more elusive than ever, whilst the scale of suffering and death continues to worsen, as many of those infected in the late seventies and early eighties become symptomatically ill. It is a moment of intensely painful contradictions, as for example the Lesbian and Gay Studies movement rapidly gains academic respectability, while all the resources of cities as large and sophisticated as New York and Paris cannot sustain a reliable weekly or even monthly lesbian and gay press. Much of the energy which accompanied the emergence of activist organizations such as Queer Nation in the US and OutRage in the UK have run out of steam, while the AIDS activist movement continues to flounder.[2] The inability of the organizers of the 1993 Washington March to articulate the epidemic politically in relation to other lesbian and gay issues is symptomatic of a deeper failure to understand AIDS as a national tragedy which strikes to the very heart of gay culture. This is in itself evidence of the long-term fall-out of the epidemic, as many of the ablest have already died. It also reflects the vast scale of personal devastation, death, and loss throughout our communities, across every division of class, race, age, and region.

In this article I want to consider some of the international implications of current lesbian and gay political tactics, focusing in particular on the relations between Europe and the United States, where I have had most direct experience for many years. It is initially prompted by an article and a letter, both published in the gay press, which suggest much about the great difficulties we face. Writing in a July 1993 edition of the American fortnightly *The Advocate*, columnist Lance Loud quoted scriptwriter John Singleton on the subject of 'the AIDS problem in the black community, where the disease continues to claim a rising number of victims, most of them intravenous drug users.'[3] Such casual statements are typical of a country in which not even gay journalists appear to understand the actual local epidemiology of HIV/AIDS. Looking at the most recent quarterly *Surveillance Report* from the US

* First published in Monica Dorenkamp and Richard Henke (Eds) Negotiating Lesbian and Gay Subjects, *New York: Routledge, 1994.*

Department of Health and Human Services it is transparently clear that the great majority of AIDS cases amongst black, Hispanic, Asian, and Native American men in the United States has resulted *not* from injecting drug use, but from sex with other men.[4] There is surely a terrible irony here, in so far as a torrent of anti-racist rhetoric within the wider field of lesbian and gay politics has conspicuously failed to identify the single most devastating example of racism as it directly affects American gay and bisexual men. Indeed, I am only aware of a single article in the American gay press on this topic.[5] The figures on which policies should be based are not difficult to obtain. While the US AIDS activist movement has properly and honourably insisted on articulating the collective interest of everyone infected by HIV, this has in effect led to a paradoxical neglect of those who remain at demonstrably greatest risk, namely gay and bisexual men. For example, at the Eighth International AIDS Conference in Amsterdam in 1992, ACT UP (Los Angeles) distributed a detailed flyer on the subject of 'The Marginalization of AIDS Afflicted Communities of Color in the U.S.' Although there were sections on prevention and education, treatment, research, funding, prisons, and women's issues, there was not one word so much as acknowledging the mere existence of gay and bisexual men of colour. This is frankly extraordinary, given that gay and bisexual men constitute by far the largest number of cases amongst communities of colour in the United States.

The question of the reporting of statistics in the US also has wider ramifications, since as far as I am aware, the United States is almost the only country in the developed world which does not routinely publish the most recent HIV statistics alongside cumulative totals, but only AIDS figures. It should be appreciated that AIDS statistics speak of transmission events which took place on average some ten years ago. They are helpful in planning care and services, but tell us nothing about the directions in which the epidemic is moving, and may be changing directions. We can only plan and implement effective education if we understand such constantly shifting patterns of infection. Yet there is little or no debate on this vital matter in the United States. The situation is only comprehensible from the outside in relation to the emphasis all along in the US on AIDS itself, largely to the exclusion of HIV-related issues in the US lesbian and gay communities.

In cities as vastly different as San Francisco, London, and Amsterdam, only 5 per cent or less of available resources have gone for HIV/AIDS education amongst gay and bisexual men, in spite of the fact that we continue to make up 80 per cent or more of the death rate from AIDS in all three cities.[6] The professional de-gaying of AIDS service organizations around the world has had disastrous consequences, especially in the field of education and prevention, which almost invariably tends to play second fiddle to other services in such organizations. Indeed, only rarely is education properly understood as a service in the first place, let alone as an entitlement. Almost without exception, national HIV education campaigns financed by governments around the world have neglected the needs of those at greatest risk, and concentrated on those at least risk. Thus the aim of preventing a heterosexual epidemic has in most countries almost entirely eclipsed the task of fighting the actual HIV epidemics which continue to grow. At the same time the US AIDS activist movement was long since effectively hijacked by other political interest groups, and has become a platform for any number of different issues, losing its effectiveness precisely because it lost the sense of clearly defined, achievable aims and objectives. Thus American AIDS activism now all too frequently provides an unhelpful model in other countries where oppositional politics may be played out in their proper place, within oppositional political parties, rather than under the umbrella of the fight against HIV/AIDS.

Aiming at the chimerical goal of risk *elimination*, much HIV education in the US has ignored earlier and demonstrably effective campaigns which were based upon the achievable goal of risk *reduction*.[7] This has much to do with specifically American perceptions of risk, a word which in American English has largely lost its sense of relative probability, and has become more or less synonymous with the concept of danger.[8] In a period of intense environmental anxiety, the notion of risk in the US has become oversimplified, unlike in Europe, where risk is till thought of as fluctuating and variable, relative to other contingent factors. Thus in the US purely theoretical risks are frequently regarded as if they were on the same level as scientifically verifiable dangers. Thus much US HIV education tends to greatly exaggerate the actual risks of HIV transmission, as is immediately apparent from advice concerning oral sex, which is all but universally regarded as a form of safer sex in other countries, according to the criteria of risk reduction. Sadly, America's international power and prestige guarantee that US models of HIV prevention may cause great harm, and wholly unnecessary anxiety, outside the United States, by making safer sex seem a largely impossible goal. There is furthermore another more hidden irony here. As younger American men and women increasingly socialize together as never before under the rubric of queerness, exaggerated and wholly unscientific claims concerning the theoretical possibility of woman-to-woman transmission may have a feedback effect on younger men, at genuinely high risk of infection. This is not of course to question the need for effective HIV education for lesbians. It is only to question the ways in which the assumed commensurability between lesbians and gay men at the political level is frequently projected across the field of HIV/AIDS. Lesbians may be at risk from HIV via unprotected sexual intercourse with men, or from sharing needles. But there is frankly no scientific commensurability between lesbians and gay men in relation to the risk of HIV transmission. Moreover, the United States AIDS establishment is strongly resistant to the mere idea that America might learn anything from overseas colleagues. For example, I shall never forget the experience of a weighty and doubtless well-intended introduction a few years ago at a national US lesbian and gay health conference, when an assembled audience of overseas delegates were cheerfully informed that the speaker and her colleagues were there to prevent us 'from reinventing the wheel'. Behind this statement lies the familiar American inability to recognize the great variations in international experience, as well as the consequences of working in countries whose HIV and AIDS epidemiology varies greatly from the United States situation. There can be no danger of 'reinventing the wheel' for the simple reason that the epidemic is not the same in any two countries. Such patronizing and essentially xenophobic comments are unfortunately hardly rare in the US AIDS arena. Hence it is hardly surprising that there is emerging a widespread grassroots resistance to what is often perceived, however unfairly, as the imperial global ambitions of the US lesbian and gay movement, in both its goals and method.

A recent letter published in the UK lesbian and gay weekly *Pink Paper* expressed this type of resentment very clearly, in relation to the ongoing US debate about gays and the military, which has inevitably flushed through the global network of syndicated stories appearing in different national presses and on radio and TV around the world. The writer regretted that

> This wholly peripheral issue is taking up so much of our time and energy that could be much better spent on other more important issues (such as) the age of consent, homelessness, anti-gay violence and getting adequate care for those with HIV/AIDS.[9]

He also strongly criticized

> the way the gay establishment here, especially activist groups and the press, see the British gay community as some sort of ultra-loyalist, unswerving colonial outpost of gay America in much the same way as Margaret Thatcher saw Britain as being an outpost of Reaganite America.[10]

This may be simply the old, tired voice of unreflecting European leftist anti-Americanism, but it also reflects a growing international acknowledgement of the importance of national specificities in lesbian and gay issues around the world, issues which may differ as greatly as overall political systems from those that prevail in the United States.

The sheer size and confidence of the US lesbian and gay movement make it likely to lead many international debates, not least within the academy. There is thus a special and important challenge to establish international dialogue and information channels, rather than retreating back into pre-1989 Cold War postures. It is moreover always salutary to remember that every nation has its own distinct queer history, both in relation to the affirmation of homosexual desire, and the obstacles to such 'movements of affirmation'.[11]

At this point it may prove helpful to attempt a little clarification on the distinction between the terms 'gay' and 'queer'. In Britain, gay identity has been founded since the early 1970s on the assumption that lesbians and gay men share certain identifiable patterns of oppression, from specific institutions, including the churches, psychiatry, the National Health Service, political parties, and so on. Gay identity is thus distinctly different from the older 'homosexual' identity, founded on notions of a fundamental individualism, and assumed to derive directly from homosexual desire. In British English, the word 'queer' has a powerfully ambiguous meaning, sometimes a term of affection, cheerfully accepted as an identity by some throughout this century, violently contested and refused by others as an insult. Elsewhere within Anglophone culture the situation is different again, as in Australia, where the word 'queer' never has had popular associations with homosexuality, and simply means 'funny', in the sense of being amusing rather than inferior. In the UK, the emergent queer identity has stood in conscious opposition to what are perceived by many to be the shortcomings of gay and lesbian identity politics, and culture.[12]

As new post-lesbian and post-gay identities emerge and variously flourish throughout the developed world, there is a greater need than ever to be able to articulate American to non-American queer national histories, and queer national cultures. The nomenclature 'gay' has inevitable connotations of Americanness outside the US, even on the part of those born long after the Stonewall Riot. It is therefore important to recognize that the new rhetoric of queerness may obliterate national differences as easily as it may illuminate them. At the same time it remains important to be able to confidently challenge the fundamental naiveté of the position taken by the letter writer in the *Pink Paper*. For while our political and social aims and tactics may vary greatly around the world, the epidemic remains always simultaneously local, national, and international. The world of biomedical research is by its very nature international, as is the work of multi-national pharmaceutical companies who ultimately control the production and distribution of potential treatment drugs. Given the nature of our global economy, and the global network of communications in the mass media *about* us, it is clear that our analyses must be international if they are fully to comprehend local and national circumstances. This point is only underscored by the close international connections between homophobic political parties of both the left and the right, travel restrictions, religious organizations, insurance companies, and so on. Hence the immediate significance of ongoing debates about nationalism and national identities, in relation to both queer politics and the future course of the epidemics in our midst.

There is also an equally pressing reason for international experience of the epidemic from a lesbian and gay, or queer perspective, since it is becoming increasingly apparent that the few institutions which theorize and respond to HIV/AIDS on global terms do so in ways which are increasingly neglectful of the needs of gay and bisexual men, who make up the great majority of cases throughout much of the undeveloped world. For example, the United Nations is planning to unify the AIDS work it undertakes in its various departmental specialist areas, including UNICEF and UNESCO and the World Health Organization, and to relocate them under one roof. Ever since the 1991 Seventh International AIDS Conference in Florence it has also been obvious that the World Health Organization has decided to prioritize the needs of the developing world to the virtual exclusion of the situation in the developed world. Furthermore, such huge bureaucratic agencies are invariably homophobic in their wider world view. To summarize, there is simply no organization or institution on earth which is currently able to assess and respond to the needs of gay and bisexual men on an international scale, from the United Nations to the European Community, and far beyond. At a time when the very notion of 'the global epidemic' has come to refer exclusively to the epidemics resulting and potentially resulting from heterosexual transmission, who is to speak for men having sex with one another in Eastern Europe, let alone in southern Africa or in southeast Asia? Hence the great timeliness of recent queer debates about the diasporic nature of our culture, if not of our explicit political goals.

Nature and diasporas

The metaphor of diaspora is seductively convenient to contemporary queer politics. Unlike the tendency of seventies and eighties lesbian and gay theory to develop overly monolithic notions of identity and cultural politics, the concept of diaspora is suggestive of diversification, of scattering, fracturing, separate developments, and also, perhaps, of a certain glamour. It also suggests something of a sense of collective interest, however difficult this may be to pin down. It implies a complex divided constituency, with varying degrees of power and powerlessness. The concept of diaspora has been developed in recent years in especially important ways by the black British sociologist, Stuart Hall, in a series of exemplary analyses of Caribbean cultures and identities. In much of this work, Hall contrasts an older black political model which emphasizes an essential 'oneness' of worldwide black cultures, to more recent debates which have questioned this notion of a single, originating cultural past, which might yet be restored. Thus he writes with admirable sensitivity and insight of the many ways in which black culture frequently offers

> a way of imposing an imaginary coherence on the experience of dispersal and fragmentation, which is the history of all enforced diasporas. They do this by representing or 'figuring' Africa as the mother of these different civilizations.[13]

There are evidently close parallels here in the recent history of lesbian and gay culture and politics to the type of 'imaginary reunification' described by Hall. For example, it is laudable and understandable that lesbian and gay politics have sought political unity between women and men as perhaps its highest internal goal. Yet it has been less than helpful that the relations between lesbians and gay men have so frequently been simply assumed to be exactly commensurate and continuous. There have been comparatively few serious attempts to articulate the constantly shifting ideological frame which sometimes casts us together as targets of new legislation, or affects us separately as women or as men. We cannot, however, assume a given or 'natural' alliance between lesbians and gay men for the simple reason that we are not in any case dealing with stable, coherent constituencies of women and men in the first place. On the contrary, there are profound divisions among lesbians and among gay men on any issue one might care to name, from the vexed topic of gays and lesbians in the military, to 'pornography' or drug use. Hence the immediate significance of the term 'queer' in the nineties, with its accompanying sense of diversity, and its cheerful embrace of the perverse.

Yet the concept of diaspora also introduces new problems of its own onto the terrain of queer culture and queer politics, not least because homosexuality is fortunately only very rarely a reason for forced expulsion from one's country of origin, though it should not be forgotten how many lesbians and gay men are indeed only too directly affected by forcible repatriation *to* their countries of origin as a result of their homosexuality. However, it is not so much external exile that we experience, but more often a form of internal exile, more strictly akin to legal and cultural quarantine, or to the state of 'inner emigration' described in different circumstances by Hannah Arendt.[14] The actual Jewish diaspora may attract anti-Semitism because, as Zygmunt Bauman points out, Jews may be regarded as 'foreigners inside' the nation, thus producing projective anxiety and hostility on the part of those who seek to define and defend narrowly rigid boundaries of language, custom, culture, and so on. For diasporas always imply a blurring of such boundaries, a porousness of social categories, and a tragic awareness of involuntary migrations.

Wherever the nation is popularly envisaged as if it were a closed family unit, homosexuality may also be perceived as similarly threatening, a refusal of homogeneity and sameness understood as indispensable aspects of properly 'loyal' national identity. Sometimes, as in France, a seemingly democratic concept of national citizenship may be equally obliterative of national sexual differences, together with questions of race and gender. The question remains whether we can effectively articulate a productive sense of international commonality structured from the shared basis of homosexual desire, which is not at the same time itself obliterative of the great diversity of sexual identities through which homosexual desire is acted upon and lived by different people in different historical periods, and in different societies. For while we are all national subjects, our sexuality intersects in often unpredictable ways with our contingent national identities. One powerful strand of lesbian and gay politics has long sought to remove such anomalies, by recourse to civil rights legislation. Yet such politics, especially in the United States, frequently leads directly to a homogenizing, minoritist vision, which also demonstrates a marked tendency to greatly exaggerate the actual number of self-conscious, 'out' lesbians and gay men in any country. Such a political vision is likely to gravitate towards such vague ideas as the supposed 'right' to marry, and so on. These are indeed weighty and painful issues for lesbians and gay male Christians, but they are theological issues, to be decided within individual churches and congregations, and hardly compatible with the wider demands of queer politics, not least in relation to the institution of marriage, and the social and economic status of women.

Yet the sense of a queer diaspora remains stubbornly attractive, if only because it is likely to accord so well to our direct experience of overseas travel, as well as of queer culture and its constitutive role in our personal lives. Few heterosexuals can imagine the sense of relief and safety which a gay man or lesbian finds in a gay bar or a dyke bar in a strange city in a foreign country. Even if one cannot speak the local language, we feel a sense of identification. Besides, we generally like meeting one another, learning about what is happening to people 'like us' from other parts of the world. At the level of the unconscious this is also, always, a site of powerful sexual fantasy – the core of all travel literature. Yet the question remains, in what sense 'like' us? The worsening gravity of the international AIDS crisis requires that we consider such questions, since with the single exception of Australia, there is no political system on earth that has responded to our needs in this terrible emergency, precisely because we are so rarely recognized in political terms as a legitimate social constituency, or as deserving national subjects, by the state or other institutions which define 'the national interest'. This is not entirely surprising, given that it remains far from clear on what basis current lesbian and gay political 'leaders' claim to 'represent' their constituency, or how that constituency itself might best be conceptualized, beyond exhausted and inadequate notions of lesbian and gay 'community'.

Hence the many anxieties around the world about contemporary American minoritist lesbian and gay politics, and their dependence on categories and concepts such as 'hate speech', and the widespread use of addiction models to supposedly explain immensely complex personal and social phenomena ranging from drug use to HIV transmission. For example, the bulk of US prevention research is firmly committed in advance of any actual findings to the belief that unsafe sex is closely linked in a direct one-to-one causal manner to either alcohol consumption or drug addiction. A vast pathologizing literature has been amassed on this topic in the US writings on HIV education. Yet I think it is fair to say that most non-American HIV/AIDS educators find this literature, and its effects in actual policies, far more harmful than helpful. As Peter Wetherburn explains:

> Large sums of money were suddenly released ... by the United States government for research into HIV and AIDS. A proportion of this money went to fund social and behavioral research which soon emerged from being a low-status Cinderella of the high-powered American academy, to be 'where it was all at' – reputations to be made, careers advanced and accolades expected ... They assumed that unsafe sex can be explained

by isolating the personality traits of the individuals who engage in these activities ... reminiscent of the search for the 'homosexual personality' in the early part of this century. It is underpinned by the spurious notion that since [gay men] are on the whole well-informed about HIV transmission and are logical and rational and concerned for their own well-being, then those who engage in unsafe sex must be illogical, irrational, or unconcerned with their survival. Hence people who have 'unsafe sex' must suffer from some defect of the intellect (denial, depression, low-self-efficacy, poor sexual communication skills, sexual compulsiveness, etc.) or be under the influence of external factors (usually drugs or alcohol), any of which can render them helpless to their baser instincts. This agenda implicitly privileges the clinician: it is aimed at providing the medical and ancillary professions with the means to identify the individuals who are being irresponsible.[15]

I cite this article at length for two reasons. First, it eloquently embodies a series of common beliefs throughout northern Europe and Australia, based on good qualitative and quantitative research, which at the same time are regarded as sheer heresy in the United States. Second, the article appeared in one of the many lesbian and gay publications which proliferate in the UK, and not in some obscure academic journal. Yet just across the English Channel in France there is no such gay press in which a politically active gay academic might publish such work in order to reach a wider, community-based audience. This, together with the virtual absence of a French equivalent to Anglophone gay identity, is not unconnected to the tragic fact that France has the worst HIV epidemic in Europe, with a vastly disproportionate impact among French 'homosexuals'.

Another symptom of 'imaginary reunification' may be found in the widespread US political dependence on a new form of heavily biologized, neo-eugenic gay politics, typified by the national Human Rights Campaign Fund's promotion of the notion that lesbian and gay identity is hardwired to genetic determinants. This is not to question the role genetics plays in all areas of human behaviour, but it does raise the important issue of why the US gay movement should so casually adopt a position which threatens to collapse all aspects of human sexual diversity together as if they were of purely biological origin. This effectively pushes the clock back some seventy years to early twentieth century German arguments that if 'we' are different 'by nature' then it is biologically pointless to persecute 'us'. Such attempts to ground 'tolerance' in a biologistic notion of object choice which in turn supposedly explains everything about our lives and feelings is perhaps not unrelated to the wider influence of crude behaviourism within American academic and popular thought.

Such misguided political campaigns return us to the vexed issue of the relations between gay and lesbian political organizations, and those they claim to represent. Indeed, it is only too apparent in many countries, including the UK, that some twenty years of puritanical leftist and feminist lesbian and gay politics have achieved less for most self-defining lesbians, gay men, and queers than has resulted from changes and expansion within the commercial scene, including the dramatic expansion of social facilities, cable TV, the gay and lesbian press, and so on. And such differences in the ordinary, everyday quality of gay and lesbian life issues have always had the most powerful diasporic impact on our lives, as we campaign for greater freedoms on the basis of what is available to other people in other countries. Besides, the sense of international unity felt most strongly by gay men around the world these days is surely forged in relation to our direct experience of protracted illness, suffering, loss, and mourning, together with the cultural solidarity we obtain from what has always been a diasporic queer culture. Neither in the US nor in Europe has the gay political leadership responded adequately to AIDS. It is as if the epidemic were to them merely an embarrassment, something which cannot be permitted to derail the triumphalist vision of a squeaky-clean, network-TV-worthy, *Vanity Fair*-respectable, and unquestionably patriotic new lesbian and gay citizenship. Indeed, little can have had more direct effect on the explosive emergence of the new queer identity in all its national variants, than the inability of a lesbian and gay politics grounded in the seventies, to respond to the changed realities of the eighties and nineties. This is sadly apparent, for example, in the stunning inanity of political analysis on display in the recent 'Queer Nation' special edition of *The Nation*.[16] It is on the High Ground of representative political claims that new would-be power formations are emerging, much more similar in many ways to the various homophile lobbying groups of the forties and fifties than to the descendants of Gay Liberation, which as far as many people, including such influential figures as Clinton's advisor David B. Mixner, are concerned, might never have happened.

In other words, what we are witnessing is the beginning of the process whereby political formations working on the terrain of homosexuality will emerge, and either flourish or disappear, to be replaced by new, more adequate approximations to people's experience. Within Anglophone societies it seems likely that the terms lesbian and gay will retain their previous political purchase, since their goals are also yet to be achieved. But 'underneath' gay identity, as it were, we are likely to find a proliferation of innovative ways of living homosexual desire in the world. And these will, by definition, be largely invisible from the perspective of the older lesbian and gay identities, and the institutions they created. Moreover, local responses to the injustices surrounding most aspects of the epidemic are already bringing into being new, articulate groupings of men in countries such as India and the Philippines, where homosexual acts were not related to notions of identity before the epidemic. This will lead to still further diasporic diversity. For example, it is clear that there is no single answer to such questions as how one thinks of oneself if one is Indian, British, and gay. One man will identify as a black man, another as a gay Asian, while a third may reject the validity of the category of gay altogether. There can be no easy resolution to such issues, nor is resolution required. On the contrary, it is the conflict between a gay political imperative to think of its constituency as unified and homogeneous, and the actual constantly changing complexity of gay culture as it is lived, that stimulates most of our greatest challenges today.

In conclusion, a properly diasporic analysis of the epidemic from a queer perspective must, at the very least, be able to account for differences of needs and strategies in countries with different types of epidemic. For example, the needs of gay and bisexual men who made up 62 per cent of newly diagnosed UK cases of HIV infection in 1992, are quite different from those of other gay and bisexual men elsewhere in the European Community, where they may constitute a minority of new cases in different epidemiological settings. Both types of situations will be largely determined by local varieties of homophobia, but these may vary in their affects and degrees. All are likely to be equally harmful for our health. We need far, far more rigorous thinking. The potential damage to the fundamental principle of sexual choice posed by the new genetic determinist strand of gay politics is still more dangerous than the anti-activist rhetoric which opposed the emergence of ACT UP in the late eighties.[17] The entire vocabulary of 'positive images', 'sexual addiction', and so on, speaks from a set of beliefs about sexuality that are positively dangerous in an epidemic since they obscure the central fact that avoiding HIV has nothing to do with what is so laughably described as 'the gay lifestyle', but depends upon socially learned skills, and a shared morality, which might well be best understood as a form of ethical sexual etiquette. This is how homosexual desire is lived by men in the nineties. It is also vitally important that in our headlong rush for normality and 'equal rights' we do not neglect or offend our queer cultural divinities – the great iconic, transcultural figures of a queer culture that is increasingly diasporic, including to name but a few – Divine, John Waters, Derek Jarman, Pasolini, Virginia Woolf, Elizabeth Bishop, Sylvia Townsend Warner, Morrissey, Frank O'Hara, k.d. lang, and on and on. We have our own queer canon, and it is nothing if not diasporic. Indeed, this is one of its profoundest characteristics.

Conclusion

In many developed countries we are currently witnessing a widening divergence between the old Gay Liberation, leftist lesbian and gay intelligentsia, and the generation who has 'come out' since the epidemic began. This is not least perhaps because so many of the ablest men of that generation have already died long before their time, indeed, ironically, just when their wisdom is most needed. It seems to me that of all the many great achievements of the American lesbian and gay movement since the sixties, the work of treatment activists in the AIDS crisis has been the most remarkable, politically, ethically, intellectually, and most important of all, in terms of practical, direct consequences – better health and longer lives for people living with HIV.

It is inexpressibly sad to visit the great cities of the United States for European gay men of my generation, who learned so much from the great confidence and vitality of the American gay scene in the seventies. We marvel at the scale of courage, both public and private. And since our epidemics are running approximately four or five years behind those in the US, we can also see what lies ahead for our local gay cultures, as our HIV epidemics slowly and inexorably turn into AIDS epidemics. Everywhere I travel in my work I find increasing levels of stress and emotional exhaustion, expressed as symptoms of many kinds, from the flourishing of conspiracy theories and open hostility to the very concept of scientific method, to the proliferation of lesbian and gay New Ageism. Yet what has lesbian and gay politics to say on these issues? Not a lot. Certainly the astonishing achievements of organizations such as New York's Treatment Action Group (TAG) are rarely seen as even a part of the wider intellectual world of Lesbian and Gay Studies.[18]

In these volatile and painful circumstances, it seems to me that the emergent discipline of Lesbian and Gay Studies has arrived at just the right time, in order to be prepared and able to contest HIV/AIDS issues as they arise within the academy. This will range from internal HIV/AIDS education, to an assessment of how different disciplines function in relation to the management of the epidemic. The universities may now be further than ever from seats of government, but nonetheless vital areas of policy are implemented on the basis of research which only academics are qualified to design and undertake. This is not of course to say that all queer academics should immediately put down their tools and do nothing but work in relation to the epidemic. It is, however, to imply that gay male academics do indeed have at least some moral responsibility to try to find out how their specialist discipline may be involved in HIV/AIDS issues. Thus the queer teaching of literature would be incomplete if it did not possess some reflexive awareness of the role of AIDS fictions in our culture. Although we will never begin to do justice to the realities of HIV/AIDS if our work is only concerned with the public domain, at the same time, social and physical scientists also have responsibilities, especially since their disciplines have been so polluted by bad, homophobic research, which has only very rarely ever been criticized in the United States.[19]

There is a cruel and ironic paradox in the emergence of a confident, articulate Lesbian and Gay Studies movement, which is enthusiastically 're-gaying' the academy, while at the same time throughout the developed world with all too few exceptions AIDS service organizations continue to 'de-gay' the epidemic in a process quite distinct from governmental 'de-gaying'.[20] At the same time, it would seem that the US Lesbian and Gay Studies movement, which is of course the flagship of parallel manoeuvres in other countries, has retreated in recent years from intellectual involvement with HIV/AIDS issues. In this respect the 1988 Yale Lesbian and Gay Studies conference marked a high-point of academic attention, for by the time of the 1991 Rutgers conference only one out of eighty panels dealt specifically with the epidemic. It is difficult not to regard this situation as further evidence of the complex displacements and projections at work throughout the wider Queer Nation, of which the academy is but one relatively small territory.

The academy matters, however, because it remains one of the primary institutional/discursive sites where 'truth' is defined and negotiated and questioned, with unpredictable consequences for the rest of society. The great challenge here is to be able to articulate our social and cultural goals in relation to the multi-faceted nature of the epidemic. Out there in the Queer Nation a great change is taking place, and far beyond, throughout the international queer diaspora. This change has no single coherent form, but is everywhere involved with the great principle of equality in law, and an angry refusal of the violence and injustice which is sadly still so widely experienced in relation to homosexuality. On the one hand we witness the fully-fledged emergence of an immensely sophisticated fetish culture, organized around physical pleasures which are inseparable from HIV/AIDS awareness, while on the other we also find an explosion of involvement in 12-step programmes, and psychotherapeutic programmes, many of which are extremeley conservative in their depiction of homosexuality, and sex in general, widely regarded as primarily a dangerous, addictive activity. In other words, the epidemic has already generated complex, conflicting cultural responses at the level of personal lived identities, which may be either puritanical, or libertarian, and sometimes both. At the same time the contingent commercial scene of clubs, bars and so on has been dramatically expanding in many parts of the world, from the smaller cities of the US, to London, and Melbourne and Vancouver.

In these circumstances we should note that growing conflict between the broad tradition of social construction theory in the academy, and its widespread rejection among nonacademics, including many leading figures in the US lesbian and gay politics movements. This conflict revolves above all around rival notions of *choice*. On the one hand we speak confidently within the field of Lesbian and Gay Studies about 'homosexual object choice' understood to be involuntary and unconscious, and relatively fixed, though potentially mobile in the lives of individuals. It should be noted that this mobility is usually considered only from the direction of 'coming out' as lesbian or gay after previously exclusive heterosexuality, rather than in the opposite direction from homosexuality to bisexuality or heterosexuality. At the same time it is insisted with equal fervour by many others, that sexual object choice or 'orientation', is entirely voluntary, and conscious. This position is ironically shared by both moralistic homophobes, aiming to prevent the 'promotion' of homosexuality, and by some libertarians and feminists. Yet another, and far more extensive constituency holds that we have no 'choice' about our sexuality, and that identity is hardwired to biology. This position in turn is shared both by crude genetic determinists, and those who simply feel convinced they were 'born this way'.

Yet in many respects these oppositions are more apparent than real. For the assertion that homosexuality is grounded in infantile desiring fantasy (like all other forms of sexual object choice), is hardly incompatible with either the empirical observation that people may 'come out' at different ages, for many different reasons, or the strongly held sense of personal difference in childhood described by most 'out' lesbians and gay men. What does remain problematic is the enthusiastic retention of the idea that sexual object choice is *infinitely* mobile and fluid, rather than its expression, both in the lives of individuals and sexual collectivities. This is a major stumbling block to the kind of intellectual politics which are so urgently needed in response to the epidemic. The question remains why this particular fantasy of absolute sexual mobility is so devoutly upheld within some sections of the queer academy.

HIV has in many respects served to reconstitute homosexuality and identities founded upon homosexual desire. This reconstitution involves many overlapping elements, from attitudes towards sex, towards illness and death, mourning, and so on. It informs the totality of our social and psychic lives in ways that we hardly begin to understand. After all, there have never been people quite like 'us' before, at least in relation to our necessarily simultaneous focus of love, sex, and death. Never before has it been so urgently necessary to mobilize concrete policies founded upon notions of commonality and solidarity, yet never before has the very notion of lesbian and gay *political* identity been less fashionable in the academy, where it is so frequently 'deconstructed' as if it were merely a vulgar 'essentialist' error. Such a position stems from the widespread belief that gay and lesbian identities are no more than a response to some primary level of regulation. This is to ignore the fact that as the marginal yet extensive field of queer historiography demonstrates, women and men have also, always, responded positively to their own homosexuality, and developed identities which should not be regarded as merely reactive and basically passive by-products of power, understood to be universally homophobic. This is simply ahistorical. It also colludes dangerously with precisely the type of widespread academic 'de-gaying' which until recently has tended to deny or obscure the very existence of earlier historical social formations and groups based on the shared experience both of desire *and* its regulation. Always the challenge is to be able to articulate together the two currents at work in the process of forging identities, the one deriving from complex shared feelings and pleasures, the other from shared discrimination and induced shame. What is not going to change is the central presence of HIV in our midst, and the conflicting tides of fatalism and hope to which it gives rise.

If the new queer academic intelligentsia is unable or unwilling to even try to grapple with the fundamental issues raised by the epidemic, other formations will doubtlessly challenge its authority. With 50 per cent of gay men already infected in several US cities, the social and psychological consequences of the epidemic in our communities must be faced. The immediate future looks very grim indeed. If Lesbian and Gay Studies has nothing to say on the details of social policy, care, services, and clinical medicine, as well as HIV education, then it can hardly expect the wholehearted loyalty it presumably seeks from its primary constituency, including the not inconsiderable number of 'independent scholars' who have traditionally constituted the bedrock of lesbian and gay intellectual life, far away from the academy which has traditionally denied the validity of their studies. It would indeed be a tragic irony if the vanguard of Lesbian and Gay Studies were to follow suit.

Notes

1 See Derek Link, 'The collapse of early intervention at the Ninth International AIDS Conference'. *Treatment Issues*, vol. 7, no. 6 (New York, July 1993); and Edward King, 'Experts gloomy at drugs' limited benefits', *AIDS Treatment Update*, Issue 8/9 (London, June/July 1993).
2 See Edward King, 'The end of the American dream', *Pink Paper*, London, 9 July 1993, p. 12; and Simon Watney, 'Read my lips: AIDS art & activism', in Nicola White (Ed.) *Read My Lips: New York AIDS Polemic* (Tramway: Glasgow, 1992).
3 Lance Loud, 'AIDS in the Hood', *The Advocate*, Los Angeles, 27 July 1993, p. 77.
4 *HIV/AIDS Surveillance Report*, vol. 5, no. 2 (July 1993), Atlanta, Georgia: US Department of Health and Human Services.
5 Sara Simmons, 'Death by genocide', *NYQ*, 22 December 1991, p. 28.
6 Information from the Ninth International AIDS Conference, Berlin 1993. For the UK see Edward King *et al.*, *HIV Prevention for Gay Men: A Survey of Initiative in the UK* (July 1992, London: National AIDS Manual Ltd.).
7 See Simon Watney, 'Emergent sexual identities and HIV/AIDS', in Peter Aggleton *et al.* (Eds) *AIDS: Facing the Second Decade* (London: Falmer Press, 1993), pp. 13–19.
8 See Mary Douglas and Aaron Wildavasky, *Risk and Culture* (Berkeley: University of California Press, 1982).
9 John Burke, 'British gay establishment in colonial outpost of US', *Pink Paper*, London, 6 August 1993, p. 8.
10 *Ibid.*
11 See Jeffrey Weeks, *Sexuality* (London: Tavistock Press, 1986).
12 See Keith Alcorn, 'Queer and now', *Gay Times*, London (May 1992), pp. 20–4.
13 See Stuart Hall, 'Cultural identity and diaspora', in Jonathan Rutherford (Ed.) *Identity: Community, Culture, Difference* (London: Lawrence and Wishart, 1990), p. 224. See also Stuart Hall, 'New ethnicities,' in Erica Carter (Ed.) *Black Film British Cinema* (London: ICA Documents, No. 7, 1988), pp. 27–31.
14 Hannah Arendt, 'On humanity in dark times: Thoughts on Lessing', *Men in Dark Times* (San Diego: Harcourt Brace Jovanovich, 1968), p. 22.
15 Peter Wetherburn, 'Alcohol and unsafe sex', *Rouge*, 11 (London 1992), pp. 12–14.
16 *The Nation*, 5 July 1993.
17 See Simon Watney, 'The possibilities of permutation', in James Miller (Ed.) *Fluid Exchanges: Artists and Critics in the AIDS Crisis* (Toronto: University of Toronto Press, 1992), pp. 329–69.
18 See Keith Alcorn, 'We don't have time', *Gay Times* (London, June 1993), pp. 38–41.

19 See the debate on this subject in *AIDS7*, pp. 279–300. See also Peter Davis *et al.* (Eds) *Sex, Gay Men and AIDS* (London: Falmer Press, 1993); Edward King, *Safety in Numbers: Safer Sex and Gay Men* (London: Cassell, 1993).
20 See Cindy Patton, *Inventing AIDS* (New York: Routledge, 1990), chapter five; also Edward King, *Safety In Numbers*.

14 Derek Jarman 1942–94: a political death*

The death of Derek Jarman robs us not only of one of cinema's most imaginative postwar independent directors but of one of Britain's proudest and most indefatigably queer gay men. With the late Angela Carter, Jarman was the greatest poetic visionary of Britain's Thatcher era. He captured with unerring accuracy the sense of inexorably developing corruption and cruelty that since the late 1970s has increasingly characterized everyday life here.

Derek was a cornucopia of gifts, talents, skills, enthusiasms, and mysteries. A man of the early 1960s, he was always (sometimes touchingly) committed to the idea of a grand transhistorical sequence of homosexuals, from Plato onward by way of Michelangelo, Wilde, and so on. At the same time, his life had been transformed by the punk movement of the mid 1970s, which he wholeheartedly embraced. He was also an erudite antiquarian, a wonderful companion for, say, visiting old churches: as a student, he himself had been shown round most of the City of London churches by Sir John Betjeman, poet laureate and canonizer of a certain traditional vision of English life, whom he revered. Not for nothing did Jarman name his darkest film *The Last of England* (1987), after Ford Madox Brown's Pre-Raphaelite painting, which is concerned, as Derek was, with the pain of exile.

He grew up during and in the shadow of World War II, and his underlying vision of life was always sombre, Goya-esque. The sky is rarely a safe place in his films. Yet there was also a Derek Jarman whose tastes lay with the traditions and conventions of the pastoral – with Gainsborough. He had studied painting at the Slade, and in 1967 his work had been exhibited in the Tate Gallery's 'Young Contemporaries' exhibition. Then he had moved on to a successful career as a set designer, working, for example, on Sir Frederick Ashton's 1968 ballet *Jazz Calendar* and on Ken Russell's 1971 film *The Devils*. It was only in the mid 1970s that he reinvented himself as a filmmaker.

Derek was a complete original, inspired simultaneously by Andy Warhol and Kenneth Anger, by Pasolini and *arte povera*. A constant was his own peculiar Englishness. What was so rare about him was his sense of dissident

* First published in Artforum, New York, May 1994.

national identity! He belonged to the England of the Elizabethan philoso pher/astrologer John Dee, of the seventeenth-century diarist and antiquarian John Evelyn and the mystic and medical man Sir Thomas Browne, and of the metaphysical poets – John Donne, George Herbert, Henry Vaughan. As a younger friend of his remarked recently, he was never deeply involved in gay politics until they caught up with him. But in the latter part of his life he was deeply committed, working, for example, with the direct-action group OutRage from its beginnings, early in 1990 in London. He became the best-known out gay man in Britain, and the most articulate spokesman for people living with HIV.

One of the most moving aspects of Derek's response to the virus was his immediate return to painting, in 1986. As he explained to me a couple of years ago, 'I left painting behind at the moment painting left itself behind because it became conceptual and all sorts of other things … I've seemed to come in where I left off.'[1] His large, late graffiti paintings, done on and largely obliterating the silk-screened front pages of British tabloid newspapers screaming with homophobic hatred and anxiety, are a kind of defiant reply to British bigotry and puritan zeal. His anger at government complacency and institutional homophobia was articulate, effective, and courageous.

Jarman lived through several virtual deaths and resurrections in the course of his illness. When I visited him in hospital in June 1990, though barely alive he could talk only of England's melancholy lack of what he described as a 'dignified' sense of its own cultural history – always greedy for the new, hopelessly and tragically ignorant of its own real achievements and history. Derek straddled Englishness, from the Knights Templars to the Pet Shop Boys. It was wholly appropriate that his funeral service took place at the Norman parish church of St Nicholas in New Romney, not far from his cele-brated seaside garden on the bleak Kent coast at Dungeness. In 1888, when the church's vicar was threatening to 'restore' St Nicholas more or less out of recognizable existence, its preservation had been the first victory for William Morris's recently founded Society for the Protection of Ancient Buildings. Indeed, Derek might well be thought of as a kind of Queer William Morris for the 1990s.

In 1991 he had said, 'I want to be part of the final alteration in the laws on homosexuality and I want to tend my garden.'[2] In early February this year [1994] he made the decision to come off all his medical treatments: at the time, the House of Commons was preparing to vote on a bill proposing a lowering of the age of consent for gay men, from 21 to 16. Jarman had cam-paigned passionately for this bill, and had said that he was living on only to see it passed. On the morning of February 21, however, *The Times* and other newspapers were put in the position of carrying front-page stories about both the age-of-consent vote, to take place later that day, and Derek's death. In the event, a dishonourable compromise – a lowering to 18 instead of 16 – was passed. The US has already witnessed the extraordinary symbolism of 'polit-ical funerals', in which the ashes of people with AIDS are thrown onto the lawns of the White House, at their request, to protest ongoing government neglect. Derek's was a self-consciously political death.

I sometimes went to exhibitions with Derek over the years, and we once visited the National Gallery together to see a Holbein portrait, *A Lady with a Squirrel and a Starling*, that had recently been acquired for the sum of £10 million, to outraged protest from the *Daily Telegraph* and other papers. It is a marvellous painting, showing a rather plain Englishwoman, seated, with a red nose, as though she had a cold. On one arm perches a squirrel, Holbein's casual acknowledgement of the challenge posed by Leonardo da Vinci's celebrated portrait of Cecilia Gallerani with an ermine. 'Ten million pounds!' said Derek, beginning to wave his arms around enthusiastically: 'Ten million pounds! What's that? That's a tank!' (This was during the Gulf War.) 'It's just one loop of a motorway flyover! There are thousands of bloody tanks! Thousands of bloody flyovers! This is unique. It's worth a *hundred* million!'

Always struggling to scrape together the money for his next film, always immensely generous to others, Derek himself was without peer or price. He is survived by his partner, Keith Collins, and by his extensive body of work, including eight books and some ten feature films, from *Sebastiane*, 1976, the spoken text of which is in Latin, through a remarkable 1979 version of *The Tempest*, through *Caravaggio*, 1986, *Edward II*, 1991, to *Blue*, 1993. This last, made while Jarman was losing his sight to AIDS, comprises a complex autobiographical soundtrack – discussing both HIV/AIDS treatment issues and Jarman's life as an artist and gay activist – and a single, unchanging, Yves Klein blue image on screen.

As writer and performer Neil Bartlett wrote in a birthday message earlier this year, 'Some people make being gay more of a pleasure. Some people reinvent what being gay might mean. Thank you Derek.' In Derek's favourite Soho café, the Maison Bertaux, a little shrine has been set up for him, with fairy lights and a few already fading newspaper photos. That is what true cultural belonging means.

Notes

1 Derek Jarman, quoted in Simon Watney, 'Derek Jarman: Rewriting history', in *Derek Jarman: Queer*, exhibition catalogue (Manchester: Manchester City Art Galleries, 1992), n. p.

2 Jarman, quoted in Minty Clinch, 'Positive direction', *Observer Magazine*, London, 13 October 1991, p. 63.

15 Numbers and nightmares: HIV/AIDS in Britain*

Lies and lethargies police the world
In its periods of peace. What pain taught
Is soon forgotten

      – W.H. Auden[1]

Introduction

It is September, 1988. 1,500 are already dead, with an estimated 40,000 already infected by the virus. The most common cause of death is pneumonia, brought on by damage to the immune system. Herpes-related conditions are also frequently found amongst those infected. In all of this, the mass media responds with haste, sympathy, and intelligent, well informed enquiry. How is the virus transmitted? How can the epidemic best be slowed down or stopped? What chance is there for effective treatments, or a vaccine? There is a tremendous sense of public concern about the terrible effects of the virus, and the press is full of heart-rending stories. Throughout the UK media there is a strong sense of sadness and of loss. Meanwhile the government refuses to make funds available for new research, though junior minister Virginia Bottomley is pictured on the front page of one newspaper – at the London Zoo.[2] For no, this is *not* a story about HIV and AIDS in Britain, but about the fate of seals in the North Sea.

British responses to HIV/AIDS and to the seal virus could hardly differ more significantly. There has been little informed debate in the UK about either HIV education and prevention strategies, or the funding and direction of medical research. Indeed, there has been little media concern on behalf of those infected by HIV, compared to our furry, aquatic animal friends. Above a headline demanding 'Save Our Seals' the *Daily Mail* insists that: 'We have made possible a virus destroying a whole species. It is our duty to find the antidote. And there is almost no time'.[3] According to the *News of the World*, seals 'are highly intelligent mammals and show many human characteristics. They have a sense of humour, pair for life and grieve for missing mates and

* First published in Emma Healey and Angela Mason (Eds) Stonewall 25: The Making of the Lesbian and Gay Community in Britain, *London: Virago Press, 1994.*

friends'.[4] Neither newspaper has ever been so understanding of or generous to gay men in Britain, who continue to experience the most devastating medical disaster to have affected any single social constituency in Britain this century. Most noticeable is any sense of the HIV epidemic as a *tragedy* in Britain. Rather, it continues to be the pretext for almost any amount of prejudice, scapegoating, and even celebration, and this is closely related to the fact that over 75 per cent of deaths from AIDS have been amongst gay and bisexual men. Indeed, even in 1993 it is possible for newspapers including the *Sunday Times* and the *Sunday Express* to deny that there is an AIDS epidemic of any significance whatsoever in the UK, with constantly repeated calls to cut HIV/AIDS funding and research altogether, and to concentrate on 'truly' deserving causes such as cot-deaths and cancer. By such spurious analogies are our lives held to count for little or nought.

Numbers

Comparison of the figures of HIV and AIDS cases in Europe demonstrates how the epidemic is shaped by varying local factors. For example, in the north of Europe the epidemic has overwhelmingly affected gay and bisexual men, whilst in the south of Europe it has principally affected injecting drug users and their sexual partners. In the middle, France has an epidemic which affects both constituencies more or less equally. Such patterns of infection and illness reflect circumstances prior to the emergence of HIV. Thus in Britain, only 5 per cent of AIDS cases have resulted from the sharing of needles by drug users, compared to some 40 per cent of cases in France. In Britain, drug users have long been treated in a far less punitive fashion than elsewhere in Europe, and consistent with this overall policy the government has since 1986 introduced an extensive national network of needle-exchanges. The effectiveness of this enlightened strategy is immediately apparent in our national HIV and AIDS statistics.

Thus in Scotland, for example, injecting drug users made up no less than 81 per cent of newly reported cases of HIV up to the end of 1985, when testing first became widely available in the UK. By 1990 this had fallen to 40 per cent, and by 1992 to only 19 per cent. This involved a fall in annual numbers from 209 in 1986 to only 24 by 1992. By contrast, the proportion of newly reported cases of HIV amongst gay and bisexual men *rose* in the same period in Scotland from 23 per cent in 1986, to 42 per cent by 1990, with a slight fall to 38 per cent by 1992. These figures in turn reflect the comparative neglect of the needs of Scottish gay and bisexual men. It is also instructive to compare them to the overall UK statistics over the same period, which show a steady *decline* in the percentage of cases of HIV resulting from unprotected sex between men, from 93 per cent in 1985, to 69 per cent in 1990, and 62 per cent by 1992.[5]

In Britain as elsewhere it is thus important to note that we are not in fact experiencing a single epidemic which has different faces; rather, we have a series of relatively distinct epidemics of HIV running side by side, according to differing routes of HIV transmission, and differing degrees of committment to demonstrably effective HIV education and prevention work. In the UK 73 per cent of HIV cases have been amongst gay or bisexual men, cumulatively since the beginning of the epidemic, a total of 11,330. A further 15 per cent of AIDS cases have resulted from unprotected heterosexual intercourse, a total of 1,269; a further 11 per cent of cases resulted from injecting drugs use, and less than 1 per cent of cases have resulted from horizontal transmission from mother to baby, a total of 143. It is important to look at the actual figures, since they can frequently be distorted. Thus 50 cases of AIDS resulting from heterosexual transmission in one year would signify a very large percentage increase in such cases. Unfortunately in Britain there is an overwhelming emphasis on the significance of such percentage increases in HIV/AIDS cases resulting from heterosexual transmission, which are few in number, and almost no attention is paid to the vastly greater numbers of gay men diagnosed annually and amounting to several thousand cases each year.

For several years it has been widely perceived that the epidemic had, as it were, 'moved on' from gay men, into other groups. Nothing could be further from the truth. The slow epidemic of HIV amongst heterosexuals, however, is almost invariably paid all the attention, as if the goal of preventing a serious epidemic amongst heterosexuals had been established at the cost of any serious attention being paid to the plight of gay and bisexual men, who continue to make up over 60 per cent of all newly reported HIV cases annually, a total of 1,577 cases in 1991, and 1,443 in 1992. We need to understand such statistics, because they provide the raw materials on the basis of which rational policies and resourcing may be established. HIV figures provide the data necessary for developing targeted education, and to trace the possible geographical or racial changes in the course of the various epidemics. Happily there is no evidence of a disproportionate impact of HIV/AIDS amongst black and Asian communities, except in the area of paediatrics. The non-white population of the UK is 5.5 per cent of the total population, whilst black paediatric cases account for more than 50 per cent of all UK paediatric AIDS cases. This clearly shows that African mothers resident in the UK have been at greater risk from HIV than other British women. AIDS statistics in turn enable the planning and budgeting for hospital beds, treatment drugs, community care services, and so on.

Approximately three-quarters of all British HIV and AIDS cases have been in London, which reflects the special role that the city plays for British gay men, especially in a period of escalating legal moralism, and publicly acceptable homophobia. Unfortunately the government has never responded realistically to the actual, demonstrable HIV/AIDS situation in Britain. Thus to date only 1.5 per cent of the Department of Health's 'ring-fenced' AIDS budget has gone to the voluntary sector, which all along has provided most basic services to people with HIV and AIDS, from legal and housing advice, to buddying and hospice care. Only a tiny fraction of this overall budget has ever been available for targeted HIV prevention work for gay men. Hence the extraordinary paradox, that whilst the government has indeed spent many tens of millions of pounds on so-called 'HIV education' provided by its lapdog Health Education Authority and other agencies, state funding has *never* been available to support any kind of demonstrably effective, community-based Safer Sex education for gay and bisexual men, who continue to make up two-thirds of *all* new cases of HIV annually!

We were at least fortunate in Britain in the extent that before the advent of HIV we already had a fairly developed gay culture in Britain, with its own press, information services, clubs, bars, cafés, and so on. This culture moreover was largely united across party-political lines in opposition to flagrant police discrimination, everyday homophobic violence and abuse, and discriminatory legislation such as the age of consent laws. The British gay movement also benefited greatly from its close contacts with the American lesbian and gay movement, which was able to draw upon a far more developed notion of citizenship, and citizens' rights, than anything available in Britain. Paradoxically, the vulgar prejudice embodied in Section 28, and the increasing levels of anti-gay hysteria in the press have served, if anything, only to pull increasing numbers of lesbians and gay men together, and to *increase* our self-confidence, and our organizational and communication skills. Organizations such as Scottish AIDS Monitor, the Terrence Higgins Trust, Body Positive, London Lighthouse, the National AIDS Manual, and others have all to a greater or lesser extent stood in a line of direct descent from the complex world of lesbian and gay identity politics as it existed before the epidemic. The tenacity and courage of these and other such institutions doubtless explain why, together with the introduction of needle-exchanges, we in Britain have fortunately suffered less than most other European countries. For example, the rate of AIDS cases per million of the overall UK population was 21.9 in 1992, compared to rates of 73 in France, 89.9 in Spain, and 65.7 in Italy.[6]

Nightmares

In a reasonable world, national and local HIV/AIDS policies would be closely based on the most recent, reliable statistics. Sadly in Britain this has never been the case, and unlike other European countries, we lack a national strategy of any kind. The UK response to HIV/AIDS has thus been essentially *ad hoc*, with large sums of money being squandered on largely cosmetic exercises, whilst areas of fundamental need such as gay men's health education are left to a handful of hard-pressed charities, which have long been subject to regular political and press criticism for undertaking *any* kind of safer sex work which acknowledges and moreover respects gay men's various emotional and sexual needs. As we enter 1994, we face a large number of potential nightmares, in relation to almost all aspects of the epidemic, from standards of journalism in the national daily newspapers, to funding, and treatment issues. For the purpose of brevity I will restrict my analysis to those factors which predominantly affect gay men.

The false consensus

One of the most remarkable features of the UK HIV/AIDS epidemics is the scale of disagreement about their size and significance. In the early 1980s the British newspaper industry geatly exaggerated the risk of HIV infection to heterosexuals. At the same time they virtually ignored the vastly disproportionate impact of HIV and AIDS amongst gay men. The government's national intervention at the end of 1986 was both belated and inappropriate. Subsequently, however, the government was unfairly criticized for responding to HIV/AIDS *at all* by those who wish to minimize the significance of the epidemic, or who have special agendas. Indeed, it is a commonplace of UK AIDS commentary from the *Daily Telegraph* to the *Daily Express* that 'too much' is being spent on AIDS. This assertion usually divides total HIV/AIDS related spending simply by the total number of AIDS cases, disregarding HIV statistics, and refusing to recognize the need for adequately funded prevention work, epidemiology, medical and social science research, and so on.

The consensus view in 1993 is well represented by Claire Baron, Research and Liaison Officer for the British All-Party Parliamentary Group on AIDS, in a recent Conference Report concerning HIV/AIDS in Europe as a whole. Thus, according to Dr Baron, 'the epidemic in Britain, in the early stages at least, affected mainly the homosexual community which already had an articulate and educated subculture to draw on'.[7] I take this to be representative of a significant proportion of official British policy-makers, in both the statutory and the voluntary sectors. It is of course almost entirely wrong and misleading, implying that in some subsequent stage of the British epidemic gay and bisexual men have somehow ceased to make up the majority of cases. Yet it is transparently clear from available HIV statistics that gay and bisexual men will continue for the foreseeable future to make up the great majority of AIDS cases, and will remain at far greater potential risk from HIV than heterosexuals.

It is almost as if the government and state-funded agencies prefer to talk about the epidemic as it will probably be in thirty years' time, rather than as it is today in the 1990s. Furthermore, it would be most unwise to assume that all gay men have some magical access to reliable, up-to-date information about HIV/AIDS. In fact, of course, most gay men read the same newspapers and watch the same TV programmes as everybody else. I have already flagged the significance of such institutions as London's Lesbian and Gay Switchboard in training volunteers and thus providing a model for emergent AIDS service organizations in the early 1980s. In reality, the so-called 'gay community' is as complex and diverse as any other arbitrary cross-section of the UK population. Indeed, one major task undertaken by community-based Safer Sex campaigns has been precisely to try to establish HIV as an issue of *collective* interest to all gay men, regardless of our known or perceived HIV status. This is especially important since most state-funded 'official' HIV/AIDS education tends to present HIV very much as a risk faced by isolated individuals, who are exhorted to renounce promiscuity, to 'choose carefully', and so on. In effect they amount to little more than moral management, and seem almost unrelated to the major, demonstrable routes of HIV transmission in the UK. Hence the danger of a liberal consensus which operates its own homophobic agenda by denying the epidemiological reality of the epidemic in order to ignore gay men's entitlements, which should be an absolute priority given the established patterns of HIV and AIDS in Britain, where in some place one in every four gay men taking the HIV test finds he is already infected.[8]

This is what is meant by the 'de-gaying' of AIDS, namely, the denial of the massive impact of HIV/AIDS in our everyday lives, and the deliberate 'normalization' of the epidemic by many institutions, including leading AIDS charities, which prefer to support the government fantasy that HIV is some kind of 'equal opportunities' infection, rather than a disaster that on the contrary has very distinct profiles. It should, for example, be remembered that the Terrence Higgins Trust was unwilling or unable to employ a single worker responsible for gay men's HIV/AIDS prevention education until 1990, and this post could not be funded by government money! As Edward King has succinctly pointed out:

> 'By all means report that heterosexuals can and do become infected with HIV. But is it too much to ask that some sense of perspective is maintained between the hysterical extremes of those who believe that "everyone is equally at risk" and those who believe that "straight sex is safe"? Gay and bisexual men are far more at risk from HIV than anyone else, now and for the foreseeable future. It is only right and proper that this indisputable fact should be taken into account by those who allocate scarce education resources, and by those who aim to record the reality of the epidemic in Britain today.'[9]

It is therefore literally nightmarish to consider the underlying implications of the Health Minister Virginia Bottomley's decision in the summer of 1993 to *abolish* the specialist AIDS Unit at the Department of Health. The AIDS Unit had previously monitored all aspects of the UK epidemic, and directed policies which, however inadequately, at least recognized the gravity of the epidemic, and the full significance of a virus which on average takes some nine years to become symptomatic as AIDS. The moral seems to be, if you don't like the statistics you are receiving, sack the statisticians, and the problem will go away. 'The problem', however, is nothing less than the lives and potentially avoidable deaths of gay men throughout Britain. Not one British newspaper even bothered to report Mrs Bottomley's lamentble decision.

Treatment Issues

Throughout the entire history of the epidemic, British medical reporting in the press has been woefully inadequate, largely because we have no tradition in Britain of specialist critical medical correspondents. For example, the *Guardian*'s main AIDS writer was previously a Sports writer for the tabloid *Today*. Most HIV/AIDS medical reporting amounts to little more than the publishing of Health Department presses releases. At the same time, unethical stories of 'miracle cures' continue to proliferate, together with the equally unethical reporting of clinical trials and other studies in the earliest stages of development, prior to any clear evidence of either harms or benefits. The early reporting of AZT was a case in point, when greatly exaggerated claims for benefit as a so-called 'early intervention' were widely published, throughout the national and gay media. Raising expectations of effective anti-HIV treatments is particularly cruel, especially when such expectations are subsequently seen to have been largely illusory.

It should be remembered that the first decade of the epidemic in Britain was predominantly an epidemic of asymptomatic HIV, rather than AIDS. Until recently, comparatively few gay men have had much direct experience of hospitalization, acute illness, and death, as in countries such as the USA, whose epidemics are running several years ahead of ours. Set up to provide caring services, and to some extent to do HIV education, the leading charities have never been much concerned or directly involved with matters of biomedical research. Hence the emergence of the National AIDS Manual, in 1989, which aimed to place an equal emphasis on both education and medicine, as well as the provision of other services. And more recently, *AIDS Treatment Update* has emerged, again in the voluntary sector, as a regular monthly publication scanning the scientific literature critically and also accessibly.[10]

Whilst life expectancy for people with AIDS has steadily improved, it seems that a plateau has now been reached. Most AIDS symptoms can now be temporarily treated, and many prevented or delayed. But for the time being the underlying problems of precisely how HIV leads to such a bewildering pattern of illnesses is not well understood, or preventable. Yet for several years the *Daily Telegraph* and others have actively campaigned *against* any further medical research, precisely on the grounds that 'AIDS remains tightly confined to members of high-risk groups, such as male homosexuals and drug addicts'.[11] This is why it is vital to insist that we are not involved in any kind of 'special pleading' on behalf of gay men, but only recognizing an epidemiological reality which has terrible and tragic human consequences. Clearly, however, many influential figures in Britain side effectively *with* HIV, and seem more than happy to sit back and gloat over the prospect of appalling suffering and death. In the meantime most basic research is conducted by commercial pharmaceutical companies, working closely in association with the Medical Reseearch Council, and British university research departments. Whilst we cannot conjure up effective treatments by *fiat*, it is distressing that so few people are in any way familiar with the ongoing state of UK medical research.

It is therefore hardly surprising that most people with HIV or AIDS also turn to complementary and holistic medicine, and the relations between holism and more conventional medical treatments will continue to be a site of potential friction and conflict, not least because of the interventions of those who wish to fancifully deny any clinical association whatsoever between HIV and AIDS, preferring to see AIDS as a magical outcome of 'promiscuity', 'excessive' recreational drug use, and so on.[12] It is therefore of vital importance that people living with HIV and AIDS have access to the widest range of information about potentially therapeutic options open to them, and that professional boundery disputes respect the full range of genuine alternatives. We urgently need to sustain a sensible centre-ground between the extremes of those who would seek to deny any useful role to holistic medicine, and those who similarly seek to deny any role whatsoever to what they caricature as 'Western medicine'. Certainly we do not know enough about varying standards of care and service provision available to people with HIV and AIDS from hospitals and clinics around the country. News of the axing of one of London's training units bodes very ill for the future course of the medical management of the epidemic.[13] At the same time, however, it is important not to become overly fatalistic, and to note that 12 per cent of a group of 562 men in San Francisco infected by HIV at least ten years ago still have T-cell counts above 500, whilst 31 per cent of the group have not developed AIDS ten years after infection.

Funding and resources

Central government provides funds for all types of HIV/AIDS-related work in the statutory sector. This money is distributed locally by the seventeen Regional Health Authorities which in turn fund direct services in the many local District Health Authorities. HIV/AIDS funds have been 'ring-fenced' by the Department of Health, and the government claims that in 1993, £250 million pounds was spent on the epidemic. Yet as long ago as October 1991, an official Report on HIV and AIDS Related Services by the Comptroller and Auditor General, revealed that millions of pounds of supposedly protected 'ring-fenced' funds intended for HIV/AIDS work were being unspent or diverted to other purposes by Regional Health Authorities around the country. The likely ending of 'ring-fencing' in 1994 will thus only serve to make a difficult situation worse. As the voluntary sector becomes increasingly caught up in the business of 'selling' its services in the new marketplace of UK health care, charities will increasingly be forced to compete as potential 'providers'. It is, moreover, far from clear whether or not District Health Authorities will be prepared to support necessary education work for gay men which might prove 'controversial' for example to homophobic local newspapers and politicians.

A rational policy would be based, as I have argued, on easily available HIV/AIDS statistics, on the basis of which local and national needs can be calculated in the short, mid and long term. As we move into a full-scale AIDS epidemic from an HIV epidemic, it is especially important that necessarily scarce resources should be spent prudently, and not wasted. Future suffering can be avoided only by demanding adequate and properly targeted funding now. As things stand, few if any AIDS service organizations could survive without charitable funding.

Yet recent changes in government policy suggest that it is intended that instead of topping up state funding, charities should henceforth provide the basic core funding for HIV/AIDS work, to be supplemented by the state. In a nutshell, the epidemic is being privatized by stealth. Fund-raisers thus have a special responsibility not to collude with the wider process of undermining the basic principles on which the National Health Service is based. The government speaks occasionally of the need to target resources, but its own actions belie it, since it was precisely charities such as the Terrence Higgins Trust which until recently have attempted to provide HIV education for gay men, that have had severe cuts in funding. In a world where resources are always limited, we surely have an ethical responsibility to fund adequately on the basis of demonstrable needs? This is sadly nowhere reflected in British public HIV/AIDS funding policy or practice.

Gay politics and gay identity

By November 1993, there had been 5,250 deaths from AIDS in Britain. Of these, 317 were women, and 51 were infants. No less than 3,993 were gay or bisexual men.[14] HIV and AIDS have had many unpredictable consequences within British lesbian and gay life, ranging from the impressive and widespread involvement of individuals as volunteers in a host of ways, to deeply personal responses to loss and stress. The great challenge has been to articulate HIV/AIDS persuasively to the principal agenda which *preceded* the epidemic in the domain of British lesbian and gay politics and culture. This has been something of an uphill struggle, since the epidemic was evidently regarded by many as a rather inconvenient distraction from the 'higher goals' of law reform on such matters as the age of consent. Only now in the nineties is it widely recognized that such discriminatory legislation has an immediate, harmful impact in relation to the epidemic, by making it extremely difficult to produce or distribute supportive safer sex education materials and information to gay teenagers, at the beginning of their sexual careers.[15]

In reality, safer sex is not simply a 'behaviour' that is 'learned' in one go, and from which one may 'relapse'. On the contrary, safer sex is above all a *process* requiring constant reinforcement, not least because few younger gay men have had any direct experience to date of acute illness and death. For many gay and bisexual men, the UK epidemic remains largely theoretical, rather than an everyday reality. Hence the unique importance of gay culture,

from theatre and film, to TV, the gay press, and of course the whole commercial 'gay scene'. Unlike other countries, most British gay bars are owned
not by gay men, but by the major commercial breweries. Moreover, many
pub and club managers have not been prepared to provide leaflets or
condoms, for fear of somehow driving their clientele away! In such complicated and contradictory circumstances, it is especially important that gay
politics is able to take on board the *realities* of the epidemic, and to relate
these to previous political demands and campaigns. There is a real danger
that if this is not done successfully, HIV/AIDS will come to be regarded as
merely an issue for 'a minority within a minority', and the implications for
all gay men may not be recognized. It is especially important that we do not
casually drift into what might amount to little less than an HIV-related
apartheid system, with HIV/AIDS only seen as issues for the sick, from
whom everyone else must 'protect' themselves. This is why it is vital that, in
Keith Alcorn's words, we continue to fight the real epidemic rather than the
phantom one. As he points out:

> The whole UK debate continues to be dominated by a phantom – a
> heterosexual epidemic running out of control – which is summoned up
> whenever anyone questions the established wisdom. It dominates the
> debate to such an extent that epidemiologists find it impossible to
> acknowledge the importance of targetting gay men except as a means of
> preventing a heterosexual epidemic. AIDS organisations believe they are
> more likely to be judged useful if they continue to prevent this phantom
> epidemic, rather than effectively preventing the real one … In these cir-
> cumstances, it is hardly surprising that many gay men might find it easy
> to accept the belief that we are not alone in this disaster, that a similar
> fare awaits the heterosexual population which has shunned, mocked or
> ignored this slow motion tragedy, now speeding up. This is a mistaken
> belief. We are almost as alone as we were in 1983.[16]

As we move further into the nineties, it is crucial that organizations claiming to represent lesbians and/or gay men recognize the need to contest homophobic accounts of the epidemic, whether in newspapers, or the policies of
Health Authorities or charities. For example, it should be plainly apparent
that supposedly 'educational' materials for young people which do not
acknowledge that gay teenagers are potentially at vastly greater risk from
HIV than their heterosexual peers, are wholly unacceptable. For HIV/AIDS
is never only a medical or social issue. Always there is a political dimension,
since so much bad research, bad reporting and bad policy-making is rooted
in homophobic attitudes which are not necessarily explicitly stated, but
which remain all the more dangerous for remaining latent but none the less
harmful in their practical consequences.[17] In conclusion, as long as the leading political and cultural institutions of British public life continue either to
sensationalize or to trivialize the enormity of the impact of HIV in our lives,

the epidemic will effectively be allowed (and tacitly encouraged) to continue and worsen. At this point in time, a gay politics which cannot articulate the epidemic politically, in relation to other ongoing issues of concerns, is tacitly colluding with those who fatalistically regard AIDS amongst gay men as an inevitability. Nothing could be further from the truth. We can stop this epidemic, but we can only do so as a result of co-ordinated collective effort. A gay politics which fails to recognize the urgency and priority of this need has effectively forfeited any claims to the allegiances of the constituency it reports to represent. The seals of the North Sea had much better friends and allies than we do.

Notes

1 W.H. Auden, 'The Age of Anxiety', *Collected Longer Poems* (London: Faber and Faber, 1988), p. 268.
2 Nicholas Schoon, 'No new money for research into seal virus', *Independent*, London, Friday 2 September 1988, p. 3.
3 *Daily Mail*, London, Wednesday 24 August 1988, p. 1.
4 Brendan Bourne, '20 deadly truths in the battle to save our seals', *News of the World*, 28 August 1988, p. 8.
5 All statistics in this section are taken from the *AIDS/HIV Quarterly Surveillance Tables*, No. 19, March 1993, Public Health Laboratory Service AIDS Centre, and the Communicable Diseases (Scotland) Unit. Unfortunately these detailed statistics are restricted to a very limited number of public institutions, and are not available, for example, to charities or other AIDS service organizations in the voluntary sector, a typical example of British secrecy combined with sheer stupidity.
6 These statistics are taken from *AIDS Surveillance in Europe*, Quarterly Report No. 37, 31 March 1993, WHO–EC Collaborating Centre on AIDS, Saint-Maurice, France.
7 Dr Claire Baron, 'Introduction: The voluntary sector: Prevention, care and political pressure', in *Report of the 1993 Conference of European Community Parliamentarians on HIV/AIDS* (London: British All-Party Parliamentary Group on AIDS, 1993), p. 43. It is worth pointing out that not one single out gay expert on gay men's HIV education was invited to speak at, or attend, this conference. Thus the entire Euopean experience of NGO work was effectively ignored and silenced. This is sadly wholly typical of such conferences.
8 See Edward King, *Safety in Numbers: Safer Sex and Gay Men* (London: Cassell, 1993) for the most detailed available analysis of British and international HIV and AIDS statistics since the beginning of the epidemic. It is a book without peer in the UK literature on HIV/AIDS.
9 Edward King, 'Predicting an epidemic of heterosexual AIDS', *Independent*, London, 22 May 1993.
10 *AIDS Treatment Update* is published monthly by NAM Charitable Trust, Unit 52, The Eurolink Centre, 49 Effra Road, London SW2 1BZ.
11 Jenny Rees, 'Cut AIDS research urges economist', *Daily Telegraph*, London, 14 July 1991.
12 See Simon Watney, 'Hard won credibility', *Gay Times*, London, October 1993, pp. 22–3; also Keith Alcorn, 'What is the *Sunday Times* up to?', *Capital Gay*, No. 625, 17 December 1993, p. 11.
13 Simon Edge, 'HIV training unit axed' *Capital Gay*, No. 625, 17 December 1993, p. 1.

14 *Monthly AIDS Figures*, 22 November 1993, Public Health Laboratory Service.

15 See Edward King, *Safety in Numbers*, chapter 4.

16 Keith Alcorn, 'Fighting the real epidemic not the phantom one', *Capital Gay*, London, No. 595, 21 May 1993, p. 14.

17 See *Le Journal du Sida*, Special Issue, August 1992, *The AIDS Epidemic In Great Britain* (Paris: Arcat/Sida), available from the National AIDS Trust, London. For a further understanding of European HIV/AIDS policies, see Hans Moerkerk and Peter Aggleton, 'AIDS prevention strategies in Europe: A comparison and critical analysis', in P. Aggleton *et al.* (Eds.) *AIDS: Individual, Cultural and Policy Dimensions* (London: Falmer Press, 1990), pp. 181–91.

16 Art from the pit: some reflections on monuments, memory and AIDS*

In Britain as in the rest of Northern Europe, Australia, Canada and elsewhere in the developed world, HIV has had a vastly disproportionate impact upon gay and bisexual men compared to its effects on other social constituencies. One of the greatest challenges to the development of effective HIV/AIDS education, care and service provision stems from the fact that throughout the developed world powerful lobby groups – including churches, politicians, newspapers and others – continue to refuse to accept that gay men constitute a valid social constituency. Rather, we are frequently regarded simply as voluntary perverts, who have somehow 'chosen' our sexual orientation and, by extension, are thought to have 'chosen' to be vulnerable to HIV. Writing in the *Daily Telegraph*, Chaim Bermant epitomizes widely held opinion:

> When I first heard of them they were known as bum-boys. Then it was nancy-boys, and pansies and fairies, and fruits and fags and faggots and poofs and poofters and queers and gays. Gays was the name they eventually chose. Now they are reverting to queers, but given their disposition should they not be calling themselves kamikazes? I ask the question in all seriousness, for they not only seem to have a death-wish themselves, but an apparent readiness to inflict death on others.[1]

When British gay filmmaker Derek Jarman died from AIDS earlier this year (1994) two British tabloid newspapers went to the extraordinary lengths of printing 'counter obituaries', belittling the man and his work at considerable length, whilst Liz Hodgkinson writing in the weekly *Spectator* concluded:

> Healthy he would have been largely ignored, or rightly condemned as a man who knowingly had sexual relations with complete strangers, even after he contracted the AIDS virus.[2]

However warped they may be, such judgements are profoundly instructive if we are seeking to understand the ways in which HIV/AIDS have been

* First published in Tedd Gott (Ed) Don't Leave Me This Way: Art in the Age of AIDS, Melbourne: Thames & Hudson, 1994.

managed (and mismanaged) in different parts of the world. For example, it is clear that for Chaim Bermant, HIV is regarded as a voluntary condition, and gay men with HIV are automatically thought of as deliberate murderers. This is echoed by Liz Hodgkinson's evident inability to distinguish between safe and unsafe sex. As far as both are concerned, it is gay sex as such that is deadly, before and independent of HIV. This pathological hostility towards gay men is frequently projected onto us in such a way that the catastrophic effects of the epidemic are rationalized as if they were natural, inevitable and unavoidable. As I have observed elsewhere:

> This epidemic is unique in so far as its prevention has been prevented, rather than transmission. Resources and education campaigns have been remorselessly targeted at those at least risk of contracting HIV, as if the priority of preventing an epidemic amongst heterosexuals had been established at the expense of halting the epidemics that are actually raging throughout the developed world.[3]

Before the AIDS crisis, few gay men could expect to have much direct experience of death before the age of retirement. Older relatives died, and there were always the shocking, unexpected accidents of disease and chance. Now all that has changed in ways that are still frequently hard to acknowledge or make sense of. My address book already contains forty-two names of friends and colleagues who have died from AIDS, not including more casual acquaintances. Seven gay men I knew died from AIDS between February and July 1994, ranging from close, lifelong friends, to people who nonetheless make up the ordinary, taken-for-granted fabric of our social lives.

Friends with whom you shared a few precious, intense months, or years; friends you slept with two or three times and continued to see regularly in the bars and clubs, reassuringly; friends who helped you make sense of the world, and enlarged it for you; friends of friends, and so on. Some have lost more this year, some less.

In the early years of the epidemic many of us read accounts by American gay men about the scale of loss in their personal lives. Such accounts often seemed almost embarrassing, because they were seemingly exaggerated, and at the same time lacking in affectivity – the deaths were described flatly, almost without an emotional response. Indeed, I well remember running into a well known gay activist in a clothes shop on Christopher Street in New York in the late 1980s. He poured out the story of how he'd set out to go to the funeral of an ex-lover, but instead had gone shopping, unable to face yet another funeral. 'You haven't lived', he explained, 'until you get used to *not* going to your best friends' funerals.' Five years later I understand his words and actions only too well. Writing now in the summer of 1994 in London, where the epidemic is running approximately five years behind the time-scale of mass infection and rate of disease progression in the US, I also understand something of the inner conflicts he must have been experiencing. There are only so many funerals one can attend in a month.

Many of us are now experiencing what amounts to a tidal wave of death, as increasing numbers of those infected in the early years of the epidemic reach the end of the line. We remember 'early' deaths before the mid-1980s, rare, unusual, and terrible for that reason. We also remember the gradual acceleration of deaths, as names disappear from memory, because there are simply too many to recall with the clarity of memory they properly deserve.

Sometimes deaths come in such dense clusters that individual deaths can be easily forgotten, and survivors often feel themselves unreal because we've not had time to mourn equally for everyone we've known and loved who has died. Sometimes the death of a comparative stranger takes on an intensity which stands, as it were, for many others we knew and loved better. One's whole social and emotional sense of the world is transformed. For example, there is only one gay man left who knew me in New York in my twenties and early thirties, and I am far from unusual in such grim experience.

All around the world gay men are living through increasingly routinized, regular processes of the sickness, dying and death of friends, regardless of our own known or perceived HIV status. And whatever films such as *Philadelphia* may suggest, few biological families in reality respond well to the needs of gay men with AIDS. In such circumstances, the task of memorializing the dead takes on a very particular significance. Sociologists who study patterns of death and mourning talk of 'family time' as a social process of care and support in relation to the entire process of dying.[4] Yet for many (if not most) gay men who have been rejected by their families, such a luxury has never been available. Rather, we might think of the time of friendship, and gay community values, which may sustain us in ways parallel to those taken for granted by heterosexuals, for whom death generally involves direct next-of-kin. As the American writer Cookie Mueller, who died of AIDS in 1989, wrote in her last letter of friends of hers who had already died:

> These were the kind of people who lifted the quality of all our lives, their war was against ignorance, the bankruptcy of beauty and the truancy of culture. They were people who scorned pettiness, intolerance, bigotry, mediocrity, ugliness and spiritual myopia; the blindness that makes life hollow was unacceptable. They tried to make us see.[5]

Thus the questions of seeing and remembering take on a very special significance in relation to AIDS, since so many of those who have died were in any case largely invisible in their lives from the perspective of mainstream, heterosexual society. Furthermore, when so much information about people living with AIDS is obscured or distorted by journalists, priests, teachers and others, it is especially important that we who survive should be able to express something of the complex truth of the lives of those no longer here to speak for themselves. As Timothy Murphy has observed in a fine and thoughtful article:

The grief of the epidemic and the incentive to memorialise are no mere biological reflexes – they are an assertion against the levelling effect of death that persons are not replaceable, that death does not nullify presence. They can also be important, if less commonly used, vehicles of moral wisdom and social criticism.[6]

In order to comprehend the *cultural* impact of AIDS it is necessary to be catholic and inclusive. In the first decade of the epidemic much activist art was produced with a clear sense of its communicative aims and objectives, much of which continues to stand the test of time. Yet in retrospect it seems to me that a wholly understandable early emphasis on collective political action and personal heroism functioned at least in part to displace deeper anxieties and uncertainties. That is why it is always important to periodize art produced in response to AIDS, and to specify its local context, as Jan Zita Grover has pointed out.[7] We should also strive to understand the institutional and ideological dimension involved in all cultural responses to the epidemic. For example, in her exemplary analysis of the role played by American charities in stimulating AIDS-associated works of art, whether for display or for auction, Kristen Engberg has noted the emergence of a clear strategy for:

> mainstreaming AIDS fundraising efforts … Framing AIDS as simply a tragic disease to be cured while ignoring the more political aspects of the AIDS movement narrows the focus of concern to the physical body and the laboratory and renders a highly complex epic struggle wholly abstract. Everyone can be 'against AIDS' in the same way that everyone is 'for peace' … ignoring the superstructure of neglect and legalised oppression (affecting class, race and sex relations) which has made AIDS a social and political crisis.[8]

At an opposite extreme, some contemporary artists regard all forms of public memorial art as intrinsically didactic and dogmatic, and have thus aimed to produce 'counter-monuments', on the grounds that all art reduces audiences to the role of passive spectatorship.[9] Commenting on Jochen Gerz and Esther Shalev-Gerz's 1986 *Monument Against Fascism* in Harburg, Germany, designed to disappear underground, critic James E. Young asks:

> How better to remember forever a vanished people than by a perpetually unfinished, ever-vanishing monument?[10]

One might, however, equally forcefully ask how an invisible monument is supposed to recall an invisible crime against humanity? One wonders what those who were 'effaced' by the Nazis might think of a 'self-effacing monument'.[11] For the issue here is not so much memory, as *forgetting*, at the level of both the social and the psychic. One is appalled but not entirely surprised to find not a single reference to gay men, or gypsies, in Young's monumental study of public memorials to the Holocaust. This is entirely contiguous with the widespread international tendency to deplore 'the global epidemic' whilst systematically repressing all precise references to those who are most affected. Thus in Britain as elsewhere one frequently finds vague references to the 'tragedy' of children with AIDS, and 'innocent' heterosexual women, but almost never is there the slightest note of sorrow or regret for the 4,291 gay and bisexual men who make up 76 per cent of the total of 5,655 deaths from AIDS in the UK up to the end of 1993. The last thing we need in terms of our various local and national cultural responses to AIDS are the types of pretentiously over-intellectualized justifications for politically correct 'invisible monuments', or equally over-aestheticized 'self-destructing memorials' which in effect merely collude with the very processes of selective historical amnesia that effective memorial art is intended to arrest, or at least delay.

All around the world, millions of ordinary bum-boys, nancy-boys, pansies, fairies, fruits, fags, faggots, queers, poofs, poofters and gay men have contracted HIV, and by and large the leading institutions of national and international health have stood by and said and done precisely nothing on their behalf. They were not rounded up and put into cattle trucks and taken away to death camps, but their need for properly supportive HIV education has been equally systematically ignored in all but a handful of countries. In the meantime the arduous struggle to provide adequate health care, better treatment drugs, proper social services and demonstrably effective community-based health education continues amongst the (largely invisible) carnage. Old political verities count for little in this context, when socialist France has fared even worse than Thatcherite Britain.[12] Certainly there can be no single approach or strategy for representing AIDS adequately or appropriately. To take just one example, sometimes straightforward captioned documentary photography will be necessary, and in other circumstances it will be inappropriate. This is the photographer's decision. We may be sure, however, that the cultural response to AIDS will be as various as its direct experience, ranging from the lives of people living with AIDS to those who have never knowingly set eyes on a person with AIDS.

In the course of the past ten years I have been closely involved in the development of an international cultural response to AIDS – a response that has, at the heart of this terrible crisis, with so much else to be done, nonetheless attempted also to pay heed to the ethical requirement to represent AIDS truthfully. Much bad art has been produced in response to AIDS, art which is every bit as sentimental or sensationalizing or exploitative as the worst that the mass media have been able to offer. In a recent British television discussion about film censorship, right-wing Christian zealot Stephen Green from the Conservative Family Campaign, a 'pro-family' lobbying organization of strongly homophobic disposition, provided a useful definition of how he and his sort think about art. He explained simply: 'Art that is good exalts. Art from The Pit must debase.'[13] I can only hope that our aesthetic responses to the whole subject of AIDS will remain properly and adequately sulphurous.

Notes

1 Chaim Bermant, 'Practising some lethal preachings', *Daily Telegraph*, London, 3 September 1991, n.p.
2 Liz Hodgkinson, 'The joy of illness', *Spectator*, London, 16 April 1994, p. 23.
3 Simon Watney, 'Powers of observation', in *Practices of Freedom: Selected Writings on HIV/AIDS* (London: Rivers Oram Press, 1994), p. 277.
4 See for example, David Clark (Ed.) *The Sociology of Death* (Oxford: Blackwell Publishers/The Sociological Review, 1993).
5 Cookie Mueller, *Walking through Clear Water in a Pool Painted Black* (New York: Semiotext(e), 1990), pp. 147–48.
6 Timothy F. Murphy, 'Testimony', in Timothy F. Murphy and Suzanne Poirier (Eds) *Writing AIDS: Gay Literature, Language and Analysis* (New York: Columbia University Press, 1990), pp. 318–19.
7 Jan Zita Grover, *AIDS: The Artist's Response* (Hoyt L. Sherman Gallery, Ohio State University, 1989), p. 3.
8 Kristen Engberg, 'Art, AIDS and the new altruism: Marketing the (ad)just(ed) cause', *New Art Examiner*, Chicago, Vol. 18, No. 9, May 1991, p. 22.
9 James E. Young, *The Texture of Memory: Holocaust Memorials and Meaning* (New Haven: Yale University Press, 1993), p. 28.
10 *Ibid.*, p. 31.
11 *Ibid.* (illustrated pp. 32–3).
12 See Simon Watney, 'Muddling through: The UK response to AIDS', in *Practices of Freedom: Selected Writings on HIV/AIDS* (London: Rivers Oram Press, 1994) p. 3.
13 *Newsnight*, BBC 2, 12 April 1994.

17 In purgatory: the work of Felix Gonzalez-Torres*

A testimony is something other
than demographics. Neither does
testimony attempt to substitute
words for persons; that would be
mere fetishism. Testimony is witness
in front of an indifferent
world about the worth and merit
of persons.
> – Timothy F. Murphy[1]

Death is insidiously present
behind the most diverse masks,
often silent, sometimes noisy,
but always active along the paths
of existence.
> – J.-B. Pontalis[2]

Introduction: death, age, memory

A recent cartoon in the *New Yorker* by the admirable Roz Chast epitomizes a certain distinct sensibility of the '90s.[3] We are shown a balding man from behind, seated at a table, looking at the obituary page of a newspaper which we also read (as it were) over his shoulder, just as one sneakily regards someone else's newspaper on a subway train or in a crowded café. The dead are provided with summary features, but no names are given. Instead we read only: 'Two Years Younger Than You,' 'Exactly Your Age'; 'Three Years Your Junior'; 'Twelve Years Older Than You'; 'Five Years Your Senior'; and 'Your Age On The Dot.'

European readers of American newspapers are frequently struck by two aspects of their obituaries. First, by the great age to which so many Americans evidently live. Second, by the sheer numbers of AIDS deaths, especially among young men in their thirties and forties. Chast's drawing

* First published in Parkett, *New York and Geneva, no. 39, 1994.*

does not require identifiable faces, since its subject matter is not so much the dead as individuals, but rather death as it is perceived by the living. Indeed, this is precisely how many hundreds of thousands of American gay men start their every day, reminded of their survivor status – so far. The endless routine of sickness, dying and death also ages the survivors prematurely, as entire networks of friends vanish, and with them 'the wealth of accumulated memory, taste, and hard-won practical wisdom they shared'.[4] This is the immediate context that gives specific significance to Felix Gonzalez-Torres's characteristically laconic observation that 'There is a lot of memory involved in my work.'[5]

Memory also has its history, both in the lives of individuals, remembering, and in whole collectivities of memory. Such collective memories will often be in sharp conflict with one another. Indeed, social collectivities are largely constituted by such bodies of accumulating memory. This is how history is lived in social relations. However, memory is never simply transparent. As I have argued elsewhere:

> Psychoanalysis refuses any notion of direct, unmediated vision, since it understands seeing as a constant site of unconscious activity ... We cannot theorise the workings or nature of remembering without at the same time considering the systematic mechanisms of forgetting. Once we begin to think of both seeing and memory as primarily defensive and self-protective operations, saturated with fantasy, then the status of ... imagery is affected rather radically.[6]

Collective memory is also limited by concrete institutions, and the criteria they employ which privilege certain 'angles' of memory, some elements to the exclusion of others, and so on. Moreover, memory is clearly culturally organized in the preferred likeness of those who possess the power to define the past. For the individual, memory thus always involves a degree of intersection between the seemingly irreducible immediacy of recollected experience, and the tug of institutionally sanctioned 'official' memories. Thus each individual death takes place to a greater or lesser extent in the context of a wider culture of dying, in which memory and memorializing play an important function.

Exemplary bodies

British art historian Nigel Llewellyn has described how prior to the Reformation:

> The traditional belief about Purgatory had created a popular image of the afterlife as a place where the souls of the dead might be imagined residing after the decease of their natural bodies, but before the Last Judgment. Purgatory also allowed the living a sense of contact with the dead through prayer ... One of the Reformers' main grievances was

against the whole corrupt practice of indulgences ... Inscriptions on countless monuments which beseeched passers-by to pray for the dead – 'orate pro nobis ...' – encouraged this sense of contact, but such wordings were expressly forbidden by reformist statute. The ending of Purgatory thus caused grievous psychological damage: from that point forward the living were, in effect, distanced from the dead ... to balance the traumatic effect of the loss of Purgatory the Protestant churches gradually developed the theory of memoria, which stressed the didactic potential of the lives and deaths of the virtuous.[7]

As Llewellyn notes: 'Protestant monuments were designed to be read as examples of virtue. In skilful enough hands and given sufficient ambition on the part of the patron, the monumental body could invent for posterity a completely new persona.'[8]

In spite of regional and other variations, the Lutheran theory of memoria underpins the entire subsequent Anglo-American culture of death and memorial art.

There is no social constituency in contemporary Anglo-American society which is more likely to be considered to be without virtue than gay men, a situation which has been greatly aggravated by the advent of AIDS. In this context we may identify a deep, ongoing cultural crisis which co-exists with the AIDS epidemic and its many conflicting narrations. Ever since the medical classification of AIDS in 1981, the bodies of people with AIDS have been used as signifiers in an immensely complex contest concerning the supposed 'meaning' of the epidemic. We may thus detect a significant slippage at work between the field of 'scientific' medical photography, which identifies symptoms, and a wider form of what might be described as moralized seeing, according to which AIDS is a signifier of powerful non-medical meanings. AIDS thus becomes also a crisis of memory. For when the deaths of our loved ones are casually dismissed as 'self-inflicted', it is the most fundamental level of our most intense experience of life and of love that is effectively denied.

Such issues of systematic remembering and forgetting, of memorializing and calumniating gay men who have died from AIDS, are absolutely central to the work of Felix Gonzalez-Torres, now in his mid-thirties, and living at the epicentre of the AIDS crisis. His work is initially distinguished by his refusal to engage in a dualistic cultural politics which strives to counter the widespread demonizing of people with AIDS with an equally over-simplified (if understandable) tendency to heroize them. Rather, he has stepped away from contestation which is directly grounded on the bodies of people with AIDS and their representations. Instead, he has consistently drawn attention to the discursive formations which frame policy and practice in relation to the everyday lives of gay men in the AIDS epidemic. He sets out and reenacts discursive contradictions and conflicts, and all his work to a greater or lesser extent involves situations of tension between rival and conflicting potential meanings. In this respect his work does not offer the closure of meaning that has been widely understood as one marker of 'political art' in the twentieth century. While his work is focused with extraordinary conceptual precision, he is never simply didactic.

Rejecting the whole idea of any single 'truth' that might encompass the social and psychic reality of all gay men within single representations, artists such as Gonzalez-Torres, Robert Gober, Jack Pierson, Tom Kalin, John-Paul Philippe, Michael Jenkins, and others have tended to draw attention to the workings of the various social and psychic mechanisms of displacement, disavowal, and projection which are actively at work in homophobic discourses, and thus also in the larger cultural process which constitutes and maintains individual and collective subjectivities. Such work is thus intended to intervene at a level prior to the self-consciously 'political'. In effect, Gonzalez-Torres returns us to a sense of demarcation between 'politics' and a politics of representation and, in doing so, exposes the workings of homophobic discourse – in symptomatic repetitions, omissions, slippages, metaphors, substitutions, emphases, and so on – rather than opposing a supposedly universal gay 'truth' to what may misleadingly be regarded as homophobic 'lies'.

This is evidently difficult to understand for critics coming from an old Leftist political culture, which is determined to cling to the notion of economic determinism, and which denounces 'consumerism' as stupid and greedy with all the vigour it had previously reserved for those it accused of 'false-consciousness' – the ignorant masses who so routinely fail to line up to justify the messianic pretensions of the Revolutionary Party leadership. In a recent article, British artist and critic Terry Atkinson describes 'those who consume' as 'transfixed by their addiction to keep doing it'.[9] It is almost as if 'producers' and 'consumers' are imagined as distinct tribes, the former 'good' class subjects, the latter wanton hedonists. From such a perspective, all objects (including art objects) are considered primarily as commodities, functioning in a distinct economy and epoch to be known as 'Late-Capital'. Again, from this perspective both 'the audience' and 'the market' are regarded as invariant and monolithic. What is 'good' about 'good' art from this perspective would be precisely its capacity to somehow transform the viewer into a good, productive, socialist subject, rejecting the culture and values of Late-Capital. It would be closely akin to a religious conversion.

For Atkinson, Gonzalez-Torres's candy pieces can only make sense as 'an area where gluttony, a kind of subspecies of Late-Capital, might be the order of the day. Shades of Hieronymus Bosch'.[10] Yet it is hard to imagine how Gonzalez-Torres (or any other artist) is supposed to be 'effective', since according to Atkinson and his ilk: 'The problem with all our critiques of Late-Capital is that in allowing the critique, Late-Capital can feel good about itself.'[11] Late-Capital is thus depicted as an entity that can think for itself, and also feel 'better' (and presumably 'worse'?) about itself. Such a monolithic, totalizing politics can hardly be expected to recognize the bizarre comic absurdity of its own reflections on 'where Late-Capitalism sees itself'. If

Atkinson truly believes that the entire developed world is currently 'suffused with self-congratulation' one can only speculate on which nearby planet he might be living.

Such doubts equally involve his inability to begin to comprehend the historical and cultural circumstances that shape Gonzalez-Torres's project. Thus his spectacularly odd reading of Gonzalez Torres's 1989 *Sheridan Square* installation, just round the corner from the site of the 1969 Stonewall riots which marked the emergence of the modern gay political movement. Placed on a billboard at the entrance to New York's most celebrated gay strip, Christopher Street, the piece substituted for the more familiar image of the Marlborough Man, which had famously occupied the same public space for many years. The piece reads as a low double horizon against an austere black ground: '*People With AIDS Coalition 1985 Police Harassment 1969 Oscar Wilde 1895 Supreme/Court 1986 Harvey Milk 1977 March On Washington 1987 Stonewall Rebellion 1969.*' Atkinson contrasts what he describes as the 'pathos' of this piece, which allegedly 'comes from remembering the gains acquired through a tradition of political culture', to another billboard project which simply shows a recently vacated double-bed with two pillows and a duvet. For Atkinson this is also an image of 'pathos' – 'personally rich and formally bleak'.[12]

It is important to correct such fanciful interpretations, since the Stonewall riots were most decidedly not produced by any known 'traditions of political culture', at least not in the tradition of ultra-leftist party politics espoused by Atkinson *et al.* (On the contrary, Stonewall was a community-based response to immediate police brutality at a community level, and it was led not by Marxists, but by black and Latino drag queens.) Nor is the bed piece an image which can adequately be described (and thus dismissed) as merely 'personal' or 'private'. On the contrary, as Gonzalez-Torres has pointed out:

> Someone's agenda has been enacted to define 'public' and 'private'. We're really talking about private property because there is no private space anymore. Our intimate desires, fantasies, dreams are ruled and intercepted by the public sphere.[13]

Thus the Sheridan Square piece rejects a conventional 'political' roll-call of heroic achievements, and presents history in a far more complex way, out of chronological order, melding different types of events from the murder of gay San Francisco politician Harvey Milk to the formation of community-based organizations in response to HIV/AIDS. History is thus specifically not presented as a seamless progressive narrative, expressing some supposedly unified historical force or will. Rather, events and institutions coexist, as in memory, in no particular order or sequence beyond that of our own active interpretive making. The 'private' defiantly invades 'public' space.

When the *Bed* billboard was exhibited in Glasgow in 1992, similar criticisms were levelled against it, on the grounds that it was not sufficiently 'informational', that it was not sufficiently didactic. Yet what could be more powerful than the sight of a clean beautiful double bed on hoardings in a grimy, wintry industrial city? For beds are where most of us are born, where we most frequently have sex, and where, if we are lucky, we will eventually die. The image of a double bed, whose pillows clearly bear the imprint of the two people who had recently occupied it, carried over the widespread publicity surrounding the exhibition and its subject matter into the public spaces of a typical city. Gonzalez-Torres draws our attention to the sheer comfort of being in bed, and the intense pleasures we associate with bedrooms. Yet, as the *Sheridan Square* poster reminds one, the privacy of the bedroom is also intimately connected to the gender of those who sleep there. Hence the significance of the reference to the notorious (or forgotten) 1986 Supreme Court decision that American gay men have no constitutional right to privacy from direct police interference in their own homes. Moreover, the reference to Harvey Milk will also remind older gay men, and others, that Milk's assassin, Dan White, received only a three-year jail sentence on the grounds that his judgement had been impaired by an excessive intake of Twinkies, a brand of sweetmeat popular with American children. (At the time, 'twinkies' was also a derogatory term for gay men in the United States).

In Britain we refer to candy as 'sweets', and children are sensibly exhorted never to take sweets from strangers. This is just one of the many levels of meaning which operate in relation to Gonzalez-Torres's celebrated candy spills, such as his *'Untitled' (Welcome Back Heroes)* of 1991, a 400-pound stack of red, white and blue wrapped Bazooka gum, 'memorializing' the Gulf War. Other candy pieces include portraits of his boyfriend and himself, and others, in which the candy has the same weight as his subjects. Who can resist candy? Thus the metaphoric associations of his materials permit Gonzalez-Torres to construct works which share what amounts to a formal invitation to the audience to participate by slowly ingesting them, sweet by sweet. Nor should we forget in this context the gradual wasting, and loss of appetite, which is so often and so painfully experienced by people with AIDS.

Such latent implications were most powerfully mobilized in his 1991 *'Untitled' (Placebo)*, which consisted of 1,000–1,200 pounds of silver-foil wrapped candies, laid out like a huge carpet across the floor of the Andrea Rosen Gallery in New York. Like several other pieces, including *'Untitled' (Bloodworks), Placebo* immediately involves us in the cultural field of the medical clinical trials of potential treatment drugs. A placebo is an inert substance, indistinguishable from a pharmaceutical compound in comparison to which the effects of a drug may be measured, after a sample of individuals have agreed to enter a clinical trial in which they do not know whether they are receiving the potentially therapeutic drug, or the placebo. And yet a placebo is never just an inert substance, for it inevitably carries with it a profound supplement of hope. Moreover, as a participant in a clinical trial, one does not know whether or not one is taking a placebo every four or eight hours, sometimes for years on end. Furthermore, the pharmaceutical compound may eventually turn out to be an effective treatment which, by receiving a placebo, one has in effect lost the opportunity to take. On the other hand, the compound may have unintended side-effects, and even do one harm. There is also the more straightforward question of the sheer quantity of such pills one ingests in the course of a clinical trial, or any long-term therapy. There is thus a complex, shifting relationship among Gonzalez-Torres's various candy pieces, which has not been apparent to critics who regard his use of sweets as if they were traditional, fixed iconographic symbols.[14] These are works of art which enact and embody the instability of life, and its extreme unpredictability and transience. There is no false optimism here, no self-deception. Rather, Gonzalez-Torres finds and mobilizes materials which may function as analogues for experience and emotions which are not 'explained' in any extended biographical supplementary exegesis. They are works about love, desire, loss, death, and mourning, and much of their extraordinary power derives from the artist's refusal to retreat into didacticism. They are works which try to take us seriously as spectators, and which encourage us to make as many associative connections as we like in relation to the materials assembled before us, as well as in relation to previous works.[15]

Thus *'Untitled' (Placebo)* also needs to be considered in the context of its exhibition in 1991, when it was installed for five days at the end of a one-month constantly changing show entitled 'Every Week There Is Something Different', which had begun with a display of conventionally framed and displayed photographs of the carved inscriptions that form the backdrop to the Teddy Roosevelt monument outside New York's Museum of Natural History. These elicit Roosevelt's various attributes of public virtue in his roles as 'Statesman', 'Scholar', 'Humanitarian', 'Historian', 'Patriot', 'Ranchman', 'Naturalist', 'Soldier', and so on. In the second stage of the exhibition a powder-blue wooden platform was installed, unlit, in the middle of the room, whilst in the third week the gallery walls had been repainted white, and a line of light bulbs around the top edge of the platform was switched on. Every day a professional male Go-Go dancer arrived and danced for a short period of time to the almost inaudible accompaniment of his Walkman. Three of the original photos were retained on the walls – 'Soldier', 'Humanitarian', and 'Explorer'.

For the Go-Go boy in his shiny silver briefs is indeed all of these things, and more, as the piece implies. Like so many others, he is soldier, on active service, manning his post, in a war zone of homophobia, censorship, anxiety, hatred, fear and loss. He is a humanitarian in his ordinary, unremarked, everyday relation to the epidemic as it affects himself, his friends, and complete strangers, and in his insistence that he is perfectly entitled to his own sexuality, just as anyone else is entitled to theirs: an explorer who has dared to leave home, to set out against all the dreadful pressures of homophobic education and popular culture. He has come out as a gay man, explored his sexuality, and has now stepped courageously into the spotlight of exhibitionism, knowing himself confidently as an object of desire for other men, daring to be shockingly sexy in a world that must go on. And his HIV status? We don't know. Nor is this the issue. Which is precisely the point. Gonzalez-Torres is not providing us with ordinary, political analysis dressed up, as it were, in art-world terms. This appears to be his major crime, to those who expect and require 'good' political art to remain within the broad Lutheran tradition of memorializing the 'exemplary body' of the heroic man – the 'good' class hero, the good 'AIDS victim', and so on. In this 'poetics of AIDS', there is no question of a humanist/expressionist aesthetic rooted in notions of 'sincerity', For many of us, the dead are so intimately coterminous with the living that the direct meaning of both terms is radically upset.

In any case, as Stravinsky pointed out long ago, sincerity is the *sine qua non* that guarantees nothing. Rather, we may consider the great variety of strategies and modes of signification being mobilized in relation to HIV/AIDS, from Gonzalez-Torres's foregrounding of the US health insurance industry in his '*Untitled' (Blue Cross)* stacks from 1990, to the drama of police lines fighting to prevent young men from leaving the remains of their loved ones outside the President's bedroom window. Unsurprisingly perhaps, critical commentary concerning Gonzalez-Torres has overwhelmingly concentrated on his supposed 'appropriation' of Minimalism, and his rewiring of its cultural connotations. Yet how terribly desiccated and precious much seventies Minimalism looks by comparison with his work. What we should notice is the way in which he relays meanings between different works, by means of the formal development of individual elements. Thus the row of light bulbs from '*Untitled' (Go-Go Dance Platform)* from 1991 have now taken on a formal life of their own in numerous subsequent light pieces involving strings of light bulbs, just as the gently chiming curtain of glass beads that gave access to the platform has been reworked with red and transparent beads in a visually and conceptually stunning analogue of red and white blood cells, blood vessels, and medical technology. Thus the light pieces also carry with them, as it were, memories (and forgettings) of their original context and its associations. And all his light pieces, with their poetic connotations of garden parties at night, discos, the Fourth of July, as well as boxing arenas and operating theatres, also carry with them an ever more ghostly shadow of the beautiful Go-Go boy on Prince Street in 1991, proudly and expertly dancing to his favourite Pet Shop Boys remix, and by contingency on the associative field of *Placebo*, which is also a packed dance-floor…

Conclusion: A note on friendship

It would be difficult in the extreme to exaggerate the significance of the impact of HIV in the lives and identities of gay men around the world – the extraordinary uncertainty and complexity and determination to which it leads us as individuals facing a frankly appalling reality. In this respect certainly we are not like other people. In these circumstances we often feel that we owe one anther 'a terrible loyalty', to borrow from Tennyson. Without marriage and its attendant rituals and institutions, gay men's most intimate and important relationships are frequently misunderstood and undervalued by heterosexuals, who simply cannot understand what one is actually saying when one tells them that a 'friend' is sick or a 'friend' has died. When old friends of mine die now I eventually come to picture them quite easily seated on clouds in some heaven designed by Pierre et Gilles, talking, laughing, having sex. This is not denial. We know they're dead. We also know we have to continue to fight on behalf of the living. This is what Felix Gonzalez-Torres's extraordinary work is 'about.' We have rediscovered Purgatory.

Notes

1 Timothy F. Murphy, 'Testimony', in T. F. Murphy and S. Poirer (Eds), *Writing AIDS: Gay Literature, Language and Analysis* (New York: Columbia University Press, 1993), p. 317.
2 J.-B. Pontalis, 'On death-work', *Frontiers in Psychoanalysis: Between the Dream and Psychic Pain* (London: The Hograth Press, 1981), p. 184.
3 *New Yorker*, 25 October 1993, p. 124.
4 Simon Watney, 'Preface: My project', *Practices of Freedom: Selected Writings on HIV/AIDS* (London: Rivers Oram Press, 1994).
5 Robert Nickas, 'Felix Gonzalez-Torres: All the time in the world', *Flash Art*, vol. XXIV, no. 161, Nov. Dec. 1991, p. 86.
6 Simon Watney, 'The image of the body', *Figures* catalogue (Cambridge, England: The Cambridge Darkroom, 1987).
7 Nigel Llewellyn, *The Art of Death: Visual Culture in the English Death Ritual c. 1500–1800* (London: Reaktion Books, 1991), pp. 26–8.
8 *Ibid.*, p. 102.
9 Terry Atkinson, 'Rites of passage', *A & D*, 1/2, Jan./Feb. 1994.
10 *Ibid.*
11 *Ibid.*
12 *Ibid.*
13 Nickas, 'Felix Gonzalez-Torres'.
14 For example, for Anthony Iannacci the candies 'call to mind the ritual of communion, the consumption (of) the body and blood of Christ', and death itself is seen 'as part of a sublime cycle, mirroring the Christian belief in the circularity of Christ's existence and resurrection' (*Artforum*, December 1991, p. 112).
15 In this context we might also consider the ways in which the titles of other pieces by Gonzalez-Torres (such as *'Untitled' [Blue Placebo]*), and the work itself, introduces the metonymous shade of Andy Warhol, and connotations of blue Marilyns, Lizs, Electric Chairs, and so on. This is only to observe that here, as elsewhere, Warhol emerges as the most genuinely enabling of all the great post-War American artists, in relation to Gran Fury as much as to Gonzalez-Torres or Gober.

18 Acts of memory*

A generation now is hanging on for so long
we ask for explanations. Some live
into their thirties! Some, seven years
past diagnosis! Amazing cause for awe.

In one of his last published poems about AIDS, the distinguished Canadian
gay writer Michael Lynch graphically describes how, for many of us, death
has ceased to be an event; it has literally become a way of life, an era of dying
set to last well into the next millennium. Week after week, year after year, it
goes on. In modern times no other single constituency has lost so many as a
result of epidemic illness. Outside of wartime or great famine, mortal illness
and death on this scale is unknown, marking our experience as unique.

Though nothing could have prepared us for this catastrophe, certain clear
patterns of response have emerged across the international diaspora of queer
culture that tell us much about its richness and tenacity. In what has become
a highly creative, constantly changing collective memorial to our dead, we
have combined public and personal grief to put an indelible face on what
society at large has largely chosen to ignore – our gay and lesbian rites and
rituals of mourning.

Today the monuments to our loved ones are everywhere from quilts to personal altars in the picture windows of community shops, to gardens. Our private funerals, though solemn, are also celebrations of achievement and joy, at
which the histories of gay life are told by friends and ex-lovers, and in music
and readings that chronicle the history of our movement. We have also seen
public funerals of protest, where our embalmed heroes are carried aloft: a
refusal, after all, to let silence equal death.

Quieter but equally passionate symbols of our resistance and vigilance are
the ubiquitous red ribbons – the gay equivalent of the WWII black armband
– and the striking tattoos that provide an indelible, personal way of recording
our losses, one that makes it impossible for us – and the world – to ignore or

* First published in Out, New York City, 1994.

forget. AIDS is already as central to gay identity as Stonewall was to those who forged the modern gay movement in the far 1970s.

Yet the past is uniquely woven in with the present. Let me briefly consider the events of the past week in my life as an urban gay man in his early forties. Last Saturday night at Heaven, one of London's leading gay clubs, a black British drag queen introduced a live set from Crystal Waters with an eloquent memorial to US record producer Dan Hartman, who recently died of AIDS. Back in the late 1970s, Hartman had virtually invented the concept of extended remixes, and I easily recalled nights in 1979 when I danced with too many friends who are no longer alive to Hartman's all-time classic, 'Relight My Fire'.

The next day I learned of the death of the boyfriend of a colleague, a brilliant, brave young gay man, only 34 years old. On Wednesday I went to his funeral in a rather dilapidated 1950s crematorium, way out in suburban south London. As the service began, the Pet Shop Boys' 'Go West' came over the speakers, followed by M. People's 'Last Night in Heaven', k.d. lang's 'Wash Me Clean', Marc Almond's 'Meet Me in My Dreams', and Jennifer Holliday's anthemic hymn of loss, 'And I Am Telling You I'm Not Going' – the one we've all seen lip-synched a million times, and every time, it makes us cry.

The music gave us an idea of the kind of guy he had been, someone we liked a lot, cute to the nth degree. Then out we stumbled into the bright spring light to the sounds of The Three Degrees, 'Take Good Care of Yourself'. But the bad news continued unabated, and three days later I had to avoid an old friend's funeral in order to get out-of-doors for a day in the sunshine, then get off my face on Ecstasy, dancing all night, surrounded by thousands of my gay brothers and our friends, each of us travelling similar routes of loss and carnage.

Writing of the various cultural responses to the losses of the First World War, historian David Cannadine distinguished 'official' national public reactions from those that were private, spontaneous, and essentially individualistic. Thus, public war memorials were constructed throughout Europe, together with ceremonies and rituals such as Britain's annual Armistice Sunday each November, when the Queen and leading politicians lead a two-minute silence throughout the country. Similarly, in America, lonely doughboys still stand on public monuments, just as most towns and villages have their well kept public war memorials, often with a small formal garden attached, and a list of the names of the dead, who are honoured for 'giving' or 'laying down' their lives. Such monuments encouraged a local and national mourning process, transforming the dead into national heroes. On a more private level, an international upsurge of spiritualism reflected a countercurrent of private, personal need to come to terms with the enormity of death.

Certain parallels are immediately evident in the AIDS crisis, though the refusal of most governments to acknowledge gay men and lesbians as a legitimate social constituency means that we have nowhere seen sympathetic or supportive 'official' national responses. And all too often, convenient references to the 'global' epidemic obscure the actual sexual, gender, and ethnic profiles of AIDS deaths around the world. Perhaps eventually we will see a form of World AIDS Day that does not suffer from the evasions and spiritual emptiness of most current December 1st activities. Moreover, it seems increasingly unlikely that we will ever witness a complete end to the AIDS epidemic, one that might result in a cultural symbolism equivalent to Armistice Sunday, or Memorial Day in the United States.

The Names Project exemplifies the difficulties we face. Drawing on a tradition of collective, community-based domestic work, the AIDS Quilt is remarkably appropriate to a disaster so often ignored or neglected. The Quilt has been criticized on the grounds that is has ceased to be 'a giant protest sign' and has become a costly distraction from the political realities of the epidemic. Yet this strikes me as somewhat beside the point. All too often AIDS renders people anonymous, mere statistics. The great and enduring wonder of the Quilt lies in its capacity to individualize, to signify something of the kinds of people who have died. The sheer vivacity and cultural richness of our gay communities survives proudly in the exuberance and excess of the quilts, with their vast range of appliquéd objects, ranging from teddy bears to sex toys, taffeta frocks to harnesses. The Quilt also provides a remarkably powerful sense of the scale of the AIDS epidemic, as one moves along the narrow avenues between the great bolts of cloth.

If the whole thing seems overly weighted down with casual New Age religiosity, it is perhaps an understandable response when almost all official religions are deeply and venomously homophobic. Consider the all-too-typical cremation-cum-gay-commemoration I described earlier. Whether in Manchester or Minneapolis, the music is likely to range from Strauss's 'Four Last Songs' to Sylvester or Barbra Streisand, often by way of the Sex Pistols and *Parsifal*. These are deeply moving affairs, especially compared with traditional Western religious ceremonies. Funerals organized for gay men by their basically homophobic relatives, who never accepted them in their lifetime, appear designed to exclude any mention of precisely the qualities we love and will miss in our now departed gay friends. But there is the alternative spectacle of a few huddled, hostile heterosexual family members attending a true gay funeral, at which friends read and speak, many of them, of course, ex-lovers.

Our own ceremonies also provide relief of a very complex kind: that one's friend has ceased suffering, that a surviving partner can now, at last, rest. And there is a shared acknowledgement of the bonds that death has forged among the survivors. It is as if gay culture is able to articulate the value and meanings of our dead friends' lives more successfully, and with far greater emotional honesty and directness, using the raw material of popular culture, than can Western society at large.

The visual arts have also become a process and repository of mourning. Many gay artists and filmmakers have responded to the scale of our loss, from the memorializing paintings of Ross Bleckner and John-Paul Philippe to the luminous, elegiac films of Derek Jarman, Bill Sherwood, Marlon Riggs, and so many others. Such responses are evidence of an ability to understand and explain what an epidemic means to those who could not otherwise grasp it.

From the outside, the very word *epidemic* is so exotic and strange, conjuring up images of the plagues of Egypt or mysterious medical disasters in far-away places. Yet from the inside, an epidemic is only too local and concrete, requiring, above all, *practical* responses, including an acknowledgement of the psychological needs of the survivors of the first generation of gay men who contracted HIV long before anyone knew of AIDS.

I am especially fond of a small painting by New York gay artist Donald Moffett, commemorating the late Ethyl Eichelberger, a magnificent, stately six-foot-four drag star of the Ridiculous Theatrical Company (founded by Charles Ludlam, who also died from AIDS several years ago). It consists simply of a black square with the words *Oh, Ethyl* stencilled in large white letters, together with the date of his death, 8/12/90. It is entirely appropriate, and infinitely touching, that we should hear at the back of our minds the exasperated voice of Lucille Ball, forever chastizing poor, wonderful, much-put-upon Vivian Vance. For might not heaven consist of being forever able to watch our favourite reruns of *I Love Lucy*, together with our friends again?

Sprouting up alongside high art is a more popular response – what many dismiss as 'AIDS kitsch', exemplified by a panoply of merchandise sold to raise funds for AIDS organizations. Few surfaces have been spared; there are AIDS posters and T-shirts, bags, mugs with the names of loved ones, commemorative paperweights, embossed poems, and the red ribbon, which serves as a commercial prototype for designers eager to exploit its easy symbolism, making velvet and diamond-encrusted ribbons, and even red ribbons for pets.

The contrast between serious and commercial responses to the epidemic underscores how unlikely it seems that a single form of ritual response will be appropriate for all our communities. For example not all lesbian and gay Christians will approve of ACT UP–type 'political funerals', at which sullen police attempt to prevent activist mourners from parading the streets with the caskets containing the remains of friends and loved ones, or from pouring human ashes over the fence onto the lawn of the White House.

Indeed, we should not dismiss AIDS kitsch too lightly or speedily, for, however inadequately, it represents something of our need to hold the dead close, to get used to our friends being gone, and to mourn them publicly. As in previous periods of history when the death of the young was an everyday event, we need our equivalents of the lockets containing melancholy clippings of human hair, or the severe, jet commemorative brooches that adorned our great-grandparents' lapels and mantlepieces. With so many deaths stretched over so many years, it is only too easy to forget the very names of those who have played central roles in our lives. It is in answer to such amnesia that we are gradually learning to develop memorials that might register the *spiritual* dimensions of this protracted epoch of death.

Different gay communities have responded to rising mortality rates with distinct etiquettes of mourning. In countries that lack a developed gay politics, the importation of US and activist styles of mourning are often regarded as alien imports. Thus, when the well known French homosexual historian Frank Arnal died from AIDS last year, the mere idea of holding a commemorative reading and meeting at a local Paris bookshop was deemed by many to be inappropriate and even bizarre. AIDS is thus also a crisis of popular memory.

Perhaps the most touching monuments to our dead are the spontaneous memorials that register immediate local losses – markers as simple as a name spray-painted on an abandoned building or in a gay cruising area, or small, sad shrines on public view. On Hudson Street in Manhattan is what a friend of mine terms the 'ACT UP lamp shop'. For several years its colourful street-front windows have contained a constantly changing panorama of framed photos, newspaper obituaries, and other mementos of local people who have died of AIDS. Similar 'AIDS windows' dot the American landscape, and those further afield as well. Recently in London's gay Soho district, a number of shrines were set up in memory of filmmaker Derek Jarman, a much-loved man in the neighbourhood. A framed photo on a shelf, together with the already yellowing obit and a string of coloured fairy lights, appeared in one of his favourite cafés. A clothes shop painted a text from one of Derek's books on the front window.

This is how communities communicate, how the streets talk eloquently about those who passed along them. This is how neighbourhood is constituted, and how, in any tragedy, neighbours help out. Here, in the hurly-burly of city life, we find direct social registrations of the losses we endure. Our greatest challenge remains finding adequate symbolic memorials that might do justice to all the suffering and courage so uniquely expressed in these intimate, communal shrines.

One existing monument to which we might look is the celebrated Homomonument in Amsterdam, which commemorates Dutch (and other) lesbian and gay victims of the Nazis. This is a triangular public space, laid out next to the Waterkerk, with one corner dropping down in the form of steps to form a jetty, jutting out into the adjacent canal. The corners of the space are pink marble. It is at once an open space and a comfortable place to sit. Yet it does not rise above ground level. This strikes me as perfect, since it so essentially establishes a public symbolic expression of what is invariably hidden, denied, buried.

We cannot, of course, simply translate one country's monument to another and expect it to be equally successful. Nonetheless, the Amsterdam memorial provides an inkling of how we might imagine our own large-scale AIDS monuments.

Just as we cannot 'accept' death on this scale, neither can we ultimately 'deny' it. Our lives are all irredeemably transformed by death; those who survive cannot help but imagine the world as it might have been, if not for HIV. We know that it is wrong to make heroes of individuals who have died in a situation in which so much is asked of so many. At the same time, we know that our dying friends are often heroic. Our friends have fought AIDS with a determination and courage that has no real parallel, and that battle, like other wars, must be acknowledged. We may hope that the symbolic but truthful memorializing of our losses will also in time register the magnitude of the homophobia that causes so much otherwise avoidable suffering at every level of the day-to-day management of this epidemic, from health promotion, to service provision and medical care. Already, revisionist historians are casually attributing this entire epidemic to 'gay promiscuity'. When so few value us in life, it is especially important to record our everyday experiences of the epidemic from the perspective of those who cannot simply go away. We must define this history, or it will not survive us.

19 Signifying AIDS: 'Global AIDS', red ribbons and other controversies*

How does one *see*, and hence think about an epidemic? Writing in the *New Yorker* in 1994, American journalist Stan Sesser noted of a recent trip to Japan that:

> A visitor to Tokyo quickly senses that something is missing. In two weeks of walking around the city's most crowded districts ... I only once saw someone in a wheelchair ... The disabled live in their own version of a world of apartheid – a world that gives an insight into that people with AIDS, a far worse stigma, are encountering?[1]

Conversely, some Japanese visitors to New York are doubtless struck by the vast army of variously disabled beggars who have nowhere but the streets and public spaces of the city in which to hang out. The experienced onlooker in New York will also be aware of the large numbers of emaciated women and men walking with sticks or being pushed in wheelchairs – everyday sights which one may easily come to take for granted in a city which has already experienced well over 50,000 diagnosed cases of AIDS. Yet this says nothing of the many more tens of thousands living with HIV infection in New York, or of the public and private institutions struggling to provide HIV/AIDS-related care and services to those in need. Or of the more than 25,000 New Yorkers who have already died from AIDS, or of the vast and daily swelling army of the bereaved, many multiply bereaved, living through personal loss on a scale unparalleled outside of wartime experience.[2]

Behind the cumulative totals of AIDS cases in different cities and different countries and regions there are clear variations in social groups which have been affected worst by HIV, and which are at greatest risk. It is by now well established that needle-exchange facilities and appropriate ancillary services can play a dramatic role in reducing the rate of new HIV infections amongst injecting drug users and, by extension, their sexual partners. Wherever HIV/AIDS continue to proliferate amongst injecting drug users, this is

* First published in P. Buchler and N. Papastergiadis (Eds) Random Access: On Crisis and Its Metaphors, *London: Rivers Oram Press, 1994.*

invariably associated with the absence of such demonstrably effective prevention programmes. Prevention work amongst gay men varies greatly in quantity and quality around the world, with consequences that may be measured in terms of rising rates of new HIV infections (where these are recorded and published). Furthermore, the size of national epidemics is affected by contingent standards of health care provision, and so on. Thus there is no simple 'AIDS epidemic'. Rather, in the thirteen years since the identification of Acquired Immune Deficiency Syndrome, the local, national and international faces of AIDS have been intimately shaped by many social and political variables. In other words, policies set by governments and other agencies have played a major role in determining the present distribution of HIV and AIDS within specific population groups around the world. AIDS is not simply 'a natural phenomenon'. Where effective, grass-roots community-based HIV/AIDS prevention and education programmes have been established, their impact has been felt. Where such initiatives have either been neglected or, as is often the case, where they have been *prevented*, this is equally reflected in local levels of sero-prevalence.

Thus one may find markedly different levels of HIV infection in closely adjacent cities of comparable size such as Glasgow and Edinburgh. The greater prevalence of HIV amongst injecting drug users in Edinburgh sadly reflects prevailing punitive police policies in that city in the late 1970s and 1980s.[3] Indeed, one can only really understand the AIDS crisis from studying the evolving statistics of HIV infection, AIDS diagnoses and AIDS mortalities, considered locally, nationally, regionally and internationally. Yet it is precisely this understanding which most public representations of the epidemic seem to efface or obscure, by over-simplifying and over-generalizing. Thus by casual and repeated reference to 'the global epidemic' or 'AIDS in Europe', the most important specific features of HIV/AIDS are totally abstracted and erased. This is most obviously the case in reports about the cumulative totals of AIDS cases in different parts of the world, for such totals tell us nothing whatsoever about current rates of net HIV infections, or which types of HIV transmission predominate locally or even nationally. It should be frankly understood that the primary existence of the epidemic is at this initial epidemiological level of the rates of distribution of HIV and AIDS – rates which may change slowly or fast, for the better or for the worse, in relation to the availability or neglect of effective prevention and education campaigns.

Yet for many years, much public discourse on AIDS has been dominated by a 'globalist' approach which only rarely troubles itself with the clarification of exactly how HIV continues to have different impacts, according to different modes of transmission, in different countries, and different degrees of human intervention. In many countries, the needs of entire 'at risk' populations have been all but entirely disregarded by national governments of all political persuasions. In all of this, worldwide, the needs of gay and bisexual men have been most consistently and systematically ignored, with terrible, predictable consequences in terms of HIV transmission, illness and death, and the often invisible related suffering throughout the international diaspora of gay identities. In American cities such as New York it seems likely that at least 50 per cent of all gay men are already infected, whilst in Britain it is estimated that perhaps one in twenty gay men are already HIV-positive, rising to one in five taking the HIV antibody test at some central London GUM clinics.[4] Yet in Britain, as in most other countries, HIV/AIDS education for gay and bisexual men has received only a tiny percentage of the total funding for prevention and education, even though we continue to make up 76 per cent of the annual death rate from AIDS. This is not 'special pleading', but the plain epidemiological reality.

World AIDS day

Since 1988, the World Health Organization (WHO) has designated 1 December as World AIDS Day, each year it is organized around a different theme. Thus in 1994, World AIDS Day highlighted 'AIDS and the Family', following the United Nations proclamation of 1994 as International Year of the Family. In 1993 the theme was 'Time to Act', specified in publicity materials as 'a day of action designed to raise public awareness of HIV and AIDS'.[5]

Yet as Edward King has pointed out:

> That was 1993, twelve long years and hundreds of thousands of deaths since AIDS was first recognised. Those on the front lines had been acting for years, actually, and often in the face of inaction or obstruction from the public health system. What a nerve for that same public health system now to turn round and declare that it was finally Time to Act! Thanks for nothing. I can't even bring myself to say better late than never.[6]

World AIDS Day publicity materials typically consist of masses of abstract data, and pious declarations against 'denial', 'prejudice', and so on. But denial *of what*, and *by whom*? An 'educational' quiz included in the 1993 materials produced by the London Borough of Camden Social Services Department asks if five statements are true or false:

1. Women are safe from HIV as long as they use a contraceptive.
2. You can get HIV from wooden toilet seats, but not plastic ones.
3. Injecting drug use will give you HIV.
4. HIV only affects certain groups in our community.
5. You can get free condoms from family planning clinics.[7]

The officially 'correct' answers to these questions tell us much about the ways in which World AIDS Day encourages us to think about the epidemic. Thus the answer to question 1 is 'false', since 'condoms offer protection against HIV and pregnancy, but other contraceptives only offer protection against pregnancy'. In this manner a simple message about condoms is confused with questions of pregnancy and other means of contraception – hardly relevant to local gay and bisexual men, who made up no fewer than 90 per cent of new cases of HIV in Camden in 1993/94, and 90 per cent of newly diagnosed AIDS cases in the same period. Question 2 is also 'false', but a ridiculous distraction from the central issues, since in neither case is anybody at any risk whatsoever. Question 3 is also 'false' which is reassuring, since injecting drug use is so frequently understood to be intrinsically a risk for HIV, rather than the practice of sharing needles. The official answer to question 4 is also 'false', since, we learn, 'HIV can and does affect people from all sections of the community'. In this manner the prevailing 'equal opportunities' approach to AIDS obscures the fact that all along HIV has been *overwhelmingly* concentrated amongst gay and bisexual men, and injecting drug users and their sexual partners. Yet this is apparently not an officially acceptable 'fact'. Question 5 is, happily, 'true'.

The National AIDS Trust leaflet for 1994 World AIDS Day informs us that in Britain, as of March 1994: 'at least 21,718 people had contracted HIV. Of these people, 9,025 had developed AIDS, of whom 6,031 had already died.'[8] Such information is little more than strategic disinformation, as it fails to make plain that 13,134 of the HIV cases were amongst gay and bisexual men, the second largest group of 1,770 cases being men infected by sexual partners abroad, or as it fails to establish that 6,792 of the UK total of 9,025 AIDS cases were again amongst gay and bisexual men, followed by 588 men infected by unprotected sex with HIV-positive women.[9]

Rather than clearly establishing the similarities and differences between the experience of, and responses to HIV/AIDS in different parts of the world, the ideology of World AIDS Day sets up a fictive unity in the name of 'the global', as if HIV/AIDS were everywhere the same. The concept of 'Global AIDS' was originally elaborated in a series of documents produced by the Global Programme on AIDS, within the World Health Organization in the second part of the 1980s.[10] In essence it has four major characteristics. First, it takes the regional as its fundamental category of priority for thinking about HIV/AIDS. Second, it is extremely homophobic, as much in its silences and omissions as in anything explicitly stated. Third, it mobilizes a generalized neo-liberal discourse against 'discrimination', with frequent appeals to notions of common 'humanity' and so on. Fourth, it derives directly from a generalist tradition of public health policy-making which is primarily concerned with *total* health-care provision. Its cultural manifestations are usually couched in terms of vague notions of 'compassion', 'tolerance' and 'solidarity'.

But solidarity *with* and *between* whom? And who is 'tolerating' whom? For example, it is far from clear that prejudice against injecting drug users is globally uniform, or related in any significant way to homophobia, misogyny or racism. AIDS does not simply cause an abstract cloud of generalized 'prejudice'. Rather, it mobilizes deep cultural forces which may vary greatly within and among different nations. Of course one needs to understand the regional patterns in order to encourage and to organize adequate national and international responses. Yet it frequently seems that in reality, the World Health Organization has imposed an extremely restrictive model of the epidemic at the heart of its Global AIDS Programme, which specifically refuses to acknowledge the urgent needs of gay men around the world, including those whose identities are formed in other traditions of sexuality. Solidarity is urged with the interests of prostitutes and injecting drug users, especially in so far as they are tacitly deemed responsible for the 'spread' of AIDS into what is imagined as a global heterosexual population, but never with gay and bisexual men. Whilst it is doubtless diplomatically necessary that World Health Organization agencies work with governments which have very different track records on human rights issues, especially in relation to homosexuality, it seems that the Global Programme's response has simply been to ignore gay men's needs altogether, whether in the developed or the developing worlds.[11] In this context the rousing triumphalism of a vision of 'global solidarity' around such issues as the United Nations, nuclear war, and AIDS, as 'one of the glories of our era' rings rather hollow.[12] In a nutshell, for 'global' read 'heterosexual transmission'.

Translated into local British terms, and duplicated more or less exactly throughout the developed world, World AIDS Day is described as

> an annual day of observance designed to expand and strengthen the worldwide effort to stop the spread of HIV and AIDS. Its goal is to open channels of communication, promote the exchange of information and experience, and forge a spirit of social tolerance.[13]

In Britain, World AIDS Day is coordinated by the National AIDS Trust whose 1994 publicity materials explain the significance of the theme of AIDS and the Family, noting that:

> Each nation must tailor the theme to reflect its own situation and pattern of epidemic. This is ever more true at local level. Unlike many countries in the world, the UK epidemic mainly affects men who have sex with men. Although families are of course affected, often as carers.[14]

Yet equally one might say that the UK epidemic is also extremely like that in many other countries, but this would not fit with the overall heterosexual bias of Global AIDS-speak. It is also notable that we only learn of abstracted 'men who have sex with men'. Has anyone ever existed who thinks of himself in such terms – for example, 'Hello, I'm a Man Who Has Sex With Men'? Most striking of all is the sense of an almost biological divide between 'families' and these 'men who have sex with men', as if gay men were not as fundamentally a part of families as anyone and everyone else. It seems that families can 'care' for us (assuming that we are HIV-positive), and that is our only permissible relationship to them, conveniently dying.

'Highlights' of World AIDS Day 1994 in London included:

> A candlelight vigil on the South Bank outside the National Theatre at 6.00 pm on December 1st for 45 minutes organised by the National AIDS Trust. Leading actors and actresses including Sir Anthony Hopkins, Dame Judi Dench and Helen Mirren, and opera diva Lesley Garrett have been approached to read out names of those who have died from AIDS. A 120-strong all-girl school choir will sing music by Vaughan Williams.

> The second Concert of Hope at Wembley Arena ... organised once again by George Michael, with Princess Diana, patron of the National AIDS Trust, as the guest of honour.[15]

Yet why hold a vigil outside the National Theatre, an institution which exercises neither power nor authority in public AIDS policy-making or practice? And whilst it is of course heartening that celebrities are prepared to take part in such ceremonies, it is far from clear what exactly they are intended to signify. If AIDS deaths are special from other deaths, it is because of objective factors of neglect, legal discrimination, the censorship of health promotion materials, government cuts in voluntary sector funding, mismanagement, and so on. The best intentions are evidently being mobilized but to no clear purpose. For example, whilst it is also heartening that massive fundraising concerts can be organized and broadcast, it is never specified *why* such funding is necessary in the first place, or to what agencies funds will be directed, or on what criteria.

Furthermore, the overwhelming heterosexual bias of the working ideology of 'Global AIDS' ensures that some of the most glaring examples of the effects of racism are never discussed. For example, HIV has had a vastly disproportionate impact amongst American black gay and bisexual men, in direct relation to the all but total official neglect of their entitlements to HIV/AIDS education.[16] The Global AIDS Programme frequently extols the virtues of community-based HIV/AIDS education and services, but this is more in recognition of the unlikelihood of most governments responding well to any aspects of human sexuality, rather than from a recognition of the needs of those who are doubly neglected as the direct result of racism combined with homophobia. For HIV is decidedly not an 'Equal Opportunities' virus. It does *not* affect everybody equally, and least of all does it do so at the global level. Commenting on the 1992 World AIDS Day theme of 'A Community Commitment', Edward King pointedly invites us

> to guess which community was mysteriously missing from the WHO's official list of communities, which included lots of non-communities or pseudo-communities such as social clubs or geographically defined communities. ... Yup, you guessed who was missing?[17]

Plus ça change.

Red ribbons

Since 1992, British World AIDS Day materials have come heavily draped with the image of red ribbons, described by the National AIDS Trust as 'an international symbol of concern about AIDS'. In 1992, the NAT offered some 'ideas on opportunities and uses for red ribbons'. These included advice to:

> Get your family/friends/colleagues/people you meet on the bus to wear one. Wear one yourself!!!
> Order enough for your employees to wear them.
> Hang big ones out of your window.
> Tie them on your windscreen wiper or bumper.
> Tie one around your portable phone/fax/computer/notepad.
> Put one on your pet's collar.
> Give them out in shopping precincts.
> Tie them around parking meters, fence posts, railings, etc.
> Use them in foyer displays.
> Do something far too outrageous to mention in print.[18]

Such gushing nonsense tells us much about the enthusiasm with which Red Ribbonism has been adopted in the UK. The familiar image of a red ribbon signifying 'AIDS awareness' goes back to the work of New York artists, curators, critics and others who formed themselves into a group called Visual AIDS in 1988. Visual AIDS met informally at first, with monthly meetings, out of which various cultural projects emerged, including the Witness Project, and a slide archive of AIDS-related artworks, housed at the Artists' Space in New York. In response to the US Vietnam Memorial Day in 1989, Visual AIDS developed the now widely adopted Day Without Art, when American museums annually align themselves with the AIDS crisis with specially curated exhibitions, the closing off of galleries for a day, the temporary display of paintings with their fronts to the wall, and so on.

In the early spring of 1991, the United States was at the height of the Gulf War and awash with media-fuelled jingoism, often expressed by yellow ribbons, emblematic of US nationalism. In response, Visual AIDS adopted red ribbons, understood as a public art-work, aiming to draw attention to the underfunding of HIV/AIDS services, by contrast to the lavish cost of the military defence of Kuwait. Visual AIDS Director Patrick J. O'Connell insists that the Red Ribbon Project was not designed 'to point fingers at who didn't do what', but aimed instead to draw attention to AIDS 'as a national issue'.[19] Whilst the sale of red ribbons in bulk has raised much needed cash for US AIDS charities, its level of semiotic generalization has also been widely criticized. American gay writer John Weir, for example, argues that: 'People who are truly living with or dying of AIDS or caring for sick lovers or friends don't need gentle reminders about their situation'.[20]

Yet this does not of course include the great majority of Americans or Britons. Furthermore, the significance of ribbons will change in different local contexts. After tennis star Pete Sampras and others wore red ribbons at Wimbledon in July 1993, journalist Peter Bond complained in London's *Evening Standard* that:

> Gay campaign fanatics are harassing stars and sports heroes into appearing on TV with an AIDS red-ribbon emblem pinned on their clothes, it is claimed. The symbol is supposedly a 'pride badge' showing that the wearer is sympathetic to those suffering from the disease. But the A-shaped motif has a less innocent aim: representing gay unity manipulating public opinion towards homosexuality ... many celebrities are being coerced by *threats* into displaying the emblem in front of the cameras with gay bully boys in Britain as well as in America saying: 'We'll make your lives misery if you don't' ... Ian Hislop of BBC2's *Have I Got News For You*, says: 'It makes me so annoyed. At the BAFTA dinner, there was a ribbon waiting on each plate. I refused to put mine on.'[21]

A week earlier the *Sunday Express* had roundly castigated the wearing of red ribbons, claiming that:

> This fashionable obsession with AIDS is more than offensive, it's actually dangerous. It deflects attention from other, more urgent, causes.[22]

Predictably, Ian Hislop, the editor of *Private Eye*, also turned up in the *Mail on Sunday*, again repeating the tale of his shocking intimidation at the BAFTA dinner earlier in the year:

> Having just lost a close relative to a disease that is equally incurable, though much less fashionable, I decided not to conform. If I felt like making a point about leukaemia for example, could I wear an L shape on my lapel in order to let everyone know?[23]

Such frivolous comparisons between HIV and other, non-infectious, uncontroversial illnesses only serve to demonstrate how little journalists such as Hislop understand about AIDS. If leukaemia were preventable, and if prevention measures were routinely neglected, and if people living with leukaemia were discriminated against in law, then and only then might the analogy with AIDS be relevant. It is, however, significant that other patient groups, including women with breast cancer, have developed parallel 'ribbon projects', which aim to associate other colours with other diseases and other medical conditions. This proliferation of 'disease symbols' cannot articulate shared needs or goals, because each symbolized disease is placed in relations of potential *rivalry* to every other symbolized disease – for funding, research, media attention, etc.

Hislop also complained in the *Mail on Sunday* that 'AIDS charities dominate media events and on these occasions the red ribbon has become de rigueur',[24] a comment significantly echoed in Simon Garfield's account of the history of red ribbons, in which he reports that within months of the 1991 Tony awards, red ribbons were 'de rigueur at every awards ceremony, every tribute'.[25] This is history rewritten from the venomous perspective of old press clippings rather than direct research, which would demonstrate how very few celebrities in Britain or the USA have ever in any way associated themselves with HIV/AIDS issues, even at the highly abstracted level of red ribbons.

It is, however, undoubtedly the case that the manufacture and marketing of the red ribbon motif has had decidedly distasteful aspects. For example, for several years the American West Coast gay magazine *The Advocate* has carried advertisements for commodities such as a transparent lucite paperweight containing a 'hand embedded ribbon' – a snip at $25 + $4 for shipping, handling and sales tax. One may also purchase a 4" × 11" table sculpture, inscribed underneath (conveniently out of sight?): 'To All Those who May Have, Cared For, Or Have Been Touched By AIDS'. This 'beautiful glass art piece' as it is described in the advertising blurb, supposedly

> symbolizes the need for awareness and offers a tribute to the broken hearts and the tears that have been shed due to the AIDS crisis. Excellent for the home or office to provide a visual representation of the need for awareness, compassion and remembrance. Allows each of us the opportunity to engage friends and family in conversation about AIDS and to educate those around us.

'Compassion' could be yours for a mere $149 + $4.95 for shipping and handling.

Meanwhile in Britain in 1992 a private businessman, Andrew Butterfield, had set up a charity named Red Ribbon International to make and distribute red ribbons. Butterfield was displeased with the way in which the National AIDS Trust had set a red ribbon within a triangle as its 1992 World AIDS Day logo, and complained of 'the ease with which it could be associated with the gay Pink Triangle, once again marginalising the AIDS issue which the Red Ribbon is breaking away from'.[26] In other words, to the man who controlled the marketing of red ribbons in Britain until 1994, AIDS is an issue which must be protected at all costs from the taint and guilt by association of any connections with gay men.[27] So much for the gay 'fanatics' and 'bully boys' supposedly conspiring to convert Britain to wholesale sodomy through the sporting of red ribbons, according to the UK popular press.

This type of apparent profiteering has no simple or inevitable reputation to the meanings people associate with red ribbons, least of all on the part of those who wear them. For the red ribbon has indeed achieved its own measure of success, at least in the numbers of people seen wearing them every day in London and the larger cities of the UK. We cannot possibly know precisely why people choose to wear red ribbons, but in a recent random sample consisting of the first five people I came across wearing ribbons one chilly morning in south London in late November 1994, one was a young female nurse working on an AIDS ward, two were young women who explained they had gay friends with HIV, one was a young gay man, and one a middle-aged gay man. All expressed versions of the belief that AIDS is a public issue with which they identified. The young gay man said he thought the red ribbon more important than Armistice Day poppies, 'because people are dying unnecessarily now'. This view may be typical, or exceptional. In either event, red ribbons are widely worn with the best of intentions, even if these may seem woolly and vague to the better informed, who can hardly be expected to think of red ribbons as much more than a distraction, more or less irritating or heart-warming according to mood. And indeed it was moving to see Martina Navratilova and all the other 1994 Wimbledon finalists wearing red ribbons before such a vast television audience. Red ribbons may not say enough, but they say something, and it is up to us to articulate the fundamental issues at stake in the AIDS crisis in such a way that this is unambiguously what red ribbons will come to mean for those who select to wear them. Rather than blaming red ribbons for not explaining everything that by now ought to be more widely understood about HIV/AIDS, we should strive to make public discussion of HIV/AIDS clearer and better informed. Let's campaign to make red ribbons indeed emblematic of injustice in the AIDS crisis, whether that involves the neglect of gay men's needs in the UK, or the neglect of injecting drug users elsewhere in much of Europe and the United States.

After all, there have been terrible losses, and for many these require public and private signification, for personal emotional reasons as much as for any other more overtly political or educational purposes. Inadequate as it may often seem, red ribbons do in part testify to the scale of our losses, and constitute a cultural revival of public forms of mourning, affirming the importance of those who were rarely valued in their lifetimes, whose deaths remain almost entirely unregretted in the public discourse of the mass media and the other leading institutions of public life throughout the world. This is, however, a genuinely global issue to which it remains unlikely in the extreme that the World Health Organization will ever turn its attention, and least of all on any future World AIDS Day.

Notes

1 Stan Sesser, 'Letter from Japan: Hidden death', *New Yorker*, 14 November 1994, p. 63.
2 See Simon Watney, 'Acts of memory', *Out*, New York, September 1994, pp. 92–7.
3 See Simon Garfield, *The End of Innocence: Britain in the Age of AIDS* (London: Faber & Faber, 1994), Ch. 5.

4 See Edward King, *Safety in Numbers: Safer Sex and Gay Men* (London: Cassell, 1993; New York: Routledge, 1994), Ch. 1.

5 WAD 93, Press Pack, National AIDS Trust, London.

6 Edward King, 'Whose life is it anyway?', *Pink Paper*, London, Issue 355, 25 November 1994, p. 16.

7 Camden Social Services, London, *World AIDS Day*, December 1993, p. 2.

8 National AIDS Trust, *World AIDS Day: 1 December 1994*.

9 Public Health Laboratory Service, London, *Quarterly AIDS and HIV Figures*, 94/1, 25 April 1994.

10 For example, Jonathan Mann, Geneva, *Global AIDS: Into the 1990s* (World Health Organization, 1989), GPA/DIR/89.2.

11 I am not aware of a single WHO document which specifies the needs of gay men, though we continue to make up the greater number of HIV and AIDS cases in many parts of the world. The Panos Institute in London is currently undertaking an initial survey of gay men's needs in the developing world, the first of its kind.

12 Mann, *Global AIDS*, p. 7.

13 National AIDS Trust, Resource Pack, London, 1 December 1994.

14 *Ibid.*

15 'World AIDS Day', *Gay Times*, London, November 1994, p. 44.

16 *HIV/AIDS Surveillance Report*, CDC, Atlanta, Georgia, USA, Vol. 6, No. 1, 1994, p. 22.

17 Edward King, 'Comment: World AIDS Day', *Pink Paper*, Issue 335.

18 National AIDS Trust, London, *WAD 92, World AIDS Day Newsletter*, Second Issue, October 1992, p. 2.

19 Personal communication.

20 John Weir, 'The red plague: Do red ribbons really help in the fight against AIDS?', *The Advocate*, Los Angeles, Issue 628, 4 May 1993, p. 38.

21 Peter Bond, 'AIDS bully boys' star symbol is so sinister', *Evening Standard*, London, 12 July 1993, n.p.

22 *Sunday Express*, 4 July 1993, n.p.

23 Sharon Churcher, 'The tyranny of the AIDS pride badge', *Mail on Sunday*, London, 11 July 1993, n.p.

24 *Ibid.*

25 Simon Garfield, *The End of Innocence*, p. 255.

26 *Ibid.*, p. 259.

27 At a later date, Butterfield attempted to obtain trade mark protection both for red ribbons and the phrase 'AIDS Awareness' and by so doing lost any support he may still have enjoyed within the larger agencies that had previously funded his company.

20 Concorde*

On Saturday 9 April [1994] the *Lancet* published the final results of the three-year Anglo-French clinical trial known as Concorde, which compared the effects of AZT as an 'early intervention' drug for asymptomatic people with HIV, and as a potential treatment drug at later stages of HIV-related illness. These results confirm the preliminary findings which were published a year ago, establishing that there is no advantage from taking AZT early rather than late. As Edward King has concluded:

> People who took AZT early had on average a small increase in their CD4 cell count, and in the short-term were less likely to develop minor HIV-related symptoms. However, when the researchers looked for more substantial effects over the long-term there was no clear advantage to taking AZT early. In particular, early AZT did not seem to delay the onset of the more serious infections that indicate that a person has developed AIDS. There was also no difference in survival between people who took AZT early and people who took AZT later in the course of infection. (*Pink Paper*, 8 April 1994).

The Concorde trial conclusively demonstrates that in relation to asymptomatic HIV infection, AZT may result in a modest increase in CD4 levels, but does not delay the onset of AIDS. For those with symptomatic HIV infection, AZT may initially delay the onset of further symptoms, in particular HIV-related dementia, for which it is also an effective treatment, though side-effects are more common amongst those starting with AZT later. These results are not surprising, in so far as they support the findings of several other trials, as well as the evidence of widespread clinical usage of the drug, in Britain and elsewhere. In other words, this final, detailed statistical breakdown of the available evidence only confirms what was already widely known and accepted. Why then all the fuss?

The controversy surrounding AZT, its cost and its effects, takes us back to the mid-eighties, at a time when there was far more optimism about the

* First published in Gay Times, *May 1994.*

possibility of a 'magic bullet' treatment for HIV infection. Indeed, as long ago as February 1986, Julian Meldrum warned in *Capital Gay* against the kind of media hype surrounding the drug, whilst a leading US researcher warned bluntly that 'This is not a cure.' By March 1987, AZT had gained official US approval for use, in spite of widespread complaints about what was regarded as excessive profiteering by the its manufacturer, the UK-based Wellcome Foundation (in those days known as Burroughs–Wellcome). The rush to license AZT is described in detail in Bruce Nussbaum's book, *Good Intentions* (1990).

Sadly, the entire history of AZT has been bedevilled by conflicting claims concerning on the one hand its supposed beneficial efficacy, and on the other its supposed harmful consequences. It is, however, important to note that exaggerated claims of clinical benefit came from Wellcome and the mass media, rather than from doctors working in the HIV/AIDS field. At the same time some gay health advocates, including Martin Delaney from San Francisco's Project Inform, and Duncan Campbell in Britain, insisted that AZT was indeed the long-awaited 'early intervention' drug for which everyone had been praying, and that it was therefore of vital importance that everyone at any risk from HIV should be tested, in order to obtain the drug. Such optimism was of course understandable, but in the absence of reliable long-term data it was also premature. It was this initial exaggeration of the potential *benefits* of AZT which led in turn to the equally unhelpful exaggeration of the supposed *harms* caused by AZT on the part of those who insisted that it was in effect little more than a form of poison. Indeed, to this day some insist that AZT is itself the 'cause' of AIDS, and one of the more helpful findings of the Concorde trial is its decisive refutation of such claims, rooted in crude conspiracy theories rather than hard science.

Meanwhile, in the real, complex world of patient management, the vast majority of doctors, especially outside the US, were cautious about AZT, and sceptical about the way in which it was originally licensed. Thus the Concorde trial was designed to evaluate AZT in the long term, in such a way that there could be no confusion between the effects the drug might have on surrogate markers for HIV disease progression such as CD4 counts, and actual clinical benefits to individuals. Thus in November 1988 a large meeting took place at the Body Positive Centre in London, between the trial's principal scientific investigators and the subjects of their research, in order to establish a proper dialogue about matters of great urgency for those already infected. As I said in my talk that day:

> Nobody involved in any way with this epidemic has chosen the situation in which we all find ourselves. We are facing an unprecedented situation … If 'informed consent' is to mean anything at all, it must surely involve information which does not simply derive from the pharmaceutical industry and government funding agencies. Without debate and discussion there can be no real consent, since choices between different options cannot be made … We cannot predict the course of our own individual

and irreducible experience of HIV infection from abstract statistics. None the less we need such statistics in order to effectively direct resources and information to groups and individuals most in need.

Now, six long years later we have the statistics, and they make it more apparent than ever that neither potential benefits nor potential harms of untested drugs should be exaggerated in significance. Sadly this has never been apparent to the mass media, who continue to regard HIV/AIDS research as if it primarily affects the stock-markets rather than people with HIV/AIDS. For most UK medical correspondents, HIV/AIDS are regarded as *theoretical* issues, and there is little sense of the epidemic as a vast *human* tragedy.

Back in 1988 everyone hoped that AZT might indeed prove of benefit to those with asymptomatic HIV infection, at a time when the available evidence was conflicting. In 1994, the Concorde trial directs our attention back again to the design and aims of clinical trials, and the wider conduct of HIV/AIDS medical research. Happily, unlike those involved in US trials, all those who participated in Concorde continue to be followed up and monitored. Although its results were of course disappointing, Concorde at least established a relation between researchers and their subjects which has greatly benefited all subsequent research protocols in the UK, by guaranteeing both accessibility of information, and the fullest consultation. All the more reason, then, to reject the continued hyping of supposed 'miracle drugs' and 'wonder cures', from whatever source they derive. As Mark Harrington observes in a recent article in *Le Journal du SIDA*:

> The refusal to squarely face the setbacks and surprises which are characteristic of scientific progress in any field, especially AIDS, makes it harder to develop strategies to overcome the setbacks and learn from the surprises.

The results of Concorde provide sad news, but the interests of people with HIV/AIDS will not be served if false hopes continue to be stimulated by cruel and irresponsible media reporting. As treatment activist Mike Barr concludes, people with HIV do not need:

> condescending disingenuous-but-well-meaning assurances about the impending triumph of medical science. People with HIV need conclusive answers from rigorous, well-designed clinical studies and comprehensive inquisitive immunological research. They need an accurate pathogenetic model. They need drugs that work.

It is only when exaggerated and often frightening claims of harm or benefit are rejected, that we may establish the type of reasonable hope which can sustain us in the long haul towards making HIV a 'chronic manageable infection'. But that day has sadly not yet arrived.

21 AIDS awareness?*

In early January 1995, Radio Four's arts omnibus programme *Kaleidoscope* concluded a series about taboos in contemporary Britain with a brief discussion of AIDS. The presenter began, ominously enough, with reference to the idea that it is now widely accepted that there is a 'gay ghetto'[1] Am I simply being a pedantic old fart when I point out the distinction between the ghettos in which Jews were confined against their will by early modern European states, and the emergence of a modern, confident lesbian and gay culture for which we have had to struggle very hard indeed for the past twenty-five years? Such questions of language are not merely academic exercises, for their outcome shapes how we understand our own individual histories, as well as our collective achievements. Since the 1970s this is more or less what many of my generation have thought of as a politics of representation. As I've written elsewhere: 'In a modern media culture, you don't know who you are if you don't know how you are represented, by whom, and for what purposes'.[2]

Launching into the subject of AIDS and representation, the BBC presenter mentioned Susan Sontag's 1986 *New Yorker* story 'The Way We Live Now', about a group of people who 'can't bring themselves to use the "A-word"'. We were then told of European artists who are apparently 'wrestling with the issues' of AIDS in their work. These unnamed artists were promptly represented by, of all people, Sir Howard Hodgkin, who did some timid, wishy-washy abstract illustrations for Sontag's ubiquitous tale when it was reprinted in Britain a few years ago by Faber & Faber as a fund-raiser. In all of this, what strikes me as most extraordinary is that nobody seems to have noticed the initial, bizarre choice of Sontag's story, as the central literary gateway into the epidemic, to not so much as mention gay men, *whilst* ostensibly writing about the epidemic in a city that has now seen more than 50,000 deaths from AIDS. Yet in the story nobody dies. Nobody gets tested. Nobody has the faintest idea about treatment issues. In other words this is 'literary AIDS', an epidemic of rumours. Maybe this is why it evidently appeals to so many UK commentators. Nor does it seem to have appeared

* First published in Icon, *Oxford, no. 1, 1995.*

odd to most people that British readers, living through a very different type of epidemic, were expected to be able to make sense of our national experience of AIDS through American lenses. Howard Hodgkin is a rich and successful, if vastly overrated painter, whose recent 'coming out' should not obscure the fact that for many decades he has said and done precisely nothing in public on behalf of other gay men. Thus AIDS emerges as a topic to which we may respond, tastefully, but which is seen to lack any real specificity of its own. AIDS is simply 'another tragedy', another example of implacable death. Stephen Daldry, Director of the English Stage Company, then proposed *Angels in America* as 'the play of the decade', praising it specifically because it was 'not just about AIDS as a major medical crisis, but somehow incorporated into that debate the whole state of America'.[3]

All well and good you might think, until one begins to reflect that by this type of logic, anything dealing with AIDS issues is automatically thought to be better if it also takes on all sorts of other, extraneous issues. How many more bloatedly pretentious allegorical plays and films and novels do we have to endure, which use AIDS primarily to make pious general points about the state of the world – about practically anything it would seem but the only too grim, concrete social and political issues confronting us immediately and directly in relation to the ongoing, disastrous mismanagement of the UK HIV/AIDS epidemics? As Harriet Gilbert pointed out in the same programme, as far as TV is concerned: 'AIDS adds a kind of frisson to adultery stories'. All well and good, until one notices that it is gay and bisexual men who continue to make up some 75 per cent of newly reported HIV and AIDS cases in the UK each year, whilst a total of less than 5 per cent of state funds for HIV/AIDS education has ever gone towards gay men's health education. Vast bonfires of money have been squandered in the name of 'AIDS awareness' in this country.

In other words, we now face a curious British liberal consensus which is only too eager to acknowledge AIDS as a 'tragedy', whilst in effect actively colluding with the very forces which serve to worsen the epidemic. Frankly, I don't get much of a 'frisson' flicking through the more than fifty RIPs scratched through my address book. In the mid-eighties I wrote and lectured and broadcasted a great deal on the subject of AIDS and representation. The aim of this work was strictly functional. It aimed to clarify issues that were at the time widely misunderstood, in order to encourage better research, better services for those in need, better care, and also better journals. Much of that work had an impact in both the statutory and non-statutory sectors of HIV/AIDS work in Britain and elsewhere.

At the same time, however, it quickly became clear that questions of AIDS and representation by the late eighties had already become widely detached from their original motivating goals, and were being in effect fetishized, as if 'getting the language right' were an end in and of itself, independent of the interests of people living with or otherwise threatened most by HIV. For example, there is a bitter irony in being lectured sternly at conferences by keen Cultural Studies types about why we must never talk about 'AIDS victims', 'the AIDS virus' or 'high-risk groups' and so on, as if these were issues which began and ended in *languages*, as if everyone with AIDS must at all costs always be presented as more or less hysterically happy, healthy and carefree, and as if HIV were some kind of 'equal opportunities virus', affecting everybody equally. In this manner, concrete political and other practical goals became *gradually* subverted into 'AIDS awareness'.

By 'AIDS awareness' I refer to the politically correct body of beliefs and attitudes concerning HIV/AIDS that seemingly dominate current UK liberal thinking (such as it is) about the epidemic. 'AIDS awareness' is everywhere, like some miasmic anti-intellectual contagion, from the ongoing work of the Health Education Authority and the National AIDS Trust, Radio Four, and far beyond. 'AIDS awareness' has ingested some aspects of the work of writers and critics such as Cindy Patton, Jan Zita Grover, Douglas Crimp, myself and others, but in a highly selective and invariably de-politicizing manner. As a system of beliefs it may fairly be described as an ideology, and as such it may be seen to possess at least five consistent characteristics.

First, unlike the epidemic, 'AIDS awareness' is overwhelmingly generalist in outlook. Its constitutive belief is that 'AIDS affects everybody', or words to such effect. It interprets the recognition that anybody may be at potential risk from HIV via known modes of transmission, to mean that everybody is at equal risk from HIV. Second, it is committed to a picture of 'the global epidemic', as if there were only one epidemic – rather than many, moving at different speeds within and between different population groups around the world, in relation to different levels of demonstrably effective prevention work, such as needle-exchanges, community-based, supportive education produced by and for gay men, and so on. Where these are neglected or prevented, rates of seroprevalence rise. By globalizing AIDS, local issues may be overlooked.

Third, 'AIDS awareness' relentlessly de-gays the epidemic, which is read primarily as 'a heterosexual problem', in relation to which (and preferably from a global perspective) gay men's realities and needs can be regarded as secondary or even tertiary. This is the direct consequence of the initial misleading notion of a unitary, global epidemic, in which all national and regional variations are erased, and the real epidemic conveniently replaced by a massive abstraction. Fourth, 'AIDS awareness' in all its variant forms and versions is relentlessly normalizing. It cheerfully encourages people to hug children with AIDS. It invites 'tolerance', often at vast expense, in terms of generally vapid and insulting mass media advertising campaigns. It demands an end to 'prejudice', yet it never specifies quite which prejudices it might mean, or where such prejudice comes from, or what consequences prejudice leads to in everyday life. Above all, it refuses to imagine any kind of collective reaction or response to the heavily abstracted ills it chastises. Fifth, it is always highly individualistic. It gladly emphasizes that people can always (supposedly) say no to sex. It sees AIDS as a 'tragedy' faced by isolated individuals, usually surrounded primarily by family units. It is usually glibly optimistic, and has little or no interest whatsoever in treatment issues or research, or choices facing people with HIV/AIDS in different parts of the world. Nor is it interested in any statistics save those which provide cumulative totals of cases. It mainly deals with AIDS figures rather than HIV figures, and seems largely unaware of the significance of the latter, as they change over time, in directing resources to prevention work where it is most needed.[4]

It is, however, significant that 'AIDS awareness' almost invariably relates HIV/AIDS to issues concerning reproductive technology and birth control, largely because AIDS has proved to be one of the few ways in which sex educators have been able to raise issues about condom use in a period of intense political pressure against sex education as such. Thus have the needs of gay and bisexual men been effectively hijacked in favour of those at the slightest statistical risk from HIV transmission via unprotected vaginal sex, throughout the developed world. 'AIDS awareness' thus concerns a largely imaginary, global epidemic, everywhere the same, in which the solutions are *equally* universal – 'love', 'understanding', 'sympathy', and so on. Least of all is 'AIDS awareness' able to acknowledge or deal with the realities of cumulative loss, though it does offer loving messages of 'support'.

And this, I'm afraid, is where we've got in Britain in 1995, with masses and masses of 'AIDS awareness' flushing around, exemplified by Red Ribbons, the most eloquently ambiguous signifier of its muddled message. By contrast, those attempting to develop and sustain community-based HIV/AIDS education to those at greatest need find that their work is all but impossible to fund within the new 'client culture' of health and service provision in the UK, where 'AIDS awareness' projects are eminently saleable, because eminently respectable, and not because they have any real significance or point whatsoever. In effect, NHS and other 'reforms' ensure that public funds are least likely to go where they are most needed in the field of prevention work concerned with sexual transmission, whilst the supposedly 'independent' charities follow suit. Thus is AIDS education blandified, and a vast gulf opens up between the epidemic as it is imagined and represented, and the various epidemics as they are actually lived.

Discourse analysis remains an invaluable tool in our analyses of the many forms of 'weasel-AIDS-speak' flourishing throughout the mass media, from notions of so-called 'diseases of choice' to the softer rhetoric of 'AIDS awareness'. But the epidemic does not stand still, just as government-led policies are likely to remain as volatile and largely unpredictable as are most governments, of all known political persuasions. Those of us who initiated the international debates about AIDS and representation in the long mid-1980s could never have imagined that ten years later we would need to oppose the rigid orthodoxy of an 'AIDS awareness' which in effect distracts attention away from the real, ongoing issues. I think it is still extremely important that we are nimble in our various decodings of the ways in which HIV/AIDS issues are represented throughout our national cultures, not least because our 'politics of representation' is potentially able to alert us to new contradictions and emergent ideas and tendencies within specific population groups. For unless we can successfully challenge the working, normative ideology of 'AIDS awareness' we are simply going to have to accept that *at least* 1,500 gay men are going to contract HIV in the UK each year for the forseeable future, and that in effect there is nothing whatsoever we can do about this, or about treatment and other service provision issues, or any other aspects of public or 'independent' policy making and implementation. How many more gay men have to die before their community comes to recognize that this is an unacceptably high trade-off for a lowered age of consent, the annual inanities of World AIDS Day, and the occasional polite, banal radio or TV Special?

Notes

1 *Kaleidoscope*, BBC Radio Four, 6 January 1995.
2 Simon Watney, 'Lesbian and gay studies in the age of AIDS', *NYQ*, No. 21, 22 March 1992, p. 42.
3 *Kaleidoscope* (note 1).
4 See Edward King, *Safety in Numbers: Safer Sex and Gay Men* (London: Cassell, 1994; New York: Routledge, 1994).

22 Moving targets: some reflections on the origins and history of gay men fighting AIDS*

When I'm in heterosexual company I find that if the topic of the epidemic comes up in conversation, most people always say the same thing. They tell me how 'wonderfully' gay men have responded to AIDS, how 'marvellously' the 'gay community' has united. They don't want to know *anything whatsoever* about the epidemic, but they do like the idea that there is a plucky little community out there on the brutal heath of Tory England, 'bravely' holding its own.

I wonder. Looking back, I can see that the degree of my own personal involvement with HIV/AIDS was unusual, to the extent that so many of my closest friends were American, and my life and career were both very much trans-Atlantic long before the announcement of AIDS in 1981. Looking back a little closer, it also strikes me how comparatively few of my gay contemporaries got involved in HIV/AIDS work. Those of us who formed the first and second generations of British NGOs (Non-Governmental Organizations) came almost without exception from the pre-AIDS gay movement which emerged in the wake of Gay Liberation.

For many years in the 1980s I attempted to steer the Terrence Higgins Trust towards properly discharging its responsibilities for health promotion. The Trust's first paid health education worker had extensive experience in Africa and spent her several years in office liaising with other feminists. And next to nothing was done. As a volunteer group leader it was fantastically depressing. There was next to no budget. The gay press was often uneven and unreliable in its coverage of AIDS in the 1980s and mainstream lesbian and gay politics has never shown the slightest trace of interest in AIDS, unless of course the luvvies wanted a press release run off for them. Gay men have attended benefits by the million, seen Lily Savage until we gag, and karaokied until we dropped – for money. But rarely has there ever been much sense of interest in who gets the money, or what is done with it.

An increasing number of us have seen friends and lovers through the harrowing journey of illness and death, but still, huge numbers of gay men I meet have had little or no direct experience of the epidemic whatsoever.

* First published in F***sheet, The Journal of Gay Men Fighting AIDS, *London, no. 19, November 1995.*

Properly planned and funded HIV/AIDS education for those at greatest risk in Britain was never even a remote possibility until long after the re-gaying of AIDS from 1990. It could not be done in the public sector for political reasons, and the NGOs were not prepared to risk losing their funding because of controversial work. In this way the newspaper and media industry effectively dominated UK social policy on AIDS and anyone working in AIDS has to recognize that many thousands of cases of HIV should properly be regarded as having been avoidable. That is to say that if proper, or even half-way decent, community services for health promotion had been available to gay men in the 1980s, thousands of men would not have become infected. This is why AIDS simply *had* to be re-gayed.

In one important sense, then, GMFA emerged initially from the ruins of the old Gay Men's Health Education Group at the Terrence Higgins Trust – pulled out from the crumbling Gothic edifice of the THT by Peter Scott and his wily cronies. But it was also rather more than that, for just as OutRage expressed something fundamental about gay politics in 1990, so GMFA equally expresses something vital of these times. Indeed, at both the 1990 and 1992 European Conferences on AIDS, British speakers successfully pushed a 're-gaying' agenda which continues to reverberate, though not without resistance, as here, from conservative homosexuals who have always appeared to prefer following the coffin to 'rocking the boat'.

My main concern in the early years of 're-gaying' was to win the argument. The statistics were blindingly obvious, but people had to be persuaded to see the epidemic in relation to their own lives. In all of this, what Edward King terms 'applied epidemiology' remains absolutely crucial to our knowledge of the epidemic. There were in fact pitifully few people involved in this endless, exhausting, and it must be said often extremely depressing uphill work. Now most of that has changed, thank God, thanks to the huge energies of the staff and volunteers of GMFA (and, to be fair, many others) and it is extremely important for longer-term, older AIDS workers to accept that we are no longer 'out there on our own', at least in the same way that we were five, or even three years ago.

My greatest worry at the moment is that a huge number of gay men are still only too happy to delegate responsibility for 'fighting AIDS' onto other people, as long as it's not them. In my experience, even the most senior journalists in the UK gay press often have no idea whatsoever about even the most elementary aspects of HIV/AIDS prevention or treatment issues. The denial of resources of gay men for HIV education in the 1980s and early 1990s was, I believe, incomparably the most important political issue facing our 'community' in those years. Those of us who tried endlessly to find new ways to explain this were patronizingly congratulated for our 'sterling efforts', and ignored. This situation has not substantially changed.

As is possibly apparent, I am a rather old-fashioned British liberal. Whatever other strategies we may develop, the continued mobilization of collective, community values amongst gay men will remain paramount. That is to buy, effective responses to AIDS don't just drop out of the sky, they have to be made in relation to changing needs. GMFA began with a solid commit ment to assessing those needs and trying to respond to them and that's what probably remains most important about the entire enterprise; GMFA is not about One Big Idea precisely because we proceed from the recognition that there's not just one type of gay man.

In my work as the Director of a small AIDS education funding agency I come across applications from all round the world, made by men joining together in a political articulation of shared needs, organized around the notion of gay identity. This is not a 'magic wand', but it is the indispensable prerequisite for other forms of organization. This World AIDS Day is about Rights and Responsibilities. In this context we can see only too clearly the global scale of the neglect of gay men's needs in this crisis. This is the same in countries where we make up a minority of cases as in countries where we continue to make up the majority. GMFA thus seems to me to be the local expression, if you will, of a far wider assertion on the part of some sections of the gay community all around the world – the assertion of the intrinsically ordinary right to sexual choice and to life itself. How can we 'fight AIDS' if we are not fully and passionately committed to life?

This is equally the case in relation to both treatment and educational work. It is certainly deeply depressing that treatment activism in Britain continues generally to mean anti-HIV theories of the Duesberg/GAG variety. Colleagues and friends in other countries are aghast. It is as if there were no truth, and worse still, as if 'the truth' didn't matter. Certainly debates about the medical aspects of HIV in Britain have only rarely considered questions of treatment as an issue of urgency. Indeed, perhaps the gravest damage caused by the Murdoch press *et al.* looking back, was the wholesale impor- tation of conspiracy theories into the field of the epidemic. Every voice became suspect. I think this has done incalculable harm, especially to the great majority of gay men who read the *Mail* or *The Times* or the *Mirror* every morning. This bad situation has only been made worse by the extremely low levels of AIDS analysis on the part of ostensibly gay men working inside the mass media supposedly as out gay men – journalists who often seem to take any opportunity to trash and belittle the community from which their careers emerged.

Yet, as George Eliot warned long ago in *Felix Holt*, indignation may be a fine war-horse, but it still has to be ridden: 'by rationality, skill, courage, armed with the right weapons, and taking definite aim'.

This is every bit as true of GMFA today as on the Sunday in March 1992 when 15 or so gay men met at Peter Scott's invitation to form the organiza- tion. The effects of HIV/AIDS throughout our culture seem almost beyond estimation and they change all the time, in the lives and feelings of individu- als and generations of gay men. For example, who if not GMFA is going to respond adequately to the growing scale of sheer loss and grief and their effects, amongst increasing numbers of gay men? Who if not GMFA is going to be able to force the difficult questions about why so many of us suffer such extreme splits between sex and intimacy? Who if not GMFA is going to be able to encourage us all to love ourselves and one another a lot more than we have been used to?

In the meantime there is no real evidence that any of the political parties really understands the issues raised by HIV/AIDS. Nor is the fantasy of a National Plan especially helpful, unless it means properly resourcing demonstrably necessary local initiatives. The mass media remain hopelessly unreliable, and most of the old left has retreated happily into a shiny new pro-family morality, which is what it always did best anyway. In the meantime, we of course continue to understand far more about our lives and our feelings than anyone else can and this is our greatest single resource. We know of the isolation and usually rather furtive initial sex of our early teens, and the romanticism and growing self-confidence of our later teens. We know about the sexual experimentation and starter-marriages of our twenties and the renewed sexual experimentation and serial relationships that tend so often to follow from the starter-marriages. We may go on to long-term open or closed relationships. We may change our sexual repertoire altogether. As we grow older, many of our relationships also contain strong elements of parenting in them and so on. These are the ordinary, difficult, wonderful, everyday narratives of our lives, and it is on this terrain, or not at all, that we will win this war.

23 'Lifelike': imagining the bodies of people with AIDS*

> A youngster hardly twenty three hangs on,
> sustained by a hateful necessary tube
> taped up to his forehead, exiting his nose,
> so ancient no one visits anymore.
> – Michael Lynch, 'Late May – Toronto'[1]

> Scared families are flocking to leave a council skyscraper branded Britain's
> first 'AIDS Ghetto'. One great-gran said relatives are too frightened to visit
> because many of her neighbors – half are gay – are dying from the HIV virus.
> Other residents at Birmingham's Clydesdale Tower are so scared of touching
> the lift buttons they don protective gloves.
> – Frank Curren, 'Our Hell Living in AIDS Ghetto'[2]

Throughout the history of the HIV/AIDS pandemic, questions concerning
the proximity of those known or thought to be uninfected to the bodies of
people living with HIV or AIDS have played a central role in public discourse. The populist press has always reported on the AIDS crisis as if HIV
were miasmatically contagious, and furthermore, as if the presence of people
living with HIV or AIDS in the community is intrinsically surprising and
therefore noteworthy. Characteristically, the *Daily Star* recently quoted
'young mum Michelle Bishop, 26', who lives on the twenty-sixth floor of a
Birmingham tower block with her six-year-old daughter, Danielle: 'I've lived
here five years and I'm desperate to leave. There are many people
living here with AIDS and I'm living in fear and want to get out.'[3]

Such reporting remains far from unusual in the UK, where HIV has had a
disproportionately limited impact compared to most other European countries –
largely as the result of early community-based HIV education developed in the
1980s by and for gay men, and the government's introduction of widespread
needle exchanges since 1986. In a country with a total population of approximately fifty-eight million, there have been twenty-five thousand reported cases

* *First published in Andrew Perchuk and Helaine Posner (Eds)* The Masculine Masquerade:
Masculinity & Representation, *Cambridge, Mass.: MIT Press, 1995.*

of HIV to date, and approximately ten thousand cases of AIDS. In this context, it is important to note that the mass media's representation of people with AIDS will always be linked to shifting national levels of sero-prevalence – responding to the overall rate of new cases in the national population. Where HIV and AIDS remain comparatively rare, there is likely to be less pressure to modify representations that emerged at the earliest stages of the epidemic. Thus, proximity is indeed an important factor in our understanding of the representation of people with AIDS – especially in relation to perceptions of risk.

Yet such perceptions are organized in very different ways for different sections of the population. HIV/AIDS education developed for heterosexuals has generally tended to problematize the HIV status of one's sexual partner. The straight AIDS message regards its target audience as uninfected, and thus 'at risk' from familiar, dangerous types of people – bisexuals, junkies, prostitutes, 'the promiscuous', and so on. Materials produced by and for gay men, however, usually proceed from a pragmatic acknowledgment that many gay men are already infected – as many as 50 per cent it is estimated in some US cities. The gay AIDS message thus tends to emphasize the fact that risk may be *to* one's sexual partners, not simply *from* them. It is not difficult to follow the displaced anxieties that continue to inform much public and private AIDS commentary, anxieties about having intimate physical contact with somebody who has been 'polluted' by equally direct prior contact to a member of the deadly *dramatis personae* of heterosexual HIV dread, bisexuals, junkies, and so on. Unpacked, the logic of the anxiety frequently seems to be the fear that one is having sex with someone who has had anal sex, or who has had sex with someone else who likes anal sex.

It is, frankly, pointless to complain at this stage of the epidemic that such fears and representations are largely groundless and irrational, for it is precisely their irrationality that sustains them. At the same time, however, we also live with a tenacious legacy of counter-representations, often mobilized by people with HIV/AIDS, working to correct the demonizing processes at work elsewhere. Since the early years of the epidemic, people living with AIDS have been involved in a long-term contestation of representations deemed to be misleading, 'stereotypical', and so on.[4] A complex politics of representation has played prominently in the history of HIV/AIDS, as rival sets of images mobilized rival explanations of the crisis. The image of someone with AIDS is, thus, inescapably caught up in a dense field of conflict, in which all too often the sadistic oversimplifications of racists, misogynists, and homophobes are countered by equally oversimplified idealizations. While it is undoubtedly just as important as before to refuse and refute casual, unthinking talk of 'AIDS victims', for example, this stance becomes absurd to whatever extent it makes anyone living with AIDS feel he or she can't talk about the too commonly shared experience of being victimized, or if it further obscures the objective processes of systematic victimization.

Positive bodies

When the Benetton clothing company recently produced an advertisement
showing ex-president Ronald Reagan's face ostensibly covered with the
Kaposi's sarcoma lesions commonly associated with AIDS, a colleague
reportedly said that Mr Reagan 'feels sickened that his image is being used
in such a disgusting fashion'.[5] Photographer and art director Oliviero
Toscani, who created the ad, defends his actions, saying: 'I did this because
Reagan disregarded alarms about the AIDS threat when he was President.'[6]
One is obliged to point out that Toscani has employed specific signs of physical deformation in order to demonize Reagan in precisely the same way that
others have used those same signs to demonize people with AIDS in general.
In either case, AIDS is held to be intrinsically disgusting – supposed 'evidence' of depravity and immorality, or, as in the Benetton ad, of government
neglect and hypocrisy. Both the *Daily Star* and Benetton share the popular
assumption that AIDS is indeed shameful.

Such routine transformations of the physical appearance of people with
AIDS into cyphers or emblems of supposed moral worth hardly serves to
clarify most people's perceptions of their own personal risk. Yet we should
not simply complain that AIDS imagery targeted at heterosexuals presents
HIV as a distant risk: In fact abundant epidemiological evidence demonstrates that, throughout the developed world, heterosexuals who have unprotected sexual intercourse are demonstrably far less likely to contract HIV
than gay men. What is noteworthy is that the dominant imagery of AIDS has
not yet adjusted to accommodate changing medical information. For example, epidemiological surveys now suggest that 'a substantial proportion [of
HIV-positive individuals] will probably be free of AIDS 20 and 25 years
after HIV-1 infection'.[7] Such reliable reports provide grounds for cautious
optimism for the many millions living with HIV throughout the developed
world.[8] The extreme fatalism that characterizes most populist AIDS discourse *requires* that AIDS be painful, hideous, and uniformly fatal. Yet
for the HIV-positive 'non-progressor', things are very different. Thus
Jonathan Grimshaw has eloquently described 'the paradox of having on the
one hand something wonderful – more years of life than one had anticipated.
And on the other hand the idea of life as a sentence, as a prisoner might be
"sentenced" for life.'[9]

Behind all this lies the physiological question of HIV status, one's own
and that of one's sexual partners – whether it is 'known' or just 'perceived'.
For most heterosexuals HIV is understandably felt as rather remote, because
for most heterosexuals it is indeed rather remote. Consequently, the fantasy
that the epidemic can be stopped by magically identifying all so-called
'AIDS carriers' remains potent. Indeed, the very notion of the 'AIDS carrier'
itself speaks volumes about the ways in which early commentators successfully framed the supposed 'meaning' of the epidemic (for heterosexuals) in
terms of the need to avoid whole classes of people. If you inhabited one of

the groups heterosexuals were meant to avoid, things were, of course, rather different. For gay men, HIV status has become a presiding issue in all our social and amorous transactions – not because we seek to avoid HIV, but because it is literally unavoidable.

Throughout the entire history of the epidemic, doctors, epidemiologists, government officials, and many others have called on gay men to come forward for HIV testing. This is somehow imagined by analogy with the national blood-transfusion service as a 'responsible' and even 'manly' thing to do, a matter of common sense. But *whose* common sense, and *of what*? Any gay man having sex with another man whose HIV status he doesn't know faces the extremely high probability that he or his partner, or both, are already infected. In gay men over 25, this has long been an everyday fact of life, something you learn to 'get used to'. In the United States, most gay men over 30 will have friends and acquaintances at all stages of HIV-related illness, and a decade of funerals behind them. In Britain, AIDS deaths appear only in the register of mortality statistics, and there has been no mass media recognition of the ways in which the epidemic is experienced in all its complexity from the perspective of those for whom death is increasingly a part of 'everyday life' – 'everyday life' as another, distant planet as far as journalists are concerned. It remains important in Britain to depict AIDS in all its awful complexity, since its reality is not lived as directly and widely as in America. This is especially important in relation to younger gay men, who are unlikely knowingly to have any direct contact whatsoever with HIV or AIDS.

The 'good news' about increased life-expectancy prospects for the already infected also signals a new challenge to gay health educators, since it seems likely that more people are likely to remain unknowingly infectious far longer than we had previously calculated. For some, the answer to such issues will be HIV testing. For others it will be an equally principled decision to continue living with uncertainty – the dominant mode of psychic reality for most gay British men in the 1990s. We know the medical evidence, and it is not good. We live our life as best we can. Love affairs end. Ardor cools. Opportunity beckons. In such respects, gay men are hardly unique.

It would be difficult, if not impossible to do justice to the emotional complexity surrounding the entire question of HIV testing among gay men. For heterosexuals, however, 'AIDS testing' is invariably sensationalized and sentimentalized. As a gay man, it is difficult to think of a more spectacularly nauseating species of journalism than the oft repeated spectacle of the star (or more often starlet) describing his or her terrible anxieties before getting HIV-test results back. One gasps at the innuendoes: Forbidden love? Sexual pleasure? God forbid! And always, always, always, they are negative. When my friends test, here in London, one in four is statistically likely to be positive. This is how *we* think of 'positive bodies'.

'I have AIDS'

Diseased Pariah News is published in San Francisco. It describes its mission as 'a quarterly publication of, by, and for people with HIV disease. We are a forum for infected people to share their thoughts, feelings, art, writing, and brownie recipes in an atmosphere free of teddy bears, magic rocks, and seronegative guilt.'[10] I ask myself which heterosexuals I know would begin to understand the notion of 'seronegative guilt', let alone the different registers of meaning it evokes in gay men who think or believe themselves to be negative, or gay men who suspect they are possibly infected, or those who suspect they are probably infected, or those who know they are 'positive', *Diseased Pariah News* has a regular hot porno gay PWA centrefold, and its most fabulous (and practical) regular column is 'GET FAT, don't die!'

In a story by my late friend and colleague Allen Barnett, a gay man learns:

> that the body can recall things on its own. There were nights when he felt the recent dead getting into bed, climbing over him as if they had just come from the shower. He felt their bodies against his own, or beneath him, a sack of balls loose between their legs, wet hair on the nape of their necks. He could feel the way each of them used to push into the mattress on their way to sleep. It was even comforting to have them there, to be remembered by them before they got up to lie briefly, like this, in someone else's bed. There were dead men he could still arouse himself for.[11]

And, presumably, there were dead men for whom feelings of arousal were simply too painful to imagine, or to follow, or to follow through on.

There is furthermore a dimension of political and ethical solidarity closely involved in gay men's relations with one another's HIV statuses, since HIV is overwhelmingly the most important issue facing our various communities, though this is rarely acknowledged by the ostensible lesbian and gay political 'leadership' organizations in Britain or the United States. They in turn seek admission to the cleaner airs of 'official' national politics, and HIV has long been an embarrassment to Rainbow Coalitionists. Hence, we should also recognize the discursive impact of the research subject who speaks from 'science' back into everyday life. In this manner Mark Harrington's presentation at the 1994 Tenth International Conference on AIDS in Yokohama exemplified a very different order of political intervention, welcoming delegates, and thanking the organizers for asking him to speak on the vexed topic of 'When to Begin Antiretroviral Treatment?':

> The topic is obviously a timely one, not only for the AIDS field in general, but also for myself in particular. Some of you were in Amsterdam two years ago and may have seen me present slides of my left auxiliary

lymph node biopsies in April 1992, in situ hybridization of which demonstrated, in the words of one of my doctors, that my lymph node was 'crammed with virus'. At the time I had somewhat over 600 CD4 cells; they are now, two years later, somewhat over 400, and I remain asymptomatic.[12]

He then delivered a paper concluding that, from the perspective of people living with HIV: 'all the advances in high-tech virology and immunology have yet to be applied or confirmed in well-designed studies which provide *clinical evidence of benefit.*'[13]

A powerful poem by my late best friend, Charles Barber, graphically describes what it is like to be treated for such advanced symptoms of HIV disease as CMV retinitis. He is describing the type of catheter routinely inserted into the chests of people with AIDS whose regular veins can no longer take injections or IV drips:

> The dream.
> Finally well,
> Over me lies his arm;
> The hole in my chest a lip-smudge,
> Stamped, sealed.
> Grotesque,
> Life-supporting,
> Deforming and healing;
> Not a cure; insistent I be
> Life-like.[14]

At a time when the metaphor for people with HIV as 'living timebombs' remains widely in use, we can only speculate about the extent popular 'concern' about AIDS is about imaginary 'fallout' rather than about the real, substantial issues of risk and death among gay men, injecting drug users, and their sexual partners.[15]

While comparisons between the signs of leprosy and plague in previous centuries and current representations of people with AIDS provide interesting parallels, all too often they are used to obscure or deflect attention away from what is unique to HIV/AIDS in the late twentieth century. This has less to do with lay perceptions possibly bearing traces of premodern notions of the body's 'humors', than with institutionalized homophobia and racism, with the complete inability of late-twentieth-century public political discourse to acknowledge the actual sexual choices and diversity of the populations politicians claim to represent. The answer to these and other current dilemmas does not lie in pretending that HIV is some kind of 'equal opportunity' virus, as it is so often depicted. There is a truth that precedes representation, and it is faithfully mapped in the many epidemiological tables that measure changing patterns of public health and illness. How those tables are themselves translated into public discourse is thus a central question for AIDS activists who wish to establish policies firmly based in the real epidemic rather than in the domains of collective cultural hallucinations.

This is why the question of how we imagine the bodies of people with AIDS matters. More than most, such bodies are inspected, evaluated, weighed, measured. More than most, they deserve the ordinary decencies of privacy. While the 'truth claims' made from the position of speaking 'as' a person with HIV or AIDS guarantees nothing about the accuracy or utility of what is said, nonetheless the claim has a fundamental validity. How we imagine the bodies of people with AIDS is always a reflection of how we all regard our own bodies, and that regard is charged with a dimension of sexual object-choice, which is as fundamental as any question of age or race or gender.

Notes

1 Michael Lynch's poem, 'Late May – Toronto,' appeared in *Tribe: An American Gay Journal*, 1 (Spring 1990), p. 44.
2 Frank Curran's 'Our Hell Living in AIDS Ghetto' appeared in the *Daily Star*, 29 Aug. 1994.
3 As reported in the *Daily Star* (London) 29 Aug. 1994, p. 44.
4 For example, see Michael Callen, *Surviving AIDS* (New York: HarperCollins, 1990).
5 Tim Miles, 'Reagan fury over Benetton AIDS ad'. *Sunday Express*, 26 June 1994.
6 *Ibid.*
7 'Long-term survival in HIV-1 infection', *British Journal of Medicine*, 30 July 1994, pp. 283–4.
8 The survey quoted and others drawing similar conclusions were conducted in the developed world; consequently, inferences from these data may only be drawn with respect to the developed world and may or may not be applicable to the Third World.
9 Jonathan Grimshaw, '"Life" for a non-progressor,' plenary talk given at Second International Conference on Biopsychosocial Aspects of HIV and AIDS, Brighton, England 7–10 July 1994.
10 *Diseased Pariah News*, 4 (1991), p. 1.
11 Allen Barnett, 'Philostorgy, now obscure', in *The Body and its Dangers* (New York: St. Martin's Press, 1990), p. 52.
12 Mark Harrington, 'When to begin antiretroviral treatment?' paper given on Thursday, 11 Aug. 1994, at the Tenth International Conference on AIDS, at Yokohama.
13 *Ibid.*, emphasis in original.
14 Charles Barber, 'Thirteen Things About a Catheter', in Rachel Hadas (Ed) *Unending Dialogue: Voices from an Aids Poetry Workshop* (Boston: Faber & Faber, 1990), p. 23.
15 For example, Gill Swain, 'AIDS TIMEBOMB: Where life really is for living'. *Daily Mirror* (London), 22 June 1994.

24 The politics of AIDS treatment information activism*

Introduction

AIDS treatment activism emerged in the United States (US) in the second half of the 1980s as a response to at least two major factors: the direct experience of acute illness and death presented by the HIV/AIDS epidemic and a lack of confidence in the capacity or willingness of the medical and pharmaceutical industries to act in the interests of people living with HIV or AIDS. Against a background of profoundly negative social perceptions of the constituencies worst affected by AIDS in the developed world, gay and bisexual men and injecting drug users and their sexual partners, the question of how medical information is generated, by whom and for whom became of major significance for those involved – especially those infected and their immediate friends, families, carers and communities.

This chapter discusses the context in which obtaining and disseminating reliable, up-to-date information in an accessible form emerged as a key issue among AIDS activists and describes and analyses the development of treatment information networks in the wider context of treatment activism, first in the US and subsequently in Britain. The author draws on personal experience and research on both sides of the Atlantic and on recently conducted interviews with key players in establishing and running AIDS information networks in Britain (Edward King, Mark Harrington, Peter Scott and Keith Alcorn). The struggle for a measure of control over information about AIDS and HIV is part of a wider strategy to secure health for individuals, groups and communities which involves a direct challenge to the, at best, benevolent paternalist attitudes of the medical, pharmaceutical and public health establishments and to widespread prejudicial attitudes and behaviours which undermine people's health.

How to make treatment choices in an epidemic

For people living with HIV and AIDS, choices about treatment are bedevilled by the fact that, since the beginning of the AIDS crisis in 1981, rival

* First published in Paul Bywaters and Eileen McLeod (Eds) Working for Equality in Health, London: Routledge, 1996.

and incompatible explanations of almost every medical aspect of the epidemic have flourished, from theories concerning modes of transmission and infectivity, to wider questions of the genesis of the epidemic, its extent and the entire field of potential treatments and cures. It remains an interesting question why AIDS has attracted so many 'cranks', conspiracy theorists and anti-rationalists of many different persuasions (Harris 1995). Certainly the situation has not been helped by the generally poor levels of medical journalism throughout the history of the epidemic. In effect, since the isolation of HIV in 1983, the public narratives 'handling' the scientific aspects of AIDS have tended to focus on 'miracle cures' and rivalries between individual scientists, rather than the medical needs of people living with HIV or AIDS.

On the one hand, the mass media have tended to be overwhelmingly fatalistic about AIDS, creating otherwise avoidable stresses for the infected, and on the other hand, the mass media have constantly thrown up seemingly 'scientific' AIDS stories which are frequently unverifiable, or reports of the earliest stages of *in vitro* research. Thus the field of public scientific information on HIV/AIDS has long been muddled with contesting claims. Treatment issues are trivialized as the epidemic itself is sensationalized. All of this is not unconnected to the negative attitudes widely exhibited towards communities most affected by AIDS in the developed world (King 1993; Watney 1994).

These contested claims are frequently presented in the mass media as taking place between 'AIDS heretics' or 'AIDS dissidents' and a supposedly sinister, and complacent 'AIDS establishment' (Harris 1995). However, as Edward King, Editor of *AIDS Treatment Update*, the British monthly AIDS treatment newsletter, has pointed out:

> There really isn't a single 'conventional' view on AIDS for 'dissenters' to disagree with … The vast majority of scientists are convinced that HIV plays a key role in causing AIDS, and that people who are not infected with HIV are not at risk of developing AIDS. However, beyond that there is little consensus. Some researchers think that HIV only causes illness in the presence of other factors. Others think that such co-factors might speed up HIV's harmful effects, but that HIV can still cause illness even in the absence of co-factors. So here again there is actually a range of opinion, not a party line.
>
> (King 1994)

The use of the term 'AIDS dissidents' suggests the notion of a rigid, conservative, orthodox, scientific establishment, challenged like Goliath by plucky, vulnerable, hard-done-by radicals. In practice, however, as King argues:

> the most radical responses to AIDS have come not from AIDS dissidents, but from those working from the inside to challenge the medical model which existed before AIDS. AIDS treatment activism has sought

to provide options for people with HIV, and help individuals to make up their own minds about those options. For example, activists have fought to make experimental drugs available as early as possible, through compassionate clinical trial designs and expanded access schemes, so that people with HIV or AIDS at least have the opportunity to take them if they so wish.

(ibid)

In effect, the many different lobby groups within the arena of debate about treatment options and research into HIV/AIDS may be roughly divided into those who are, to mimic the language of another controversial health debate, 'pro-choice', and those who are 'anti-choice'. For example, those who proselytize against involvement with what they term 'Western medicine', as if it were monolithic, are, in effect, reducing choice for people with HIV or AIDS, just as clearly as those who deny any causal agency between HIV and AIDS provide only the dogmatic assertion that AIDS is somehow caused by the use of recreational drugs or homosexuality and exhibit little or no concern for treatment as an urgent issue for the infected. In reality, surveys clearly demonstrate that most people living with HIV or AIDS use both conventional and complementary medicines, and other therapies, on the basis of informed choices (Barton *et al.* 1994). Such choices are, in any case, often far from easy. For example, whilst one may be looking for beneficial synergistic effects of drugs used in combination, equally it is often the case that different types of drugs which may seem individually advantageous may have harmful consequences when used together. Both the initial need to make choices in the absence of medical understanding of the disease and the subsequent pollution and hijacking of sources of reliable information by lobbies with agendas which precede and exceed HIV/AIDS, have raised questions about how medical information is produced and disseminated.

The emergence of treatment activism

Treatment activism emerged in the US where the epidemic is running approximately five years ahead of the epidemics in Europe. It is also important to recognize that the UK epidemic is disproportionately small by international standards of comparison. Thus, until very recently, Britain has primarily experienced an epidemic of asymptomatic HIV infection, prior to the onset of AIDS, whereas the United States has had a far wider, large-scale experience of symptomatic illness and death. By the end of 1994, 260,000 Americans had already died from AIDS (Centre for Disease Control and Prevention 1994), whereas in Britain, with approximately a quarter of the population of the United States, there had been approaching 7,000 deaths (Communicable Disease Surveillance Centre 1994). These figures alone speak of a vastly different social experience of AIDS between cities such as New York and London.

Given this background and the well known inequalities of American health care provision, it is not surprising that the demand for reliable medical information, couched in practically helpful terms, emerged first in the United States, as increasing numbers of hitherto largely healthy young people sickened and died without effective treatments. Paradoxically, the private, commercial nature of medical provision in the United States had also long encouraged a more generally active role on the part of many patients and patient-groups, in relation to the authority of individual doctors and whole areas of clinical medicine, from paediatrics to oncology. Thus AIDS treatment activism emerged in the mid-1980s in New York and rapidly elsewhere in the United States, within the longstanding American political tradition of voluntary associations, banded together as citizens with specific common goals. Amongst these was a recognition of the need for accessible, reliable, up-to-date information about all and any research that might have some practical therapeutic significance.

A number of community-based periodicals appeared in the mid-1980s in order to 'translate' relevant findings, routinely written up and published in the many different professional scientific journals such as the *British Medical Journal* or the *New England Journal of Medicine*, into pragmatically useful lay terms. The first of these periodicals was *AIDS Treatment News*, which was founded by John S. James in May 1986, initially as a bi-weekly column in the *San Francisco Sentinel*, a local San Francisco gay newspaper. As he explained, back in 1986: '"Beautiful death" ideas were strong in San Francisco, and treatment information was regarded as quackery, false hope which interfered with the process of accepting death' (James 1989: xxix). *AIDS Treatment News* was, and remains, a non-profit organization, with a small staff, and few resources, aiming to 'contribute to public understanding of how opportunities have been lost in AIDS treatment development, and how past and present problems can be corrected. A humane, informed, and articulate public and professional consensus can save lives' (James 1989: xxxvi).

Very similar motives and aims informed and encouraged the emergence of the AIDS Coalition To Unleash Power (ACT UP) in New York in 1986 (Kramer 1995). However, for ACT UP, treatment information activism was intimately connected to the strategic targeting of institutions understood to be blocking research, or the provision of treatment drugs available in countries such as Britain but unlicensed in the USA. Recognition of the immediately harmful consequences of the market economics of American health care and medical research led initially to the straightforward demand for access to potential treatment drugs, via the provision of more widely available clinical trials. Large numbers of people with HIV had already been recruited into initial clinical trials and the question of the medical ethics of informed consent was widely discussed and written about (Levine *et al.* 1991). Action to secure access to treatment information thus connected closely to campaigns targeting individual pharmaceutical corporations and relevant government departments of the Centers for Disease Control (CDC) and the Food and Drug Administration (FDA), ironically the very departments which had been set up in the 1920s to protect Americans from being exploited, and possibly poisoned, in the search for effective treatments. As playwright Harvey Fierstein explained in a fund-raising letter on behalf of ACT UP in 1988:

> There are times – and I believe this is one of them – when a community has no choice left but to demonstrate to make its voice heard. Quite frankly, I am afraid of what might happen if we don't protest, if we don't take to the streets, if we don't force the government to hear our plea.
>
> (Fierstein 1988)

Hence, in the mid-1980s in the United States, treatment activism involved both the provision of information *and*, frequently, the provision of hard-to-obtain drugs via the appearance of Buyer's Clubs, which varied greatly in the quality of the (often imported) drugs they provided and sold. And from its origins, the People With AIDS Coalition in New York, led by Michael Callen and Michael Hirsch, provided regular treatment data in its publication the *PWA Newsline*. Only subsequently did the goal of providing treatment information become separate from direct treatment advocacy.

From treatment activism to treatment information

As ACT UP grew and developed, however, it also became vulnerable to the wider forces of political sectarianism, which saw in AIDS only another example of government neglect or cupidity and recognized no specific medical agenda or priorities. Indeed, as early as Spring 1988, some perceptive AIDS activists were already complaining that:

> Our message is weakened and made partisan when individuals and groups use ACT UP's energy, enthusiasm and demonstrations to promote their non-AIDS political and social agendas regardless of how worthy … Was ACT UP set up to oppose the Reagan administration's foreign policy in Central America? … ACT UP is not affiliated to any political party. When we participate in ACT UP demonstrations we are neither for nor against the Contras, the Sandanistas, the Israelis, the Arabs, nuclear power plants, ICBM's, high tariffs, low tariffs or saving the ozone layer or the dolphins. We are AIDS activists busting our asses to change government policies that are allowing a generation of gay men to die.
>
> (Bramson 1988)

What had been intended as a coalition between the worst affected social communities had become in effect a coalition of left-wing causes. Indeed, by

the early 1990s it was frequently argued that the demand for universal socialized medicine in the USA should be the top priority and all questions of
HIV/AIDS research should be placed on hold. It was at this point that ACT
UP's Treatment and Data Committee resigned and set up their own independent organization, the Treatment Action Group (TAG). Only in this way
could expert, pragmatic, achievable demands, which addressed the fact that
large numbers of people were dying from AIDS now, be formulated and
campaigned for.

Summarizing the current situation in relation to community-based
HIV/AIDS US treatment information, leading TAG activist Mark Harrington
observes that now:

> most large and many smaller community-based organisations around the
> country routinely publish treatment updates. Among the most reliable
> are Gay Men's Health Crisis (GMHC)'s 'Treatment Issues', 'TPA News'
> from Chicago and 'Critical Path' from Philadelphia. Also of note are
> local and regional AIDS treatment directories such as AIDS Treatment
> and Data Network's 'The Experimental Guide' for New York, New
> Jersey and Connecticut, or the Community Consortium's 'Directory of
> HIV Clinical Trials in the Bay Area'. The American Foundation For
> AIDS Research's important and pioneering Directory has now been
> closed, unfortunately. Niche newsletters include the PWA Health
> Group's 'Notes From The Underground' and San Francisco's 'Diseased
> Pariah News' with its important 'Get Fat, Don't Die' column. The New
> York-based Treatment Action Group (TAG)'s 'TAGline' is also a niche
> newsletter, in that it focuses on research policy rather than on ground-
> breaking treatment information per se. In this, and like TAG's periodic
> reports, it grows from the tradition of activist broadsides, pamphlets and
> factsheets which were used by ACT UP/New York in 1988–1992 and
> particularly its Treatment + Data Committee with a weekly 'T+G
> Digest' and the annual 'AIDS Treatment Research Agendas'.
>
> (Harrington 1995)

Harrington concludes that many US treatment newsletters have yet to fully
come to grips with defining and promulgating standards of what is considered 'reliable' data. Many continue to publish articles based on anecdotes or
speculation which, while not necessarily to be excluded, need to be clearly
distinguished from the domain of scientific rationality. Noting the continued
need for accurate, up-to-date data, Harrington insists that:

> Treatment advocacy needs to continually revisit its original founding
> principles and see which remain relevant (PWA empowerment and
> involvement within research, inclusiveness of clinical trials, availability
> of expanded access programs, continued emphasis on opportunistic
> infections and cancers) and which need rethinking (prohibition of

placebos, use of clinical endpoints in efficacy trials, criteria for acceler-
ated approval, reliance on surrogate markers, the assumption that a new
drug is necessarily better, etc.). Is it possible to ground a vigorous treatment advocacy movement within a framework of realistic (as opposed to
Utopian) expectations, and if so, how? There is a lack of historical
memory and an insufficient ability to train, mentor and encourage new
treatment activists.

(*ibid.*)

The scale of this task may become more apparent if one considers the sheer
volume and complexity of HIV/AIDS research in progress around the world,
in need of constant processing and evaluation. For example, the handbook
listing papers and poster presentations at the Ninth International AIDS
Conference, in Berlin in 1993, came to 672 pages, with an average of some
ten different references per page.

The American AIDS information newsletters have now become a central
network both for the forging of research and treatment policies and individual decision making – a network which now spills over into e-mail and
beyond. Moreover, American models of AIDS activism and advocacy work
have been widely influential in other countries with less pronounced and
confident traditions of community action coupled to medical scepticism,
such as Australia, Canada and the United Kingdom. Yet, of course, the
institutions controlling and regulating medical knowledge differ greatly in
different countries. Only in a handful of cases has American-style
AIDS activism taken root in other parts of the world, such as Paris, where the
epidemic is as catastrophic as in most American cities (European Centre for
the Epidemiological Monitoring of AIDS 1994) and where the direct effects
of illness and death are thus far more widely experienced than in London
or Edinburgh. Thus in '*Action*': *La Lettre Mensuelle d'ACT UP*, the
regular publication of ACT UP/PARIS, treatment information and treatment
advocacy remain closely connected behind the slogan '*Info = Vie*'
(Information = Life).

Treatment information activism in Britain

Meanwhile in Britain things are rather different. Writing to complain about a
recent article about AIDS in the weekly London listings magazine *Time Out*,
a doctor recently invited readers to 'think about all the politically correct
money that has poured into AIDS research at the expense of other diseases.
And think about the members of your families who have died, and what
killed them?' (Nicholson 1994).

Such attitudes reflect a widespread belief that AIDS research is somehow
conducted at the expense of other diseases and medical conditions. Not far
behind this lies the less often openly stated belief that people with HIV are
not 'like us' (meaning upright heterosexuals) and have only themselves to

blame. Indeed, throughout the Thatcher years, the UK mass media and government departments were widely and often persuasively influenced by small, extremist religious and right-wing political groups such as Family and Youth Concern, the Conservative Family Campaign and others (King 1993). In a period of intense competition in the newspaper industry, AIDS has also long been treated as if it were a theoretical issue concerning rival scientific explanations, rather than as an epidemic causing horrific personal and social consequences. Thus the wholly unverifiable assertions of a few individuals and groups with pre-existing moral or political agendas have often been advanced as if they were on the same footing as the consistent research findings of tens of thousands of doctors and researchers around the world (*ibid.*: Ch. 5). Because there is no baseline to tell us reliably how many gay men there are in the UK it is difficult to assess accurate proportions, but for many years one in four or five gay men attending central London clinics for HIV tests have found they were HIV-positive (King 1993). Moreover the pressures on gay men to take the test are immense. The scale of infection, illness and nowadays death throughout the British gay community, especially in London which has 75 per cent of all UK cases, has no British (or American) parallel in modern times, even in warfare. For example, of the 5,653 deaths from AIDS up to the end of 1993, 4,291 were amongst gay and bisexual men (Communicable Disease Surveillance Centre 1993). And in recent years, our losses have gone largely unremarked and unlamented, while attention has increasingly focused on 'heterosexual AIDS' (*ibid.*: Ch. 6).

In the early years of the epidemic the British gay press frequently reported news from the US gay press on all aspects of AIDS. Articles from the *New York Native* and *Christopher Street* were summarized within weeks in *Gay News* in London. Yet the number of cases here was small and HIV testing had not yet come into being, so there was little general interest in questions of *cure* compared to the questions of *cause*. As the epidemic unfolded, AIDS Service Organizations emerged from small groups of affected individuals, who recognized clear needs and understood that nobody was going to do anything for the gay community and that we would have to do things for ourselves. Yet groups such as the Terrence Higgins Trust (THT) never regarded the provision of treatment information as being part of their central remit. A group of doctors within the THT simply wrote brief bulletins of the latest information and had no sense of politics around the provision of information. Meanwhile Body Positive, which came into being in 1985, included treatment information in its newsletter, as did several other publications including *Frontliners*, published by and for people with AIDS.

It should also be noted that some small factions of the medical profession and journalists made aggressive attempts to stifle or otherwise invalidate the voices of complementary medicine. This led to a tendency to regard 'official' and complementary medicine as if they were wholly opposed, as if an absolute choice had to be made between the two, rather than choices from *both* options. Similarly, significant legitimate controversy concerning the costs of drugs such as AZT and the possibility of profiteering on the part of the multinational pharmaceutical corporations may also have distracted attention away from the concrete issues of treatment and treatment research goals. Meanwhile, newspapers competed with one another for ever more sensationalist stories about supposedly evil 'AIDS-carriers' and so on. However, some individuals were already connected with the US treatment activism, shipping prescribed drugs for the effective treatment of ailments such as Cyto Megalo Virus retinitis to the United States where they were unavailable and patients simply went blind. Others had close contacts from the beginning with the emergence of ACT UP and reported back to Britain in the gay press.

By the late 1980s it was apparent, however, that Britain was unlikely to see the kinds of pressure that had led to the large-scale AIDS treatment activist movement that prevailed in the USA. People would gladly campaign against drug company and health care profiteering but not in favour of particular research, treatment and information policies. This was largely because there were so few people sufficiently on top of the medical literature to be able to formulate an effective critique, if it were needed. There was no UK equivalent to the Treatment and Data Committee of ACT UP in New York and, because of their more deferential relationship with doctors mentioned earlier, British patients tended to expect far less detailed information about their options than Americans.

There was an attempt in the late 1980s to set up a Community Research Initiative (CRI) on New York lines, running clinical trials conducted from GPs' surgeries rather than in hospitals, but the competition between the leading London hospitals enforced by government policies undermined the project, since individual hospitals needed to account for patients in order to provide services. Patients could not be 'shared' and GPs were not keen to take on the long-term chronically ill for similar budgetary reasons. In Britain, AIDS activism was honourably concerned with Social Security and housing issues but not with medical policy. As in America, the institutional world of lesbian and gay politics, for example national lobbying groups claiming representational status, seemed (and seem) unwilling to advocate the 'regaying' (King 1993: 169) of HIV/AIDS, usually, it is perversely claimed, 'not to make AIDS look like a gay plague'. Moreover AIDS service organizations, on both sides of the Atlantic, have moved away from a clear identification with the gay (and lesbian) communities from which they first emerged (*ibid.*: Ch. 5). Thus treatment activists have tended to forge close personal friendships across the Atlantic, rooted in a shared political and ethical perception of the epidemic: what is most urgently needed and how to best achieve such goals.

It was in this context that the *National AIDS Manual* (NAM) was set up by Peter Scott and others in 1988, publishing its first edition in the autumn of that year. NAM came into being as the result of a sense of the general absence in Britain of reliable, up-to-date treatment information, together with accurate data and information on all aspects of the UK epidemic, providing access to further specialist resources and organizations. Most of those at the heart of NAM, including myself, had also had direct experience of the US treatment activist movement, had experienced personal losses early in the epidemic and were long familiar with the various American treatment information newsletters. NAM gained significant help from the American Foundation for AIDS Research (AmFAR), which had begun its far more modest *Treatments Directory* in 1987. NAM was established as an independent, not-for-profit company which could service all HIV/AIDS agencies, having begun as a specialist filing system for London's 24-hour London Lesbian and Gay Switchboard. The aim of NAM was to mediate between the domains of primary research in peer-reviewed medical journals and the type of over-simplified (and often sadly incorrect) data being provided from other sources, especially in relation to treatment options. Funded from sales, together with awards from the Department of Health, pharmaceutical companies, and others, NAM provides an independent voice on HIV/AIDS research.

Scott, the founding Editor of NAM, felt the need to develop a 'learning mechanism' – a form of step-by-step guide to help newcomers understand the issues involved. NAM thus emerged from the self-help model of gay community politics in Britain, with a distrust of the professionalization of AIDS health education and a sense of the publication as a teaching tool, regarding education as a process rather than the provision of what Scott has described as 'undigested chunks of raw information' (1995). The strategic intention was that the readership work out for themselves the wider politics revealed by treatment information (for example, about the inequality of access to both clinical trials and treatments between people living in London and those elsewhere).

Initially published in a loose-leaf format, and updating every ninety days, NAM rapidly became the central, reliable text on most specialist aspects of the epidemic in the UK, with a current circulation of 1,200 organizations and institutions. Whilst the mass media present AIDS treatment information either sensationally or not at all, NAM continues to provide a balanced centreground between rival and competing extremes. As in America, a number of gay doctors played a key role in the provision and checking of information. However, it should be noted that far fewer gay doctors are 'out' at work in Britain than in America, largely because of the more tenacious levels of anti-gay prejudice within the National Health Service and especially amongst consultants who determine medical students' career prospects within the leading medical teaching schools and hospitals in Britain, a topic crying out for detailed research.

NAM is thus a clear example of the type of 'second wave' HIV/AIDS charity, emerging in response to needs that were not apparent to 'first wave' charities, which had never seen the need for treatment information as a high priority. Moreover, treatment information was not regarded as a service they could sell to Local Authority and other financial 'purchasers' within the reorganized economy of British health care provision in the later 1980s and 1990s.

More recently NAM has divided into a series of individual publications, which can be subscribed to separately or together. Thus the NAM *Treatment Directory* specifically covers all aspects of HIV/AIDS-related medical research, including a detailed survey and analysis of the field of complementary and alternative therapies. NAM has also published a separate AIDS treatment digest, *AIDS Treatment Update* (ATU), on a monthly basis since 1992. This is free for people with HIV or AIDS and is the most widely consulted specialist treatment newsletter in the UK. With a circulation of almost 3,000 individual copies and 600 professional subscribers, ATU aims to provide immediately relevant material for its readership through a combination of general and special issues focusing, for example, on matters of particular relevance to women (for example, Issue 29, May 1995).

It remains to be seen, however, whether the provision of accurate treatment information will eventually translate into treatment activism of the type which in America has so successfully influenced pharmaceutical companies and others. It should be remembered that in the US it was born from a unique sense of emergency, focused largely within a particular social constituency. As yet, in the UK, involvement in HIV/AIDS treatment activism is confined to a small number of people and it is unclear whether or not it might provide a model for other 'disease-communities'. As Edward King, Editor of ATU says:

> ATU aims to provide an environment and, as it were, tools to enable treatment activism to emerge. In the absence of a treatment activist movement in Britain, we wanted to provide a pre-requisite for the emergence of such a movement, based on what is securely known, and most up-to-date. But even after three years there's no indication it has resulted in any more treatment activism in Britain. Perhaps something we did or didn't do caused this. Perhaps people think it's all being done by us for them? Or it may be that activism requires more people with a different personal investment in getting involved?
>
> (King 1995)

It should also be noted that the domain of AIDS treatment information in the UK remains heavily contested by conflicting and frankly incompatible lobbies. For example, small groups such as Gays Against Genocide (GAG) can relatively easily obtain wide-scale press and television coverage for views that are based on the belief that pharmaceutical companies and, in effect, the entire medical profession together with all existing AIDS agencies, are deliberately trying to kill people with poisonous drugs, and that HIV has no role whatever in relation to AIDS or any other aspect of human health (McKerrow and Woods 1993). Picketing organizations such as the Terrence

Higgins Trust and publicly branding individual doctors and AIDS workers, including myself, as 'murderers', GAG and others have contributed mightily to spreading confusion, misunderstanding and anxiety amongst people living with HIV and AIDS.

Nor are such diversionary and divisive tactics peculiar to Britain. The author clearly remembers the poignant spectacle of a group of American AIDS workers and activists joining a protest march in Florence at the beginning of the 1991 Seventh International AIDS Conference, until it was explained to them that this was a demonstration *against* the provision of needle-exchanges, organized by an Italo-French right-wing New Age group fronted by a charismatic guru, hiding behind a public face of fashionable anti-vivisectionist concern! Such are the contradictions of AIDS treatment information in Europe. Certainly the various bureaucracies of the European Union have been at least as slow as any other major international body to recognize AIDS as a serious crisis or the need for accurate information for the hundreds of thousands of those directly affected throughout the EU, or their communities. It remains to be seen whether or not publications such as *European AIDS Treatment News*, produced by the European AIDS Treatment Group, based in Berlin, will, in time, create a well informed readership, calmly explaining AIDS for and from the position of the infected, rather than as a confusing and frightening nightmare.

Conclusion

Edward King summarizes the major contribution and achievements of AIDS information newsletters and other publications as follows:

> They've been able to get absolutely on top of the material and taken together they give you an amazingly complete picture of the available medical information and debates and choices. In the U.S. these days you have a sort of network of specialist publications, which is a long way from how they all began, when 'AIDS Treatment News' and others were all more or less seen as tools simply to inform people with HIV about current approved and experimental treatment options.

> In the U.K. it is all a lot different, since 'AIDS Treatment Update' is doing more or less exactly what the U.S. publications were doing some seven years ago. I want ATU material to be as practical as possible. We only very rarely publish anything that doesn't have immediate relevance for people facing treatment decisions in British clinics. The other thing we have been trying to do, in simple terms, is to encourage wider understanding of the complexities of medical treatment issues, whilst at the same time providing straightforward, factual, accessible information. At the same time we go to great pains to highlight the doubts and uncertainties and the conflicts of opinion that characterise much of AIDS research. I think

we probably do that better than most other people. Yet many doctors, and others, when they hear the phrase 'treatment activism', probably think of 'GAG' rather than 'NAM' or 'ATU'. What a world!

(King 1995)

The history of the provision of community-based HIV/AIDS treatment information and other forms of treatment-based activism suggests a number of initial lessons. First, the process of carefully sifting through and translating vast quantities of highly complex medical data into practical, applicable terms, has already helped transform relationships between doctors and people with HIV and AIDS. Patients are empowered in relation to their primary care providers and others and nobody need today face the frightening uncertainties that prevailed ten years ago.

Second, this history also teaches something of the ways in which treatment issues may be vulnerable to attempted hijacking from either the Left or the Right, who enter the arena with other prior agenda which are usually divisive and distracting from the specific goals motivating community-based treatment specialists. Such would-be 'entryism' is itself perhaps symptomatic of extremist political forces which have few political sites or institutions left open to them in Britain today.

Third, it demonstrates how allopathic and complementary medicine may be regarded and articulated together, from the perspective of potential clients and carers and other service providers, rather than being constantly opposed to one another, with unhelpful degrees of mutual mistrust and hostility.

Fourth, it seems increasingly clear that different national cultural features, as well as local levels of infection, play a significant role in defining and directing different types of treatment advocacy and activism. In Britain, for example, it is probable that there has simply not been the scale of problems harmfully affecting the health of people living with HIV and AIDS, compared to the situation in the United States, for example, or France.

Fifth, and finally, it teaches the need to be able to define achievable aims and appropriate strategies for realizing them. In this respect, as in many others, the movement for greater control over the production and dissemination of HIV/AIDS treatment information may provide a model for other groups of 'patients'. It was thus heartening to recently hear anecdotally that NAM's 1994 *Directory of Complementary and Alternative Therapies* is regarded as indispensable by a group of Scottish cancer patients to whom it was given. It is, of course, primarily for people living with HIV or AIDS to decide on the success or otherwise of our efforts.

References

Barton, S., Davies, S., Schroeder, K., Arthur, G. and Gazzard, B.G. (1994) 'Complementary therapies used by people with HIV infection' (letter), *AIDS*, 8, p. 561.

Brunison, II (1988) *A Plea For Common Sense*, New York: ACT UP.
Centre for Disease Control and Prevention (1994) *HIV/AIDS Surveillance Report*, 6 (2), p. 19.
Communicable Disease Surveillance Centre (1993) 'AIDS and HIV-1 infections in the UK: monthly report', *Communicable Disease Report*, December, Collingwood.
——(1994) 'AIDS and HIV-1 infections in the UK: monthly report', *Communicable Disease Report*, December, Collingwood.
European Centre for the Epidemiological Monitoring of AIDS (1994) *AIDS Surveillance in Europe Quarterly Report*, 44, December, Brussels.
Fierstein, H. (1988) *ACT UP Fund-raising Letter*, ACT UP, August, p. 3.
Harrington, M. (1995) personal communication.
Harris, S.B. (1995) 'The AIDS heresies: a case-study in scepticism taken too far', *Sceptic Magazine*, 3 (2).
James, S.J. (1989) 'Introduction. Overview: AIDS treatment research and public policy – yesterday and today', in S.J. James, *AIDS Treatment News: Issues 1 through 75, April 1986 through March 1989*, Berkeley, CA: Celestial Arts.
King, E. (1993) *Safety in Numbers*, London: Cassell.
——(1994) 'Out of the margins', *Pink Paper*, 21, p. 13.
——(1995) personal communication.
Kramer, L. (1995) *Reports from the Holocaust: The Story of an AIDS Activist*, London: Cassell.
Levine, C., Dubbler, N.N. and Levine, R.J. (1991) 'Building a new consensus: ethical principles and policies for clinical research on HIV/AIDS', *International Research Bulletin: A Review of Human Subjects Research*, 13 (1–2), pp. 1–17.
McKerrow, G. and Woods, C. (1993) 'The angry young men of GAG', *Capital Gay* 16 July, pp. 16–17.
Nicholson, D. (1994) 'HIV negative', *Time Out*, 7–14 December, p. 178.
Scott, P. (1995) personal communication.
Watney, S. (1994) *Practices of Freedom: Selected Writings on HIV/AIDS*, London: Rivers Oram Press.

25 GLF: 25 years on*

A vital resource for any living, strong social movement is its sense of its own history. Since the entire social and political scene inherited and inhabited by British lesbians and gay men today has its roots firmly sited in the Gay Liberation movement of the early seventies, there is good reason why we should this year be celebrating the 25th anniversary of the first British 'Gay Day' rally in Hyde Park, with a march to Trafalgar Square, on 28 August 1971. Whilst earlier 'homosexual rights' movements in Britain and Europe had campaigned and lobbied for equality in law, and 'tolerance', Gay Liberation looked beyond narrow parliamentarianism, recognizing that questions of sexuality affect every aspect of society, from women's wages to the school curriculum, as well as opportunities for personal happiness and fulfilment.

For many younger lesbians and gay men today, I suspect that the heady days of the Gay Liberation Front (GLF) movement must seem remote and rather peculiar – hairy hippies in frocks, ardent Maoists summoning up visions of Cultural Revolution, dour feminists criticizing other women for wearing bras or make-up, and so on. They were all certainly there, but that hardly exhausts what Gay Liberation meant to the thousands of women and men who flocked to early meetings, dances, and 'Gay Days' in the parks of London and around the country. GLF was a great melting-pot of ideas, from anarchism to the self-styled 'revolutionary' political parties of the old far left. What matters most in retrospect, however, was the shared insistence that lesbians and gay men constitute an authentic social constituency, both like and unlike others, defined in relation to shared oppressions, but also by shared *pleasures*.

It is widely understood that GLF provided the initiative behind a wide range of institutions founded by and for lesbians and gay men in the seventies, such as the national Switchboard movement, and the emergence of the modern gay press, which in turn nourished our original responses to HIV and AIDS in the early eighties. In retrospect, it is sometimes tempting to contrast too sharply the history of the emergence of the modern lesbian and gay

* First published in Pink Paper, London, June 1996.

'movement', from the parallel history of the emergence of the modern lesbian and gay social 'scene'. Indeed, GLF always insisted that the regulation and policing of homosexuality, in public or in private, was equally of political significance. This came from direct experience. For example, if you went to any of the small clubs of the late sixties or early seventies you were always given a meal ticket together with your admission. This was not because lesbians and gay men were starving, or greedy, but to satisfy the requirements of the law. Thus the music stopped at eleven, and everyone had to sit down to eat plates of nasty spam and limp lettuce leaves. Often the best bars and clubs had no alcohol licence at all.

By comparison, lesbian and gay life in Paris or Amsterdam seemed heavenly indeed, and given the large numbers of gay British visitors to such cities, I'm convinced that much of the deeper popular impetus behind GLF related far more to the dramatic contrast between British and mainland European experience, than to the direct influence of the United States. Cheap trans-Atlantic air flights didn't become available until some years after GLF, and whilst Stonewall may have provided the rhetoric, it was the widespread first-hand experience of less sexually repressive European social democracies, especially France and Holland, which provided the basic model for what many thousands were seeking in their own lives and home-towns in the UK. Of course, some preferred what they saw as the 'anti-capitalist' purity of leftist politics, to the supposedly 'decadent' gay scene, whilst others found all questions of politics tedious. But for most people in any way involved in either, the relations between the 'gay movement' and the 'gay scene' were always very much a two-way street.

We also knew in 1971 that fifty years earlier, Holland had been every bit as sexually repressive as Britain, and that the similar social changes we sought could not simply be effected by parliamentary means. Yet always in Britain there was the central factor of *class*. Far, far fewer ordinary middle-class lesbians and gay men were involved in the fledgling British lesbian and gay movement than in the United States, and indeed this is still reflected in the marked distinction in the listings sections of the gay press between gay 'business' and 'professional' organizations, and gay politics. The organizational skills of the far left also meant that British lesbian and gay politics were always very vulnerable to 'entryists', seeking to convert us to the higher political goals of world revolution, and so on. Indeed, it was not until the emergence of OutRage in 1990 that it became possible to launch a coherent lesbian and gay activist politics which was not constantly being distracted by other issues which often had nothing to do with sexual politics. It was as if *our* politics were not seen as sufficiently valid or pressing, and I still get annoyed with people who complain about the supposedly 'apolitical' nature of the contemporary gay scene, as if politics begins and ends with political parties. The moralism and puritanism of the Left are still as much with us today as they were twenty-five years ago, however much their emphases may have shifted.

It is fashionable these days in some jaded circles to decry all notions of gay identity and gay community, but this is of course nonsense to most of us, as we struggle along with our friends to meet the ever-changing and largely unpredictable challenges of everyday life. Contrary to sadly misguided opinion, we are not 'confined' to ghettos. Rather, we have collectively constructed an enormous social world, of great complexity, for ourselves, and with little or no support or encouragement from others. And this, after all, is one of the many things GLF set out to *achieve*, of which we should be *proud*. Now there are new problems, which we couldn't have imagined in the seventies, to which we need to respond. This is how living social movements develop and grow over time, and is entirely unsurprising. Lesbian and gay culture continues to generate challenging new visions of how we might live and relate to ourselves and to one another, whilst the old questions of sexual choice, pluralism, diversity, and consent never of course go away. As the tiresome, worldly cynicism of the eighties and early nineties fades, together with its shallow intellectual and political aims of continual 'deconstruction', surely it's about time for a bit of *reconstruction* – rebuilding our somewhat battered and wounded constituency so that it can continue to meet our needs, including the need to understand and learn from our own history.

26 These waves of dying friends: gay men, AIDS and multiple loss*

Cities are our gardens, with their stench
and contagion and rage, our memory, our
sepals that will not endure
these waves of dying friends
without a cry.
                              – Michael Lynch, 1989

A witness accomplishes things that were not intended.
                              – Czeslaw Milosz, 1991

Introduction: theorizing loss

Those with sharp eyes attending the Eighth International AIDS Conference
in Amsterdam in June 1992 might have noticed, among the material promoting the many thousands of talks and papers, a small but significant cluster of
posters and other presentations dealing with the growing experience of multiple loss among gay men (Amsterdam 1992). For example, from San
Francisco, Michael Gorman and others reported on suicide as the leading
cause of non-AIDS mortality in a cohort study of local men, regarding suicide in the dry, defensive language of the social sciences as one aspect of 'the
natural history of outcomes secondary to HIV itself' (Gorman *et al.* 1992). In
other words, we are invited to distinguish between the *primary* medical
symptoms of HIV infection, which are by now well established, and the *secondary* social symptoms caused by proximity to illness and death among
one's friends and acquaintances on a constant, recurrent basis, over time.

A paper from Washington suggested from US data that young men who
have attempted suicide 'engage in twice as many risk behaviours as those
who have not attempted suicide' (Cunningham 1992). Another paper from
Los Angeles identified a wide range of characteristics, understood to constitute what is now increasingly understood as 'Multiple Loss Syndrome'

* First published in Peter Horne and Reina Lewis (Eds) Outlooks: Lesbian and Gay Sexualities
and Visual Culture, *London: Routledge, 1996.*

(Jacoby Klein 1992). These include: feelings of numbness, anger, isolation, guilt, abandonment, disbelief, depression, etc.; inability to emote; the expression of feelings of loss, by pessimism, cynicism, fatalism or insecurity; socially irresponsible behaviour with self-destructive overtones; withdrawal from support systems; preoccupation with one's own mortality; pathological grief symptoms; panic, self-doubt, loss of control; and resentment over never-ending memorial services. The 'coping mechanisms' also recorded in the paper seem almost pitifully inadequate for the scale of suffering in the situations with which they are supposed to help individuals to cope. They include involvement with support systems; lighting a candle to represent loss; volunteering to help the less fortunate; attention to self-care, grooming, exercise, nutrition and so on; and finally establishing a 'new place in life for the deceased'.

Writing from the perspective of a gay man living with AIDS, Leon McKusick identified three distinct processes involved in Multiple Loss Syndrome (a term discussed below) (McKusick 1992). First, grief and bereavement, 'feeling pain, disengaging from the dead and re-engaging with the living'; second, a process akin to Post-traumatic Stress Syndrome, involving either the intense re-experiencing of tragic events, or conversely, a protective dissociation, with symptoms of excessive coolness and numbing. Third, he describes burn-out, concluding on the subject of the need fully to feel and explore loss, in order to be able to readjust to the world of the living, and to redirect a sense of hope from the dead, as it were, to those who are still alive. This reinvestment involves new ideas, new people, a whole new start to life. It is thus implicit that mourning on such a constant and protracted scale constitutes a completely transformative personal experience, after which one will never again be the person one was 'before'.

Writing this article, and others, is for me a part of an ongoing process of mourning, and in turn part of the far wider attempt on the part of so many of my generation to 'make sense' of what has happened to us (Watney 1994). This requires us to overcome reticence. Indeed, the strong feeling that one should not speak in public about questions of personal loss might be seen as one of the primary symptoms of multiple loss, whether or not one considers this a discrete, clinical syndrome. Here I want to explore some aspects of the ways in which multiple losses may be experienced, and to suggest that while distinct patterns of emotional and behavioural responses may indeed be established and classified, these do not necessarily lock together in any immediately apparent and uniform fashion. For example, the same scale of loss which may drive one gay man into workaholism and unsafe sex, may render another incapable of work or sex of any kind. Furthermore, such symptoms may change unpredictably over time. While there may at first sight seem to be some advantage in drawing an immediate parallel between the primary medical symptoms of Acquired Immune Deficiency Syndrome (AIDS), and the secondary socio-psychological symptoms of a closely associated Multiple Loss Syndrome, the analogy strikes me as initially misleading, and part of a wider contemporary tendency to conceptualize supposedly distinct syndromes (Air Hijack Victim Syndrome, Falklands War Syndrome), rather than considering and confronting death and disease as necessary aspects of the human condition. Neatly classifying our various responses to the AIDS crisis as a syndrome, we run the risk of finding yet another way *not* to talk about pain (Scarry 1985; Sedgwick 1993; Hacking 1995).

Seroprevalence and multiple loss

In Britain we are still in many respects in the 'early stages' of the full-scale experience of high AIDS mortality rates. It is thus of some practical signifi-cance to consider multiple loss as an experience which will predictably sadly affect increasing numbers of gay men, and others, in the coming decade, in order to be able to plan and resource adequate service provision and other forms of community-based support for those in need. At the same time it is equally important not to exaggerate the scale of multiple loss in the United Kingdom, compared to countries such as the United States, Canada or France, where HIV is far more widely prevalent among the various well known risk groups, and where levels of immediate loss are already being experienced among gay men on a scale which we are, fortunately, most unlikely to experience in the United Kingdom.

Within the United Kingdom, the effects of AIDS-associated mortality have been overwhelmingly concentrated among gay men (King 1993). Thus, as of the end of 1993, 76 per cent of all reported AIDS deaths had been of gay and bisexual men, a total of 4,291 fatalities. The next single largest number of deaths in any other social constituency was the 381 heterosexual women and men infected by 'high risk' partners. These made up 7 per cent of the total. In other words, in the United Kingdom HIV/AIDS have had an impact among gay and bisexual men which is incommensurate with the effects in other risk groups, let alone among heterosexuals (Public Health Laboratory Service AIDS Centre 1994). Of the 9,218 cases of AIDS diagnosed in the United Kingdom since the beginning of the epidemic, 7,334 resulted from unprotected sex between men, or 80 per cent of the total figure (Public Health Laboratory Service AIDS Centre 1994). No less than 74 per cent of these cases have been among gay and bisexual men aged between 25 and 44, and it is therefore in this group that we may also reasonably expect the experience of multiple loss to be most concentrated, bearing in mind that another 21 per cent of HIV and AIDS cases have been among men over 45.

With some 75 per cent of all British AIDS cases being in London, it is also clear that multiple loss is fundamentally an urban phenomenon, closely related to the networks of friendships established over many decades in the lives of gay men in London. Taking the North West Thames region of London alone, we may note that 840 men aged between 15 and 64 died of AIDS in the years 1991–2, compared to 54 women (Ward and Hickman 1994). The great majority of these men were gay or bisexual, and it is within their immediate social environment that multiple loss is most frequently experienced, often by men living themselves with HIV or AIDS. It should, moreover, be understood that AIDS thus threatens to corrode the most fundamental level of social 'belonging' in most gay men's lives, namely those bonds of friendship and shared personal histories that constitute our sense of gay identity. All too often it is imagined that gay identity functions in this crisis like some kind of magical prophylaxis, whereas in reality self-confidence and self-esteem may be radically undermined rather than strengthened by the prolonged experience of illness, suffering and death all around one. For AIDS devours not only one's past, in the sense of ex-lovers and friends from one's earlier life, but also one's future, especially perhaps in the loss of so many of those younger friends who in happier times one might casually imagine as the friends of one's own middle and old age. That is, if you are not yourself infected. In this context I well remember the words of an old friend of mine, now in his late forties, while nursing his first lover (with whom he had lived for many years two decades ago) through his final illness in the early 1990s. Describing to colleagues at work within an academic institution that a 'friend' was dying, he was met with little understanding or sympathy. 'Friendship' among gay men is not frankly widely understood outside our own communities, just as the scale of our losses is rarely acknowledged by most heterosexuals, who seem often to prefer to imagine that HIV is some kind of 'equal opportunities' virus, affecting everybody equally, as so much official AIDS education continues misleadingly to insist.

Thus, for example, we may note a widespread cultural concern about so-called 'killer viruses' and their theoretical implications, in films such as *Outbreak*, and the writings of Richard Preston concerning the Ebola virus, while the actual, extensive impact of HIV among gay men is never publicly acknowledged, let alone regarded as tragic, or even regrettable (Preston 1995). Indeed, AIDS is frequently presented to heterosexuals as a 'warning' of other potential threats in such a way that the direct impact of HIV itself is displaced or ignored. Hence it is still possible for a leading British medical journalist to write casually of HIV as a virus which is:

> not particularly infectious, but its delayed action combined with its transmission during the most compulsive human activity can cause the complacency and denial that make it such a great threat.
>
> (Connor 1995)

For most heterosexuals in the United Kingdom, HIV is indeed a most remote statistical possibility, and this is precisely why they are generally so ill-equipped to understand or comment upon the situation confronting gay men, as the third decade of the epidemic in our midst looms into sight. Thus throughout the extensive social scientific and popular medical literature of AIDS we may find frequent references to the supposed dangers of 'denial', referring to the imagined refusal or inability of gay men to recognize the 'realities' of the epidemic, and to avoid *all* possible risk of infection. By this logiu, gay men are thus deemed personally responsible for contracting HIV, while at the same time there is no consideration whatsoever of the possibly contradictory impact the epidemic has had in our lives. Nor is there any consideration of the many years of irresponsible journalism which has repeatedly insisted that there is no association whatsoever between HIV and AIDS, and even in effect that there is no such thing as an 'AIDS epidemic' at all (King 1993).

Rarely is there any understanding of the great difficulties facing gay men entering intimate personal relationships against the background of epidemic illness, which for many remains largely anecdotal and distant. Nor is there much interest in how we sustain our relationships over time, or the specific difficulties of ending relationships. So-called 'denial' is sternly admonished, but there is rarely any question of how gay men manage to 'get through' the epidemic, or any note of sorrow or loss concerning those who don't. 'Complacency' is a marvellously convenient term for those who have not felt or exhibited the slightest concern for gay men's lives throughout the entire history of the epidemic. Writing of the 270,000 military fatalities among British armed service personnel in the Second World War, and the 60,000 civilians killed in air raids and so on, historian David Cannadine has observed that death in postwar, peacetime Britain tends to be thought of as 'either general and in the future, or individual in the present' (Cannadine 1981). AIDS has been posed as a largely abstract, imaginary horror for most heterosexuals, and there has been little attempt to consider it 'from the inside' as it were, as it affects those for whom HIV has long been a complex everyday reality, continually changing in its significance and meaning. Besides, 'denial' is a singularly inappropriate and insensitive term with which to try to make sense of the wide range of ways in which fallible human beings may respond over time to the escalating prevalence of HIV and AIDS within a relatively small social constituency such as gay male society. Who is to say what the 'reality' of HIV should be to a teenager 'coming out' in 1996, or to an older gay man who may have already lost over forty personal friends and long-term acquaintances, who are likely to include many ex-lovers and ex-sexual partners who subsequently became 'friends', with all the ordinary complexity the word implies. How is one supposed to live an ordinary, 'healthy' gay life with the knowledge that up to 20 per cent of one's community may already be infected, and that the worst years, in terms of deaths from AIDS, still lie ahead? It seems to me that these things are not currently being sufficiently discussed within the field of gay culture, from theatre and film to the gay press.

Such problems are exacerbated at a time when some gay intellectuals can still claim that AIDS is merely 'one issue among many' facing gay men, as if questions of reducing HIV transmission, and dealing with illness and death on an unparalleled scale in modern times were somehow strictly comparable with such issues as anti-gay discrimination in public housing or in the workplace (Annetts and Thompson 1992). Such issues are of course of great importance, but they are not commensurate with AIDS. These same attitudes are also reflected in the fashionable Wanna-Be-Julie-Burchill school of so-called 'post-gay' and 'anti-gay' journalism, which significantly flourishes in publications such as *Time Out* and the *Independent* and the *Guardian* newspapers, which are only too predictably happy to publish 'post-gay' or 'queer' journalists attacking the very idea of gay collectivity, or community values of any kind. In an epidemic, such attitudes also amount to cultural symptoms of the crisis in our midst, complex displacements of anxiety, uncertainty, and so on. Such attitudes also usually stem from those who have happily been largely spared the full impact of disease and death in their immediate social environment, and for whom spurious comparisons between incommensurate issues may often form their own type of personal defence against an otherwise unbearable reality.

The challenge here is not so much that of dealing with 'denial', imagined as a voluntary personal fault, as of meeting the dangers posed by the very psychological mechanisms that may serve to make life tolerable in the context of unevenly experienced illness, when the direct experience of asymptomatic HIV infection is far more common among gay men than that of death. Indeed, the crude social amnesia and exaggerated emotional detachment on the part of those gay men who complain that 'too much' is said about AIDS are themselves probably best understood also as displaced cultural symptoms of the epidemic, as it unfolds in our midst. This unevenness of experience of *all* aspects of HIV/AIDS is one of the major characteristics of the situation in the United Kingdom, unlike that in countries with much higher levels of seroprevalence. Thus the probability of multiple loss may be roughly calculated from local seroprevalence rates as they translate unpredictably into the daily lived experience of individuals and groups. With approximately 12,000 cases of AIDS in Britain up to mid-1995, and around 6,000 deaths, it is impossible accurately to assess how many gay men are currently experiencing multiple loss, though it is certainly several thousand. To this figure should be added the many thousands who have many friends living at various stages of HIV infection and related pre-AIDS illness. As the epidemic develops in time we may thus detect a common narrative, involving the gradual multiple experience of HIV illness, and AIDS, prior to the experience of death on a large scale. It is thus of the greatest importance that we recognize the essentially *slow-motion* impact of the epidemic among gay and bisexual men, bearing in mind that the average rate of progression from HIV infection to symptomatic illness is ten years, with a further uncertain future involving many potential different sequences and combinations of illnesses in the lives of people with AIDS.

We should therefore expect widespread cumulative emotional distress from the largely unpredictable course of illness and death surrounding us. At the same time, we should recognize the wide disparity of the experience of illness, death and mourning among gay men in Britain. Furthermore, it is statistically unlikely that younger gay men will have shared the same experience of illness and death as older gay men. This may serve to make death harder to talk about, and to share. In the coming decade, however, death will increasingly affect those moving through their twenties and into their thirties, as infected contemporaries sicken and die. It should be noted that for several years approximately 1,000 gay men annually are discovering that they are infected. Indeed, one reason for criticizing those who wilfully exaggerate the actual numbers of gay or homosexually active men in Britain is that exaggerations such as 'one in ten' obscure our understanding of the likely future impact of the epidemic. While many of those who find themselves infected each year will not necessarily be cases of recent infection, it is none the less only too tragically clear that in the absence of more effective anti-retroviral treatment drugs, a steady rate of symptomatic illness and death will remain dispersed among gay men for at least another twenty years. The cumulative effects of such terrible losses can hardly be imagined, which is precisely why we need good research as this stage of the epidemic, in order to be able to respond to future needs.

The steady death rate from AIDS among gay men is also likely to have important consequences for HIV education and prevention work, not least in relation to the growing potential for personal fatalism which the long-term experience of the epidemic may induce. And since illness and death are not evenly distributed among gay men, especially outside London, it is also likely that HIV and AIDS will remain largely theoretical for many gay men, whether or not they are actively involved in the social gay scene. Thus individuals experience the risk of HIV in very different ways, according to complex changing personal experience. For some this may result in feelings of magical invulnerability. For others it may conversely lead to the feeling that with so many of one's friends infected, or ill, or dead, one has no right to be alive and uninfected oneself. Future health promotion campaigns will need carefully to monitor and evaluate the changing perceptions and experience of the epidemic in the gay community, since it is clear that no single strategy can be adequate. If gay men think that such work is already taking place on an adequate scale, they are sadly deluding themselves. Education which was effective at one stage of an epidemic may be irrelevant or even counterproductive at later stages. In this context, the likelihood that multiple loss may increase some gay men's potential vulnerability to HIV must be considered very seriously.

At the same time we may be confident that nothing will be clarified or adequately explained by those who claim there is a type of 'death-wish' intrinsically connected to homosexual desire, and always of course conveniently unconscious (Guibert 1991; Gehler 1994). How gay men managed to survive before the advent of HIV is never of course considered by such fatalistic theories, which present illness and death as the direct by-products of individual or collective gay pathology, 'problems' only for those who are innately 'predisposed' to premature death. From such a perspective the entire personal impact of the epidemic among gay men can be largely, if not entirely, ignored, together with any serious consideration of ongoing HIV education or treatment research, since presumably nothing can be done to help the innately 'predisposed' to protect themselves or one another. Such attitudes are frequently combined with the assertion that safer sex is really very simple and easy, and that vast amounts of well-researched, effective education work have been developed for and by gay men. Nothing could be further from the truth.

Representing loss: negotiating life

No two deaths are ever the same. To live through the slow, and frequently painful, deaths of close friends, one after the other, and sometimes at the same time, over many years, is an experience for which nobody can be adequately prepared. For many of us, the epidemic has unfurled in more or less distinct stages, including stages in our experience of death. First, the early deaths, isolated, inexplicable, shocking, surrounded by mystery. These were the deaths that motivated many into HIV/AIDS-related work in the voluntary sector in the early and mid-1980s. Then deaths began to accumulate, though still scattered: sudden deaths, entirely unexpected deaths, as well as deaths which were fought long and hard, to the very last breath. Many now have quietly prayed for many friends to die. Many have marvelled at the strength of young hearts in prematurely aged and emaciated bodies. Deaths overlap. Sometimes the death of a comparative stranger is felt more deeply than that of an old flame. Names disappear, and surely few have time to honour all the anniversaries of deaths. Many weeks and even months would be packed with little else. Sometimes entire groups of friends are swallowed up as if they had never existed. Looking through old photos one becomes aware of a growing army of the dead. You learn to avoid certain streets, certain towns, certain cities. Often bars and clubs feel intolerably thick with ghosts, though they usually encourage one to have a good time. To avoid ghosts it is necessary to find new social haunts, but nowhere remains ghost-free for long. Then you learn to stop trying to avoid them, for their messages are important. I keep a kind of personal iconostasis where I work, with photographs of the living and the recently dead, and some now long-dead. We develop our own private rituals. There are some deaths, or dyings, one just cannot deal with. As a gay man in my mid-forties I find I am currently most deeply upset by the continued new infections and illness among younger friends and colleagues, from the generations which followed mine, which had been the generation of Gay Liberation in the early 1970s. They feel in a way like our children, and it sometimes seems that our most brilliant children were also the most vulnerable. Thus one also comes to mourn for futures that can never be, as much as for the 'pre-AIDS' past, which now seems all but unimaginable – locked far away behind gates guarded by angels holding blazing torches. For many, drugs serve their efficient narcotic function, blocking off the intolerable – for a while.

And sometimes, when death has become more or less completely normal, and is almost taken for granted and continuous with everyday life, death may, as it were, 'reach out' in ways that we have hardly begun to consider. Certainly morbidity and frankly self-destructive behaviour are likely to be frequent symptoms of cumulative loss. Some may indeed become wholly stupefied by the scale of death around them, while others painfully learn to adapt, make new friends, retain their sexual appetites, their self-confidence, and so on. As we move through the last years of the second decade of the epidemic, it is more apparent that the long-term emotional impact of HIV and AIDS is likely to be increasingly deeply felt among more gay men, as the direct impact of illness and death becomes inexorably wider, and the gaps in experience begin to narrow, like the isolated rings of ripples from individual raindrops on the surface of a pond, gradually overlapping as the rain sets in.

It is precisely in order to avoid fatalism and morbidity that we need to be thinking and talking more about death and dying in our communities at this stage of the epidemic. We have not chosen this terrible catastrophe. We do our best to control it. But it is there, and it is not going to vanish overnight. Somehow we have to come to be able to live with AIDS deaths without letting death overwhelm us. Alongside the struggles for effective health promotion, and better treatment drugs and services, we should also recognize the serious danger of widespread HIV/AIDS-associated clinical depression and other forms of mental illness throughout our communities. Bland talk about 'burn-out' does not begin to do justice to the complexity of the issues involved, not the least of which concerns the ways in which cumulative loss may undermine gay identity, returning individuals to private hells of shame and loneliness from which we thought we had long since escaped. Yet our contemporary gay and 'queer' culture seems to find it infinitely easier to deal with body-building than with soul-searching. Nor does the world of lesbian and gay politics seem to have anything much to say on these growing problems associated with cumulative loss in our communities, and has more or less surrendered the whole issue of 'feelings' to a motley crew of New Age gurus, who doubtless provide some people with some help.

For example, I have been struck by the reading of a late Victorian prayer by Henry Scott Holland at three funerals or commemoration ceremonies I have attended in the past year:

> Death is nothing at all. I have only slipped away into the next room. I am I, and you are you. Whatever we were to each other, that we still are ... Put no difference in your tone, wear no forced air of solemnity or sorrow ... Why should I be out of mind because I am out of sight? I am waiting for you, for an interval, somewhere very near, just round the corner. All is well.
>
> (Scott Holland 1992)

I think this is an appalling prayer. I think it makes mourning impossible, because it so trivializes and sentimentalizes death. At each of the three occasions on which I heard it read, in relation to the lives of socially active, politically committed, gay men I wanted to shout out loud: '*No*! Death is *not* "nothing at all". It's the pits, the worst. You are not who you were, as I am not who I was. You are dead, and I am devastated. All is not well at all. They are not just there having a quick smoke in "the next room" before opening the door to come back in. And I will be as embarrassingly "emotional" as I fucking well choose!' Providing only false consolation, the Scott Holland prayer (and the New Age culture that it typifies) strikes me as a positive barrier to mourning, and the slow, painful acceptance of loss that mourning involves, if it is not to turn into melancholia, unable to 'cut off', unable to incorporate the dead person into one's new, changed, diminished life.

Thus the cultural challenge of adequately memorializing the dead is always intimately connected to the widely shared yet generally private, individual experience of grief and cumulative multiple loss. Yet what kind of memorials might we need? Certainly it would be a disaster if we were to drift into a kind of victim mentality, along the lines of vague and generally misleading metaphors of the Holocaust. Surely lesbian and gay culture already suffers from more than its share of 'victim politics', with regular ritual shamings of the 'impure', and so on, and its upside-down hierarchies of victimhood status. Yet with so much grief in our private lives, we need opportunities for its shared expression, as well as the need to celebrate and affirm the significance of the lives of those who have died. We may perhaps eventually be able to rescue something meaningful from the annual platitudes of World AIDS Day, but at present our only two major national memorializing projects are both imported traditions from the United States – the Candle-lit Vigil, and the UK Quilts Project, and while both have doubtless provided many with a means of public mourning, neither has seized the national imagination at the level of national cultural symbols. Indeed, it may well be that they were, as it were, 'premature', arriving in Britain from a country which has experienced a vastly higher death rate from AIDS than the United Kingdom.

Perhaps some of our most effective memorials will be essentially local, like the light shop in New York's West Village, whose windows contain an ever-changing display of photographs and obituaries and personal tributes to local people who have recently died from AIDS, or like the images and texts by Derek Jarman which appeared in shop-windows up and down Old Compton Street in the heart of London's West End gay 'village' the day after he died. A street that he had travelled almost daily for many decades now mourned his passing, and even today, more than two years later, there is still a shrine with fairy-lights behind the counter at his favourite Soho café, the Maison Bertaux which he, like me, had known since the 1960s, when it had been under the formidable rule of old Madame Bertaux herself, and next door there was a very proper hardware store, with neat, diligent apprentices.

Derek would fight his way to the upstairs tea-room even after he could hardly walk (Watney 1994).

Many will by now be familiar with the types of secular funeral and commemorative ceremonies which are such a feature of the immediate social gay response to the epidemic. For example, I suddenly recall walking through West London two years ago behind a magnificent horse-drawn glass catafalque carrying an ex-lover to the crematorium, and the wonderful release in the chapel as Barbra Streisand belted out 'Comin' In And Out Of Your Life', using our culture to affirm our lives and our feelings. Or, more recently, walking into another packed chapel, to the wonderfully appropriate and infinitely moving strains of Lou Reed's 'Take A Walk On The Wild Side'. In this context it is perhaps also worth considering the way in which so much recent techno music has, in effect, revivified and reconstructed so many of the gay disco 'standards' and anthems of the pre-AIDS era as new re-mixes, insisting as it were on the unbroken continuities of pop music and dance culture. Such continuities affirm the underlying tenacity of gay culture, and its deeper will for life and happiness, in spite of the growing presence of death all around us.

In such circumstances we should probably at least try to observe the anniversaries of our friends, or else life itself can begin to seem unreal and devoid of value or purpose, because we have been unable to integrate our dead into our new, changed lives. Questions of spirituality are much in the air, and it seems important not to 'give' this ground over wholly to purveyors of psycho-babble, or to spurious New Age religiosity. One of the measures of the strength of our culture will be reflected in the ways we learn to take care of ourselves and of one another, emotionally, and in every other way. Gay culture and self-confidence is very young, and we have little to draw upon by way of models. Nor can it be sufficiently pointed out that nothing quite like this has ever happened before – the steady haemorrhaging of a significant percentage of a marginalized social constituency which is itself widely blamed for the disaster in its midst.

At a time when mental health care and service provision is under fire throughout the statutory sector and the National Health Service, existing institutions should recognize the strong likelihood of steadily increased demand for both emergency service provision and for long-term counselling, group-work, and so on. For just as we were initially most at risk from HIV at the beginning of the AIDS crisis at a time when nobody knew HIV was out there, so today we are also most vulnerable to the long-term emotional and psychological consequences of living cheek by jowel with death in an epidemic of such duration, from all the varieties of clinical depression, to frankly suicidal behaviour. I can only conclude that it is our capacity to seize onto life and joy and happiness that will be most needed to carry us through the grim years ahead. We go clubbing on Friday night not out of 'denial', but in order, among many other things, to mourn. This is the complex nature of urban gay life in the 1990s, and it is already inseparable from the epidemic in its midst. How we are to share all this, and come through, only time will tell.

References

Amsterdam (1992) Eighth International AIDS Conference Abstracts, *Track D: Poster Social Impact and Responses*, D465.

Annetts, J. and Thompson, B. (1992) 'Dangerous activism', in K. Plummer, (Ed.) *Modern Homosexualities: Fragments of Lesbian and Gay Experience*, London: Routledge, pp. 227–36.

Cannadine, D. (1981) 'War and death, grief and mourning in modern Britain, in Joachim Whaley, (Ed.) *Mirrors of Mortality: Studies on the Social History of Death*, London: Europa, p. 238.

Connor, S. (1995) 'The terror is infectious', *Independent*, section two, London, Thursday 20 April 1995, p. 31.

Cunningham, R. *et al.* (1992) 'AIDS risk behaviour: a new way of committing suicide?', Eighth International AIDS Conference, Amsterdam.

Gehler, M. (1994) *Adam et Yves: enquête chez les garçons*, Paris: Grasset.

Gorman, M. *et al.* (1992) 'Suicide as the leading cause of non AIDS mortality in a cohort of men in San Francisco', Eighth International AIDS Conference, Amsterdam.

Guibert, H. (1991) *To The Friend Who Did Not Save My Life*, London: Quartet.

Hacking, I. (1995) *Rewriting the Soul: Multiple Personality and the Sciences of Memory*, Princeton, NJ.

Jacoby Klein, S. (1992) 'AIDS related gay grief: an update including multiple loss syndrome', AIDS Project Los Angeles, Eighth International AIDS Conference, Amsterdam.

King, E. (1993) *Safety in Numbers: Safer Sex and Gay Men*, London: Cassell; New York: Routledge, 1994.

Lynch, M. (1989) 'Cry', *These Waves of Dying Friends*, New York, Contact Publications, p. 82.

McKusick, L. (1992) 'The epidemiology and psychology of multiple loss in our communities', session 61, Eighth International AIDS Conference, Amsterdam.

Milosz, C. (1991) *The Late Show*, BBC-2, Monday 25 November.

Preston, R. (1995) 'Back in the hot zone', *New Yorker*, 22 May, pp. 43–5.

Public Health Laboratory Service AIDS Centre (1994) *AIDS/HIV Quarterly Surveillance Tables*, 25, Data To End September.

Scarry, E. (1985) *The Body in Pain: The Making and Unmaking of the World*, Oxford: Oxford University Press.

Scott Holland, H. (1992) 'Death is nothing at all' in Liz Stewart (Ed.) *Daring to Speak Love's Name*, London Hamish Hamilton, pp. 141–2.

Sedgwick, E.K. (1993) 'Epidemic of the will', *Tendencies*, Durham, NC, Duke University Press, pp. 130–43.

Ward, H. and Hickman, M. (1994) *The Epidemiology of AIDS and HIV in North West Thames*, London: Academic Department of Public Health, St Mary's Hospital Medical School.

Watney, S. (1994) 'Acts of memory', *Out Magazine*, 15, New York p. 92.

27 The political significance of statistics in the AIDS Crisis: epidemiology, representation and re-gaying*

Summary

I begin this essay by considering ways in which HIV and AIDS statistics have been gathered and presented by epidemiologists in official tables and charts. I examine how journalists and others have frequently based misleading accounts of the epidemic on selective reporting of statistics, which in turn reflect other forms of bias. I propose that epidemiology should be understood as a primary system of representation, mediating between the lived experience of the consequences of HIV infection and wider social beliefs, attitudes and behaviour, including public policies. In conclusion, I look at some of the ways in which targeted HIV/AIDS education for those at greatest risk has been widely neglected, whilst the needs of those at least risk have consistently drawn the most attention and resources. Throughout the AIDS crisis, the field of epidemiology has been the site of several complex biopolitical struggles in relation to a wide range of issues, from questions concerning the aims and methods of medical research (including clinical trials), to questions of social service provision and prevention strategies. These struggles demonstrate the importance of recognizing that statistics should be public rather than governmental property, and that epidemiologists have ethical responsibilities as social scientists to make the significance of their findings widely and accessibly available. Nor should the methods or reporting of national epidemiological research be subject to partisan political pressures from government or government agencies.

Introduction

Much attention has been paid in the history of the AIDS crisis to the roles played by language and visual imagery, from photography to feature films, in mediating and representing the epidemic.[1] Indeed, sometimes it has seemed as if the goal of changing and improving the words and images generated in response to HIV/AIDS has had a higher priority than concrete issues of social and medical

---

* First published in Joshua Oppenheimer and Helena Reckitt (Eds) Acting on AIDS: Sex Drugs & Politics, London: Serpent's Tail, 1997.

policy and the provision of care and services. Yet the primary purpose for a cultural critique of the uses of language and imagery in relation to HIV/AIDS should always be immediate questions of social policy. Social policy, in turn, is a site of conflicting demands, based on different and opposing values. For example, a vocal lobby has long campaigned for sweeping cuts in government funding for all aspects of the epidemic, on the grounds that HIV is a 'self-inflicted' illness, and that it has received 'disproportionately' high resources in relation to other medical conditions such as heart disease or cancer.[2]

It is important to understand that such opinions express deeply held beliefs and prejudices, which are deployed by academics, journalists, and lobbyists in order to directly influence public policies. When such views prevail, real harm may result. The fight against such prejudice is not simply an abstract battle for 'truth', but a politically necessary struggle for specific goals. Furthermore, many of the controversies surrounding almost all aspects of the epidemic are in one way or another related to statistically based claims and counter-claims. In this respect, the ways in which HIV and AIDS statistics are gathered and published take on special significance, since they provide us with the most scientifically accurate pictures of the epidemic. Statistics such as numbers of newly reported cases of HIV infection, average life-expectancy and mortality rates provide the key data from which we build our understanding of the epidemic and its progress. Understanding the role of statistics is particularly important in relation to the introduction in the 1990s of a form of market economy within the British National Health Service (NHS). Whilst the enforced competition for funds from NHS 'purchasers' of services, such as health authorities, for 'providers' of services, such as charities, may be seen as harmful, the system must, for the time being at least, be made to work as well as it can. Epidemiology provides vital information on the basis of which projects competing for scarce funds may be evaluated by professional purchasers. It is on the grounds of statistics, and their interpretation, that actual policies are funded and put into practice, in a wider social climate of considerable public confusion and misunderstanding concerning HIV and AIDS. Whilst health care systems differ in different countries, it is nevertheless significant that the British experience is typical rather than an international exception, especially in the provision of prevention resources to those at least risk from HIV, rather than to those at demonstrably greater risk.

Facts and figures

British epidemiological surveillance of AIDS began at the Public Health Laboratory Service (PHLS) and the Scottish Centre for Infection and Environmental Health (SCIEH) in 1982. Epidemiological surveillance of HIV began two years later, after the introduction of blood tests for the recently discovered retrovirus. Summaries of statistics are published monthly, with a *News Release* every six months, and detailed *AIDS/HIV Quarterly Surveillance Tables*, which are distributed to leading state agencies including the Health Education Authority and the Medical Research Council. Unfortunately these statistics are not distributed to HIV/AIDS charities who are equally involved in the national management of the epidemic. Throughout the developed world, government agencies provide similar services, whilst wider regional and global statistics are produced by agencies including the European Centre for the Epidemiological Monitoring of AIDS, UN AIDS, and the World Health Organization. American HIV/AIDS statistics are published by the Centers for Disease Control and Prevention (CDCP), in Atlanta, Georgia.

It is on the basis of changing patterns of infection and illness that epidemiologists are able to make mathematical projections concerning the likely course of the epidemic. Statistics are gathered in relation to factors of age, class, gender, sexuality, ethnicity, and mode of HIV transmission. Such statistics do not transparently disclose the changing mathematical 'truth' of the epidemic. Attention, in most official epidemiological reporting, is given in accordance with contingent social factors and institutional pressures (such as entrenched prejudice). Thus, of the thirty-two sets of tables in the most recent British *AIDS/HIV Quarterly Surveillance Tables* (no. 13, to March 1996), there are eight which consider heterosexual transmission from different perspectives. Only two tables consider specific aspects of male-to-male transmission, although these constitute 69 per cent of new AIDS cases in the first quarter of 1996. Simply put, epidemiology focuses in greater or lesser detail on its social targets according to determining factors which are best understood as biopolitical. In the accompanying notes published with the *AIDS/HIV Quarterly Surveillance Tables* the reader is informed that:

> For the UK, the proportion of AIDS cases attributable to sexual intercourse between men has consistently declined, from 95 per cent of those reported by the end of 1985, to 69 per cent of those reported in the first quarter of 1996. Over the same period, the proportion of cases attributed to heterosexual exposure has risen from 4 per cent to 23 per cent.[3]

The intended meaning could hardly be more clear: AIDS amongst gay men is on the decline and AIDS amongst heterosexuals is on the increase. This has been the editorial tendency of the PHLS publications for many years. Yet a closer look at the actual figures reveals any such conclusion as extremely misleading if left without further qualification. Initially, we should examine the difference between HIV statistics and AIDS statistics. AIDS statistics are extremely useful for the planning and costing of services, including hospital treatment, but they tell us nothing about the state of current HIV infections. Hence the importance of making the careful distinction between HIV and AIDS statistics, recognizing that they look at different aspects of an epidemic which essentially moves in very slow motion. Unfortunately, the separate publication of Scottish statistics from those from the rest of the UK does not facilitate our understanding of overall patterns of infection and illness. Taken together, however, figures for newly reported cases of AIDS in Britain in 1995 show 1,248 cases resulting from male-to-male transmission, and 408 cases resulting from heterosexual transmission (202 men and 206 women). However, of these cases of heterosexual transmission, only 18 had resulted from exposure in Britain from a partner with no obvious risk factor.[4]

Turning to HIV statistics, the picture is depressingly similar. There were 2,709 newly reported cases of HIV in Britain in 1995, of which 1,540 resulted from male-to-male transmission, and 777 from heterosexual transmission, of which 523 occurred abroad. This hardly supports the widely assumed view that HIV and AIDS are somehow less of a problem for gay men than for heterosexuals. Yet it is precisely this view which has dominated prevention and education campaigns in the UK. We thus see that blanket comparisons between percentage increases in cases of HIV or AIDS resulting from male-to-male and heterosexual transmission are likely to be highly misleading. A relatively small increase in cases amongst heterosexuals may result in a percentage increase which is then contrasted to the more or less steady rate of male-to-male cases, as if the former were larger and more in need of intervention than the latter. In reality, nothing could be further from the truth. It's clear that if some trends are emphasized to the exclusion of others, a false picture of the real epidemic is manufactured and promoted. Moreover, male-to-male cases are not given a fraction of the ancillary detail provided for cases of heterosexual transmission, according to a wide variety of ascertainable risk factors.

Knowledge of these could help in the design of targeted health promotion interventions. In the past few years, new tables have been published concerning younger gay men, but much less data is provided about the risk factors involved in male-to-male transmission than is routinely provided in relation to heterosexual transmission. Far more information is available about the 669 cases of HIV in children than about the 16,542 cases amongst gay men. This is not to argue that too much information is provided about pediatric HIV and AIDS, but merely to underscore how little is provided about the social group most devastated by illness and death. If the types of data one might reasonably expect to be provided as the basis for prevention work amongst those at demonstrably greatest risk is not collected, one can only assume that this is because they are not thought to be sufficiently important. The implication of such selective data gathering and reporting is that all gay men are the same, without significant variant risk factors in relation to patterns of infection. This, in turn, suggests that nothing could be known about how we become infected, an assumption which would never be acceptable in relation to heterosexuals, especially if they were experiencing a devastating epidemic in their midst.

Data are collected in relation to heterosexual transmission of HIV as if this reflected a major epidemic, whilst the absence of data concerning gay men implies that HIV is somehow no longer a catastrophe for us. Such largely unconscious attitudes also explain the way in which the PHLS has frequently advanced the highly misleading notion of a 'plateau effect' in relation to HIV/AIDS amongst gay and bisexual men. Whilst comparative rates of increase may have shifted, this should not be allowed to mask the actual figures from which such statistical artefacts are derived, which demonstrate only too clearly the vastly disproportionate impact of AIDS and HIV on gay men in Britain, as in many other developed countries. I do not want to belittle heterosexual or other modes of HIV transmission, but I do want to call for a more sophisticated (and accessible) articulation of the ways in which different constituencies are affected by HIV in the UK.

Similar problems of omission sadly afflict the reporting of HIV and AIDS statistics which reference race and ethnicity. In the only table which deals with these issues, HIV and AIDS statistics are conflated, and detailed annual statistics are not provided. Instead, cumulative totals of cases are published in such a way that it is impossible to see whether or not there have been changes in rates of HIV transmission within different British ethnic groups, in relation to different modes of transmission. The available statistics are thus unusable for prevention and education campaigns, which should be their *raison d'être*. Official epidemiologists may recognize the role their own statistics might play in relation to the needs of prevention workers on the front line of the crisis. Why else should detailed statistics be gathered, if not to help target resources to sites of greatest demonstrable need? Yet in Britain they are prevented by departmental directives from gathering just the kind of information relating to factors of race and ethnicity which would be of most practical use.

All too often, state agencies such as the CDCP provide summaries of statistics about the epidemic which amount to strategic misinformation in so far as they only provide AIDS figures with an absence of the more important HIV figures. These summaries are usually accompanied by sensationalizing generalizations which tend to obscure more than they reveal, as in the conclusion that: 'AIDS is the leading cause of death among all men between the ages of 25 and 34 in New York City, Newark, Los Angeles and San Francisco'.[5]

This sounds dramatic, but tells us nothing about the things we most need to know: who is getting sick and how they were infected. In this manner the direct effects of homophobic evasion obliterate the real epidemic, which is replaced by statistical abstractions based only on cumulative totals of AIDS cases. Without regularly updated information about patterns of HIV transmission, effective prevention work cannot easily be designed and undertaken. Yet ironically it is precisely these detailed statistics which in most countries are hardest to obtain.

Statistics into stories: reporting HIV/AIDS

A useful and fascinating book could be written about the ways in which journalists have translated epidemiological data concerning HIV/AIDS into newspaper features, editorials, and stories. Certain clear trends may be retrospectively observed over time, and thus clarified.

In British journalism, HIV and AIDS affect only 'people' or 'individuals', never gay men or African immigrants and refugees. Thus, in 1986, *The Times's* science editor noted: 'Current estimates indicate that more than 20,000 individuals in the UK are believed to be infected'.[6] In 1987, Andrew Veitch reported in the *Guardian* that 'another 22 people died from AIDS last month',[7] whilst in 1988, the *Independent*'s Health Service correspondent informed readers that 'a further 32 people died of AIDS last month'.[8] Summary statements such as the ones cited are sometimes qualified with more detailed information, but none the less there is a noticeable tendency towards statistical generalizations, with misleading emphasis placed on percentage increases in the rate of heterosexual transmission, which is thus exaggerated out of all proportion to other modes of transmission.[9] There are literally thousands of examples of this type of journalism.

Uncertainty about the future course of heterosexual transmission was entirely understandable in the 1980s, before it became overwhelmingly clear from many years of statistics that an epidemic amongst heterosexuals was not going to take place. This uncertainty was made all the more confusing as a direct result of the taking up of rival 'positions' about AIDS on the part of rival newspapers seeking to capture readership with deliberate breaches in objectivity. Thus, throughout the 1980s and early 1990s some papers would routinely exaggerate the risks of heterosexual transmission, whilst others denied that HIV could be heterosexually transmitted at all. This uncertainty and confusion has caused much real harm.

I am not aware of any straight newspaper journalist in the UK in the 1980s who reported HIV and AIDS statistics reliably, without disguising their underlying significance: the deaths of thousands of gay men. This was often justified on the grounds of avoiding 'scapegoating', as if this made it legitimate to entirely ignore the human centre of the UK epidemic, colluding with the contingent political tendency to refuse funding for gay men's health education throughout the 1980s. All of this was reported in the national British gay papers, but the dailies were unimpressed.

Conspiracy theories have always played a part in AIDS journalism, escalating in ambition at a time when there was genuine medical uncertainty, but subsequently remaining impervious to scientific evidence. For example, in the summer of 1996, the *Sunday Times* is still seemingly committed to its former policy of denying any clinical association between HIV and AIDS and denying that there is or ever has been an AIDS epidemic anywhere in Africa. There have been, however, several other types of conspiracy theories which have flourished in the tabloids and beyond. The first concerned the origins of the epidemic, and blamed anything from the KGB to the CIA to meteors. Subsequently there were medical conspiracy theories, usually of a highly sensationalist kind. For example, for many years doctors with HIV ('AIDS Doctors') were subjected to extensive media witch hunts, and were deemed to be intrinsically dangerous, and therefore beyond the protection of professional confidentiality. These in turn melded with stories about how the key doctors, together with medical researchers, and frequently community activists (the 'AIDS establishment') were harassing and intimidating those who denied any clinical association between HIV and AIDS ('AIDS dissidents'). These 'dissidents' claimed that doctors were deliberately killing or harming their patients with bogus treatments. This type of conspiracy theory feeds back directly into earlier beliefs that AIDS is a form of genocidal warfare against particular population groups, as has been argued by some black radicals in the United States (including Spike Lee).[10] For some, there simply is no epidemic. For others, HIV remains a 'self-inflicted illness'. As recently as 1993, the *Guardian*'s weekly Pass Notes column recorded of AIDS: 'One early theory had it that it originated in US or Soviet laboratories specialising in biological warfare. Isn't that a bit far-fetched? No more so than HIV–AIDS'.[11] Yet by 1993, it was already overwhelmingly clear from epidemiological evidence that the clinical association between HIV and AIDS was scientifically verified. Moreover, besides Robert Gallo, the scientist who discovered HIV, I am not aware of a single leading HIV/AIDS research scientist who has ever claimed that HIV explains all the many variations of illness experienced by most of the infected.

It is plain that epidemiology has not been well reported in the national British press. Journalists cannot be held entirely responsible for this, since epidemiologists themselves have rarely entered into public debate about the nature of the epidemic and the effectiveness of policies. Ironically, it is the very newspapers which themselves in the 1980s vastly exaggerated the potential threat of HIV to heterosexuals in Britain, which now claim that it was gay men who exaggerated the risk of heterosexual transmission, in order to obtain government funding. Furthermore, newspapers maintain that these same (always unnamed) gay men somehow determined official Cabinet Committee policies leading up to and beyond the national 1986 mixed-media AIDS education campaign, based around images of icebergs and tumbling tombstones, and accompanied by a leaflet-drop to every household in the land. It may, however, be fairly said that some lesbians and gay men within AIDS service organizations actively colluded with the de-gaying of AIDS education, just as they refused to provide treatment information services.[12] It is worth recalling the cautionary note in *New Scientist* in 1993, which quietly pointed out that epidemiological predictions from 1989 and 1990

> were astonishingly close to the numbers now emerging. In 1992 there were 1,573 cases in Britain. The last prediction by government scientists ... predicted 1,600 cases for 1992, with upper and lower ranges of 950 and 2,800 ... All we know is that this epidemic is unstable, unpredictable from place to place and dangerous. Caution is the only rational response – which means drawing a fine line between doom-mongering

and idiotic complacency. Newspapers may not think this makes for good copy, but they must get their facts right.[13]

Sadly, nothing suggests that this much-needed fine line has yet emerged, let alone widened into the established 'common sense' of journalistic understanding of the epidemic.

Re-gaying AIDS I

Writing in a letter to the *Independent*, Edward King sets out most cogently the rationale behind the 're-gaying' of AIDS:

> By all means report that heterosexuals can and do become infected with HIV. But is it too much to ask that some sense of perspective is maintained between the hysterical extremes of those who believe that 'everyone is equally at risk' and those who believe that 'straight sex is safe'? Gay and bisexual men are far more at risk of HIV than anyone else, now and for the foreseeable future. It is only right and proper that this indisputable fact should be taken into account both by those who allocate scarce education resources, and by those who aim to record the reality of the epidemic in Britain today.[14]

Little reliable statistical evidence was available in the mid and late 1980s and at the same time there was abundant evidence of the possibility of heterosexual transmission. This possibility threatened to turn into a widespread probability if AIDS continued to be treated only as a 'gay plague', affecting only members of 'high risk groups'. In the mid and late 1980s, the 'straight sex is safe' line was widely promoted in several national newspapers. I and others[15] criticized the category of 'high-risk groups' in an attempt to explain the realities of the epidemic in terms of specific high-risk behaviours. We could not have predicted that this would prove a blessing to the lobby which proclaimed that 'everyone is equally at risk'. HIV was presented by them as a general, abstract peril, and for this position to be credible it was necessary to ignore the actual epidemiology.

It is still not widely understood, even amongst British gay men, that only a tiny fraction of available resources for HIV/AIDS education in the UK was ever made available to projects for gay men. The great difficulties experienced by many of us attempting to develop safer sex education in the voluntary sector in the late 1980s obliged us to contrast our experience of the epidemic with the ways it was routinely portrayed in the mass media. Whilst Cindy Patton introduced the notion of the 'de-gaying' of AIDS as early as 1986, this had referred to the refusal of American health care professionals to acknowledge the pioneering work of gay and lesbian activists in the earliest years of the epidemic. This was not posed as an epidemiological argument, as it was later by myself, Edward King, Peter Scott, and others. This work was subsequently institutionalized in a series of major research projects in the early 1990s, documenting in great detail the neglect of gay men's needs.[16] King, together with Michael Rooney and Peter Scott, revealed in a widely influential 1992 report that two-thirds of public agencies undertaking safer sex work were providing nothing whatsoever for gay and bisexual men.[17]

In reality, re-gaying has involved repeated and patient explanation of the predictable human and economic costs of policies which continue to neglect education for those most demonstrably vulnerable to HIV. Epidemiological arguments thus lay at the heart of re-gaying, described by Edward King as 'applied epidemiology'.[18] As I observed in 1991, 'The perception is that AIDS has, as it were, 'moved on' from gay men. Nothing could be further from the truth, as the most recent statistics demonstrate only too clearly'.[19]

The emergence of 'AIDS prevention activism' in the UK, in organizations such as Gay Men Fighting AIDS (GMFA), was the institutional embodiment of the principles informing the re-gaying of AIDS. Such institutions were needed to undertake sometimes controversial research and health promotion interventions, from which the older AIDS charities at that time distanced themselves. The arguments involved were widely reported in the gay press by Keith Alcorn, Edward King, Peter Scott, myself and others, but never permeated through to the straight press, which was still vainly disputing inaccurate 'positions' amongst themselves, without any interest at all in the crisis confronting gay men. Re-gaying was directed primarily in relation to the agencies and public institutions managing the course of the epidemic from the top. Ironically, it was the introduction of some degree of market choice in the field of health promotion which permitted the re-gaying of AIDS where it most matters – in public policy and resourcing. A 1996 report, prepared by two experienced HIV/AIDS administrators from the statutory sector, notes that 'Being explicit about the epidemiology behind targeting allows providers to understand clearly the types of bid that will be welcome, and enables commissioners and providers to engage in strategic debate'.[20]

Some gay commentators have criticized the re-gaying of AIDS on the grounds that it somehow leads to the neglect of heterosexuals in other countries.[21] Such objections fail to understand the sheer scale of official refusal to provide resources for gay men's work in countries where gay men have all along made up the majority of cases, as well as in countries where we constitute a disproportionately affected minority. There is no single, universal, educational answer to the challenges of HIV/AIDS prevention, and demands for simple transcultural solutions are themselves symptoms of a naïve globalism which has its political roots elsewhere in contemporary leftist theory. Hence the continuing importance of repeating that there is no single, unified, global epidemic. Rather, as has long been apparent to those working in this field, there are distinctly different epidemics within any given country, moving at different speeds within different sections of the population, in relation to different modes of transmission, and different degrees and types of pre-vention work.[22] For example, where injecting drug use is aggressively policed, and clean injecting equipment is not readily available, HIV trans-mission is likely to spread rapidly amongst injecting drug users who have effectively been obliged to share needles. If needle-exchanges are intro-duced, rates of infection fall incrementally. Similarly, where gay men's needs are neglected, rates either stay stable, or even rise, as was scandalously the case until recently in Scotland. Yet as Keith Alcorn pointed out in *Capital Gay* in 1993, none of this is widely understood because

> The whole UK debate about AIDS continues to be dominated by a phan-tom – a heterosexual epidemic running out of control – which is sum-moned up whenever anyone questions the accepted wisdom. It dominates the debate to such an extent that epidemiologists find it impossible to acknowledge the importance of targeting gay men except as a means of preventing the heterosexual epidemic.[23]

The success of re-gaying in Britain has been entirely pragmatic. It has been a remarkable achievement on the part of determined campaigners and activists working within and between the statutory and voluntary sectors, who were able to mobilize epidemiology as the primary justification for their intended changes in official policy. That this should have been necessary is one measure of the extent to which British responses to the epidemic were deflected by influential currents of moralism, bigotry and prejudice in the 1980s. The response that 'AIDS affects everyone equally', which was widely held in professional HIV/AIDS circles until very recently, ended up address-ing nobody in particular, and least of all those at greatest risk.

Re-gaying AIDS II: media reactions and misunderstandings

The consequences of not acknowledging the communities most affected by HIV/AIDS is not widely understood amongst British journalists. Recently, Tom Wilkie reported in the *Independent* that 'globally, in 1996, AIDS is a disease of heterosexuals'.[24]

In a bizarre new twist to the journalistic spectre of a phantom heterosexual epidemic running out of control, Wilkie proposes that although

> gay men remain the most affected group in Western countries and the death toll amongst them is terrible … if there is any consolation or com-fort to be gained from this tragic waste of human life, these men did not die in vain, in so far as their deaths have acted as a global early-warning signal. A touching analogy is with the delicate canaries that coal-miners used to take with them down the pit, because these fragile birds were more exquisitely sensitive to danger than the miners themselves.[25]

Quite how the deaths of hundreds of thousands of gay men in Europe and North America is supposed to help heterosexuals in the developing world is not vouchsafed. Besides, only someone far and safely away from the direct, long-term realities of the epidemic as it is experienced by gay men could expect it to provide any kind of consolation or comfort, whilst the analogy to canaries is as absurd as it is distasteful and insensitive.

Similarly disturbing are the comments of cultural critics such as Jenny Gilbert, dance critic of the *Independent on Sunday*, who recently complained of a fund-raiser for AIDS at Convent Garden:

> Why AIDS? Why not multiple sclerosis? The reason is that we have a strong gay lobby, and a large gay presence in the arts. No wonder people complain that the arts serve their own interest.[26]

Perhaps Ms Gilbert is aware of another incurable epidemic, currently prevalent in Britain? As soon as gay men are seen to organize on our own behalf, we are dismissed as self-serving conspirators. Behind such modish contemporary attitudes lies a total ignorance of the real HIV/AIDS situation. In an epidemic, such an ignorance reveals an indifference to our deaths which is a reliable indicator of attitudes towards our lives.

More subtle, but equally unpleasant, were the comments of the *Independent on Sunday*'s television critic, Lucy Ellmann, in response to the December 1995 broadcast of the very first programme made to document the tragic consequences of the de-gaying of AIDS in Britain, and to explain the agenda of re-gaying. As far as Ellmann was concerned, the programme merely:

> made the newly fashionable point that, at least in Britain, AIDS is still a gay disease, and the government's 'Iceberg' campaign was misleading and ineffective. So my 10 years of abstinence was all for naught. And I'm rapidly tiring of those twee red ribbons, which look like fashionably crossed legs. They seem to signify the latest method of AIDS prevention: cross your legs and think about fund-raising.[27]

'Newly fashionable'! I wonder where? Thus she casually dismisses a major political struggle waged by a handful of gay men with very few social or political allies, in a period of widely sanctioned homophobia, with almost no support or interest from the liberal intelligentsia or the British left. I point this out to underscore the point that the most significant democratic political dimensions of the AIDS crisis have taken place in institutional and discursive arenas with which few on the traditional left are at all familiar – including the field of epidemiology. What is so typical, and insufferable, about Ellmann's comments, is the way she instinctively turns the subject of AIDS to herself, as if her experience were what the epidemic is all about: poor old Lucy! She used those nasty condoms all those years, or perhaps was even frightened into celibacy. How one's heart breaks for her noble self-sacrifice. Lucy is furious, but unlike us, she is not furious about the scale of stupidity and injustice manifested in public policy throughout the history of British HIV/AIDS education, with predictably tragic consequences amongst gay men. She's furious with the annoying little red symbols which irritate her so much. Gay men's lives, my dear? An entire programme? How passé, how boring! This, apparently, is the way in which significant swathes of British public opinion respond to AIDS. It seems to be connected to a strong sense amongst some heterosexuals that they were deliberately misled into unfounded anxieties about AIDS, which indeed became a symbolic site for a wide range of sexual concerns in the 1980s.

Back in 1987, the now sadly defunct *London Daily News* advertised 'a fascinating new survey' of how 'AIDS has altered Londoners' sex lives', with an enormous bold-type headline, underlined in the original: 'No Sex Please We're Scared To Death'.[28] To me this serves to underline the vast empirical gulf between most heterosexuals' experience of the epidemic, and the experience of gay men. From the earliest days of the epidemic, gay community-based AIDS educators have struggled, with almost no resources until very recently, to develop health promotion strategies for gay men which were the very opposite to the messages beamed at heterosexuals. Government campaigns presented HIV as a threat to isolated individuals from dangerous strangers. Preposterous goals of lifelong monogamy, or celibacy, were widely advocated, alongside condom use. For gay men, such strategies would have been catastrophically misguided, not least because the sheer prevalence of HIV in our midst means that monogamy wouldn't constitute meaningful prevention. Community-based AIDS education in Britain was based on the clear principles of achievable risk reduction, whilst 'AIDS awareness' campaigns for heterosexuals were based on the incitement of fear, and aimed at total risk elimination.

Yes, we were there in the private statistics, but rarely in the public reporting of them, or subsequent commentary or consideration. Those few of us who pointed out from the late 1980s that gay men's health education was being disastrously and scandalously neglected, were heard with indifference, disbelief, or embarrassed silence. Nor was there ever support for re-gaying from within the institutional vanguard of lesbian and gay politics, or the British civil rights movement, or any party political position. We set pragmatic, well reasoned, achievable goals, targeted to the various public and private institutions in whose power the direction of resources for health promotion lay, and for years and years we slogged away, until we were successful. This was a long, drawn-out process. It was, of course, a process which should never have had to take place at all, if public policy had followed available epidemiological evidence, rather than the more powerful pressures of ideology, politics, and prejudice. We will never know how many gay lives were lost because no relevant campaigns reached them. But we can be sure that had resourcing for targeted education been allocated in a manner proportionate to major demonstrable epidemiological trends in Britain, France, the United States, and numerous other countries, many lives would have been saved.

Conclusion

Epidemiology is not a unified science. It comprises many schools of thought, following different lines of emphasis. In postwar Britain, epidemiology has tended to be sensitive to statistical associations between factors of class, region, and occupation, in relation to long-term patterns of health, ill-ness, and life-expectancy rates.[29] In this respect British epidemiology has reflected the prevailing ethos of socialized medicine in an industrial, class-based society. Sadly, in comparison with its recognition of gender as a major factor in public health, British epidemiology has not been sensitive to sexuality. In an important recent article, Professor Ronald Frankenberg noted that:

> Classical British epidemiology … is devised, in contrast to that of the United States, by physicians (together with the occasional biological convert) and for physicians. The considerable power and effectiveness of its arguments come neither from its verbal rhetoric nor, unlike that of neighbouring France, from its biological base, but from the clarity of definition of its variables and their irrefutable mathematics.[30]

Frankenberg is critical of the way in which 'pure' statistical epidemiology lacks any immediate connection to notions of application, and that even more interventionist forms of epidemiological description can only imagine people via unwieldy abstractions such as 'lifestyle', which are understood as totally individual and voluntary. Hence in the dominant academic literature of HIV/AIDS epidemiology, the only practical goal is to tell people to hurry up and change their 'lifestyles'. 'Failure' to do so is interpreted as a personal fault, with much attendant talk of 'recidivism' and 'relapse', and a reliance on simple and quantifiable explanations, such as drug use, for complex human behaviour.[31] Neither classic nor interventionist epidemiology shows any understanding of human sexuality or sexual desire, which are simply treated like any other 'behaviours'.

The consistently low quality of levels of journalistic reporting of HIV/AIDS statistics, with little or no recognition of the significant differ-ences between HIV and AIDS figures, strongly suggests that the system of public epidemiological press releases is not effective. This is not to say that epidemiologists have a responsibility to advocate specific types of prevention programmes. However, like other scientists, social and otherwise, epidemiologists do have an ethical responsibility to ensure as far as is reasonably possible that their findings are initially reported to the public in ways that cannot easily be sensationalized or misinterpreted. This requires that epidemiologists should not be subjected to government pressure either in the aims of their work, their methods, or the conclusions they reach.

Throughout the AIDS crisis there has been a degree of dialogue between state epidemiological agencies, and community-based prevention workers. Categories of reporting have, as a result of such dialogue, grown more sensitive to factors to which educators have drawn attention. Furthermore, epidemiologists have been hampered in their work by direct and indirect government interference concerning issues which are held to be politically sensitive. In this way, necessary long-term scientific research may be sacrificed to short-term political expediency. Epidemiologists have followed methods which might be relevant to short-term epidemics of infectious disease, but which are woefully inadequate to long-term epidemics, in which risk factors change over time, in the lives of vulnerable individuals and whole groups. Whilst the concept of 'risk group' may indeed imply a spurious cohesion of all members, responses to HIV/AIDS should alert us to the fact that the term continues to play a vital nominative role in situations where those at real risk of harm are already pariahs of one kind or another. Paradoxically, in Britain, humane postwar policies towards injecting drug users had provided them with an identifiable place on the social map, as far as epidemiologists were concerned. The introduction of needle-exchanges around the UK since 1986 (with a resulting steady, detectable decline in new drugs-related HIV infections) is an excellent example of 'applied epidemiology'.[32]

Unfamiliar with gay men as a social constituency, epidemiologists have often been unable to imagine the situation facing community-based education and prevention workers. This difficulty has been compounded by the new gulf between biomedical administration within the National Health Service, and those who implement strategies 'on the ground'. When the directions and resources for primary prevention are controlled by politicians, as was the case with HIV/AIDS education in Britain throughout the 1980s, there are serious grounds for alarm. Historians will doubtless debate why it was the case that Thatcherism responded comparatively well to the needs of injecting drug users in the UK, and so badly to African women resident in the UK and to gay men. In the meantime, the least we may expect is that epidemiologists will find collective means of ensuring that their voice is unambiguously heard when government policies that are ostensibly intended to alleviate or reduce harm, are demonstrably misguided and actually working to increase harm. The expansion from a social epidemiology of class and gender to a social epidemiology sensitive to the full range of sexual and other primary social identities in Britain is long overdue. Its absence has already contributed to public misunderstanding and mismanagement of HIV/AIDS education in the UK.

Notes

1 See Simon Watney, *Policing Desire, Pornography, AIDS & The Media*, (London: Cassell, 1987; Minneapolis: University of Minnesota Press, 1996).
2 See Simon Watney, 'Figure skating', *Gay Times*, London, October 1994, p. 38.
3 PHLS AIDS Centre – Communicable Disease Surveillance Centre, and Scottish Centre for Infection & Environmental Health, Unpublished Surveillance Tables No. 31 March 1996, Notes to Tables 10–12.
4 PHLS AIDS Centre, *Six Monthly AIDS and HIV Figures*, July 1996, Table 1.
5 *Safetynet*, Current Statistics November 1993, Centers for Disease Control and Prevention, Atlanta, Georgia, USA.
6 Science Editor, 'AIDS cases in Britain double in 10 months', *The Times*, London, Saturday 14 June 1986, n.p.
7 Andrew Veitch, 'Forecast of 4,000 deaths as AIDS kills 22 more', *Guardian*, London, 10 March 1987, n.p.
8 Nicholas Timmins, 'Recorded cases of AIDS double', *Independent*, London, Tuesday 12 January 1988, p. 3
9 Peter Wilsher and Neville Hodgkinson, 'At risk', *Sunday Times*, London, 2 November 1986, p. 25.
10 Simon Watney, 'Conspiracy theories', *Gay Times*, London, March 1993, p. 14. See also Nat Hentoff, 'Conspiracy theories: J Edgar Hoover to Spike Lee', *Village Voice*, New York, 22 January 1993, n.p.
11 'Pass Notes No. 295: AIDS', *Guardian*, London, 30 November 1993, p. 22.
12 Edward King, 'HIV prevention and the new nurology', in J. Oppenheimer and H. Reckitt, *Acting on AIDS* (London: [??221] 1997).
13 'The numbers game', *New Scientist*, 29 April 1993, n.p.
14 Edward King, 'Predicting an epidemic of heterosexual AIDS', *Independent*, London, Tuesday 25 May 1993, p. 17.
15 Simon Watney, 1987. See also Simon Watney, 'Preface: My project', *Practices of Freedom: Selected Writings on HIV/AIDS* (London: Rivers Oram Press; Durham: Duke University Press, 1994).
16 For example, Michael Rooney and Peter Scott, 'Working where the risks are: Health promotion interventions for gay men and other men who have sex with men in the second decade of the HIV epidemic', in B. Evans, S. Sandberg and S. Watson (Eds) *Working Where The Risks Are: Issues in HIV prevention* (London: Health Education Authority) pp. 13–65: Edward King, Michael Rooney and Peter Scott, *HIV Prevention for Gay Men: A survey of initiatives in the UK* (London: North West Thames Regional Health Authority, 1992); Edward King, *Safety in Numbers: Safer sex and gay men* (London: Cassell, 1993. New York: Routledge, 1994). Peter Scott, *Purchasing HIV Prevention: A No-nonsense quide for use with qay men and bisexual men* (London: Health Education Authority, 1995).
17 Edward King, Michael Rooney and Peter Scott 1992, *op. cit.*
18 Edward King, 'Fucking boyfriends', *Fact Sheet* No. 4a, 1994, Gay Men Fighting AIDS, London, January/February 1994. See also Edward King, 'Bridging the gap between science and AIDS service provision', in L. Sherr, P. Catalan and B. Hedge (Eds) *The Impact of AIDS: Psychological and Social Aspects of HIV Infection* (London: Harwood, 1996).
19 Simon Watney, 'State of emergency', *Gay Times*, April 1991; reprinted in Simon Watney, 1994, *op. cit.*, pp. 187–90.
20 Andrew Ridley and Stephen Jones, *Criteria for prioritizing HIV prevention services*, The HIV Project, London, HIV Seminar Notes, No. 5, December 1995, p. 4.
21 For example, Toby Manning, 'Media hype', *Positive Times*, London, Issue 18, August 1996, p. 13.

22 See Simon Watney, 'Signifying AIDS', in P. Buchler and N. Papastergiadis (Eds) *Random Access: On Crisis and its metaphors* (London: Rivers Oram Press, 1995), pp. 193–210.

23 Keith Alcorn, 'Fighting the real epidemic, not the phantom one', *Capital Gay*, London: No. 595, 21 May 1993, p. 14.

24 Tom Wilkie, 'Beware false comfort for heterosexuals', *Independent*, London, Friday 21 June 1996, p. 19.

25 *Ibid.*

26 Jenny Gilbert, 'Dancing with tears in their eyes', *Independent on Sunday*, London, 11 February 1996, p. 15.

27 Lucy Ellmann, 'He's been tangoed!', *Independent on Sunday*, London, 10 December 1995, p. 14. Referring to Nigel Evans' film, *The End of Innocence*, broadcast earlier that week on BBC2.

28 Advertisement, *Guardian*, London, 6 May 1987, n.p.

29 See D.J.P. Barker and G. Rose, *Epidemiology for the Uninitiated* (London: British Medical Association, 1992).

30 Ronald Frankenberg, 'The impact of HIV/AIDS on concepts relating to risk and culture within British community epidemiology: Candidates or targets for prevention', *Soc. Sci. Med.*, Vol. 38, No. 10, 1994, p. 1327.

31 See Simon Watney, 'AIDS and social science: Taking the scenic route through an emergency', *NYQ*, New York, Nos. 11 and 12, 12 and 19 January 1991: reprinted in Simon Watney, *Practices of Freedom*, pp. 221–7.

32 Edward King's book, *Safety in Numbers*, is the *locus classicus* of this whole debate. It is a book that every thoughtful gay man should read.

28 Lesbian and gay studies in the age of AIDS*

> Being blithe about transgression quickly becomes a way of forgetting that people actually suffer, and so of putting the (moral) emphasis in the wrong place. Prometheus didn't think that transgression was a good idea: he thought that elitist knowledge was unjust.
>
> – Adam Phillips, *On Flirtation*

> There are two central goals of an undergraduate college education in the liberal arts: to produce students who can reason and argue for themselves, conducting a Socratically 'examined life', and also to produce students who are, to use the old Stoic term, 'citizens of the entire world'.
>
> – Martha Nussbaum, 'The Softness of Reason'

Introduction

I'd like to begin with a couple of anecdotes, and some basic research.

On a trip to a major US city, a friend of mine who is a full-time AIDS worker met a graduate student studying at a leading local university. They struck up a friendship, and had sex a few times. The American talked a lot about current Queer Theory – the 'tyranny of identity', the 'shattering of the self', and so on. My friend was puzzled that the American, who is of Hispanic origins, dismissed all aspects of social identity as fictions which are merely 'performative'. Six months later my friend was back in the United States, and looked up the student. It was 1995. Sadly his news was not good. He had been recently diagnosed HIV-positive, and his health was poor. This well educated young man, attending one of the most prestigious universities in the developed world, living at the epicentre of the AIDS crisis, could talk the night away about Lacan and Derrida, but he knew absolutely nothing about any single aspect of AIDS medical science or related social science. He knew *nothing whatsoever* about treatment issues.

* *First published in Andy Medhurst and Sally Munt (Eds)* Lesbian and Gay Studies: A Critical Introduction, *London: Cassell, 1998.*

A few months ago I had a bit of a panic about an article I'd agreed to write for a book. Since agreeing to do it I'd been ill myself and had to convalesce for many months. The article was to be about mass media responses to AIDS, and it suddenly occurred to me that if I phoned around a few academic departments with credentials in the field of Lesbian and Gay Studies I would probably find somebody doing interesting work which might be published in my place. I gave up after about half a dozen calls, all reporting back more or less the same message: 'Sorry, nobody studying AIDS here.' In fairness, I was directed to some excellent work by young art historians, but this was not what I was after.

Thinking about this article, I decided to undertake a fast quantitative survey of the literature. I took down from my shelves twelve available anthologies of Lesbian and Gay Studies materials, six British and six American, all published in the 1990s. In all, I counted a total of 233 articles, of which twenty-five were about some aspect of HIV/AIDS. In three recent special 'queer' issues of respected academic journals there was a total of thirty-nine articles, of which three were about HIV/AIDS. Moreover, out of a total of ninety items broadcast in the British lesbian and gay TV series *Out On Tuesday/Out* between 1989 and 1992, only six dealt with the epidemic.[1] This was widely regarded at the time as the 'cutting edge' of contemporary British queer culture.

In this article I want to explore some of the implications of these and other anecdotes and evidence. It is by now clearly apparent that throughout the Anglophone world there are distinct institutional and discursive historical barriers between the separate (if often overlapping) domains of lesbian and gay politics, the lesbian and gay press (where it survives), lesbian and gay community-based HIV/AIDS work, and Lesbian and Gay Studies. This is by no means necessarily a bad thing. With limited resources and varying goals, it may well be the case that territorial specialization and targeting is inevitable. Yet it is surely strange that all the combined energies and enthusiasm of the emergent field of Lesbian and Gay Studies has so far had so little to say about our intimate lived experience of the epidemic. For example, many lesbian and gay AIDS specialists feel abandoned by much of contemporary lesbian and gay politics, as well as by the Lesbian and Gay Studies movement, which often seems to prefer to view the epidemic through the binoculars of arcane literary theory, rather than from the perspective of establishing and fulfilling urgent, practical research needs.

This article is written in the belief that it is important that we sometimes pause to consider both the quality and quantity of the dialogue and interaction between the different sectors of our wider movement. It is vital that we should be able to meaningfully articulate together the various changing aims and strategies of these different sectors, and the many different currents and undercurrents of thought that inform them. Furthermore, it would of course be unwise and naïve to imagine that AIDS is only present in the curriculum by direct, named reference. Indeed, we should by now have come to expect complex displacements and dissociations related to AIDS in the lives of individuals and entire generations of lesbians and gay men, in relation to a catastrophe to which Lesbian and Gay Studies has responded with great caution.

None of the above is perhaps especially surprising, not least because so many of our responses to AIDS are in effect 'private'. Yet what does this tell us about working assumptions concerning the relations between 'private' and 'professional' life? How have we drifted into a situation in which almost everyone working in HIV/AIDS education argues the need to develop and evaluate appropriate Safer Sex materials for gay men rooted in our collective experience, whilst many within the Academy seem increasingly hostile to the very idea of community-based lesbian and gay identities, as if these were an embarrassing form of philosophical error, rather than a most remarkable political and cultural *achievement*? From the constantly beleaguered sector of community-based HIV/AIDS education and service provision, it does seem hard to understand why the queer Academy has found it so seemingly difficult to engage constructively and supportively with much the worst catastrophe in the (albeit brief) history of our common movement.

This is turn raises questions concerning the commonality of international Lesbian and Gay Studies. Whilst with notable exceptions the epidemic is largely invisible in terms of research or writings about it in Lesbian and Gay Studies departments in Britain, Australia and the United States, this doubtless reflects many different local circumstances, and should not be taken as simply an invariant international phenomenon. Nor is the current situation explicable in terms of a lack of potential research funding. Thus in Britain, for example, far fewer undergraduate or graduate students have had much direct experience of illness or death in their immediate social circles than in Australia or the USA, though this would not necessarily guarantee a lack of interest in the subject of AIDS within UK-based Lesbian and Gay Studies. There may also be complex inter-generational issues at stake. Certainly there are major differences between the curriculum and the teaching of Lesbian and Gay Studies in Britain and the US, not least at the level of actual lived identities. For example, in Britain, academics working in the field describe themselves as lesbians or gay men, whilst in the United States the nomenclature of queer is far more widespread as a term denoting individual and collective identity.

AIDS has been extensively studied under the rubric of many well established academic disciplines including most noticeably medicine, psychology, and sociology, but in the domain of Lesbian and Gay Studies it usually undergoes a strange sea-change, like so much else besides, and becomes curiously abstracted and transformed into a largely theoretical issue, which may enter the curriculum as an example of other wider debates concerning 'abjection', or 'otherness', or whatever. Yet it remains significant that most lesbians or gay men working on questions of sexuality and AIDS do so either outside Lesbian and Gay Studies, or outside the Academy altogether.

The historical background

The greatest single social and political achievement of the international Gay Liberation Front (GLF) movement of the early 1970s was to usher in a vast range of new possibilities concerning how lesbians and gay men might live lives free of legal and other forms of acute discrimination. Rejecting the older, pre-Wolfenden homosexual culture of concealment and fear which had been so much a product of the legalized persecution of homosexuality, GLF celebrated sexual diversity and insisted on the equal validity of all forms of consensual sexual behaviour. Throughout the Anglophone world, very large numbers of lesbians and gay men worked to establish the first lesbian and gay newspapers and magazines, 24-hour switchboards, housing agencies, support groups, and so on, as well as professional organizations for doctors, teachers and so on, together with Trade Union groups and sections within established political parties, churches, and so on. At the same time there was a slow but steady growth of commercial clubs, bars, restaurants and so on, together with the emergence of an entire culture produced by and for lesbians and gay men in the form of theatre, film and dance companies, independent publishing houses, and so on. Indeed, it is extremely difficult for younger lesbians and gay men to comprehend that almost none of the everyday institutions that we take for granted today were available twenty-five years ago.

Alas, very little scholarly historical research has been undertaken concerning the emergence and development of either 'the gay movement' or 'the gay scene' in the 1970s. Subsequent commentators have accused GLF of promoting a supposedly 'universalizing discourse of identity and rights'.[2] Yet such accusations remain unsubstantiated assertions for the obvious reason that there is no evidence whatsoever that would support the proposition that lesbian and gay identities were imagined or experienced in the 1970s as two invariant, monolithic constructions, accepted willy-nilly by *all* 'out' lesbians and gay men. For the many hundreds of thousands of lesbians and gay men who were deeply involved in the social and political struggles of the 1970s and 1980s, it is frequently galling in the extreme to be glibly informed that academics (usually American) somehow invented the critique of sexually grounded identities in the late 1980s and 1990s.[3]

In other words, the modern world of lesbian and gay culture is still very much in its infancy. For example, we have not yet lived to see a generation of confident 'out' lesbian and gay pensioners, though that day is not now far off. Inevitably, the relations between the different generations of a recently emergent social movement are likely to be subject to considerable strain and stress, as younger women and men frame new demands and react against the perceived authority of their predecessors. This situation is further complicated by the contingent history of the wider, changing relations between women and men. Yet what we have gained far outweighs anything we might have lost. The widely felt sense of commonality between substantial numbers of lesbians and gay men in their teens and twenties in the 1990s could hardly have been imagined two decades ago, just as 1950s 'homosexuals' could not have imagined the sense of collectivity developed by the first generations of 'out' lesbians and gay men in the 1970s and 1980s, reflected in the tremendous range of social groups listed in the back pages in any regular lesbian and/or gay male newspaper or news magazine.

However, the development of the modern lesbian and gay movement has been deeply fractured and fragmented by other contingent political and social factors. Of these, the three most conspicuous are, first, the political impact of feminism and gender-based politics and culture; second, the often contradictory impact of the larger political disposition of Reagan-Thatcherism; and third, AIDS. Lesbian and gay and post-gay identities grounded in homosexual desire and behaviour have all been profoundly shaped by these huge influences, in an enormous variety of ways. Thus campaigns against sexual censorship have united some women and men together, and divided others, on both sides of the debate. Similarly, AIDS has united many lesbians and gay men, and divided others. So much for the fantasy of a supposedly uniform lesbian or gay identity, imposed on all!

The proliferation of lesbian-only, and gay, and mixed initiatives has led to a wide variety of different and sometimes conflicting perceptions across the wider arena of lesbian and gay culture and activism. AIDS workers have frequently found fault with the lesbian and gay press, and lesbian and gay politics, just as some lesbian and gay activists have complained that 'too much' attention is paid to AIDS. Meanwhile, it is sometimes asserted that the emergence of the thriving commercial gay scene of the 1990s is nothing more than a reflection of negative and essentially exploitative commercial interests. Such a crude verdict stands in a long tradition of ultra-leftism within the lesbian and gay 'movement', substantial sections of which were always more of the old self-styled Marxist revolutionary left, than of sexual politics. In the main, however, the lesbian and gay political movements after GLF were remarkably practical in their demands and their strategies. Lesbian and gay sexual politics were never only concerned with lesbians and gay men: always there was also a wider critique of the organization and power relations of sexuality as a whole, with all its constantly changing forms and identities. Some prominent lesbian and gay politics may have disliked and even despised the commercial gay of the 1970s, but every large-scale political movement contains its share of puritans, and it is simply untrue to assert, as one contemporary British critic who was not around at the time claims, that: 'there was a complete split between the politicos and the "scene queens", a split dating back almost 30 years' (Woods 1995: 15).

Apart from the far left, there was always a constant to-and-fro traffic between the 'movement' and the 'scene' in the lives of most politically active lesbians and gay men in the twenty years after Stonewall. Besides, such totalizing criticisms of the gay scene in the 1970s or today are usually based on the naïve supposition that lesbian and gay culture should somehow be immune to the impact of wider ongoing social changes – as if lesbian and gay culture, unlike the rest of society, should somehow have remained totally free and unpolluted by any of the influences of Reagan-Thatcherism which we would expect to find at work in relation to the constant process of the making and remaking of all contemporary social groups and formations. It is certainly important not to over-emphasize the size or the impact of either the most conservative wing of 'assimilationist' politics within the wider historical lesbian and gay movement, or its opposite revolutionary socialist wing. In reality, few have ever argued against targeted political campaigns designed to reduce or end anti-gay legal discrimination, whilst at the same time few 'out' lesbians or gay men have ever believed that issues of sexual politics begin and end in Westminster, or Washington, or Sydney, or Ottawa. The great majority of those who have ever been heavily involved in lesbian and gay politics or culture have also been extensively involved in a multitude of ways with the gay scene, and this is as true of OutRage or Queer Nation or ACT UP as it was of GLF.

It is against this complex, little-understood historical backdrop that the Lesbian and Gay Studies movement (LGSM) was painstakingly established, in different countries, in relation to different local conditions and local histories. The origins of this movement, in relation to the field of further and higher education, lay in a convergence of many different social forces, ranging from the work of earlier community-based 'independent scholars' to the production of community archives in many cities, and the role of 'out' lesbian and gay academics working within the university system in the wake of GLF. The Women's Movement provided a powerful model for a political movement that aimed as far as possible to be non-sexist in principle and in practice. Feminist academics had also successfully established the validity of Women's Studies within the academic curriculum, though not of course without considerable resistance and continuing contestation. In Britain there was a close relationship between the emergent terrain of Lesbian and Gay Studies and the emergent terrain of cultural studies. For example, it is worth recalling that the first issue of *Working Papers in Cultural Studies* from the University of Birmingham, which launched the Cultural Studies movement, appeared in Britain in 1971, at the height of GLF activism (Dyer 1971: 53–64). Moreover, that first issue of *WPCS* contained an article by Richard Dyer about Tom Jones, the popular Welsh singer and symbol of glamorous working-class male heterosexual masculinity, alongside articles by Stuart Hall, Roland Barthes, and others. In the face of later claims that GLF initiated some kind of unitary gay identity, which was believed to be based on some timeless trans-cultural subjective 'essence' of homosexuality, it is well worth pausing to reflect on the sophisticated and prophetic questions with which Dyer concluded his article:

> Rather than seeking to explain why Tom Jones is popular, in itself rather a trivial question, one is saying, given that Jones *is* popular … what does this tell us about the kind of society we live in? Given that he is like

this what can we suppose (and set up for further research) about
contemporary culture and consciousness? (p. 64)

In Britain, one powerful and influential strand of Lesbian and Gay Studies
has long been concerned with posing such questions in relation to the position of lesbians and gay men within British culture, and in relation to the
cultural forms developed by lesbians and gay men ourselves. This tendency
has also been strongly shaped by the historical and theoretical work of
Jeffrey Weeks, Stuart Hall, Michel Foucault and others. Profoundly informed
by psychoanalysis (but not necessarily Lacanian), this style of Lesbian and
Gay Studies proceeded in the course of the 1970s and 1980s to develop the
implications of Dyer's originating and immensely invigorating questions. It
provided the central political and intellectual ground of Lesbian and Gay
Studies in Britain and Australia, and remains influential throughout the international LGSM diaspora.[4]

How, then, have we moved from the open-minded eclecticism of the early
LGSM, with its involvement in questions of anthropology, historiography,
sociology and so on, to the present arid domain of compulsory theoretical
abstraction, with its rigid orthodoxies and its remorseless anti-idealism? This
tendency is far more marked in the United States than in Britain, and a full
historical analysis of the international LGSM would doubtless need to be
sensitive to the many ways in which local national political and cultural circumstances have been introjected into the heart of different national LGSM traditions. Certainly the widespread nihilism of much American Queer Theory
reveals a deeper sense of exclusion from any ordinary (heterosexual) opportunities for involvement in democratic politics. Moreover, the scale of catastrophic
loss from AIDS in the USA is also doubtless reflected in a host of complex ways
in Queer Theory and queer studies, in ways which are significantly different
from the situations obtaining in countries such as Britain, where the size of the
epidemic has been proportionately smaller, or in countries where homosexual
transmission has accounted for a smaller percentage of overall cases.

Lesbian and gay studies in the age of AIDS

At the end of a lengthy and sometimes illuminating recent analysis of theories of spectatorship in film studies, Caroline Evans and Lorrains Gamman
launch what I take to be a currently fashionable assault on the very notion of
sexual identities. Apparently unaware of any of the actual, complex history
involved, they cite as if it were evidence, the unsubstantiated claims of film
critic Alan McKee, writing in the journal *Screen* in 1993, of 'the identity politics of (the) 1970s … where a transcendental and essential "gay identity"
stabilized homosexual projects' (p. 38). From here it is only a skip and a
jump to the familiar ritual denunciation of lesbian and gay identities as an
illusion, a deception, a false ontology – followed by much excited gushing
about the supposed virtues of 'multiple, shifting and changeable' sexual

subject-positions, which is apparently how many bright young contemporary queers think about themselves.[5]

In effect, the struggles in the 1970s to establish 'theory' as an important element within our understanding of sexuality has ironically led to a narrow stranglehold in much of the Academy by forces which are overtly hostile to lesbian and gay identity politics of any kind. This is especially marked in the United States, where even more than in Britain, contemporary university education consists increasingly of learning by rote, with little reward for intellectual curiosity, or scepticism concerning received wisdoms. Indeed, there can be few more transparent examples of discursive 'regulatory regimes' than American Queer Studies, in which students are herded through a curriculum that in effect often denies the validity or authenticity of any kind of communitarian or collective lesbian and gay culture or politics. I happen to think that this is a very regrettable situation, and that furthermore it explains much about the troubled relations between Lesbian and Gay Studies and the epidemic.

Sadly, much of contemporary Lesbian and Gay Studies seems always to know in advance what it is going to discover. Thus the lives of actual lesbians and gay men are neatly evacuated from the intellectual range of enquiries, and are replaced by fetishized 'texts', which have to stand in for real people. For those of us who worked hard in the 1970s to establish the idea of a 'politics of representation', it is often an unhappy and astonishing experience to witness the extent to which such an approach has come to obscure any clear representations of politics. Much of the current confusion seems to derive from the theoretical assumption that language is the *only* mode of consciousness. Yet what after all is sex, if not a mode of primary communication concerning meanings and feelings that exceed and are not necessarily available to language, save in a *post hoc* mode? What concerns me most in all of this is that constant attacks on the very notion of lesbian and gay male identities developed within the privileged, hot-house world of academia, are grossly irresponsible in the immediate context of the AIDS crisis, and the types of necessary, communitarian identity politics which provide the most reliable forms of resistance and mutual protection.

From the outside, much of the current Lesbian and Gay Studies movement often looks not unlike any other self-congratulatory academic tea-party, with the highest stockades and the most daunting ditches all around it, aggressively refusing access to all but the queerest of the queer (as defined from within). From the outside, nothing could be more remarkable than an academic tendency which has been debating sexual identity and identities for more than a decade, as if this has no connection whatsoever with AIDS! In retrospect, it would appear that there have thus been two simultaneous yet almost entirely unrelated sets of academic and intellectual debates being conducted about (homo)sexual identities since the early 1980s, and it is to these that I now turn.

First, there has been a long debate, grounded above all in a philosophical critique of 'essentialism', which has interpreted lesbian and gay identities as if they are nothing more than responses to oppressive (heterosexual) power, as if all sexual identities were primarily products of 'regulatory regimes'. We are thus urged to combat 'naïve' notions about fixed, or even stable sexual identities. From this perspective, human sexuality is always and everywhere polymorphously perverse, and if you think you are exclusively attracted to either the opposite or the same sex, then you are no more than a helpless and deluded victim, and most certainly not a happy, liberated queer. In this view, identities are always known in advance, in order to be denied. The mutable and inevitably deeply contingent historical forms and dispositions of human sexuality are read as if 'gay identity' somehow involved denying the *ultimate* provisionality of sexual identities. I emphasize the word 'ultimate' because it seems to me that there is all the difference in the world between the insistence on the provisionality and contingency of sexual identities in the longer historical duration, and a certain style of deconstructionist denial of the validity of the category of sexual identity itself on the grounds that such identities are 'merely' provisional, and of their nature 'essentialist'.

It is as if the category of 'the subject', especially the sexual subject, has taken the place within the liberal academic imagination formerly held by 'the ruling class' and its many avatars within the thought-structures of the old far left. Such an approach to sexuality can only take place if the identities under attack are highly abstract and generalized, and largely projective. This can only happen if the whole debate has, in advance, been effectively disconnected from any direct involvement with ordinary human lives, in all their grinding confusion and perplexity. In place of the (always provisional, always to-be-constructed) collectivity of lesbian and gay political and social identities, we are offered only the spectacle of heroically 'transgressive' queers, bravely seeing off dragons of essentialist error, and other thought-crimes – whilst all around them the world in which they live is constantly changing, not least in response to an epidemic which so manifestly disproportionately affects those involved in such debates. This relentless denial of the (always provisional, always to-be-constructed) validity of lesbian and gay identities is frequently evinced with much the same bracing intellectual self-confidence that I well remember being used in the 1970s by those who were then dismissing our identities as merely a froth of 'false-consciousness' in Britain and the United States. These days, however, in Britain, the more fanatical anti-gay deconstructionist position is more widely espoused by journalists than by academics, and feeds back into the Academy via the publishing explosion associated with the LGSM.[6] 'Anti-gay' politics in Britain amongst men who formerly defined themselves as gay is what happened to queer politics in Britain. It delights in a blatantly snobbish contempt for 'ordinary' lesbians and gay men, who are frequently portayed as more or less uniformly stupid, mindless 'consumers', unable to think or care about anything except body-building, tattoos, body-piercing, designer-clothes, house music and drugs. When the epidemic is mentioned, it is as personal tragedy, but never as a political issue. For example, it is noticeable that the 'anti-gay' tendency in British sexual politics has never had any involvement or shown public concern over HIV/AIDS treatment issues. In fact many leading 'anti-gay' politicos have consistently belittled the work of already belea-guered AIDS service organizations, which provide much-needed and reliable treatment information. This is not the place, but work needs to be done in relation to the historical, cultural mapping of the self-styled 'AIDS dissident' movement, and queer and 'anti-gay' politics and the constituencies they may represent.

The other major debate about lesbian and gay identities has taken place within and outside the university system, but almost entirely outside the aca-demic field of Lesbian and Gay Studies. This other debate has been over-whelmingly concerned with HIV/AIDS prevention and education – work which could not be trusted to be undertaken with any sense of urgency by most heterosexual academic sociologists and psychologists. It has been a debate about the relations between gay male identity, and sexual behaviour – above all, with the adoption and maintenance of safer sex. It has therefore also been closely connected to the development and evaluation of safer sex education, which is likely to need to change over time, as the epidemic changes, not least in relation to the availability of adequate resources for pre-vention work, and appropriate campaigns.[7] This second debate about lesbian and gay identities has taken place in the gay press, in books and journals and conferences and magazine articles, and has frequently drawn upon the insights and arguments of the LGSM.[8] It has also been undertaken in acade-mic departments of sociology and education studies.[9] Statistics play an espe-cially important role in the AIDS crisis, not least in relation to our ability to detect changing trends and patterns or new infections, and their possible rela-tions to other determining factors.[10] At the same time, however, there have been important and sometimes heated debates about the methods and values of conventional mainstream 'behavioural' studies within academic departments undertaking HIV/AIDS-related research. For example, some researchers regard sexual behaviour as if it were just like any other, with lit-tle or no sense of what the study of sexuality tells us about the great com-plexity of human sexual behaviour, not least in relation to the role of the unconscious.[11] Yet as far as I can tell, little of any of this has been considered under the rubric of the LGSM on either side of the Atlantic or Pacific.

To take one example, there was an immensely important international debate focused on the values and beliefs associated with the use of the term 'relapse' in relation to gay men's sexual behaviour for several years from 1989 until about 1992. This was not merely a semantic squabble about the use of words. Rather, it drew attention to a previously unacknowledged divi-sion between those who thought of safer sex simply as an 'event', and those who recognized it as a *process*.[12] This in turn reflected profoundly conflicting attitudes towards unsafe sex. Yet this debate never 'crossed over' into the mainstream of the LGSM, and like other such debates it went largely unheard beyond the immediate environment in which contestation had taken place, such as AIDS service organizations around the world producing gay men's health education campaigns, and the social studies tracks of the annual International AIDS Conferences, and in specialist publications. Throughout the early 1990s there has also been a heated international debate about sexual identities in relation to 'negotiated risk', and the potential danger of developing so-called 'AIDS education' campaigns which might have the effect of increasing risks.[13] It is surely in retrospect significant that little if any of the above has been of much interest to the LGSM, with the significant exception of questions concerning lesbians and safer sex. The 're-gaying' of AIDS in the 1990s has not taken place with the support of either the mainstream world of lesbian and gay politics, or the LGSM, yet the 'de-gaying' of AIDS was arguably the most important social and political issue facing gay men all around the world from the late 1980s until today. In Britain it remains significant that much 'anti-gay' opinion has also criticized the 're-gaying' of the epidemic, and cheerfully advises us not to trust wicked scientists.[14] This is turn reflects a wider ignorance of and/or hostility to scientific method in its entirety as one of the many regrettable symptoms of postmodernism. The recognition that science is neither neutral nor necessarily benign is used to justify a wholesale rejection of all things scientific, and this is particularly tragic at a time when it has been so important for us to engage with scientists in the development of potential treatment drugs, or prevention campaigns. Indeed, it is precisely because activists have understood that science is *not* neutral that we have been involved in the biopolitics of AIDS all along.[15]

Conclusion

What, if any, conclusions can be drawn from the above? We may perhaps detect a few trends. Certainly there is an air of unpleasant snobbishness in some academic pronouncements concerning 'ordinary' (i.e. non-academic) lesbian and gay lives, as if having read Judith Butler and Jacques Derrida placed one far above the unsophisticated masses, with their quaint and amusing beliefs about themselves and one another. Ultimately this probably doesn't matter very much, because it affects so very few people, and is part and parcel of the nature of the institutions of further and higher education these days. Yet identity politics do matter, not least because they continue to provoke so much hostility from those who would seek to return us to a largely imaginary past in which 'politics' were unpolluted by such vulgar issues as gender or sexuality or race. They also matter *personally*: for whilst all sexual identities may be (or may become) restrictive to some people, it is equally important to emphasize that they may also provide refuge and stability, whilst providing us with our most intimate sense of psychic and social belonging in the world. Needless to say, much of the lesbian and gay cultural agenda of the 1970s and 1980s looks narrow and didactic ten or twenty years on, yet this hardly justifies a total rejection of the history of the wider social movement of which we are all, willingly or unwillingly, a part.

The challenge is not to denounce such identifications, but to explore them, and their significance in the complex process of the forging and reforging of identities. It is terribly easy to pose as a romantic. Outsider, forever 'transgressing' against the evil norms of liberal humanism, or 'crude essentialism', or 'bourgeois society' – it is rather more difficult to understand the real world, and the possibilities it provides both for growth and fulfilment and for misery.

It would undoubtedly be a sad day if an over-intellectualized Lesbian and Gay Studies movement drifted into a cynical politics which threatens to end up in direct conflict with the lives of most lesbians and gay men, getting along as best we can, involved with our communities at every level, from our 'families of friends'[16] to our involvement with all the institutions that frame our lives. 'Coming out' is most decidedly not just 'another' closet, if you've ever been in or come from the closet. To pretend otherwise is to disengage oneself from issues of the most immediate and pressing relevance to most lesbians and gay men, not least in relation to AIDS. It also signifies a certain loss of short-term historical memory, which I have no doubt is also intimately associated with the epidemic, if in ways we have barely yet begun to understand.[17]

Hence the importance of insisting that our identities are never only negative responses to 'regulatory regimes' – they are also and always shaped by the forces of life-affirming pleasure and sexual love. We need to be able to understand the constant interaction between these two sets of processes at work in the forging of individual and collective sexual identities. It is only in a banal and unhelpful sense that they can be dismissed as fictions since, as Jeffrey Weeks observes, without them 'We would have no basis to explain our individual needs and desires, nor a sense of collective belonging that provides the agency and means for change' (1995: 99). The British psychoanalyst Adam Philips has felicitously described 'the new pieties of the contemporary sexual enlightenment – that it is more truthful and better not to know who you are, that it is preferable to shift and float than to know, stop or stay' (1994: 124). Far from having been no more than an 'essentialist error', the emergence of lesbian and gay identity politics around the world has been one of the most remarkable social advances in the post war period. Frankly, you either accept the validity of gay and lesbian identities, or you oppose them. There is no half-way house on this particular road. Nobody begged us to go out and have Gay Liberation, or OutRage or Queer Nation or ACT UP. Nobody forced us at gun-point to form the modern lesbian and gay press, or the many national and international organizations which represent many different aspects of our lives as 'out' lesbians and gay men. Shame and concealment may be a modish stance for some daring 1990s dandies, but for most they remain involuntary sources of pain and unhappiness. Gay Pride may be a rather rough-and-ready old idea, but at least the sexual politics of the 1970s and 1980s didn't spend *all* its time and energy in misplaced anger and campaigns against ourselves, unlike many of today's queer and 'anti-gay' moralists, who pour out of the gyms to denounce supposedly brain-dead 'muscle-Mary's'. Can anyone seriously believe that 'coming out' merely delivers one into the hands of new systems of oppressive power? What exactly are these terrible 'regulatory regimes' we are warned about, and to which the dreadful illusion of sexual identity makes us so vulnerable? How does any if this relate to the pressing and constantly changing demands of the epidemic in our midst? How are we to study AIDS?

Notes

1 See Colin Richardson, 'TVOD: The never-bending story', in P. Burston and C. Richardson (Eds) *A Queer Romance: Lesbians, Gay Men and Popular Culture* (London: Routledge, 1995), pp. 241–4.

2 Steven Seidman, 'Identity and politics in a "postmodern" gay culture: Some historical and conceptual notes', in Michael Warner (Ed.) *Fear of a Queer Planet: Queer Politics and Social Theory* (Minneapolis: University of Minnesota Press, 1993), pp. 105–43. See also in much the same vein and reaching similar conclusions, Kenneth Mackinnon, 'Gay's the word – or is it?', in V. Harwood *et al.* (Eds) *Pleasure Principles: Politics, Sexuality and Ethics* (London: Lawrence & Wishart, 1993), pp. 109–24.

3 For example, see Paul Burston and Colin Richardson, 'Introduction', in *A Queer Romance, op. cit.* See also Simon Watney, 'Emergent sexual identities and HIV/AIDS', in P. Aggleton *et al.* (Eds) *AIDS: Facing the Second Decade* (London: Falmer Press, 1993), pp. 13–29.

4 The history of this international movement remains in urgent need of analysis.

5 Such attitudes are closely connected to the influential writings of, amongst others, the US academics Judith Butler and Leo Bersani.

6 For example, the various books and many articles by British journalists Paul Burston and Mark Simpson and other publications from Cassell and Routledge.

7 For an overview of the vast literature on this subject it is most helpful to start with Edward King's *Safety in Numbers: Safer Sex and Gay Men* (London: Cassell, 1993 New York: Routledge, 1994).

8 See Dennis Altman, *Power and Community: Organizational and Cultural Responses to AIDS* (London: Falmer Press, 1994). See also Simon Watney, *Practices of Freedom: Selected Writings on HIV/AIDS* (London: Rivers Oram Press, 1994; Durham, NC: Duke University Press, 1994) and Jeffrey Weeks, *Invented Moralities: Sexual Values in an Age of Uncertainty* (London: Polity Press, 1995).

9 For example, in Britain, the Institute of Education at the University of London, or the School of Behavioural Sciences at Macquarie University, Sydney, Australia.

10 See Simon Watney, 'The political significance of statistics in the AIDS crisis: Epidemiology, representation and re-gaying', in Helena Reckitts and Joshua Oppenheimer (Eds), *Acting on AIDS* (London: Serpent's Tail Press, 1997); (available on the Internet: eking@dircon.co.uk).

11 See Simon Watney, 'AIDS and social science: Taking the scenic route through an emergency', in *Practices of Freedom*.

12 See Peter Davis and Project SIGMA, 'On relapse: Recidivism or rational response?', in P. Aggleton *et al.* (Eds) *AIDS: Rights, Risks and Reasons* (London: Falmer Press, 1992 pp. 133–42. See also Michael Rooney and Peter Scott, 'Working where the risks are', in B. Evans *et al.* (Eds) *Working Where the Risks*

Are: Issues in HIV Prevention (London: Health Education Authority, 1992), pp. 13–65.

13 See Susan Kippax, R. W. Connell, G. W. Dowsett and June Crawford, *AIDS: Sustaining Safer Sex: Gay Communities Respond to AIDS* (London: Falmer Press, 1993).

14 For example, see Mark Simpson, 'Unholy trinity', *Time Out*, 8–15 February 1995, p. 90.

15 See contributions by Edward King, Peter Scott and Mark Harrington in Helena Reckitts and Joshua Oppenheimer (Eds) *Acting on AIDS*.

16 I heard Armistead Maupin use this phrase in a British television interview some years ago.

17 See Walt Odets, *In the Shadow of the Epidemic: Being HIV Negative in the Age of AIDS* (Durham, NC: Duke University Press, 1995). See also Simon Watney, 'These waves of dying friends: Gay men, AIDS and multiple loss', in Peter Horne and Reina Lewis (Eds) *Outlooks: Lesbian and Gay Sexualities and Visual Cultures* (London: Routledge, 1996), pp. 159–70.

References and further reading

Bronski, Michael, 'Sex in the '60s, sex in the '90s. The problems of pleasure', in *Steam*, Vol. 2, No. 2, Summer 1994, pp. 132–4.

Lyer, Richard, 'The meaning of Tom Jones', in *Working Papers in Cultural Studies*, Issue One, University of Birmingham (UK), Spring 1971, pp. 53–64.

Escoffier, Jeffrey, 'Inside the ivory closet. The challenges facing lesbian and gay studies', *OUT/LOOK*, No. 10, San Francisco, Autumn 1990, pp. 40–50.

Evans Caroline and Gamman, Lorraine, 'The gaze revisited, or reviewing queer viewing', in Paul Burston and Colin Richardson (Eds) *A Queer Romance* (London: Routledge, 1995), pp. 13–56.

Gevisser, Mark, 'Lesbian and gay students choose', *Nation*, 26 March 1988, pp. 413–14.

King, Edward, *Safety in Numbers: Safer Sex and Gay Men* (London: Cassell, 1993; New York: Routledge, 1994).

Nussbaum, Martha, 'The softness of reason: A classical case for gay studies', *New Republic*, 13 and 20 July 1992, pp. 26–35.

Phillips, Adam, *On Flirtation* (London: Faber and Faber, 1994).

Rofes, Eric, 'Gay groups vs. AIDS groups: Averting civil war in the 1990s', in *OUT/LOOK*, No. 8, San Francisco, Spring 1990, pp. 8–17.

Schulman, Sarah, *My American History: Lesbian and Gay Life During the Reagan/Bush Years* (London: Cassell, 1994).

Sedgwick, Eve Kosofsky (Ed.), *Gary in Your Pocket: Stories and Notebooks of Gary Fisher* (Durham, NC: Duke University Press, 1996).

Sedgwick, Eve Kosofsky, 'Socratic raptures, Socratic ruptures: Notes toward queer performativity', in Susan Gubar and Jonathan Kamholtz (Eds) *English Inside and Out* (New York: Routledge, 1993), pp. 122–37.

Vance, Carol S., 'Anthropology rediscovers sexuality: A theoretical comment', in *Social Science and Medicine*, Vol. 33, No. 8, 1991, pp. 875–84.

Watney, Simon, 'AIDS and the politics of queer diaspora', in Monica Dorenkamp and Richard Henke (Eds) *Negotiating Lesbian and Gay Subjects* (New York: Routledge, 1995), pp. 53–71.

Weeks, Jeffrey, *Invented Moralities: Sexual Values in an Age of Uncertainty* (London: Polity Press, 1995).

Woods, Chris, *State of the Queer Nation: A Critique of Gay and Lesbian Politics in 1990's Britain* (London: Cassell, 1995).

Acknowledgement

I would like to thank Sally Munt, Andy Medhurst, and Daniel Monk for their helpful comments on an earlier draft of this chapter.

29 Imagine hope: AIDS and gay identity

'Hope without an object cannot live',

— Samuel Taylor Coleridge[1]

Introduction

Many different time-scales are at work in all our lives. For most lesbians and gay men there is the time-scale of our relations with our families, as our parents age, and our heterosexual siblings and other contemporaries raise families of their own. Then there is the time-scale of our own friendships, our love-affairs and partnerships, and the time-scale of our working lives, of where we've lived, the music we've loved, and so on. For most lesbians and gay men there is also the time-scale of the social and political history of our communities. 'Coming out' in the 1970s was very different from 'coming out' in the 1980s or the 1990s. The relative significance of all these different levels of experience will of course vary from person to person, according to our family backgrounds, and a host of different factors, including our unique, personal time-scales of individual growth, change, and development.

For gay men there is also the time-scale of AIDS, which we feel in a different and more acute way than other social groups in Britain simply because it continues to affect us so much more directly and painfully than any other social constituency. What AIDS means today is vastly different from what it meant ten years ago. Many gay men of my age will look back like me, sadly aware of the many dear friends who didn't live long enough to benefit from the new combination therapies available only in the past few years. At the same time my generation's experience of HIV and AIDS is very different from that of young gay men coming out on the gay scene today, who were born after the beginning of the epidemic.

The time-scale of AIDS and the time-scale of Gay Liberation are not the same, but in many respects they have overlapped. The gay scene onto which HIV emerged, unknown, in the 1970s was barely a decade old. Community-based institutions such as the gay press and switchboards were in their infancy. For almost twenty years lesbians and gay men have responded to

AIDS in a vast range of mainly very practical and pragmatic ways. This community-based response grew out of a particular history of community organization, at a very particular time.

For at least 20,000 gay men throughout Britain, the time-scale of AIDS is intimately bound up with the fact of our being already infected, and the great range of health-related and other personal issues this raises, not the least of which concerns one's own changing perceptions of what it means to be HIV-positive. This will vary as much as individuals vary.

Looking back, we can all doubtless sense a series of different stages in the history of the epidemic, relating mainly to particular people we knew who have died, the availability of effective treatment drugs for the infected, and the changing political climate in Britain over the years, especially as this has affected the provision of services including targeted prevention work. At the same time we are reaching the end of the first chapter in the longer history of the modern gay and lesbian movement, with which the issue of legal parity has been so closely associated since the partial decriminalization of homosexuality by the Wolfenden Act in 1968.

Modern gay identity emerged largely as a campaigning force, rooted in notions of commonality which were undoubtedly strengthened by a shared experience of discrimination in public and in private life. As the legal façade of prejudice is dismantled, it is likely that the next few decades will see a steady erosion of the cultural acceptability of homophobia, just as the overt expression of racism has become increasingly socially unacceptable since the passing of the Race Relations Act in 1965.

For any gay man of my age, looking back over the history of gay identity since the 1960s is likely to induce a certain sense of vertigo. Those of us born before the 1960s discovered ourselves as teenage 'homosexuals'. This, and 'queer', were the only terms available to us with which to think about who and what we were. We witnessed the whole remarkable process by which the word 'gay', gradually changed its meaning from being a private subcultural code word, to publicly standing for a substantial and increasingly widely accepted social constituency. Yet by the end of the 1990s it was apparent to many that gay identity was undergoing significant changes. An entire phase of modern gay history, largely associated in Britain with the issue of the age of consent, was drawing to a close. Earlier forms of gay identity had responded to much more prejudiced times than these. As wider attitudes towards homosexuality gradually become more liberal, the formation of future gay identities will in turn be profoundly affected. This gradual shift in public attitudes towards homosexuality is part of a wider climate of change in relation to many other aspects of consensual sexuality.

With such changes in mind, it is worth reflecting on the possible consequences for the future management of the epidemic, which will continue to disproportionately affect gay men for the foreseeable future. Most people no longer speak of AIDS as a crisis. It has become part of the general social and mental furniture of our times. In this chapter I want to consider something of the relationship between the emergence and subsequent history of social, lived identities grounded in the experience of living with AIDS, and the longer post-war history of changing sexual identities grounded in homosexual desire. Both were initially closely involved with identities forged in the United States, and both quickly became self-sufficient within the wider fabric of British society.

AIDS and identity

In the early years of the epidemic, people diagnosed with AIDS faced the nightmare of a diagnosis about which little was known, as well as immediate life-threatening medical conditions for which there were few if any recognized treatments. There was also widespread prejudice and discrimination. In the United States, where the first cases were identified in 1981, the government completely ignored the situation for almost a decade. Indeed, to this day there are almost no legally sanctioned needle-exchange programmes in America, and targeted prevention work for gay men has been at best perfunctory. The first US conference on targeted HIV education for gay men sponsored by the government's Centers for Disease Control and Prevention did not take place until the summer of 1999.

It is important to understand that AIDS appeared as a medical diagnosis several years before the identification of the human immuno-deficiency virus (HIV). AIDS was thus the primary term around which personal and social identities accreted. With large numbers of affected people, within a culture with a strong discourse of civil rights, the notion of People With AIDS (PWAs) represented a collective resistance to discrimination and the widely prevailing fatalism of the times, together with a strong rejection of 'victimhood' status. Thus in 1983 the National Association for People with AIDS was formed at the second US AIDS Forum, held in Denver, Colorado, which resulted in a historic policy document known as the Denver Principles.[2]

As Max Navarre pointed out:

> Because AIDS is so often perceived as a moral problem instead of a health crisis, and because of the connection between AIDS and gay men, AIDS has from the beginning been a political issue, tied to the long and bitter struggle for gay and lesbian rights. The movement of self-empowerment for PWAs has its origins in this grass-roots struggle; the Denver Principles are its manifesto. The creation of this document set the stage for a new kind of interaction between doctor and patient, between service provider and recipient … PWAs were saying no – no, we will not be characterised as victims; no, we will not be experimented upon without our complete understanding and approval; no, we will not go out with a whimper.[3]

From the very beginning there was also the question of *hope*, understood as a prerequisite of healing.

The first UK gay press reports about AIDS in the early 1980s were filed from New York, and as early as March 1983 the name of Michael Callen, one of the founders of New York's PWA Coalition, was to be found in *Gay News*.[4] Together with Dr Joseph Sonnabend, Callen authored *How to Have Sex in an Epidemic*, the founding text of safer sex education based on the principle of risk reduction. This initial PWA identity was soon, however, fractured by the identification of HIV, and the gradual availability of antibody testing from 1984 onwards. This resulted in many hundreds of thousands of people throughout the developed world finding themselves HIV-positive, but not having AIDS. I well remember attending the Second European Conference on HIV and Homosexuality, held in Copenhagen in February 1992. I was there to give a paper in which I presented the main reasons for 're-gaying' AIDS in countries where gay men made up the great majority of cases, but where, like Britain, 'resources for prevention work, and care, were not being targeted where they were most needed. Many of those attending had known one another from the old network of friendships between people who had been actively engaged in national lesbian and gay politics all over Europe, and further afield, in the years immediately before the epidemic. Most of us now came together from small organizations set up in the 1980s all around the world in response to AIDS, including organizations consisting of and representing people with HIV and AIDS.

At one of the plenary sessions a Danish activist made his way to a microphone. He was already well known to many of us as a crank. Looking round at the audience he solemnly announced: 'A new identity has come into the world. The HIV identity'. And as 'a person with HIV', he then proceeded to spout any amount of ill-informed nonsense about AIDS being caused by a collective 'death-wish' on the part of the infected. I was sitting next to a friend with HIV, who leaned across to me and whispered: 'As a person with HIV, I would like to say that the world is made of cream cheese.' I repeat this tiny incident because it seems to me to encapsulate something of the enormous complexity of issues involved in any attempt to discuss the relationship between the emergence and subsequent history of identities grounded in relation to HIV and AIDS. When people with HIV describe our own direct experience of having the virus, we speak with unique authority. But a diagnosis is not a qualification, and the fact of having HIV does not *of itself* automatically make one an expert in any other fields of knowledge.

For many years the New York weekly *Village Voice* has published an annual lesbian and gay special issue to coincide with Gay Pride events in June. In June 1989 Larry Kramer thundered away as usual in his familiar Old Testament mode, but what I remember is the cover illustration by Donald Moffett. Under the caption 'Gay Life '89' was a large, horizontal black and white photograph of a hand pulling back the strap of a T-shirt to reveal a shoulder tattooed with the one word: 'Esperanza'. Across the middle of the image, in white letters on a black rectangle, were the two words:

'Imagine Hope'. Hope? What could that mean? Hope *for what?* Of course you hoped, but it was very dangerous. If you hoped for too much you were bound to be disappointed. If you expected very little, you might even possibly be admirably surprised. This was the state of mind for many of us, ten years ago, as treatments failed, and the sick all seemed to be moving, albeit at different speeds, along a terrible Via Dolorossa of progressively more horrible opportunistic illnesses – illness, hospital, resurrection; illness, hospital, resurrection; illness, hospital, *what?* We did not entertain too much hope therefore, certainly not far-fetched hope, not hope that invited instant disappointment, and with it avoidable, unhelpful, exhausting despair.

Yet hope of some kind was also a moral necessity. My best friend, 35, and by that time almost blind, asked me: 'Is it unreasonable for me to expect to have a good summer, to feel the sunshine on my face?' His strong dancer's legs were by then little folded match-sticks under the rug stretched over his knees as I slowly circumnavigated his wheel-chair around Washington Square. Hundreds of thousands of us either in wheel-chairs, or pushing wheel-chairs. You had to find just enough hope. It was not unreasonable to think that at least the situation might remain stable, and not get worse, perhaps long enough to benefit from better treatments ahead in some nebulous future, not yet accessible, but not unreasonable to imagine as a *possibility*.

Ten years ago the scale of the American epidemic stimulated an organized activist response in the form of the ACT UP movement, alongside the older AIDS service organizations. In the late 1980s we did not know which way the epidemic was going to go. British AIDS activism was honourably and bravely confrontational with the press, against companies which discriminated against HIV-positive employees, and so on. Happily, however, we have not needed activism very often, since in most respects the British AIDS movement has generally achieved its goals in relation to treatment and services by other less confrontational means.

The moment of classic AIDS activism is now long past. Then we hoped for drugs that would work, now we hope for drugs which will keep working. Veteran US AIDS worker Eric Rofes recently quoted Seattle-based gay journalist Dan Savage on the changing AIDS situation:

> Change is scary, and we are entering a period of change that involves not just the facts of this particular virus, or of one particular sexual act, but the identities gay men have constructed around AIDS in order to survive: HIV-negative, HIV-positive, PWA, AIDS activist, AIDS educator, service provider, fund-raiser. What do these roles mean anymore? Are they still relevant? What does it mean to be a 'Person with AIDS' who isn't sick, or to be HIV-positive when no trace of virus can be found in your blood? What does it mean to have 'unsafe' sex if you're not risking death? How are these new realities going to affect not just our sex lives, but every other aspect of our lives?[5]

There is no reliable road-map for this new landscape, whether in relation to the experience of infection and illness, or in relation to prevention work.

Like many others, Rofes is very enthusiastic about the Australian notion of 'post-AIDS' identities.[6] There is a danger of getting caught up in empty semantics here, but the real point is surely that different types and generations of gay men will have very different educational needs, and that no single formulation ('safer sex', 'negotiated safety', 'post-AIDS', etc.) is ever going to resolve this in one magical formulation or strategy. The epidemic is constantly changing. We may be far beyond the original phase of 'crisis', but are we truly 'post-AIDS'? The world being what it is these days, such debates often seem terribly po-faced from the outside, as leading activists (especially in America) denounce one another, and other groups of gay men, in ever larger and angrier books.

I think we need to keep all this in perspective. Recent scandalized accounts of gay men 'bare-backing', or fucking without condoms regardless of their HIV status, are only the latest in a long line of such scare-stories concerning 'relapse' or 'slippage' which have been around throughout the whole history of the epidemic.[7] Beyond the important question of the extent to which they are literally true or false, there is the wider issue of their reception, of how much constructive thought and discussion they generate. In a sense these stories are perhaps best understood as a kind of folk narrative, operating at the level of gossip and rumour and hearsay, which provides a means of encouraging and permitting frank discussion of subjects that are generally taboo.[8] This is one of the ways in which a community communicates with itself in a crisis, about issues that are largely unspoken, and for which there is little opportunity for open public consideration and reflection.

One the most important things we should have learned by now concerns the sheer diversity of our community, from bears and leathermen, to circuit-boys, on rural gay men, or the Duckie's crowd, not forgetting the great number of people who are not effectively on the gay scene at all. There is no single 'centre' to our kind of community, no single 'cutting edge'. There is thus no universally applicable single answer to the challenge of reducing to an absolute minimum the number of new cases of infection. Inadequate as it may at times have been, AIDS education amongst gay men in the UK has obviously worked to the extent that our epidemic remains more or less stable, and small by all international standards of comparison.

With greater community focus, we could probably significantly reduce the annual figure of 1,500 new cases of HIV amongst gay men. As in the field of treatment drugs, it's important not to expect too much, too soon, in order not to become paralysed by disappointment. In the early 1990s we hoped above all for better treatments for the sick. The success of combination therapies in the late 1990s has led to a certain lessening of attention to medical issues. Yet frankly we have not the faintest idea how long the various cocktails of drugs will effectively check disease progression. For some they do not work at all. It thus seems likely that for the foreseeable future, the question of treatment drugs will be of immediate interest to those with HIV and their friends, but probably not to many others. Yet HIV will never simply go away of its own accord, and as medical circumstances change, so will the immediate physical experience of living with the virus, as well as related personal and collective identities.

Throughout the history of the epidemic large numbers of people have worked together on the basis of their shared infection and recognized shared medical and related social interests. The establishment and running of organizations such as Body Positive, and the national network of self-help groups reflect something of this extensive and admirably pragmatic constituency. Where on earth would we have been without people such as Jonathan Grimshaw and Tony Whitehead? As attention turns increasingly towards the goal of controlling the virus prior to the onset of opportunistic conditions, we are likely in the future to find a gradual weakening of the older PWA identity, with a much broader focus on HIV, though this situation may eventually be reversed for all we know in circumstances we cannot predict. One example of this international shift of emphasis comes from Vancouver, where the British Columbia Persons With AIDS Society's excellent and long-established publication *BCPWA News* changed its name to *Living+* in the summer of 1999.

AIDS and Gay Identity

In February 1998, by a majority of 313 to 130, the House of Commons voted to equalize the age of consent in Britain. There were no cheering demonstrators outside, nor parties in the streets. In the end, the result was almost taken for granted by most people. There had been bitter disappointment at an earlier stage of the campaign in the early 1990s, yet by the end of the decade the ethical and juridical arguments had been largely won. The reduction of the age of consent for gay men from 21 to 18 in February 1994 only served to draw yet more attention to an increasingly glaring anomaly. Legal discrimination against lesbians and gay men was no longer widely culturally acceptable. The law had finally recognized us as a legitimate social constituency.[9] For this, and much else besides, we are all greatly in debt to the efficient and effective lobbying work of the Stonewall Group, and in particular its Director, Angela Mason.

Although the decision of the Commons was subsequently rejected by the House of Lords, this was a great symbolic moment in the history of British sexual politics, and the result of many decades of campaigning by many hundreds of thousands of people. A long chapter in the history of the gay and lesbian movement, closely associated with the goal of legal parity, is finally drawing to a close. It is precisely because of the deep symbolic significance of the issue of the age of consent that the old moral right is prepared to fight to the last ditch. They are not gallant losers. It is hardly surprising that the *Sunday Telegraph* announced the proposed abolition of the notorious Section

28 as: 'The Law that made it illegal to "promote" homosexuality is to be scrapped'.[16]

Future generations will doubtless find it astonishing that in 1992 a government minister, Earl Ferrers, then Minister of State at the Home Office, was reported in the *Daily Telegraph* commenting that: 'When people complained that the law was discriminatory against male homosexuals, his personal view was "quite right too"'.[11] In many European countries such as Holland no minister could possibly survive in his or her job if they expressed such sentiments, since they would infringe the national constitution. In countries such as Britain and France, prejudice is more deep-grained, and has doubtless played a more significant historical role in the formation of national identity. We can hardly expect the prejudices of centuries to disappear overnight. Change will always be met with resistance, and some changes meet more resistance than others. For many people, the issue of the sexual age of consent lies right at the heart of their personal value systems. They sincerely and passionately believe that homosexuality is a wicked and unacceptable voluntary perversion. We may speculate as much as we like about the role such feelings play in the personal lives of such people, but such deeply held prejudices are not likely to change, for the simple reason that they are so deeply *irrational*.

Yet in the long run there is nothing much they can do in the face of the gradual and now irreversible loosening up of most aspects of consensual sexuality since the 1960s. The familiar style of crude twentieth-century anti-gay prejudice will not seem cool or convincing in the twenty-first century. This in turn is likely to have profound consequences for the construction of future identities grounded in homosexual desire and experience. For those of us old enough to remember the passing of Wolfenden, it is, however, difficult not to think of the whole issue of the age of consent as in many respects a regrettable distraction, a campaign we should never have had to fight in the first place. The moral necessity of the political focus on law has sadly involved a distraction of attention away from questions concerning our personal lived experience in the world. This in turn has led to a marginalizing of questions of personal growth, and the quality of our lives and relationships. Ironically it is AIDS which has put such issues back on the agenda of our everyday lives.

For thirty years the gay movement has focused honourably and indefatigably on the goal of legal rights. Most of my generation were motivated to engage in sexual politics by the simple aim of ensuring that subsequent generations of lesbians and gay men would get a better deal in early life than we had. The issue itself accepted the principle of legal parity, or you did not. Yet it could not be rushed, since behind the legislative goal there lay a number of complex and deeply controversial conflicts concerning the changing meanings of both gender and sexuality. The resistances provoked by the issue had to be lived through on a time-scale of many decades in order for the emergence of a new and broadly acceptable cultural consensus.

It was not merely coincidence that 1998 also marked the demise of the long sequence of Gay Pride festivals dating back to the origins of the modern gay movement. Thus 1999 saw the first national British annual Lesbian and Gay Mardi Gras, employing the rhetoric of Australian communitarian politics, but in reality replacing the older tradition of community-based organization with a commercial, business-led management. Much the same has happened in New York. Though its meaning has changed over time, every year since the early 1970s Gay Pride has provided an opportunity to see, laid out before one's eyes, the capillary range or organizations and groups run by and for lesbians and gay men, from ramblers' groups to bikers, from gay Tories to gay Trotskyites. The change of name is symptomatic of the end of an epoch. It speaks of a certain exhaustion, but also of our capacity for reinvention, and the reinvigoration of our particular social movement.

It is this vastly complex matrix of formal and informal connections which are implied, if inadequately, by notions of lesbian and gay community. Moreover, it is worth recalling that there was a steel-band playing on the very first Gay Pride march, and over the years the event has faithfully reflected something of the steady, confident growth of the flourishing modern commercial gay scene of bars and clubs, as well as the changes in lesbian and gay politics over the years. Thus the gay 'scene' and the gay 'movement' were brought together at Gay Pride, much to the dislike of some political sectarians, and ranting puritans of many persuasions. Indeed, bashing Gay Pride became something of a fashionable pastime amongst the politically correct of the 1990s, especially on the part of those who snobbishly wished to proclaim their supposedly superior 'outsider' vanguard status. It is equally unhelpful to try to wind back the clock and preserve what Gay Pride meant in the 1970s. Calls to restore Pride to a lost Golden Age of 'community control', with 'a combination of fun and politics' sound hopelessly naïve, and painfully inadequate to the world in which we now live.[12]

From the early 1980s the marquees and stalls at Gay Pride also increasingly provided an annual public focus for the emerging sector of non-governmental AIDS service organizations. For many years there was a vast Health Tent, sheltering a flourishing range of organizations from support groups such as Body Positive, to education campaigns, including the work of local government agencies, and community-based groups dealing with everything from complementary therapies to questions of mourning and loss.

Yet strangely, we know little about the ways in which the epidemic has really affected the inner lives of most gay men, beyond our sexual behaviour. Turning the pages of most lesbian and gay publications these days is an illuminating experience. We see crowds of ever-happy, laughing people out in the bars and clubs. We are endlessly encouraged to perfect our bodies and our homes. We read reviews of the latest music, and we have advice columns. There are letters. There are holiday features. There is also news. And there is also a steady trickle of AIDS stories, not always reliable. Yet whether or not it is explicitly acknowledged, the epidemic is always there, amid the swirling parade of promotions and ideal body-images and phone-line ads and club ads and small ads and so on. Much of our response as gay men to AIDS has been largely unconscious, but is none the less clearly reflected in a host of complex social phenomena, from the continued rise of gym culture to the widespread use of Ecstasy and other drugs. It is no less present in the lives of those who have never set foot in a gym, or who never do drugs. We may also detect an extreme splitting throughout gay male culture of questions of male prowess and sexual performance from questions of our capacity for intimacy and love. In our obsession with bodies and appearances we frequently neglect the dimension of our emotional and mental health.

Yet these issues are rarely addressed in most contemporary activist gay (or 'anti-gay') politics, with their relentless cynicism and lugubrious litanies of woe and victimhood, forever whingeing on about misery and 'oppression', without any sense of our achievements, or any practical, realistic vision or goals. The generous libertarian traditions of Gay Liberation have gradually ossified into a frozen leftist orthodoxy of ghastly, dour moralism and furious self-righteousness. It is not the gay community, or gay identity which have failed to adapt to changing circumstances, but their embittered and often condescending left-wing critics.

In the meantime, however, back in the real world, lesbians and gay men have come in from the cold now as a recognized social constituency. Real, enduring social, political, and juridical changes have taken place throughout British society, and have happened *in spite of*, and not because of, the vainglorious posturing of the far left and its allies. For the first time we have a government which acknowledges our existence as a legitimate social constituency, albeit a fluid and changing one. We are no longer locked out of national or local political debates. Participation is open to us, though this of course by no means guarantees easy success to any of our campaigns. To pretend otherwise is to wilfully turn one's back on the pressing goals of achieving real change in relation to the world we must all somehow inhabit together. Eighties-style activism may again become necessary in the future, who knows? But it is not the appropriate mode for achieving our immediate or long-term political goals today.

In any case, our recent gains mean that we *need* sexual politics less than hitherto. Things are changing fast. When Stephen Gately, popular member of boy-band Boyzone 'came out' as gay in June 1999, the traditionally venomously homophobic London *Evening Standard* reassured its readers at length as to 'Why teen pin-ups *can* be gay'.[13] In its Life & Style section the *Evening Standard* also in the previous week described at length the work of a London-based surrogate baby agency for lesbians and gay men.[14]

Only a few years ago, both stories would have been front-page scandals. We all benefit from the new spirit of openness that is currently abroad in the land. In 1999 Minister of Agriculture Nick Brown came out as gay to a largely indifferent nation, with no great media hysterics. Michael Portillo's disclosures about his past were also widely received without waves of moral outrage. Sexual identity is simply a less important issue than it used to be, and this in itself is a great gain for everyone. Homophobia is not going to magically vanish overnight, but throughout most of the Anglophone world it has far less cultural or political clout than it had ten or twenty years ago. Meanwhile new institutions such as the annual Summer Rites festival, and the growing indie scene emerge to suit new circumstances, reflecting new times and new identities. We can also expect to see the emergence of institutions reflecting the needs of older lesbians and gay men, as the first generation of the 1970s Gay Liberation movement approaches retirement age.

The lesbian and gay movement was one of the engines which helped turn Britain slowly from a post-war culture of hyper-respectability and extreme sexual inhibition, into the far more laid-back, pluralist, live-and-let-live society we inhabit today. As the initial goals of the modern post-1969 lesbian and gay movement are gradually realized, its overall identity will inevitably change, along with much of its older sense of urgency, and this will surely be no bad thing. It might even provide the opportunity for us to look more closely at ourselves, and the quality of our *personal* lives and relationships.

Conclusion

Elizabeth Bowen's 1955 novel *A World of Love* is set in her favourite social landscape – the romantic, social world of the old Anglo-Irish Ascendancy families before partition, doomed gentry whose lives of shabby gentility are about to be steam-rollered by a history their own ancestors had triggered. It is, amongst other things, a novel about ghosts, a subject to which Elizabeth Bowen was instinctively drawn. Here the ghost is Guy, killed in the First World War, whose memory haunts the tale. For his cousin Antonia:

> though a generation was mown down his death seemed to her an invented story … He and life had the same sticky temperament; they kept one another in play; they were on terms. It would be long before Guy was done with life … She recollected how he had kicked a door down when a defective lock kept him stuck in a lavatory during a tennis party – he was a participator … He had it in him to make a good end, but not soon; he would have been ready to disengage himself when the hour came, but rightfully speaking it had not … It was simply that these years she went on living belonged to him, his lease upon them not having run out yet. The living were living in his lifetime; and of this his contemporaries never were unaware. They were incomplete.[15]

I quote this passage at some length because it eloquently suggests much about the ways in which personal and social identities may be affected by questions of *loss*. It also speaks to me of a psychological dimension that I frequently meet amongst gay men, resulting from a widely shared premature experience of mortal illness and death over the course of many long years, on a traumatizing scale analogous in some ways with the experience of war. There is now a very substantial number of people who have lost many close friends to AIDS, and our experience of the epidemic is different from that of other gay men whose immediate social circles have happily (so far) remained untouched. In such circumstances, it is only too easy to find oneself spending as much time in the company of the dead as in that of the living.

Advances in treatments are frequently cited as if AIDS were now indeed a completely medically manageable, chronic illness. Against this misleadingly over-simplified blanket optimism, little or no account is taken of what an HIV diagnosis means today, as your viral load continues to rise or your CD4 count falls. HIV is about starting treatments, sticking with treatments, and changing treatments when they fail, or when they themselves make you ill. These days people with HIV are frequently exhorted to 'come out', but the analogy with disclosing one's sexual identity strikes me as misleading, if well intended. There may be many good reasons for being open and public about an HIV diagnosis, but there are also equally good reasons against. Not the least of these is the sense of control individuals can still exercise over their lives, without having to be *publicly* defined primarily in relation to only one aspect of them, however important that aspect may be *in private*.

Not everyone has a safe and supportive environment around them. Many come from previously hostile and unsupportive families. Many feel profound shame and embarrassment about their illness. And who already knows more about shame and self-disgust than gay men? Furthermore, it causes real human pain to those who love us when we tell them we have HIV. In other words, it remains as important as it ever was to respect the decision of individuals to do what they feel is best for them, in their circumstances, recognizing that these are likely to change over time in unpredictable ways. It is entirely unreasonable to expect all people with HIV to be permanently manning the barricades in the style of late 1980s activism. By the same token, we should all be immensely grateful to all those who choose to live publicly as HIV-positive, often at considerable personal cost.

We should, however, respect the decision of those who refuse, as they see it, to be reduced to a diagnostic identity. There is a vital issue here of choice, in much the same way that some benefit greatly from access to the latest reliable treatment information, whereas others do not want to be distracted from their main life tasks by what they regard as a tidal wave of complex and often confusing medical information. Again, such attitudes will often change over time. Generalizations about what people with HIV should or should not do are generally impertinent, and almost always unhelpful. After all, who would *want* to have HIV? Some people will make HIV the centre of their lives. Others will want to try to put it out of their minds as far as possible. For some these may be the right decisions, but not for others. As with most things in this life, for many the middle way is best, acknowledging HIV enough to take it seriously, and to be able to put up and sustain a fight, but not to the extent of letting it take over one's entire remaining life. This is not necessarily as easy as it may sound.

Everyone wishes AIDS would simply vanish, tonight. Yet on and on it goes. Some behave badly, most behave well. I have witnessed the whole history of the epidemic, from the first conference organized by the newly formed Terrence Higgins Trust at the Conway Hall in London in May 1983, to the present day. If we have some reasonable grounds for hope today, it is because in spite of ordinary human folly and stupidity, the AIDS epidemic has consistently managed to draw the attention and skills of an army of women and men who have generally responded magnificently to this whole, horrible business. There are people there for us. We want better treatments, but we also know these cannot be magically summoned up by acts of will. There is real comfort in knowing that well informed groups such as the Treatment Action Group in New York and the National AIDS Manual in the UK are able to draw attention to changing medical priorities, and are working with rather than mindlessly against the leading researchers in the field. Resurrections are reassuringly frequent.

Yet AIDS remains a nightmare from which we will not in the foreseeable future wake up. The financial and managerial crisis in the National Health Service is not going to go away in the foreseeable future either, with possibly disastrous consequences for the future of patient care. This is why malicious, bigoted attempts to portray HIV as a 'disease of choice' continue to be so dangerously misleading, in an age of remorseless cut-backs and triage.

As we move into the new millennium it is not possible to measure how much of the older altruistic communitarian value system associated with gay identity has survived the social and spiritual decimation of Thatcherism and its long-term fall out, which is all around us and which will take many decades to heal. Yet the basic principles of volunteerism and collective self-help seem tenacious. Ten years ago concrete medical hope was all but unimaginable. Derek Jarman confided to his diary in 1989 that he had 'fallen off the edge of hope'. Those reaching the end of available treatment options today will understand his words. Yet some now claim that we have been 'overtaken' by hope, to the extent that it has supposedly pushed fear 'out of sight, below the surface'.[16] Fear, claims Michelangelo Signorile: 'has gone back in the closet'.[17]

Signorile is the most shrewd and perceptive of contemporary gay American commentators, and is bracingly dismissive both of the 'anti-gay' position, and of 'post-AIDS' theory.[18] In this respect, however, I think he is for once mistaken. For fear does not necessarily look like a painting by Munch. On the contrary, it is likely to be displaced, and to be apparent only in symptoms which may not look like fear at all. These may have consequences as harmful as those resulting from complacency. The real challenge is not simply to keep pressing the panic-button as if it were still 1991, but on the contrary to continue to devise appropriate ways to encourage new generations of gay men, across *all* lines of class, region and race, to take this hateful virus very seriously indeed.

We will also continue to need targeted campaigns for older men whose entire sexual lives will have been lived in the shadow of the epidemic. HIV is not in any sense our fate or destiny as gay men. We cannot afford as a community to let down our guard. To continue to insist, in the face of all the evidence to the contrary, that fear is the *only* way of motivating gay men to have safer sex over the course of many years, and the likelihood of many different types of relationships, of many differing degrees of emotional intensity, strikes me as a form of inflexible, and ultimately lazy thinking. Indeed, it is a way of *not* getting directly involved with people's real, messily complex lives and emotions, where risk is actually *lived*. As Robinson Crusoe mused on his desert island three hundred years ago: 'How strange a checkerwork of Providence is the life of man! and by what secret differing springs are the affections hurried about, as differing circumstances present! Today we love what tomorrow we hate; today we seek what tomorrow we shun; today we desire what tomorrow we fear; nay, even tremble at the apprehensions of.'[19] Human nature has evidently not changed very much in the interim, nor human frailty.

In all of this it needs to be remembered that almost everybody is subject to moments of self-destructive behaviour, for a host of different reasons. Who has not gone out and got blind drunk after having a blazing row with one's family, or after discovering that you have been betrayed by a trusted friend, or that you have lost your job, or that your partner has been unfaithful? Sex has always provided ample opportunities for self-destructive behaviour, and this in itself is entirely ordinary and human. But for gay men in the age of AIDS, such behaviour can tragically involve much more than mere recklessness. Alas, it can only too easily prove deadly. Surely in such circumstances the maintenance of safer sex requires *self-confidence*, not its opposite.

Yet in many recent debates about safer sex, gut-wrenching fear is still frequently invoked as if it were somehow a magic, all-in-one answer to the challenge of reducing HIV transmission. This seems to me a most dubious and unlikely proposition, for the simple reason that our deepest human emotions are not hard-wired to our behaviour. Who is to say what makes different people most afraid, or how fear may guide their actions? Why on earth should anyone assume that fear leads *automatically* to safer sex in exactly the same way for everyone, in all circumstances? It is, however, surely the case that there is indeed a strong taboo against gay men openly *acknowledging* fear, which is rather a different thing. We mostly deal with our fears as best we can, and as always, this will differ greatly for individuals. As men, we are not necessarily very good at this.

This has different implications for uninfected gay men, afraid of infection, and those of us living with HIV, for many of whom the issue of losing libido altogether is the main issue.[20] As one gay man reflects: 'The stigma of AIDS is alive and well in me. I wonder if this is not a common problem, that deep

down inside we feel "unclean" which turns us off being turned on?'[21] It
is important to balance scare-mongering reports about 'bare-backing' with
the recognition that many positive gay men find *any* kind of sex almost
unimaginable, largely out of fear of the remotest possibility of infecting
someone else.

Above all, most of us simply want to be able to get on with our lives as
normally as possible, as we feel appropriate. Having seen so many deaths,
and so many exaggerated claims of benefit and of harm in relation to treatment drugs over the years, we are likely to be extremely prudent and cautious about all wild speculation and unproved assertions. What a luxury it
would be, though, to take hope for granted. We are nowhere near that time
yet, but it is at least *imaginable*. For all of us, but especially for those of us
infected, the epidemic is sadly very far from over. For now we soldier on.
I've had my say.

Notes

1 Richard Holmes (Ed.) Samuel Taylor Coleridge, *Selected Poetry* (London: 1996
  Penguin Books), p. 25.
2 Max Navarre, '"Fighting the victim label" PWA Coalition Portfolio', in Douglas
  Crimp (Ed.). *AIDS: Cultural Analysis, Cultural Activism* (Cambridge, Mass: MIT
  Press, 1988).
3 *Ibid.*, pp. 144–5.
4 *Gay News*, No. 261, 17–30 March 1983, p. 7.
5 Eric Rofes, *Dry Bones Breathe: Gay Men Creating Post-AIDS Identities and
  Cultures* (New York and London: Haworth Press, 1998), p. 270.
6 Gary Dowsett and David McInnes, 'Post AIDS: Assessing the long term social
  impact of HIV/AIDS in gay communities', XI International Conference on AIDS,
  Vancouver, 1996. See also Gary Dowsett's important book, *Practicing Desire:
  Homosexual Sex in the Era of AIDS* (Stanford University Press, 1996).
7 Typical of the journalistic discourse of 'slippage', see Alan Shaldrake and Ivor
  Key, 'Slippage to death. Ugly new word sums up gays' return to a lifestyle of
  casual sex', and John McEntree, 'Sympathy slipping away as well', *Sunday
  Express*. London, 15 September 1991. See also Rupert Haselden, 'Gay abandon',
  Weekend Guardian, Saturday 7 September 1991, pp. 20–2, and subsequent letters
  by myself and many others, in *the Guardian*, from Tuesday 10 September, to
  Tuesday 17 September 1991.
8 It is well worth considering such stories in relation to the structure and role of
  rumours amongst combatants during the Second World War as analysed by Paul
  Fussell in *Wartime: Understanding and Behaviour in the Second World War*
  (Oxford University Press, 1989).
9 See David Northmore, 'Lords approve asylum rights', *Pink Paper*, Issue 577,
  Friday 2 April 1999, p. 1
10 David Bamber, 'Curbs on "gay" lessons to be scrapped', *Sunday Telegraph*
  6 June 1999, p. 11.
11 Anthony Looch and Charles de Lisle, 'Campaign for consent at 21 is defeated',
  Daily Telegraph, Tuesday 21 June 1994.
12 Peter Tatchell, quoted in 'The great festival debate', *Pink Paper*. Issue 592,
  16 July 1999, p. 8.
13 Hettie Judah and John McKie, 'Why teen pin-ups *can* be gay', *Evening Standard*,
  London, Wednesday 16 June 1999, p. 31.

14 Chrissy Iley, 'Where rich, gay men go to buy babies', *Evening Standard*, London Monday / June 1999, p. 26.
15 Elizabeth Bowen, *A World of Love* (London: Jonathan Cape, 1955), pp. 64–5.
16 Michelangelo Signorile, 'Don't fear the fear', *The Advocate*, 30 March 1999.
17 *Ibid.*
18 Michelangelo Signorile, '841,085 & counting', *Out Magazine*, New York, 17 August 1998.
19 Daniel Defoe, *Robinson Crusoe* (1719) (London: Penguin Books, 1994), p. 154.
20 Peter Duffin, 'Finished at forty?', *Body Positive Newsletter*. Issue 216, October 1997, pp. 1–2.
21 'Letters', *Body Positive Newsletter*. Issue 217, November 1997, p. 11.

Index